Devils and Realist
vol. 13

story by **Madoka Takadono**
art by **Utako Yukihiro**

Cast of characters

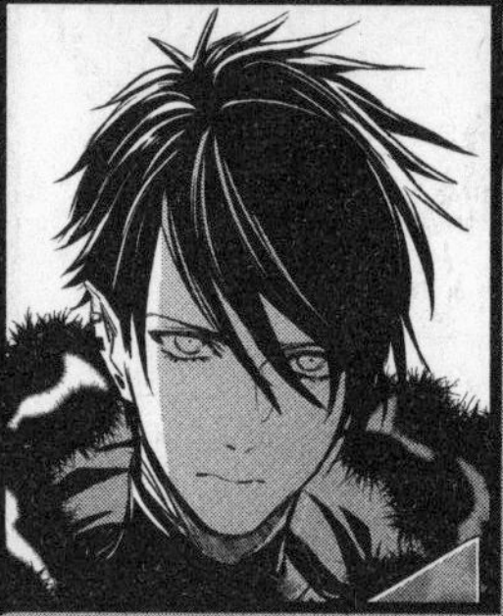

Dantalion
71st pillar and commander of 36 armies of Hell, he is Grand Duke of the Underworld. He is one of the candidates for representative king and is relied on at school as a jock.

Kevin
William's capable yet gambling-addicted butler who is also a pastor at the academy. In truth, he is the angel Uriel who has been dispatched from Heaven.

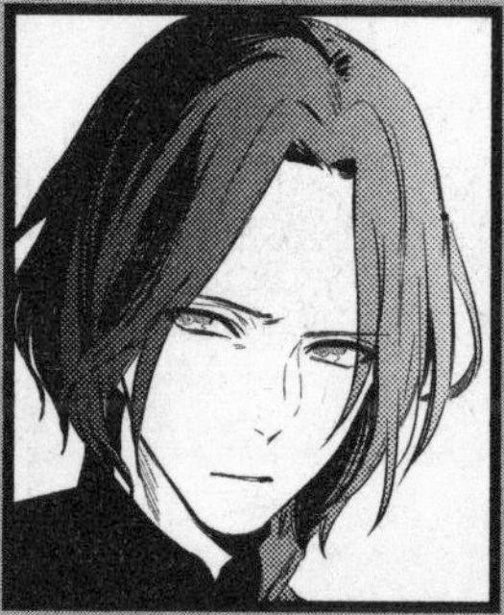

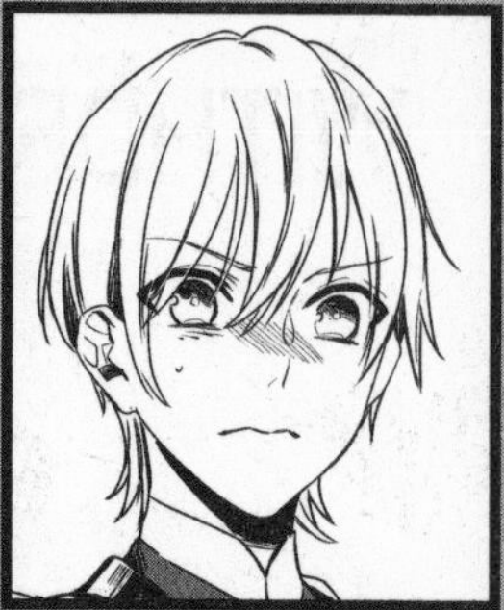

William
A brilliant realist from a famous noble family whose wealth was recently restored. As the descendant of King Solomon, he is the Elector with the authority to choose the representative of the king of Hell. He is slowly beginning to accept this role.

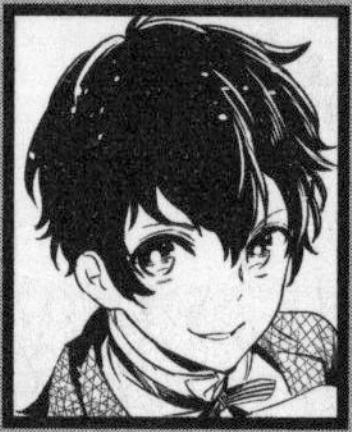

Metatron
An angel with enormous power. He encourages Uriel to join him in a heavenly conspiracy to convince Michael to go to sleep.

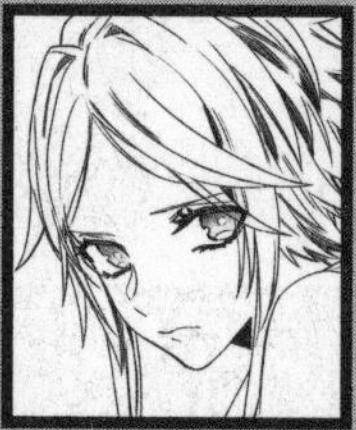

Sytry
Twelfth Pillar of Hell who leads 60 armies. Sytry is Prince of Hell and a candidate to represent the king. He is treated like a princess at school because of his beautiful appearance.

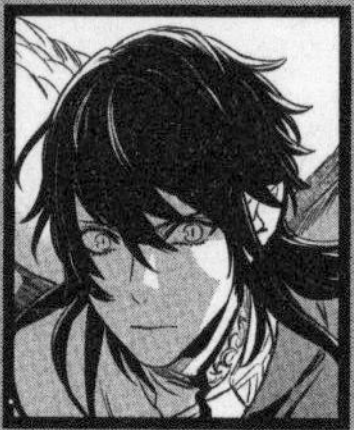

Camio
A candidate for representative king, Camio is Solomon's 53rd pillar and a Great President of Hell. He is an excellent student at school and serves as class representative.

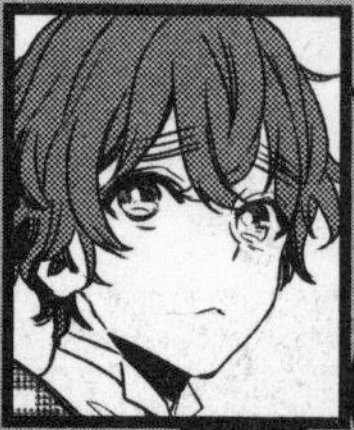

Isaac
William's classmate. Lover of supernatural phenomena.

The Story So Far

The demons Dantalion and Sytry appear suddenly before impoverished noble William to tell him that he is the Elector who will decide the representative king of Hell. After the demons join him at school as students, William lives a life more and more entangled with the doings of Hell. With his uncle's return, William's family wealth is restored to its former glory.
The demons, preoccupied with other matters, take some time off school: Dantalion, after the death of Baphomet, turns his focus on Hell. Camio, about to welcome his beloved Maria as his retainer, goes to his father Lucifer. Finally, Sytry is dragged off to Heaven by Metatron.

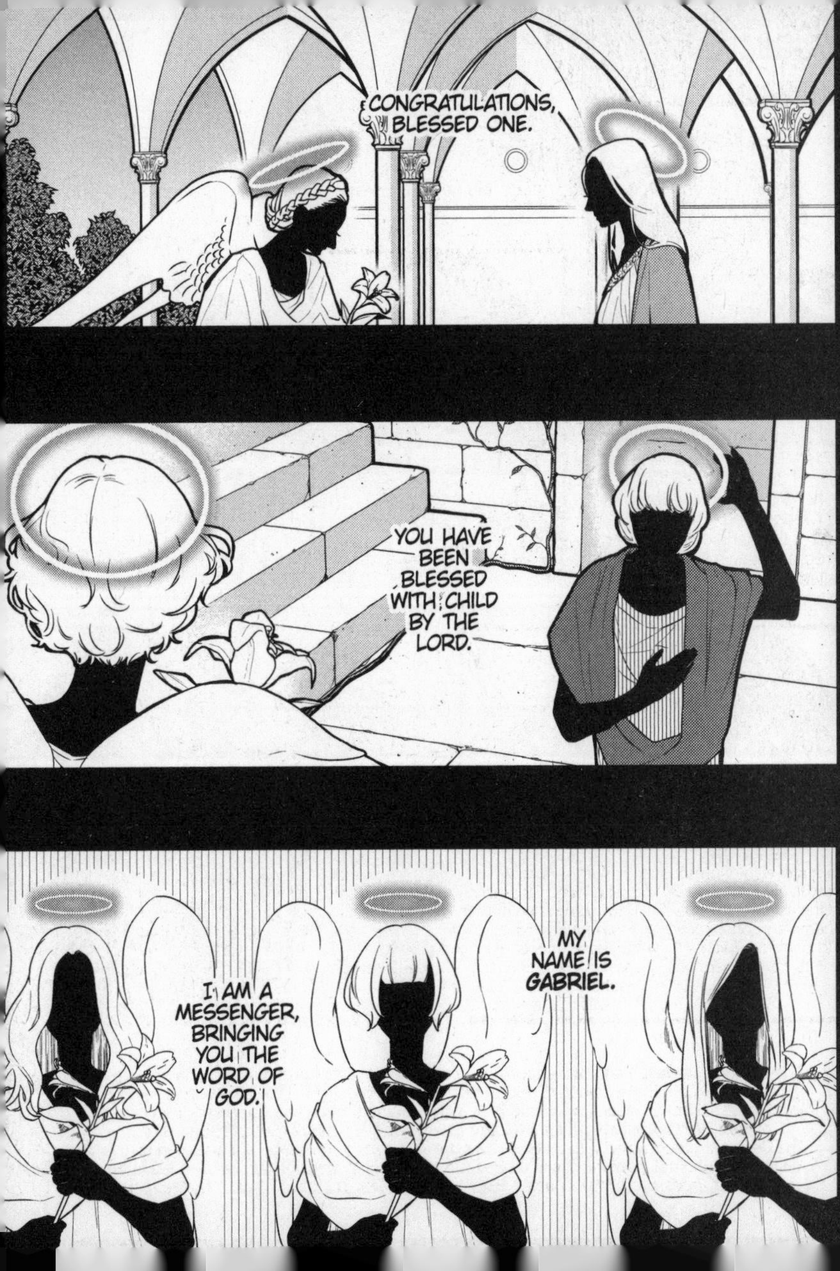
CONGRATULATIONS, BLESSED ONE.
YOU HAVE BEEN BLESSED WITH CHILD BY THE LORD.
MY NAME IS GABRIEL.
I AM A MESSENGER, BRINGING YOU THE WORD OF GOD.

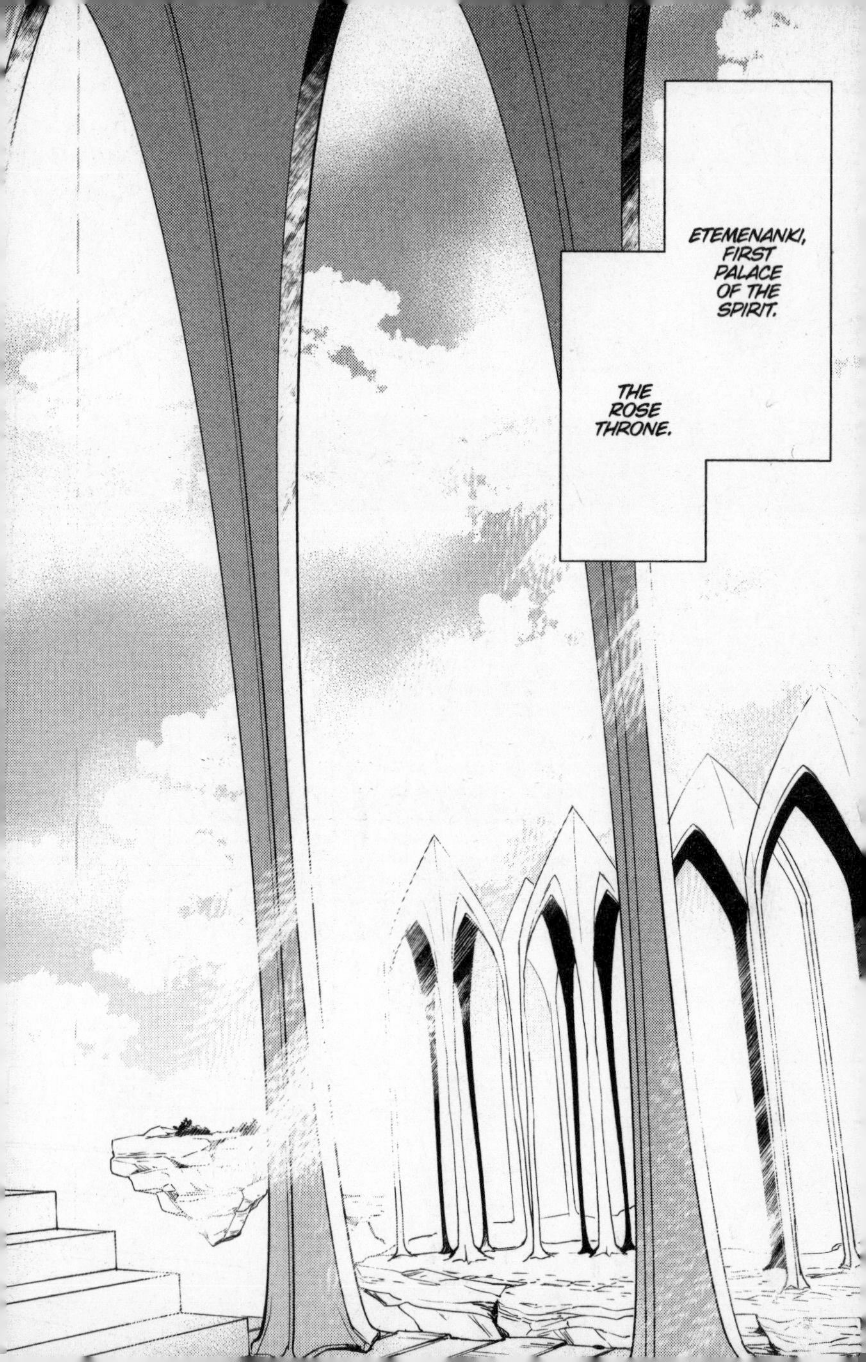
ETEMENANKI, FIRST PALACE OF THE SPIRIT.
THE ROSE THRONE.

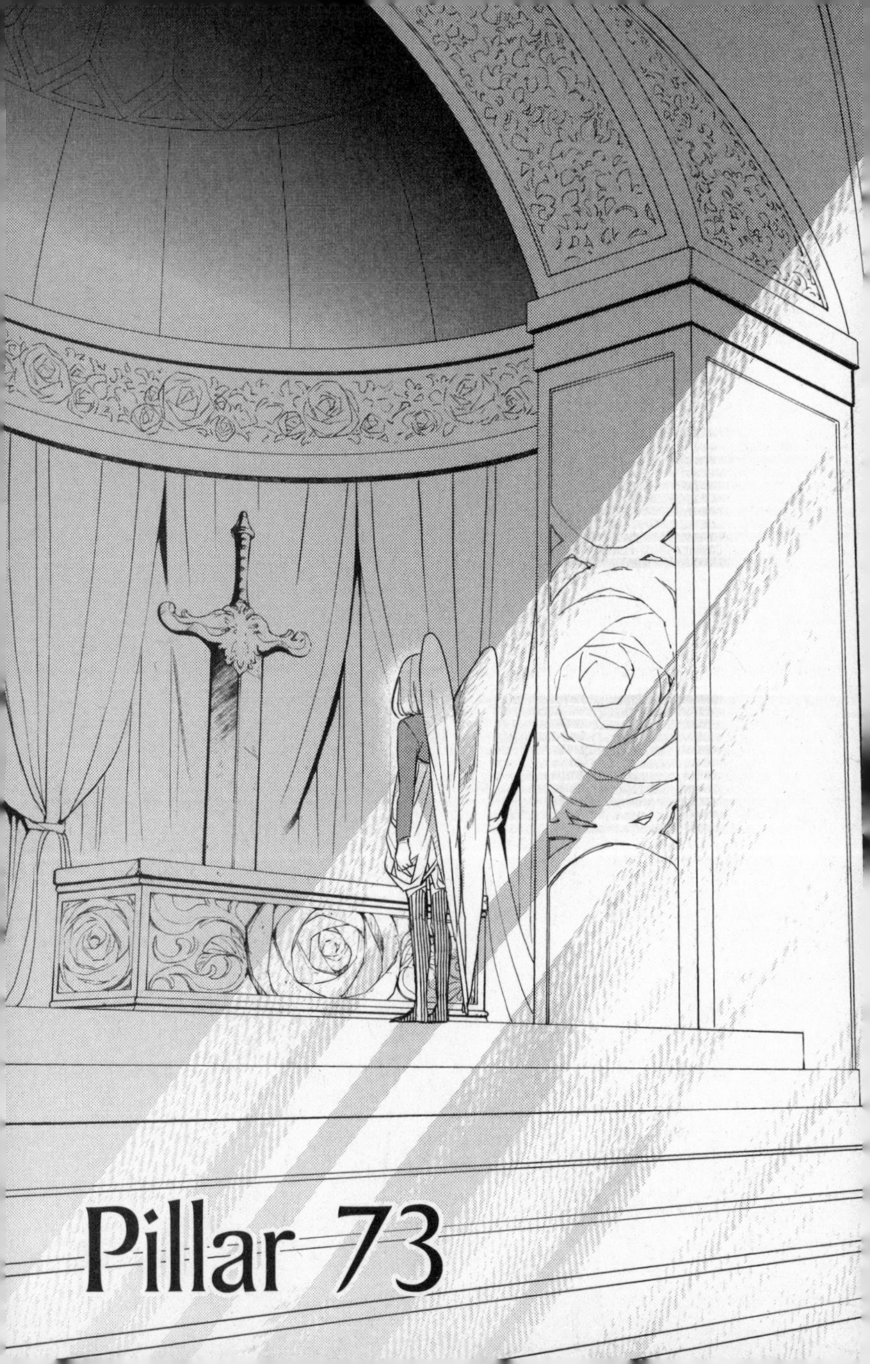
Pillar 73

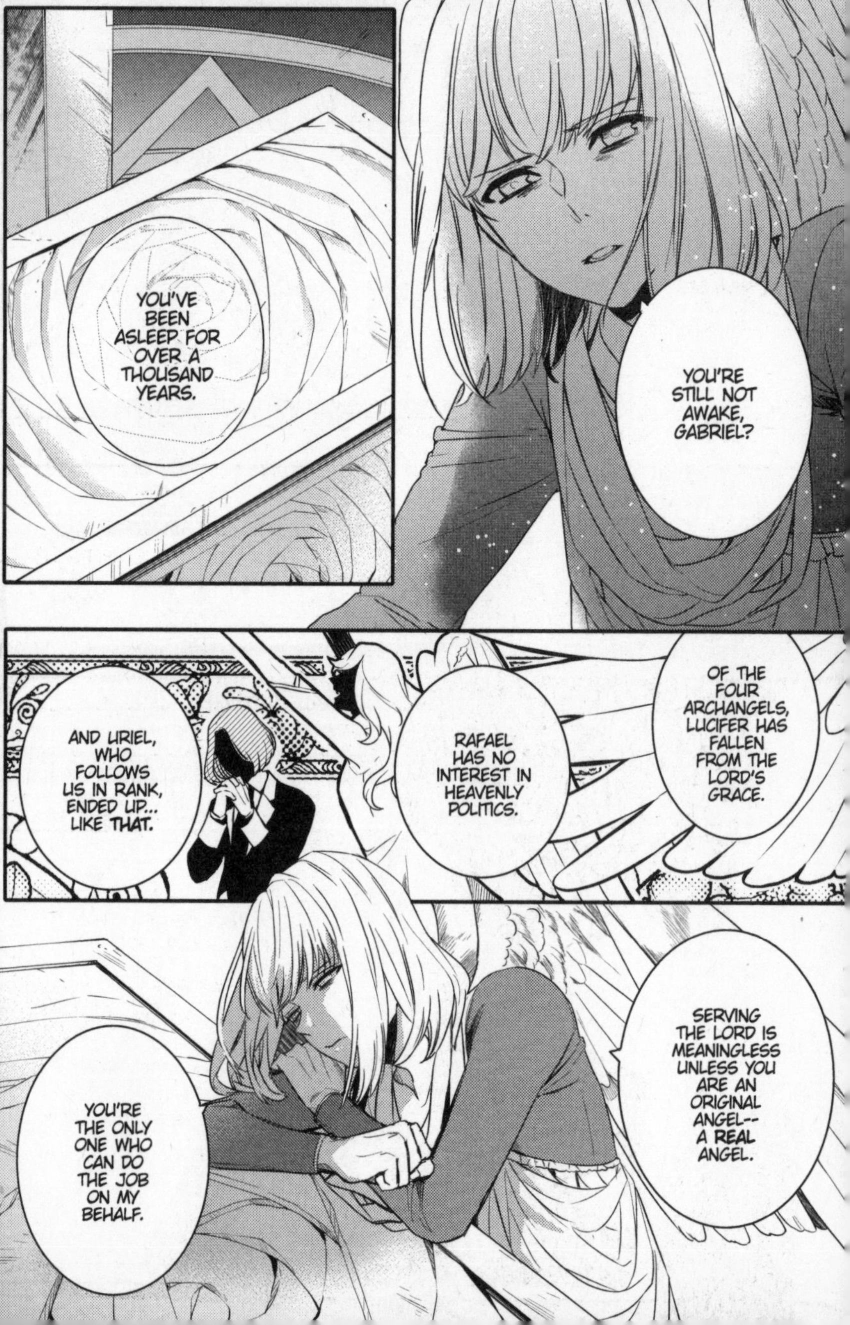
YOU'RE STILL NOT AWAKE, GABRIEL?
YOU'VE BEEN ASLEEP FOR OVER A THOUSAND YEARS.
OF THE FOUR ARCHANGELS, LUCIFER HAS FALLEN FROM THE LORD'S GRACE.
RAFAEL HAS NO INTEREST IN HEAVENLY POLITICS.
AND URIEL, WHO FOLLOWS US IN RANK, ENDED UP... LIKE THAT.
SERVING THE LORD IS MEANINGLESS UNLESS YOU ARE AN ORIGINAL ANGEL-- A REAL ANGEL.
YOU'RE THE ONLY ONE WHO CAN DO THE JOB ON MY BEHALF.

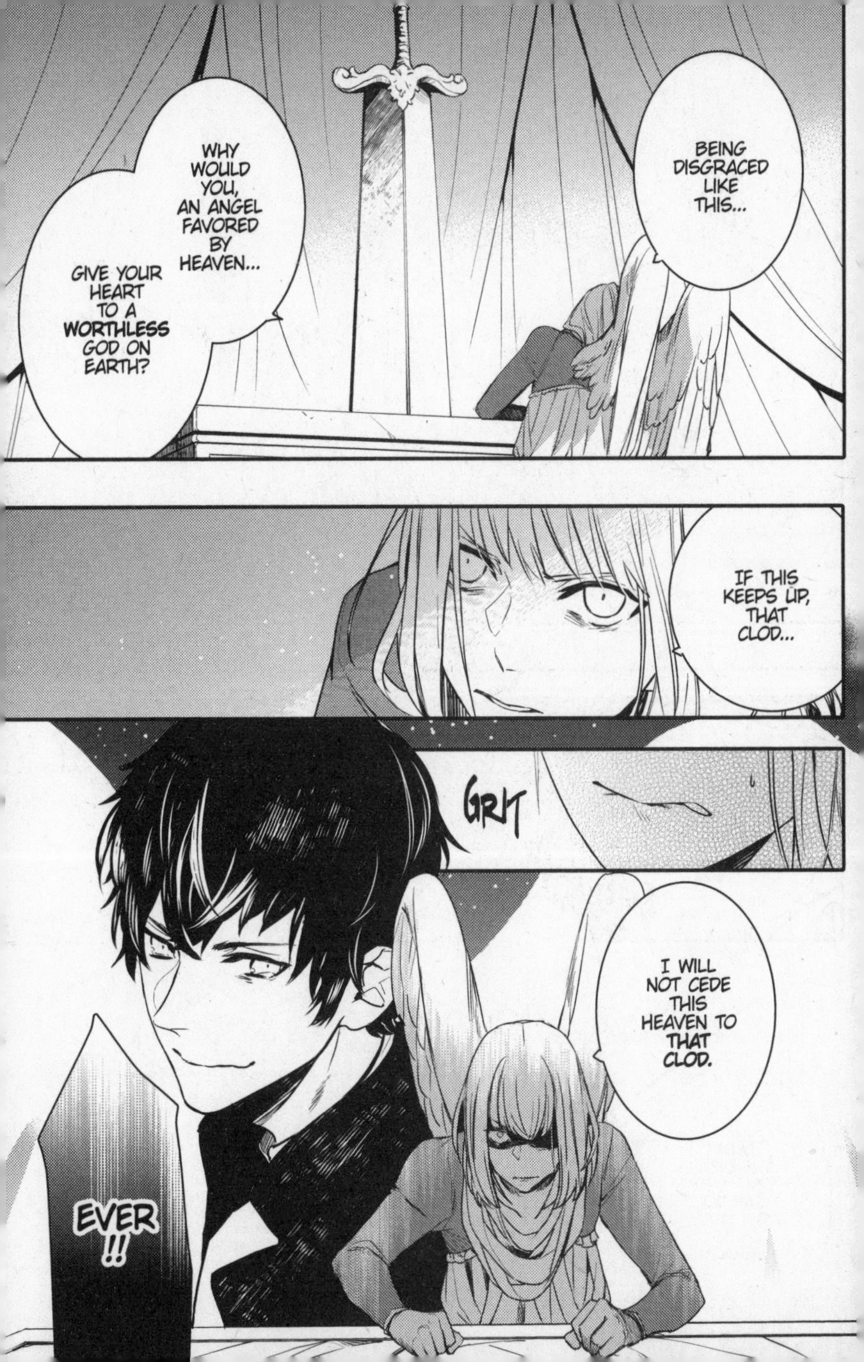
BEING DISGRACED LIKE THIS...
WHY WOULD YOU, AN ANGEL FAVORED BY HEAVEN...
GIVE YOUR HEART TO A WORTHLESS GOD ON EARTH?
IF THIS KEEPS UP, THAT CLOD...
GRIT
I WILL NOT CEDE THIS HEAVEN TO THAT CLOD.
EVER!!

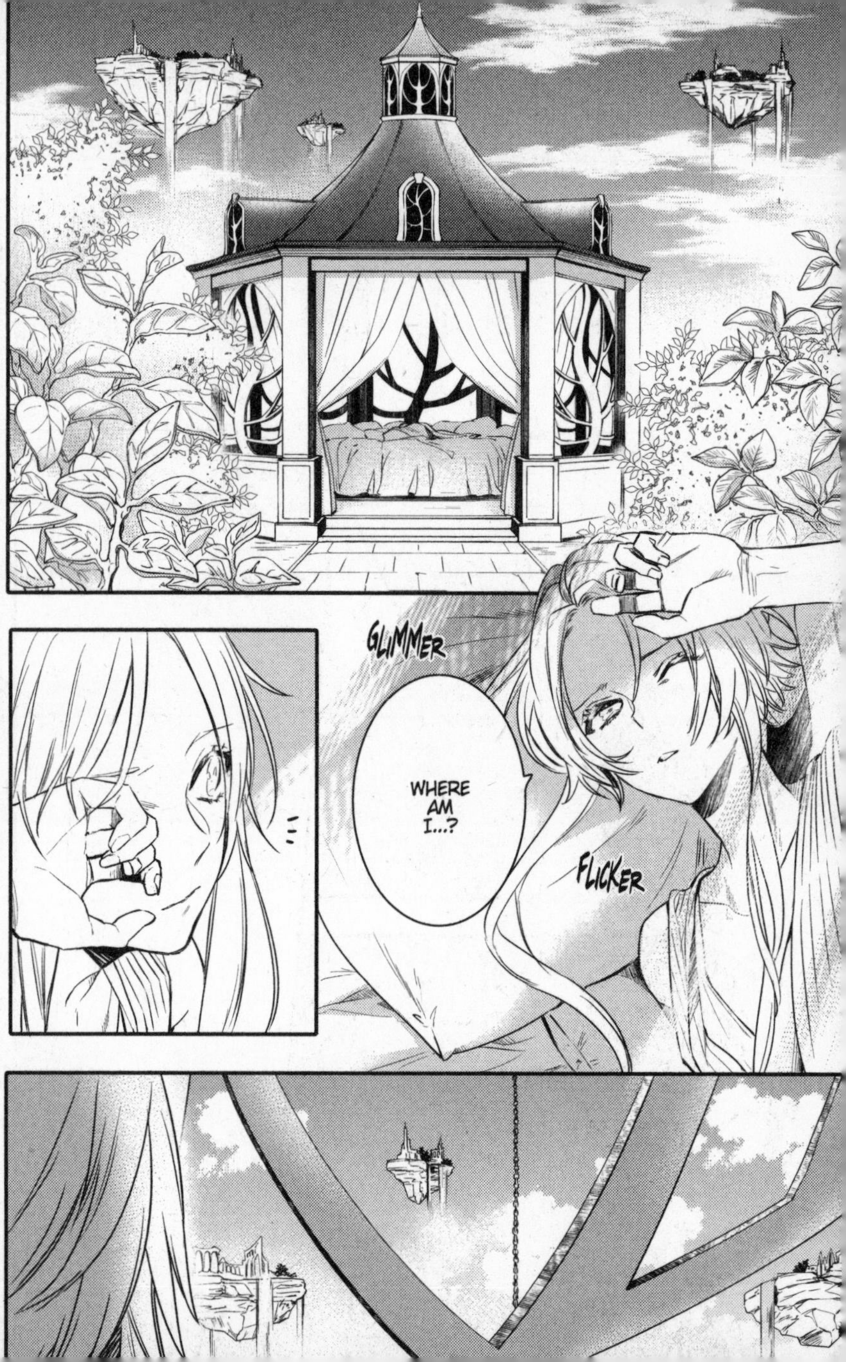
GLIMMER
WHERE AM I...?
FLICKER

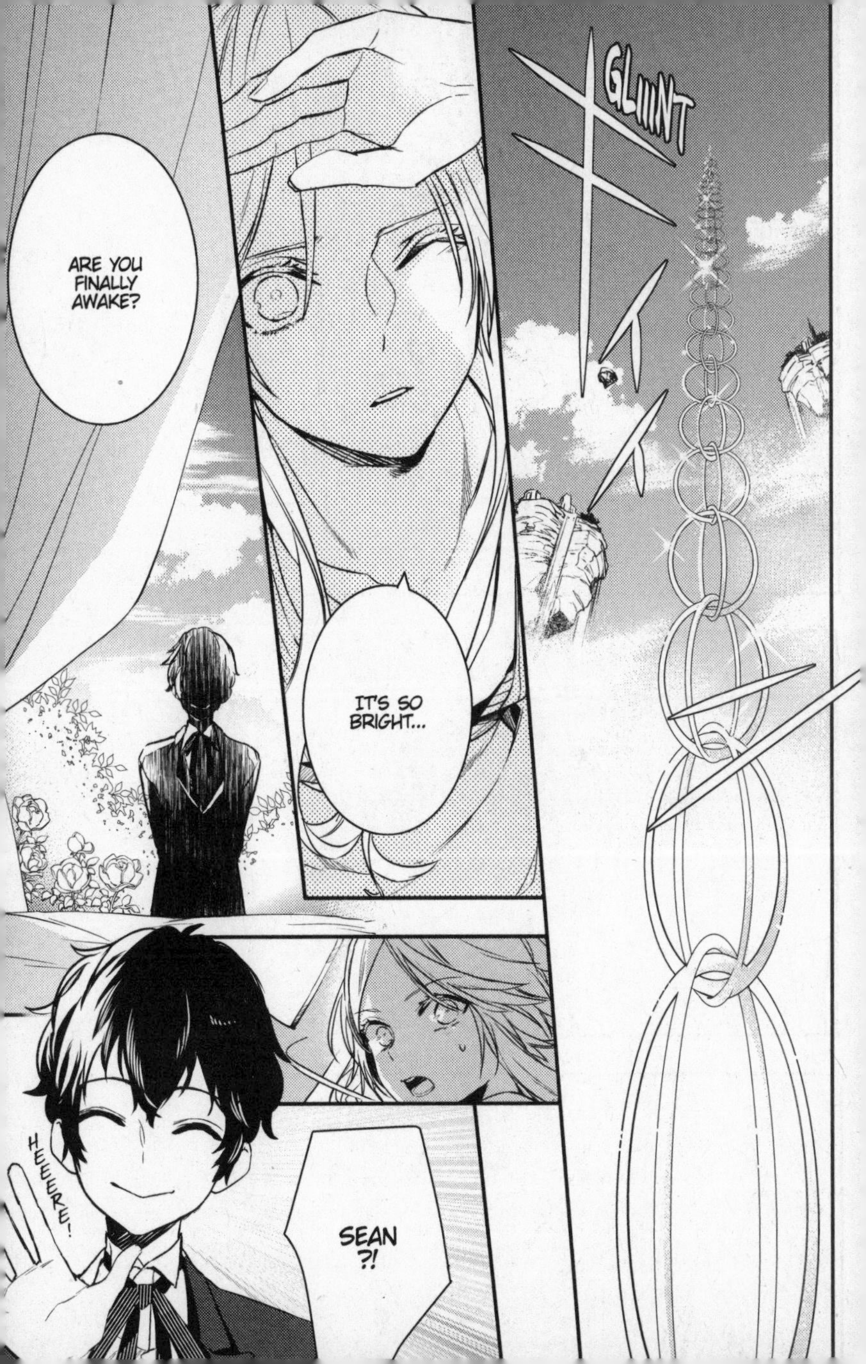

GLIIINT
IT'S SO BRIGHT...
ARE YOU FINALLY AWAKE?
SEAN ?!
HEEEERE!

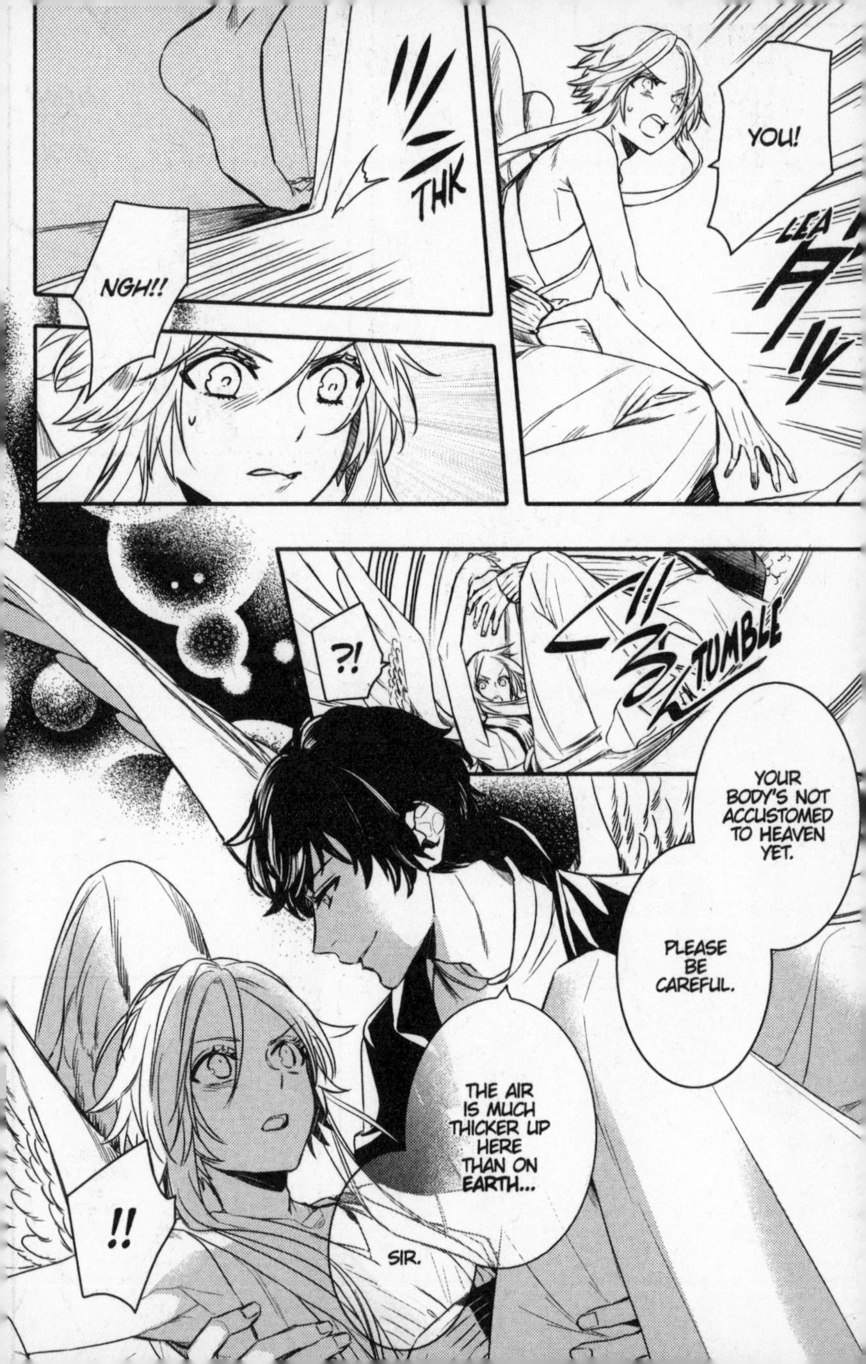
YOU!
LEA
THK
NGH!!
TUMBLE
?!
YOUR BODY'S NOT ACCUSTOMED TO HEAVEN YET.
PLEASE BE CAREFUL.
THE AIR IS MUCH THICKER UP HERE THAN ON EARTH...
SIR.
!!

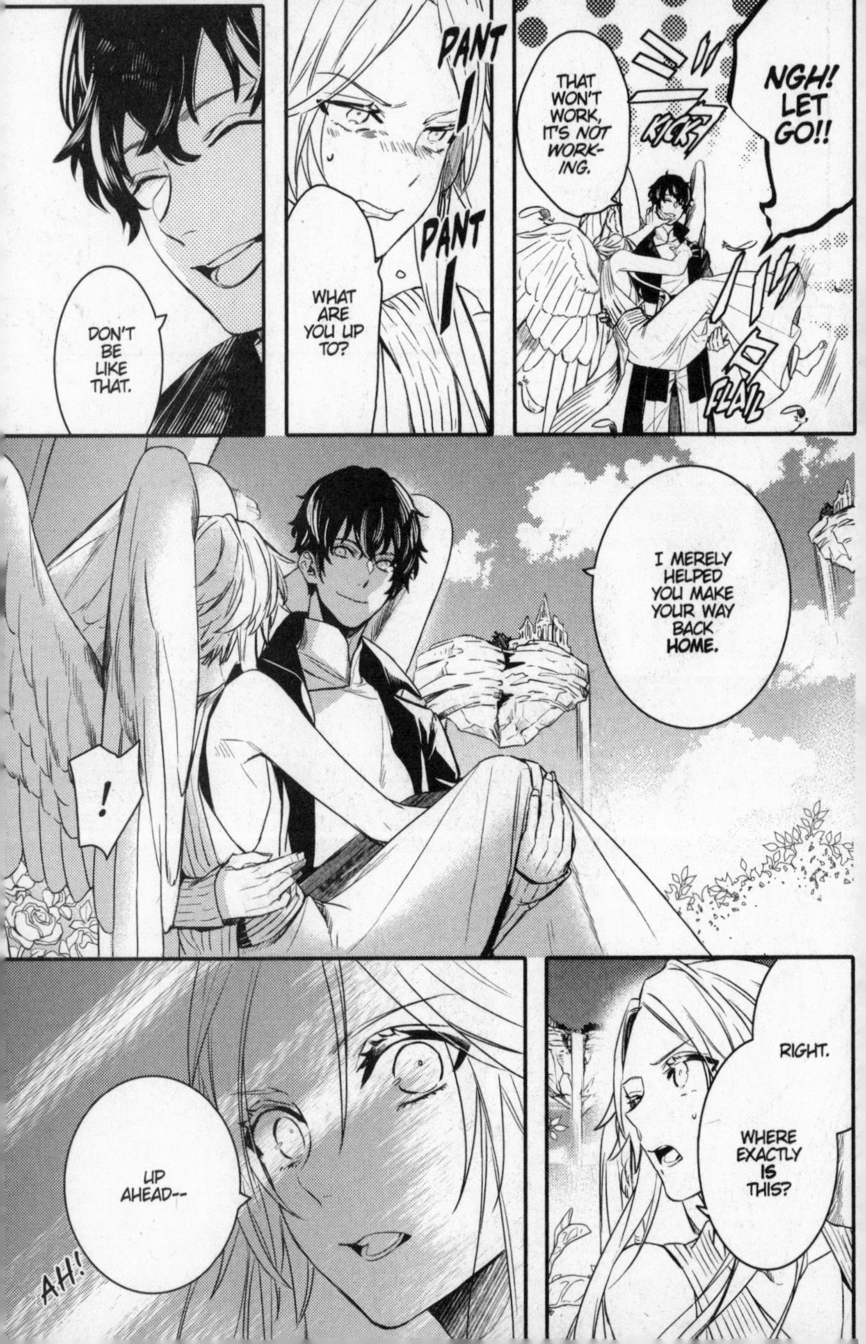
NGH! LET GO!!
THAT WON'T WORK, IT'S NOT WORKING.
KICK
FLAIL
PANT PANT
WHAT ARE YOU UP TO?
DON'T BE LIKE THAT.
I MERELY HELPED YOU MAKE YOUR WAY BACK HOME.
!
RIGHT.
WHERE EXACTLY IS THIS?
UP AHEAD--
AH!

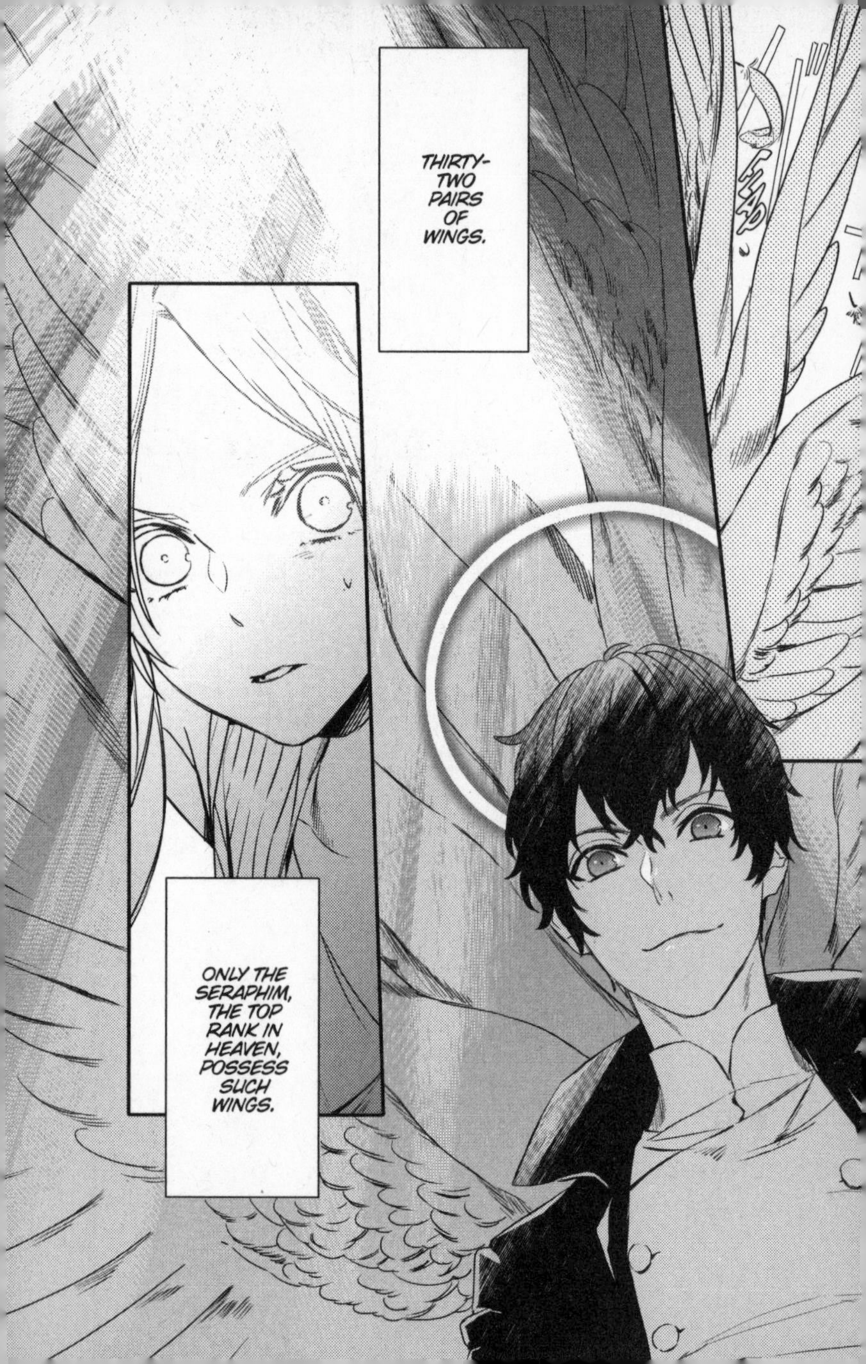
FLAP
THIRTY-TWO PAIRS OF WINGS.
ONLY THE SERAPHIM, THE TOP RANK IN HEAVEN, POSSESS SUCH WINGS.

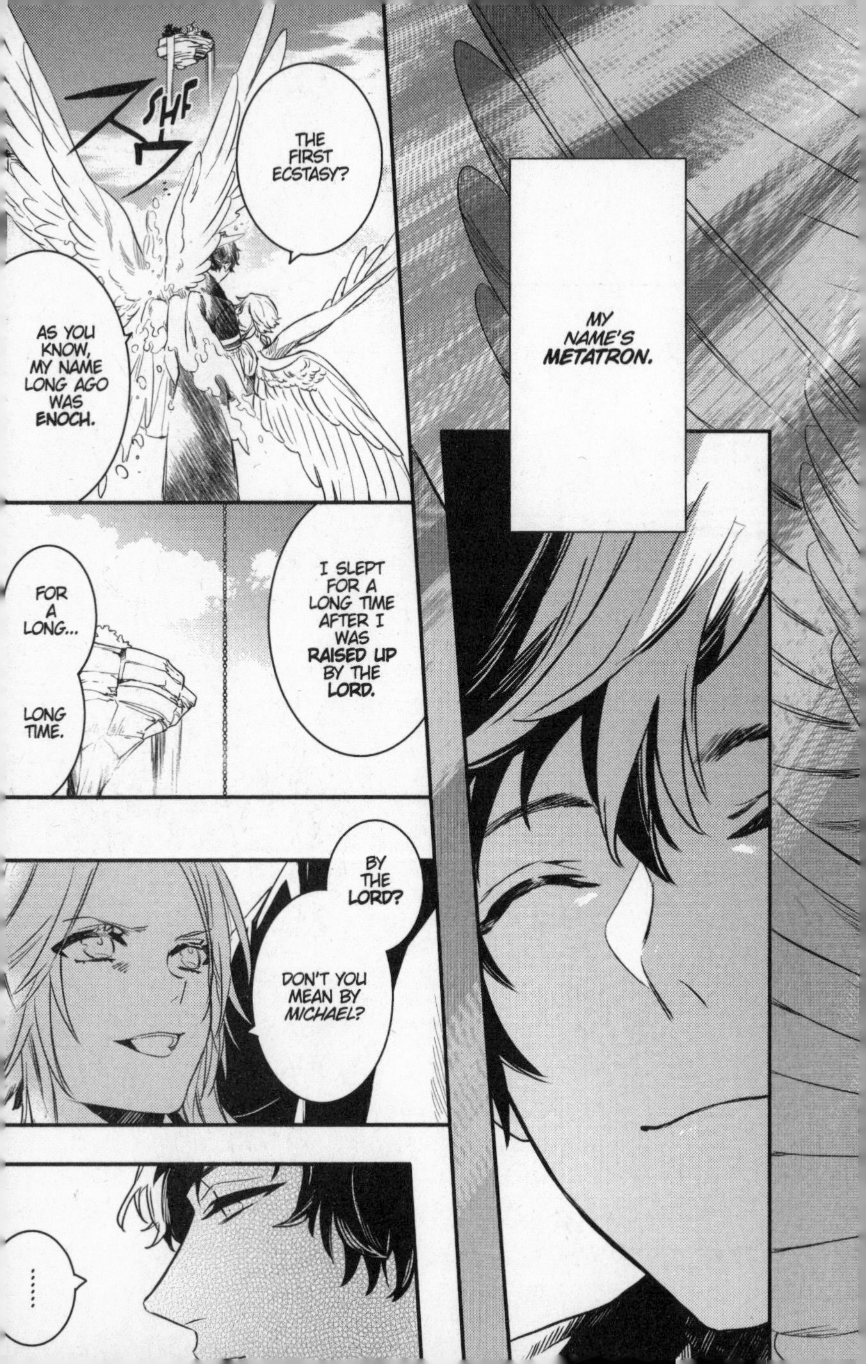
MY NAME'S METATRON.
SHF
THE FIRST ECSTASY?
AS YOU KNOW, MY NAME LONG AGO WAS ENOCH.
I SLEPT FOR A LONG TIME AFTER I WAS RAISED UP BY THE LORD.
FOR A LONG...
LONG TIME.
BY THE LORD?
DON'T YOU MEAN BY MICHAEL?
......

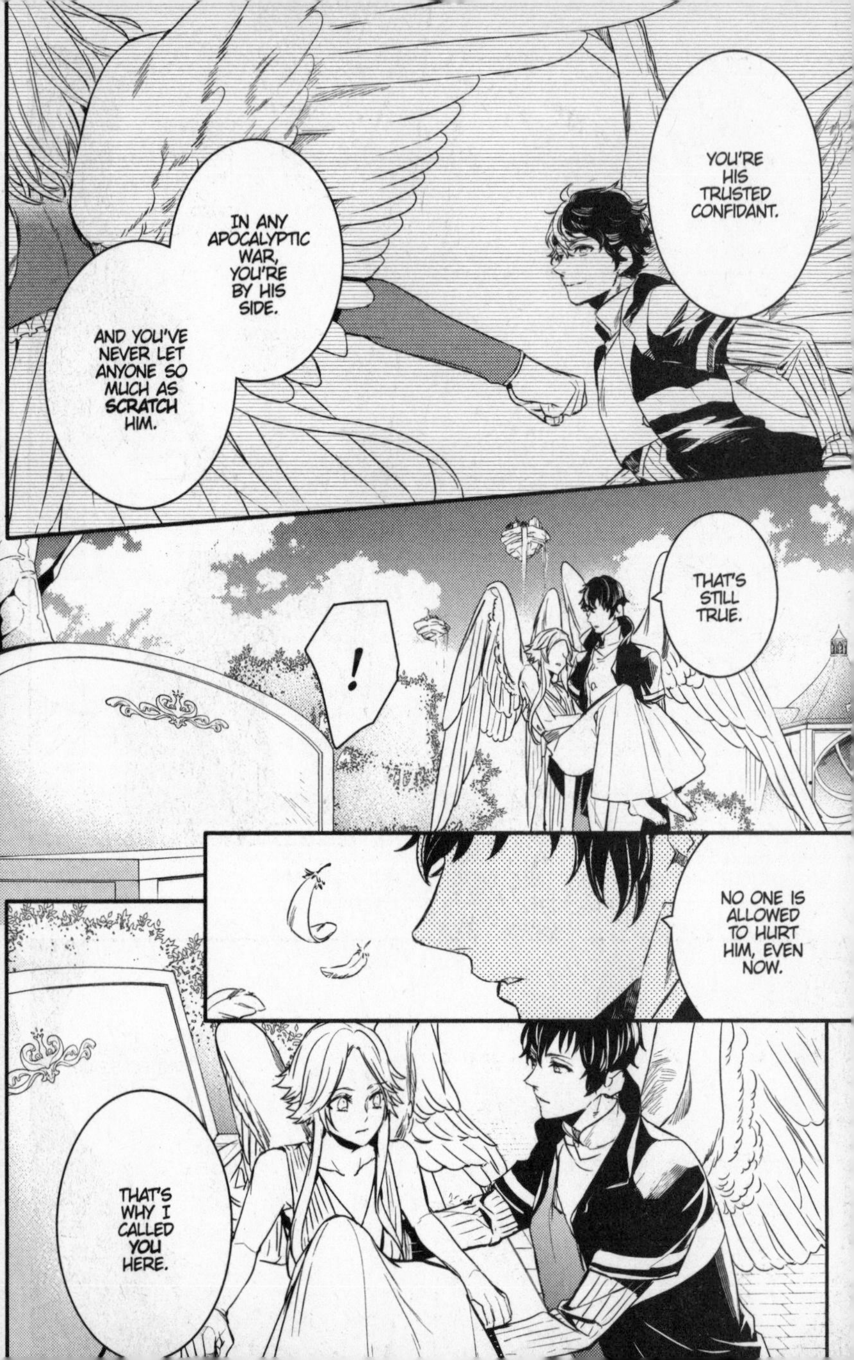
YOU'RE HIS TRUSTED CONFIDANT.
IN ANY APOCALYPTIC WAR, YOU'RE BY HIS SIDE.
AND YOU'VE NEVER LET ANYONE SO MUCH AS SCRATCH HIM.
THAT'S STILL TRUE.
!
NO ONE IS ALLOWED TO HURT HIM, EVEN NOW.
THAT'S WHY I CALLED YOU HERE.

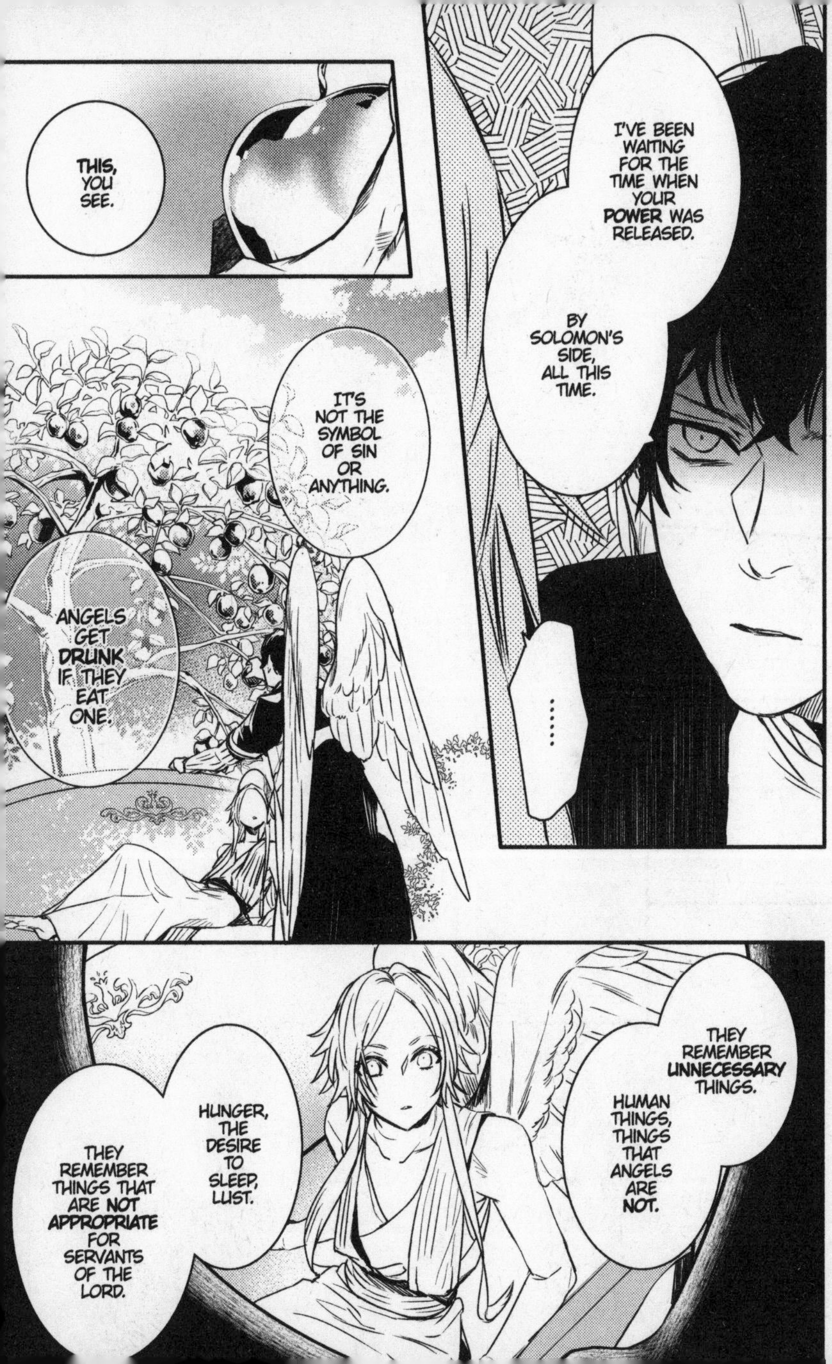
I'VE BEEN WAITING FOR THE TIME WHEN YOUR POWER WAS RELEASED.
BY SOLOMON'S SIDE, ALL THIS TIME.
......
THIS, YOU SEE.
IT'S NOT THE SYMBOL OF SIN OR ANYTHING.
ANGELS GET DRUNK IF THEY EAT ONE.
THEY REMEMBER UNNECESSARY THINGS.
HUMAN THINGS, THINGS THAT ANGELS ARE NOT.
HUNGER, THE DESIRE TO SLEEP, LUST.
THEY REMEMBER THINGS THAT ARE NOT APPROPRIATE FOR SERVANTS OF THE LORD.

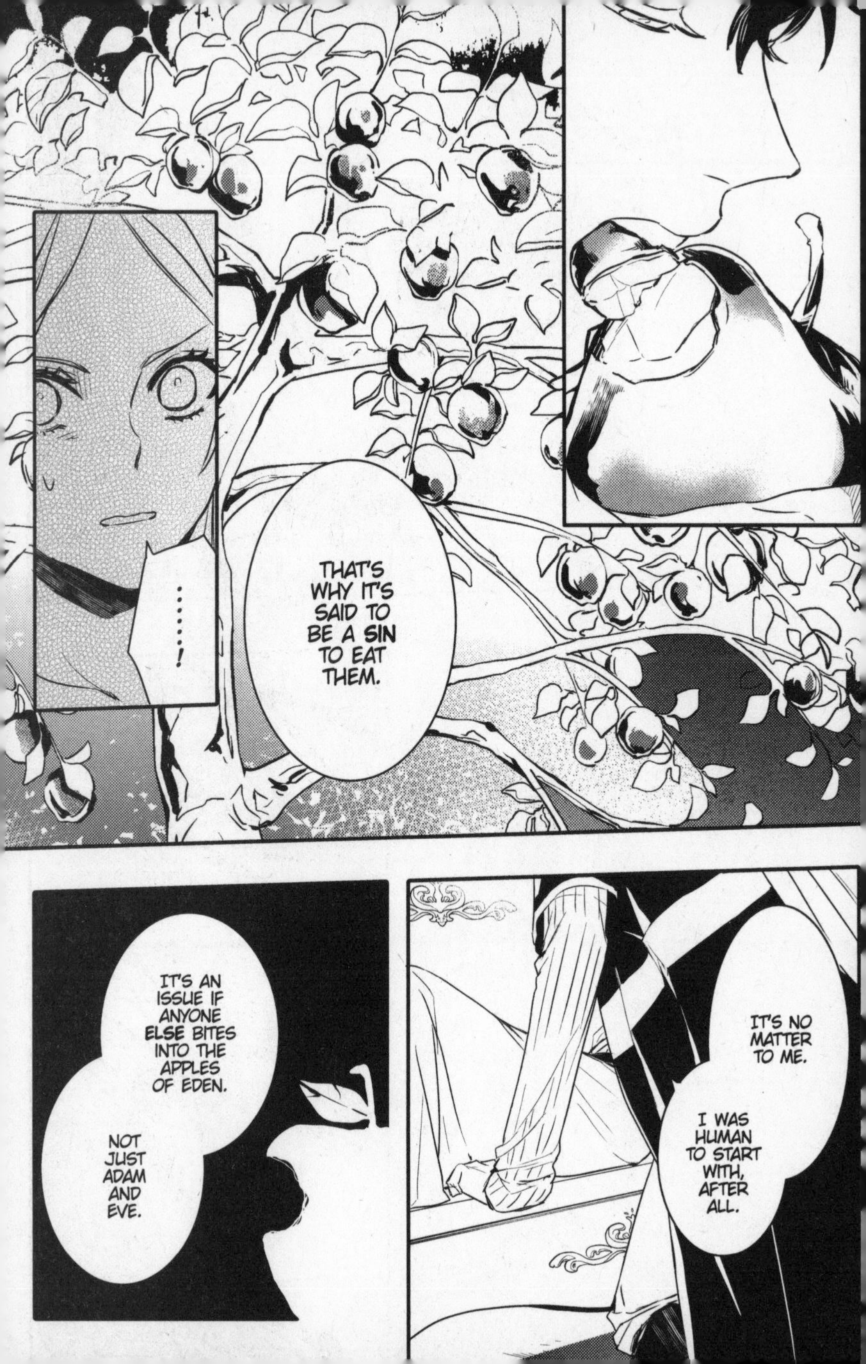
THAT'S WHY IT'S SAID TO BE A SIN TO EAT THEM.
......!
IT'S NO MATTER TO ME.
I WAS HUMAN TO START WITH, AFTER ALL.
IT'S AN ISSUE IF ANYONE ELSE BITES INTO THE APPLES OF EDEN.
NOT JUST ADAM AND EVE.

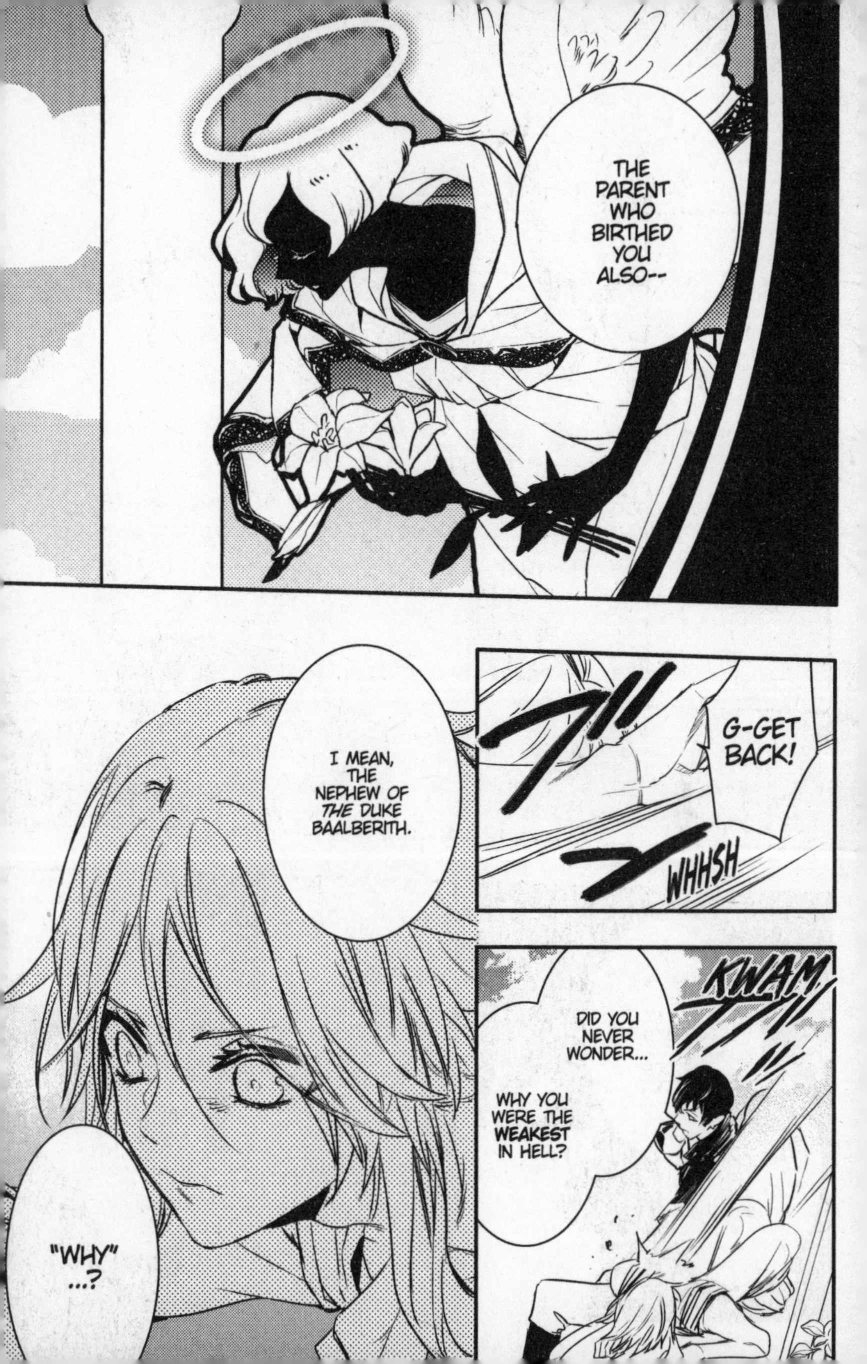
THE PARENT WHO BIRTHED YOU ALSO--
G-GET BACK!
WHHSH
KWAM
DID YOU NEVER WONDER...
WHY YOU WERE THE WEAKEST IN HELL?
I MEAN, THE NEPHEW OF THE DUKE BAALBERITH.
"WHY" ...?

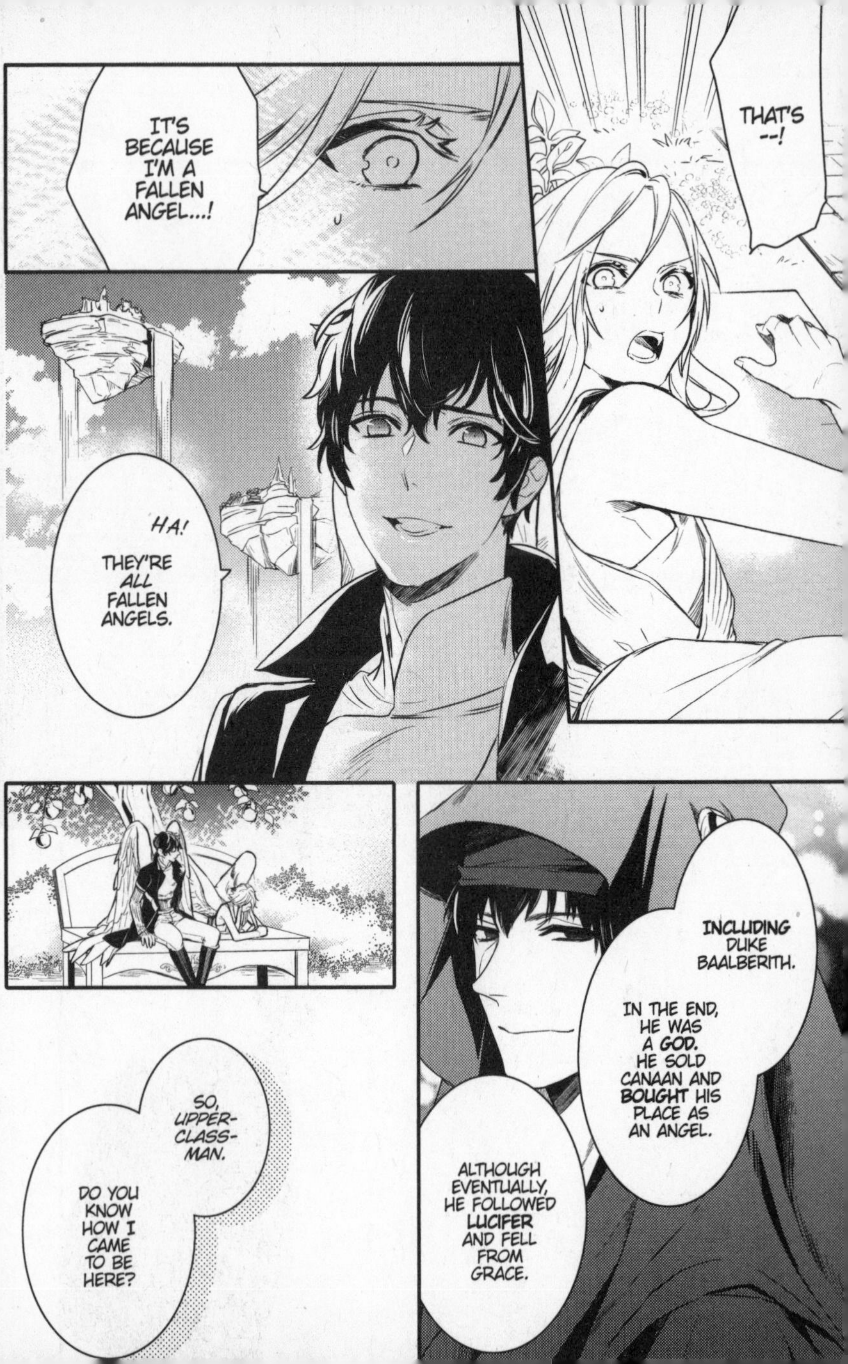
THAT'S --!
IT'S BECAUSE I'M A FALLEN ANGEL...!
HA! THEY'RE ALL FALLEN ANGELS.
INCLUDING DUKE BAALBERITH.
IN THE END, HE WAS A GOD. HE SOLD CANAAN AND BOUGHT HIS PLACE AS AN ANGEL.
ALTHOUGH EVENTUALLY, HE FOLLOWED LUCIFER AND FELL FROM GRACE.
SO, UPPER-CLASSMAN.
DO YOU KNOW HOW I CAME TO BE HERE?

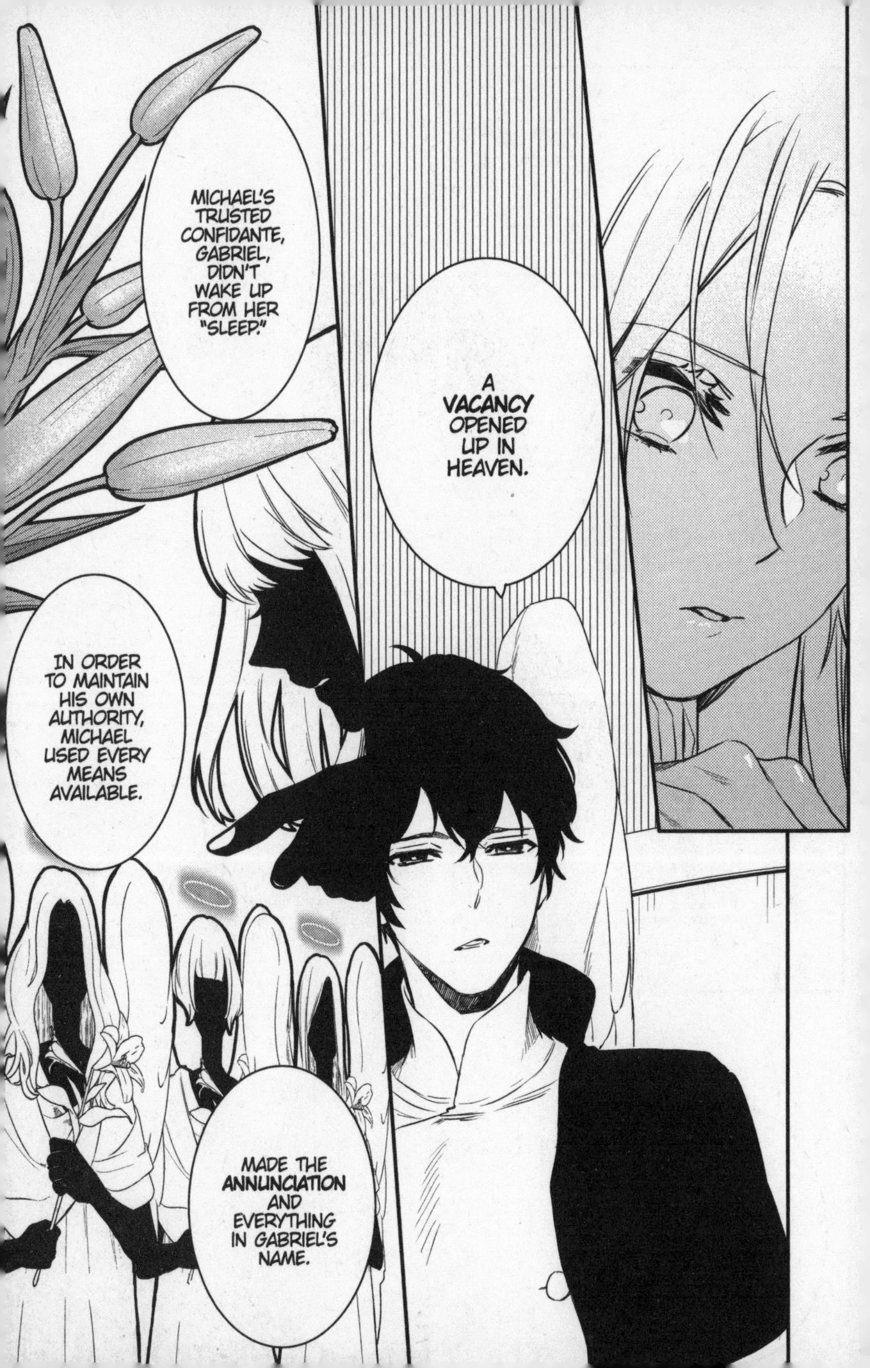
A VACANCY OPENED UP IN HEAVEN.
MICHAEL'S TRUSTED CONFIDANTE, GABRIEL, DIDN'T WAKE UP FROM HER "SLEEP."
IN ORDER TO MAINTAIN HIS OWN AUTHORITY, MICHAEL USED EVERY MEANS AVAILABLE.
MADE THE ANNUNCIATION AND EVERYTHING IN GABRIEL'S NAME.

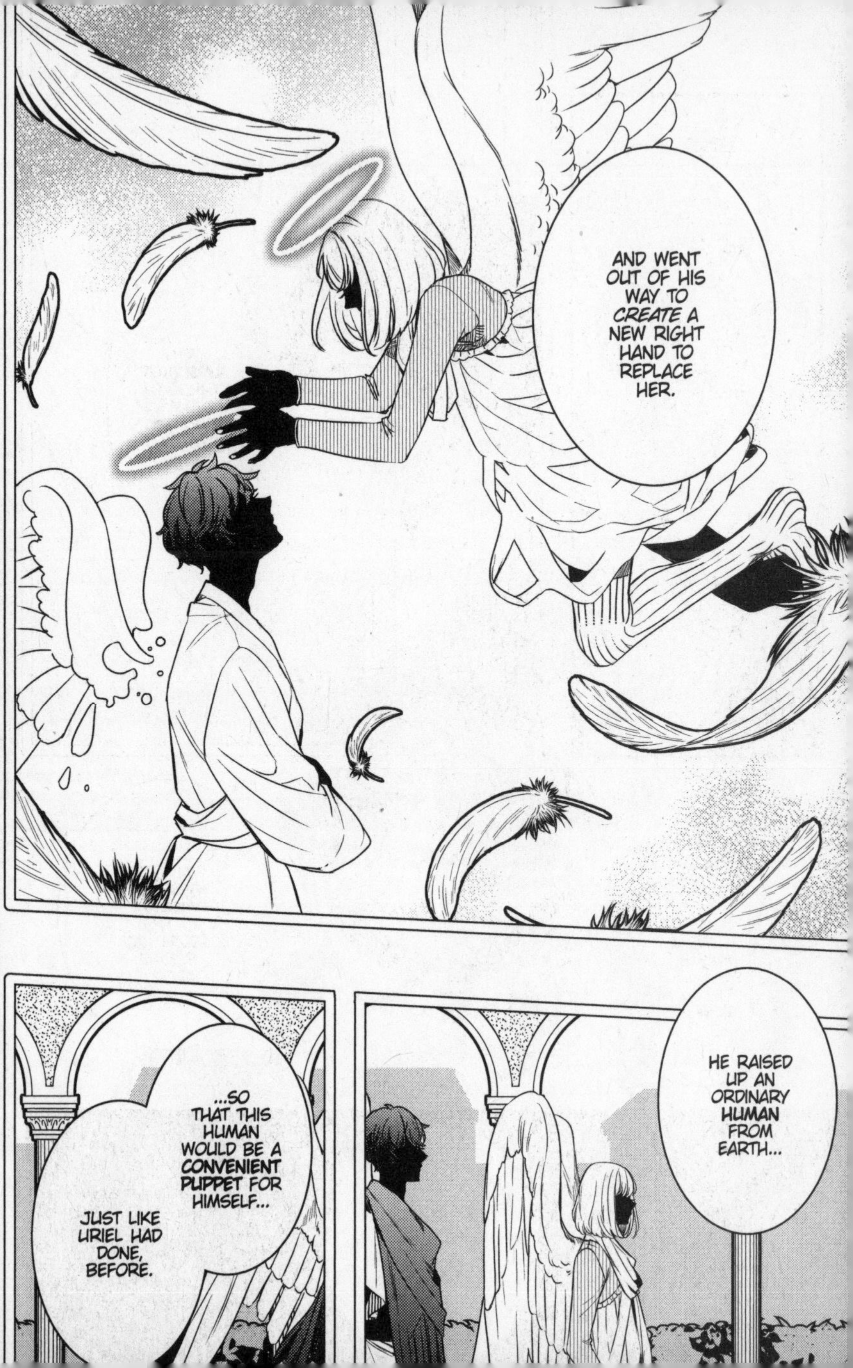
AND WENT OUT OF HIS WAY TO *CREATE* A NEW RIGHT HAND TO REPLACE HER.
HE RAISED UP AN ORDINARY HUMAN FROM EARTH...
...SO THAT THIS HUMAN WOULD BE A CONVENIENT PUPPET FOR HIMSELF...
JUST LIKE URIEL HAD DONE, BEFORE.

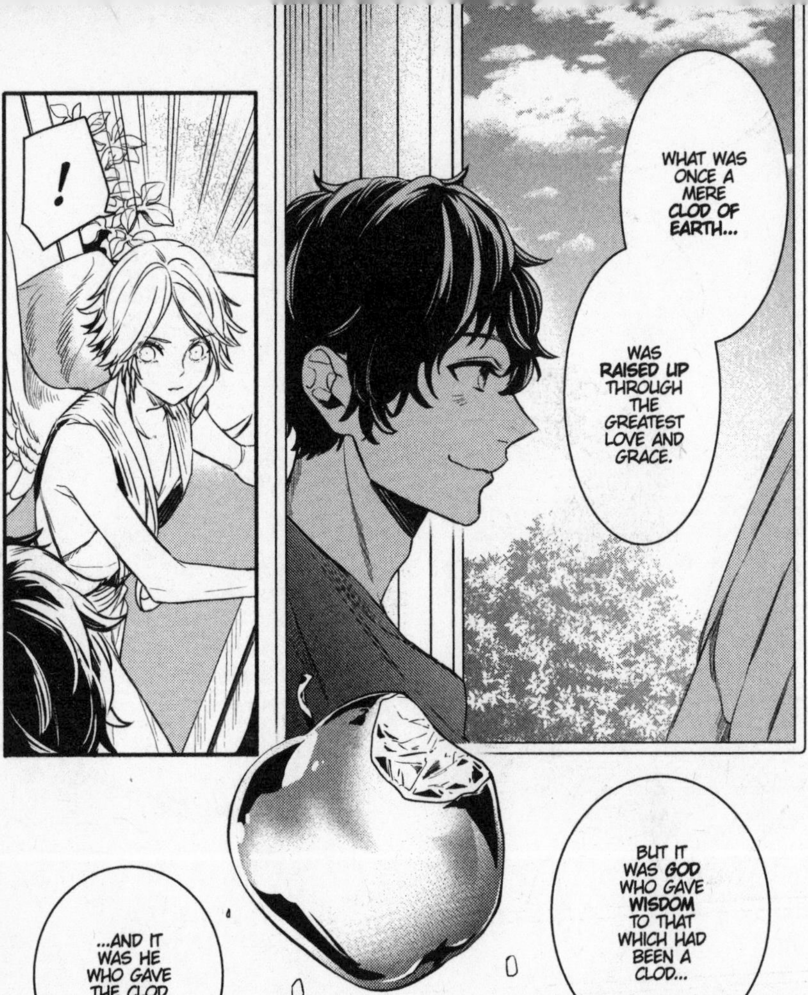
WHAT WAS ONCE A MERE CLOD OF EARTH...
WAS RAISED UP THROUGH THE GREATEST LOVE AND GRACE.
!
BUT IT WAS GOD WHO GAVE WISDOM TO THAT WHICH HAD BEEN A CLOD...
...AND IT WAS HE WHO GAVE THE CLOD POWER.

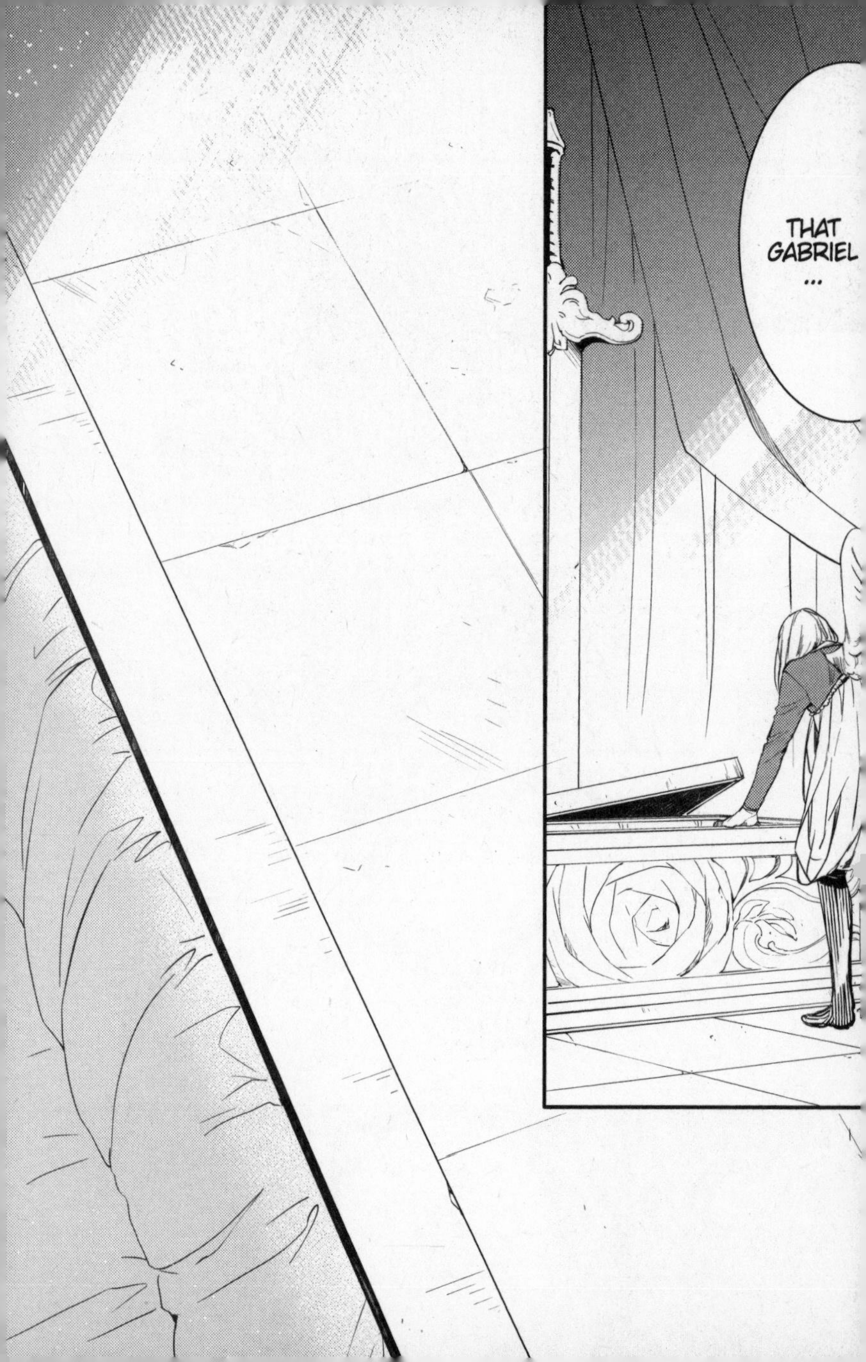
THAT GABRIEL ...

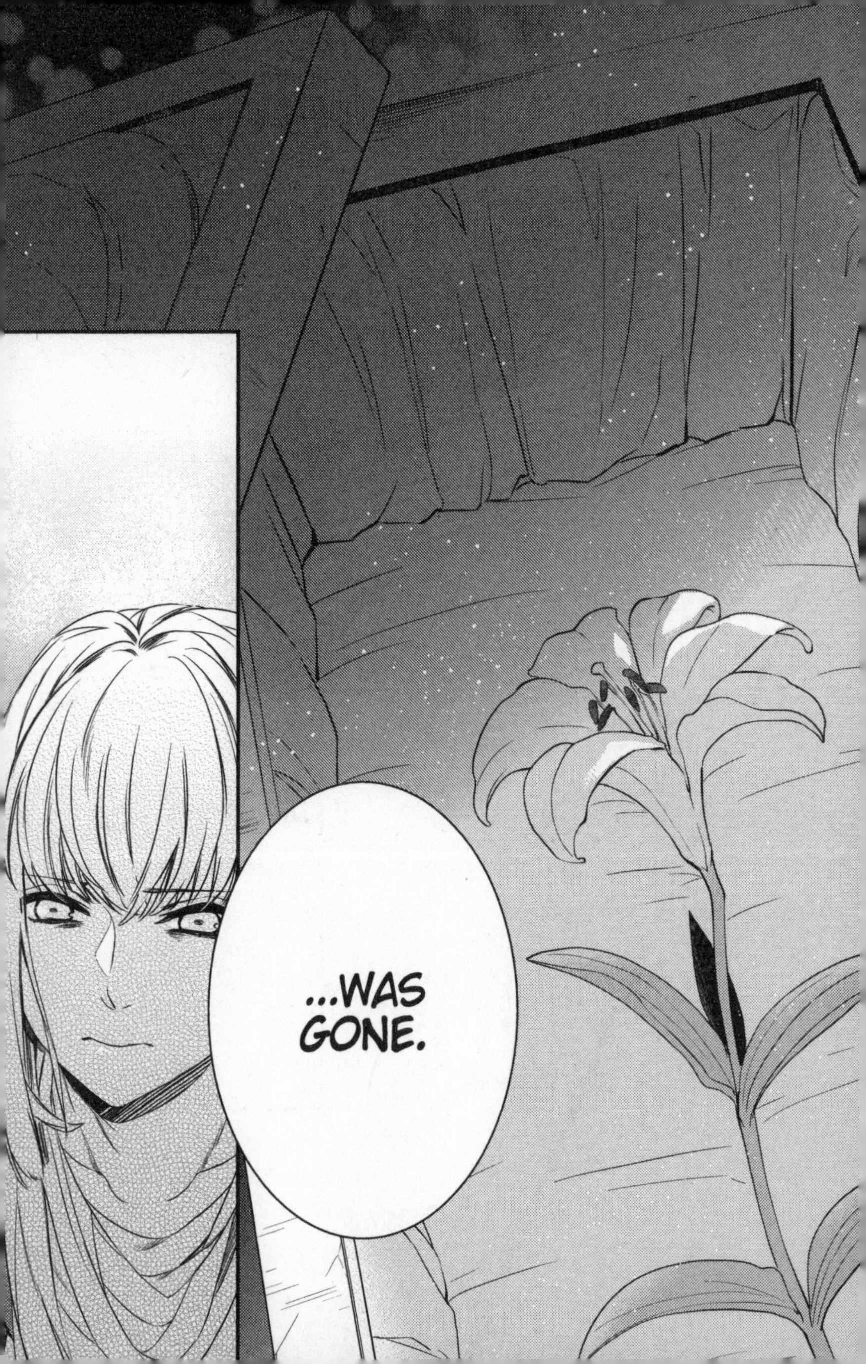
...WAS GONE.

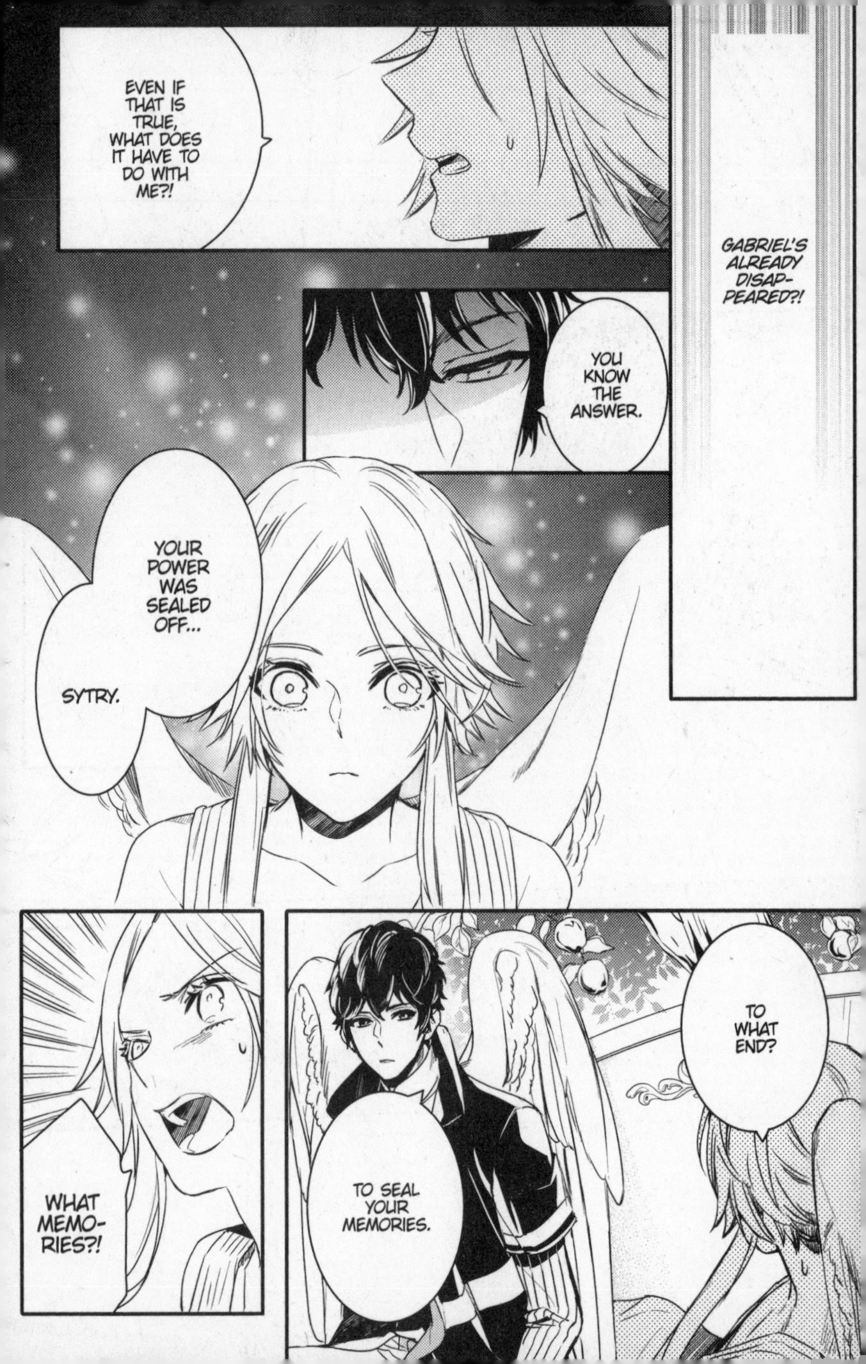
GABRIEL'S ALREADY DISAP-PEARED?!
EVEN IF THAT IS TRUE, WHAT DOES IT HAVE TO DO WITH ME?!
YOU KNOW THE ANSWER.
YOUR POWER WAS SEALED OFF...
SYTRY.
TO WHAT END?
TO SEAL YOUR MEMORIES.
WHAT MEMO-RIES?!

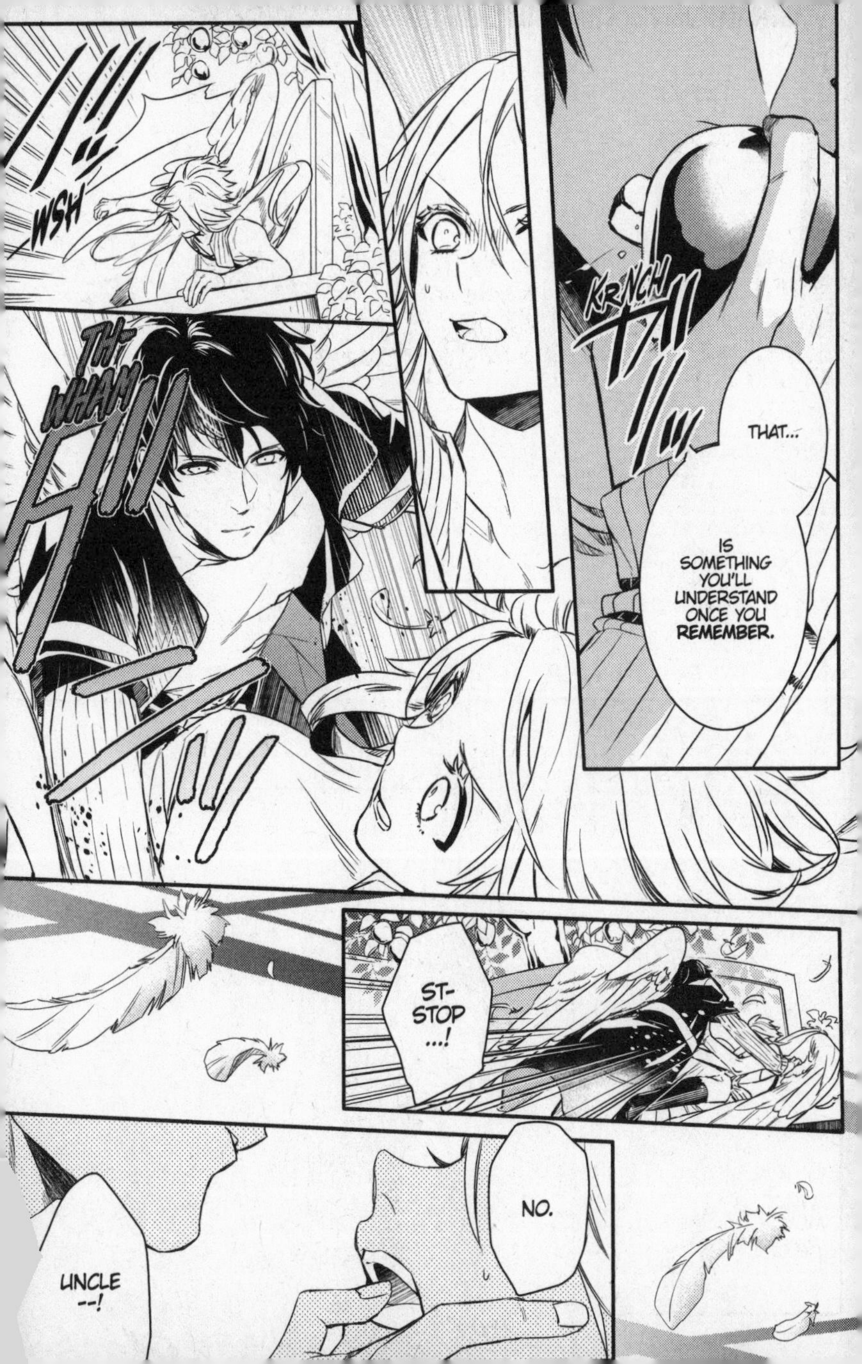
KRNCH
THAT...
IS SOMETHING YOU'LL UNDERSTAND ONCE YOU REMEMBER.
WSH
TH-WHAM
ST-STOP ...!
NO.
UNCLE --!

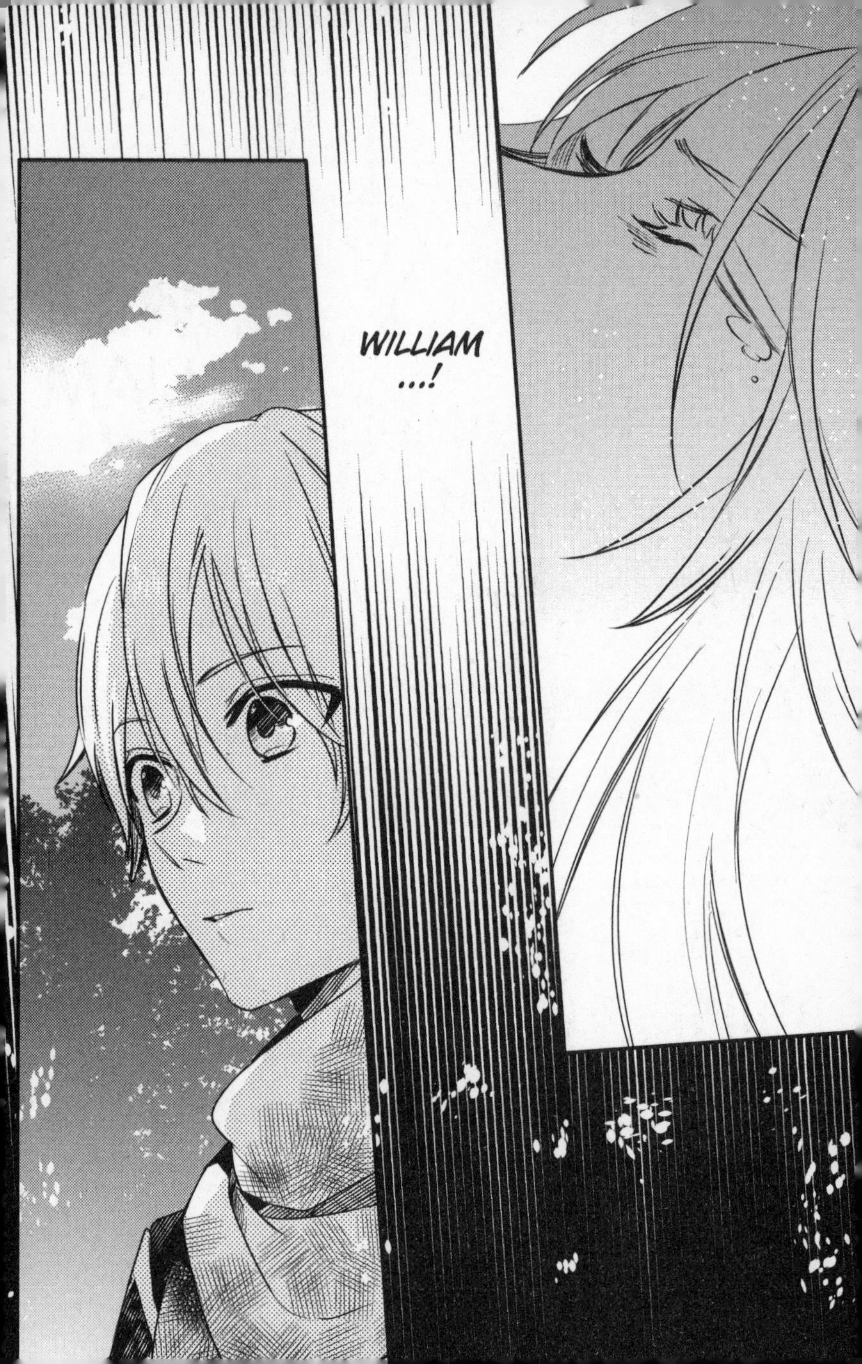
WILLIAM
...!

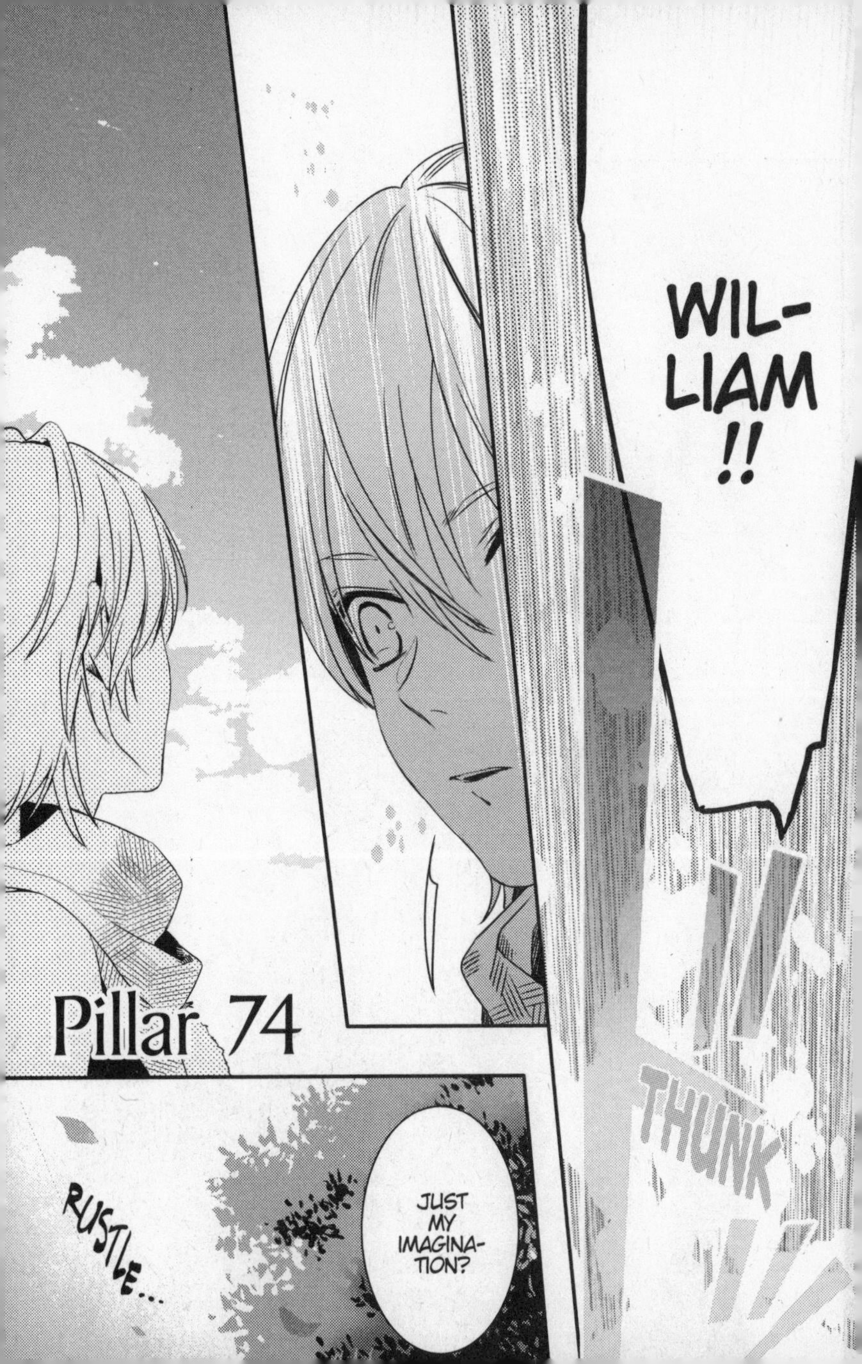
WIL-
LIAM
!!
THUNK
Pillar 74
JUST MY IMAGINATION?
RUSTLE...

Pillar 74

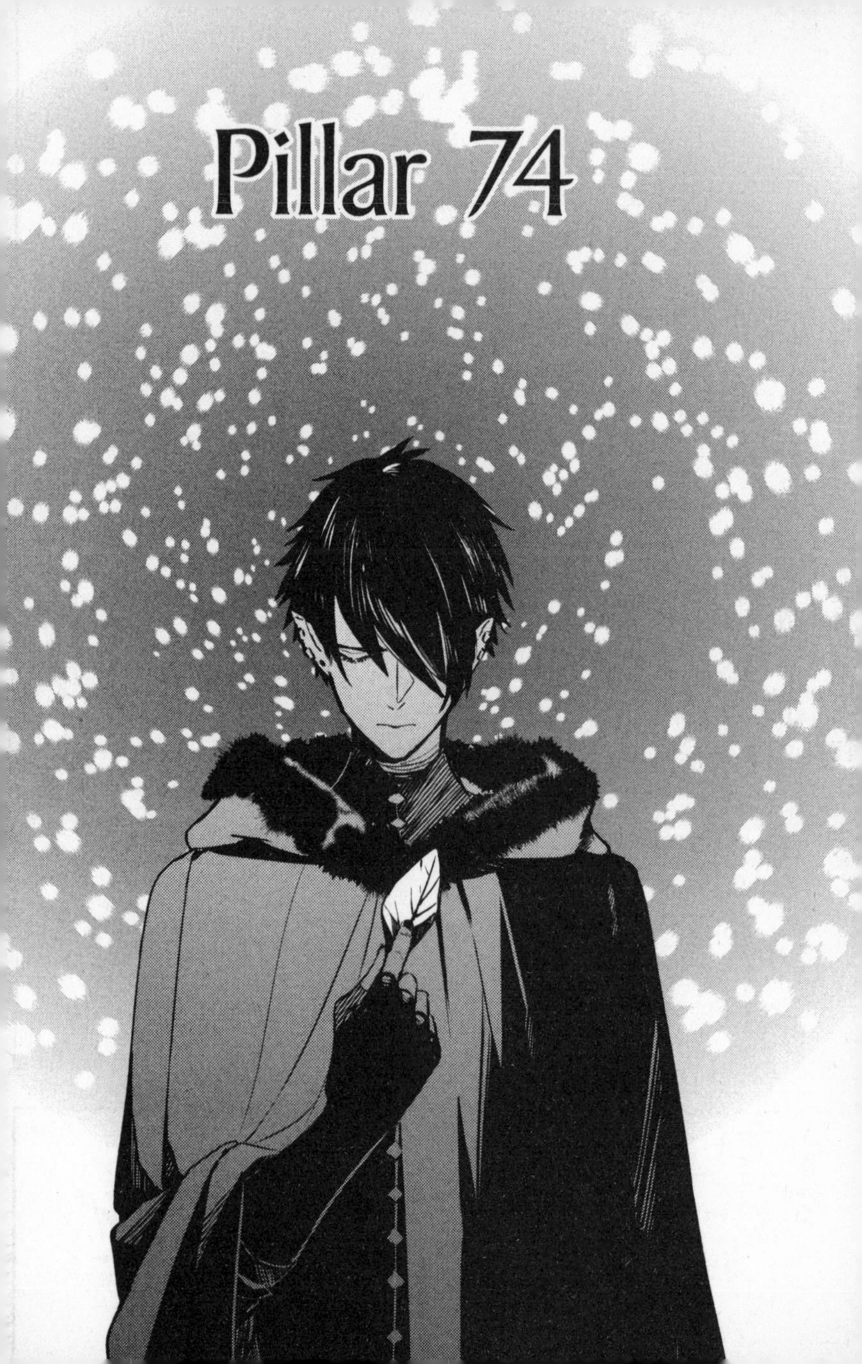

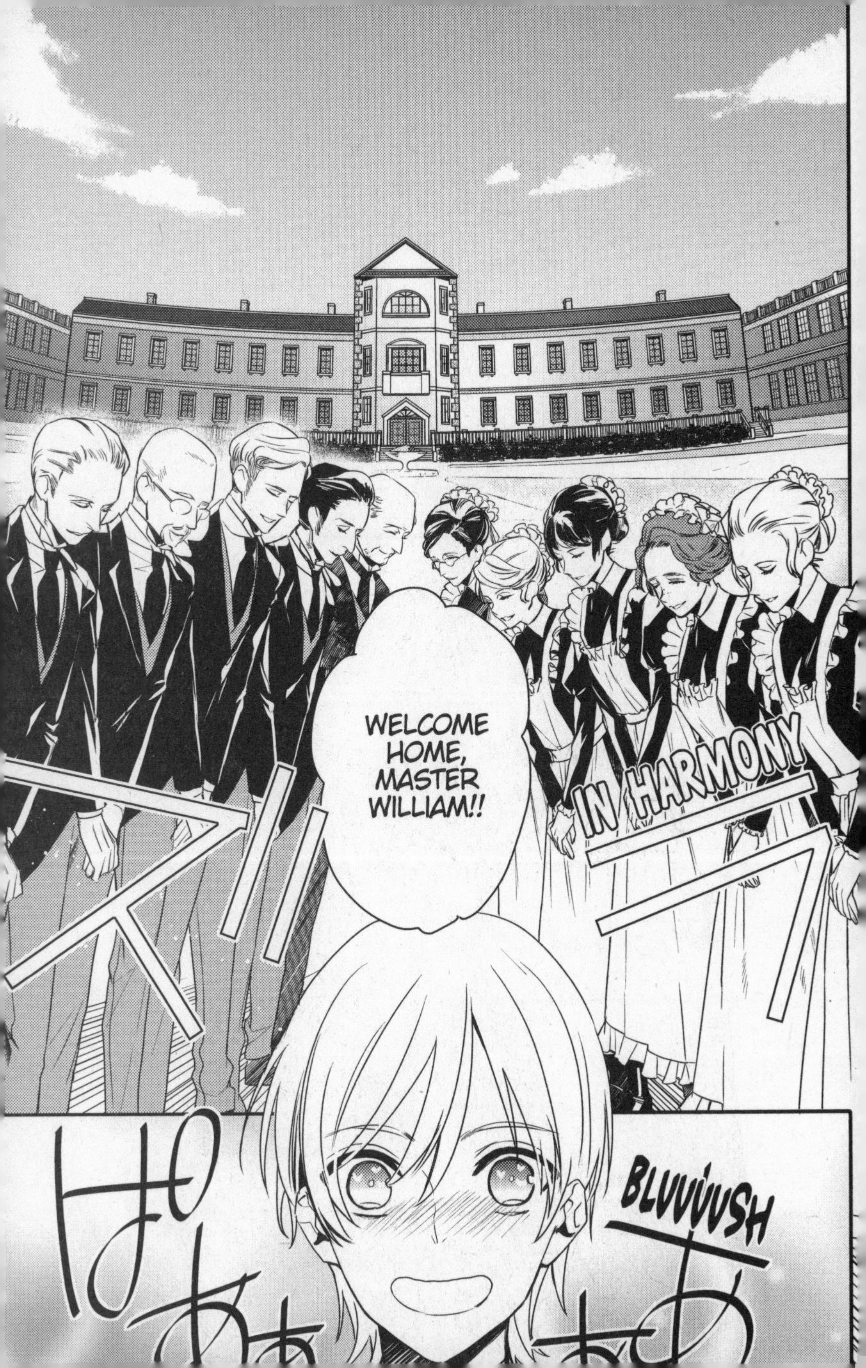
WELCOME HOME, MASTER WILLIAM!!
IN HARMONY
BLUUUUSH

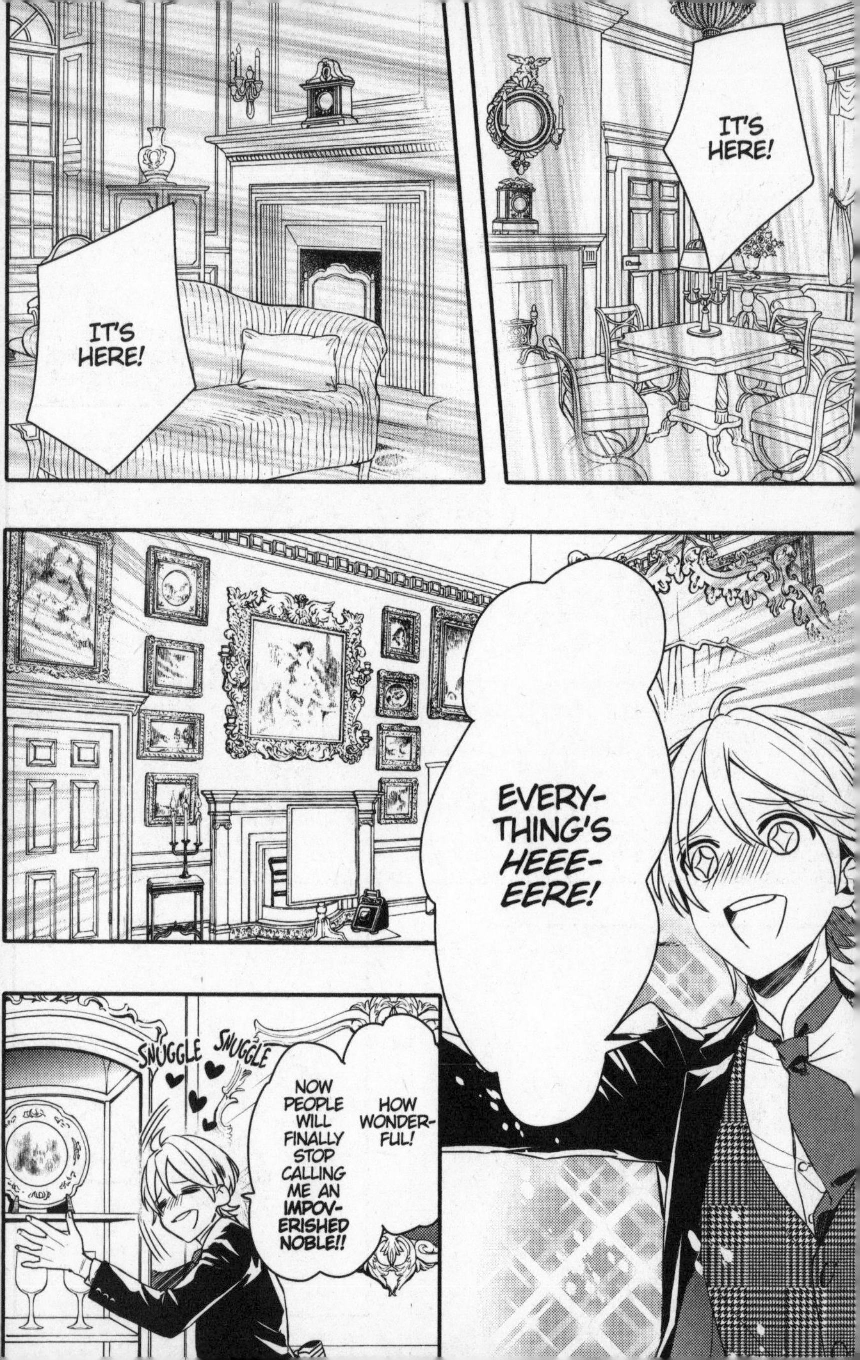
IT'S HERE!
IT'S HERE!
EVERYTHING'S HEEEEERE!
SNUGGLE SNUGGLE
HOW WONDERFUL!
NOW PEOPLE WILL FINALLY STOP CALLING ME AN IMPOVERISHED NOBLE!!

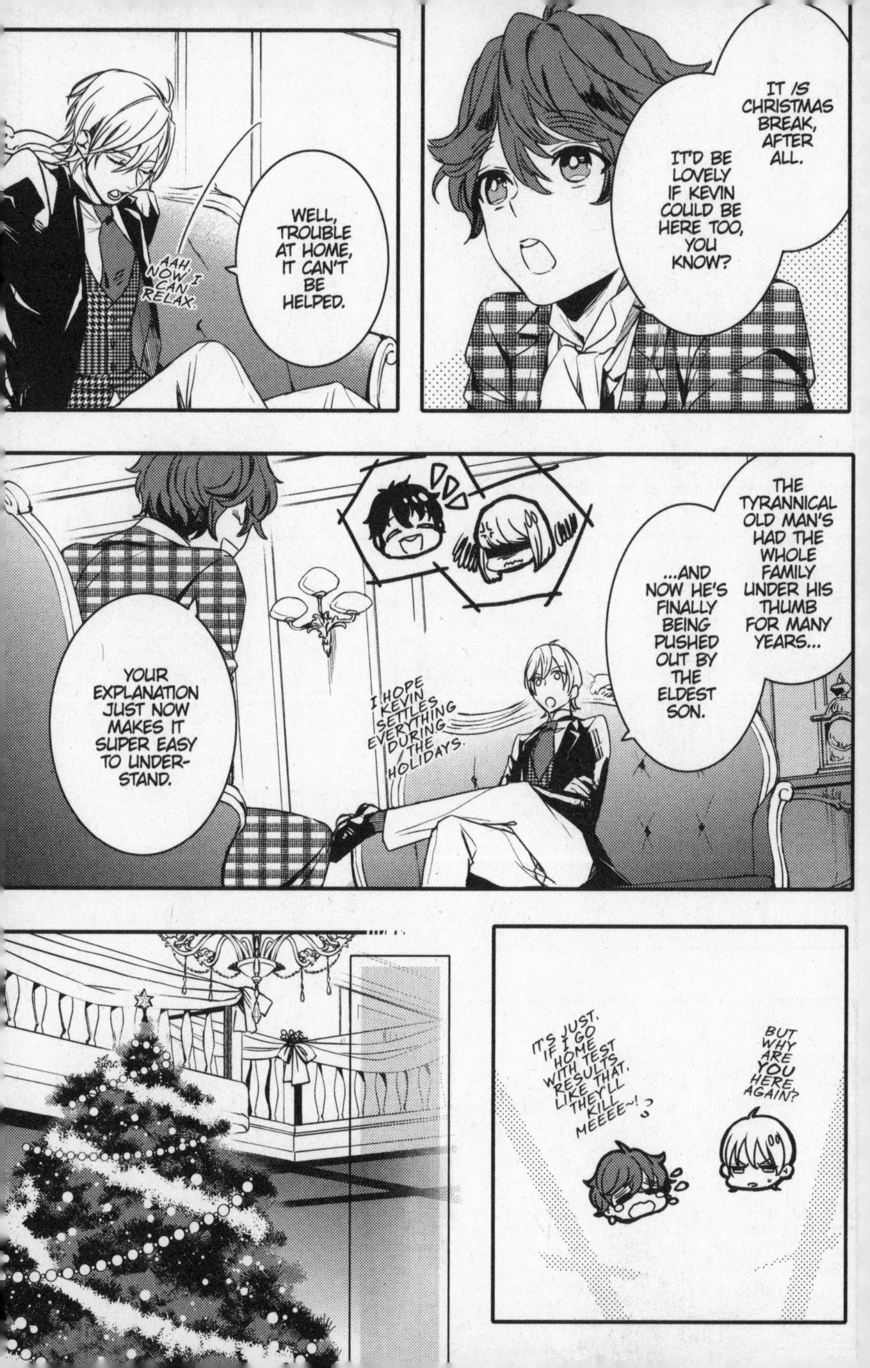
IT IS CHRISTMAS BREAK, AFTER ALL.
IT'D BE LOVELY IF KEVIN COULD BE HERE TOO, YOU KNOW?
WELL, TROUBLE AT HOME, IT CAN'T BE HELPED.
AAH, NOW I CAN RELAX.
THE TYRANNICAL OLD MAN'S HAD THE WHOLE FAMILY UNDER HIS THUMB FOR MANY YEARS...
...AND NOW HE'S FINALLY BEING PUSHED OUT BY THE ELDEST SON.
I HOPE KEVIN SETTLES EVERYTHING DURING THE HOLIDAYS.
YOUR EXPLANATION JUST NOW MAKES IT SUPER EASY TO UNDERSTAND.
BUT WHY ARE YOU HERE, AGAIN?
IT'S JUST, IF I GO HOME WITH TEST RESULTS LIKE THAT, THEY'LL KILL MEEEE~!

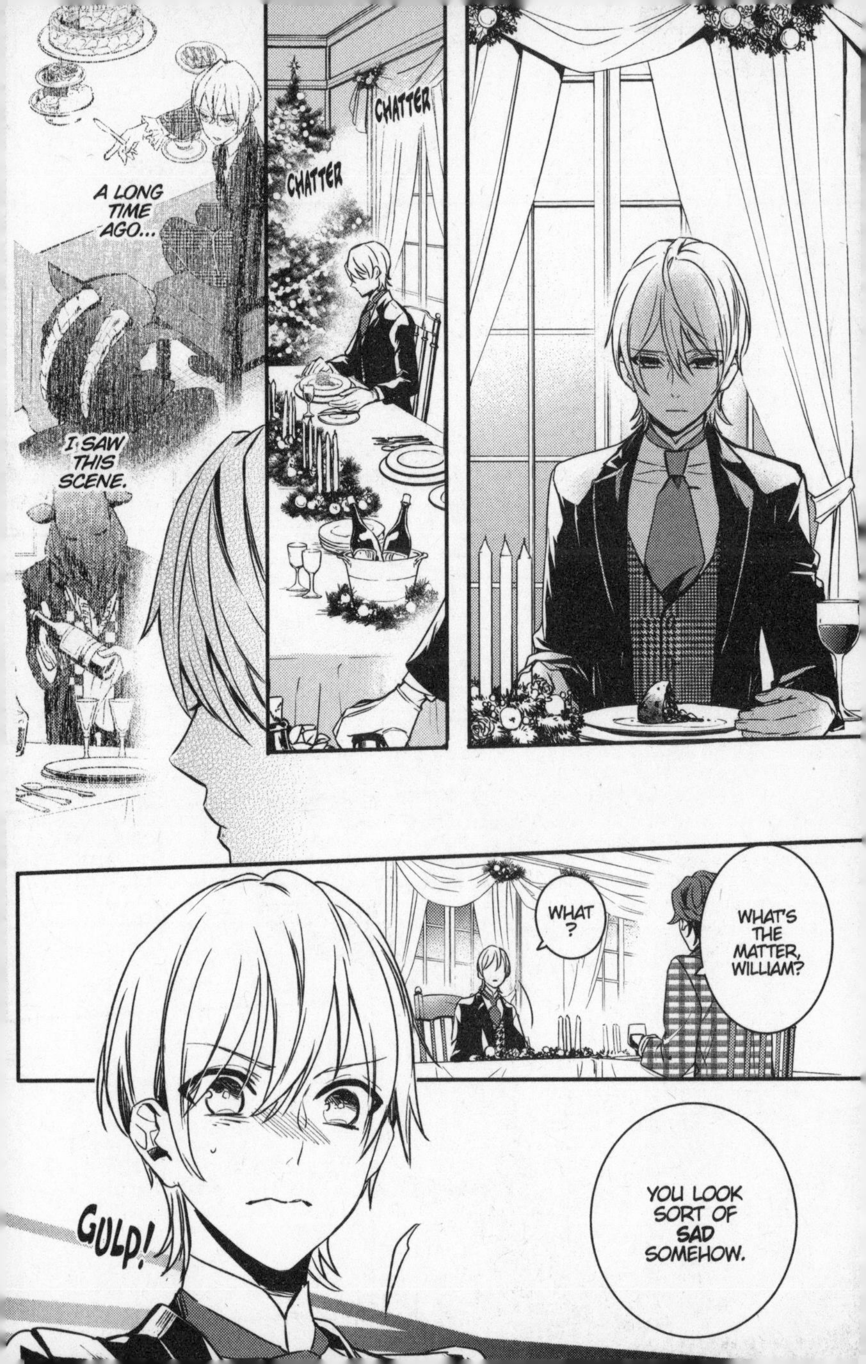
CHATTER
CHATTER
A LONG TIME AGO...
I SAW THIS SCENE.
WHAT'S THE MATTER, WILLIAM?
WHAT?
YOU LOOK SORT OF SAD SOMEHOW.
GULP!

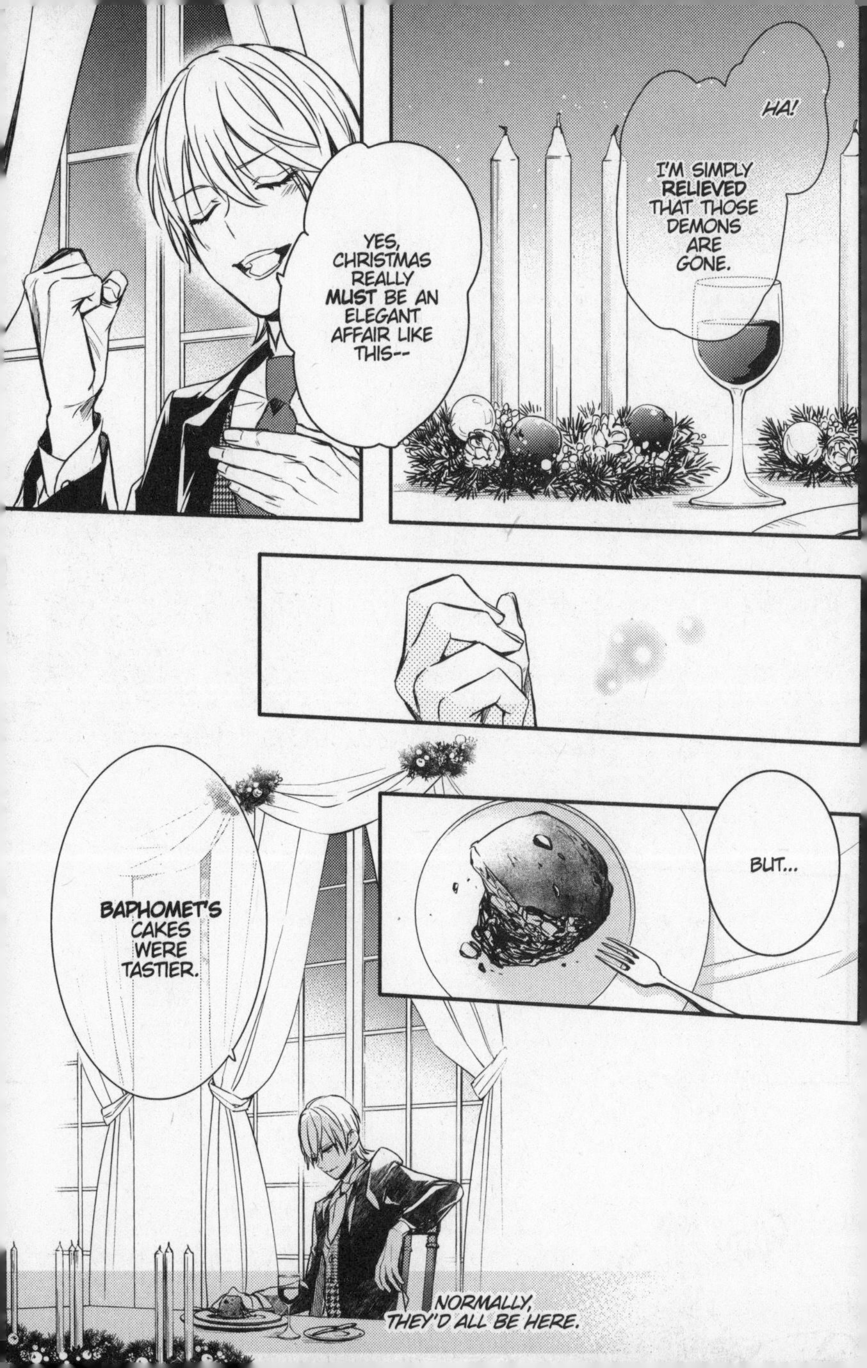
HA!
I'M SIMPLY RELIEVED THAT THOSE DEMONS ARE GONE.
YES, CHRISTMAS REALLY MUST BE AN ELEGANT AFFAIR LIKE THIS--
BUT...
BAPHOMET'S CAKES WERE TASTIER.
NORMALLY, THEY'D ALL BE HERE.

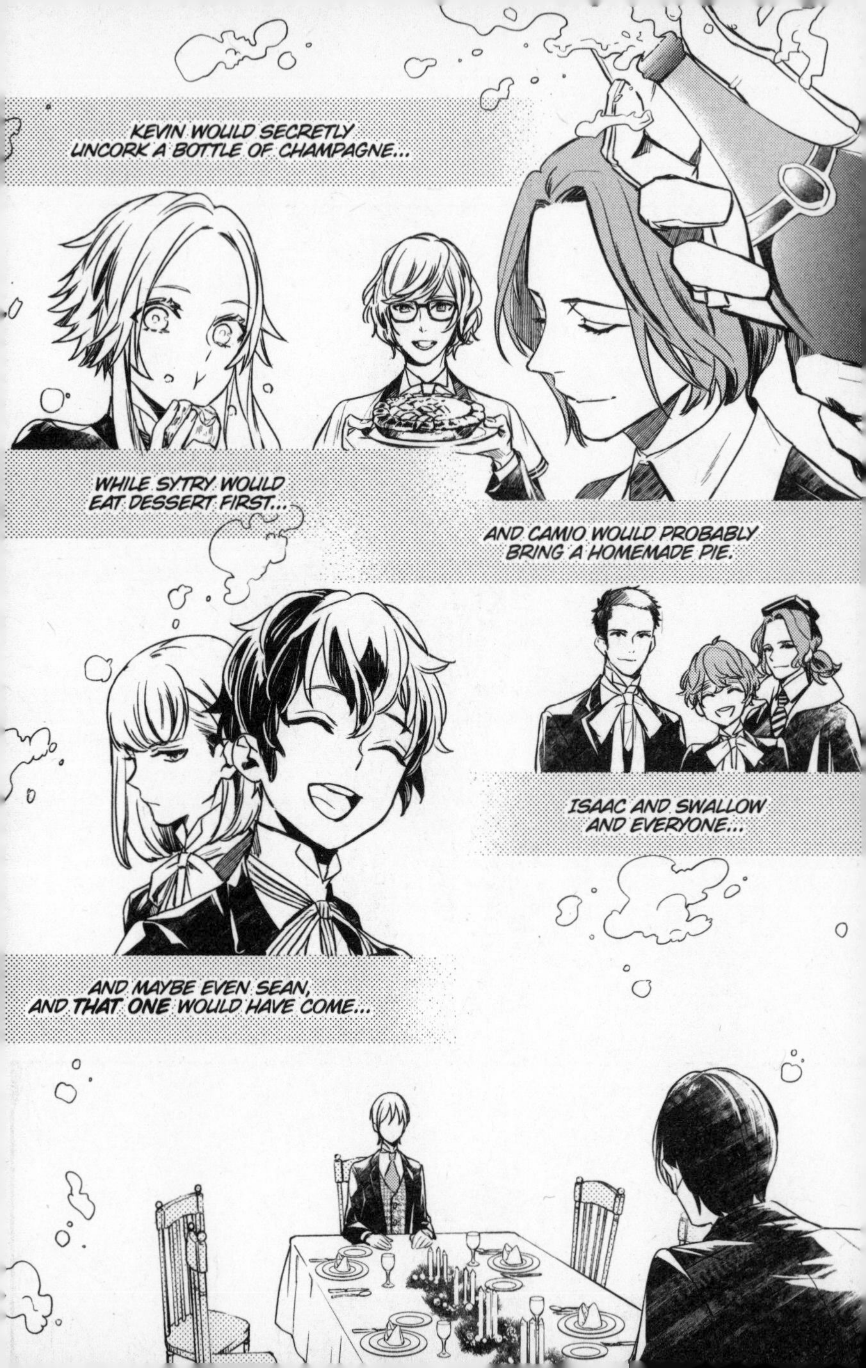
KEVIN WOULD SECRETLY UNCORK A BOTTLE OF CHAMPAGNE...
WHILE SYTRY WOULD EAT DESSERT FIRST...
AND CAMIO WOULD PROBABLY BRING A HOMEMADE PIE.
ISAAC AND SWALLOW AND EVERYONE...
AND MAYBE EVEN SEAN, AND THAT ONE WOULD HAVE COME...

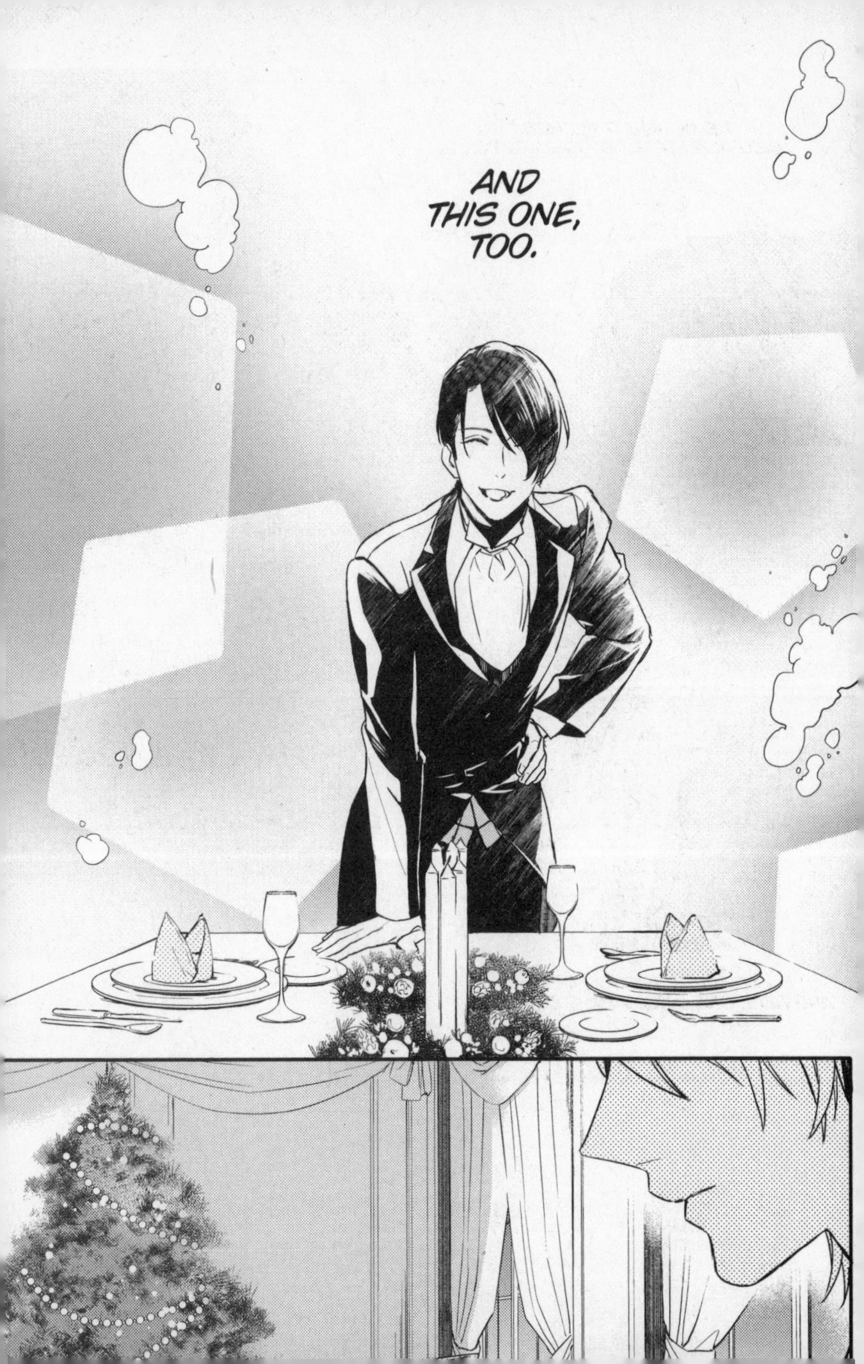
AND THIS ONE, TOO.

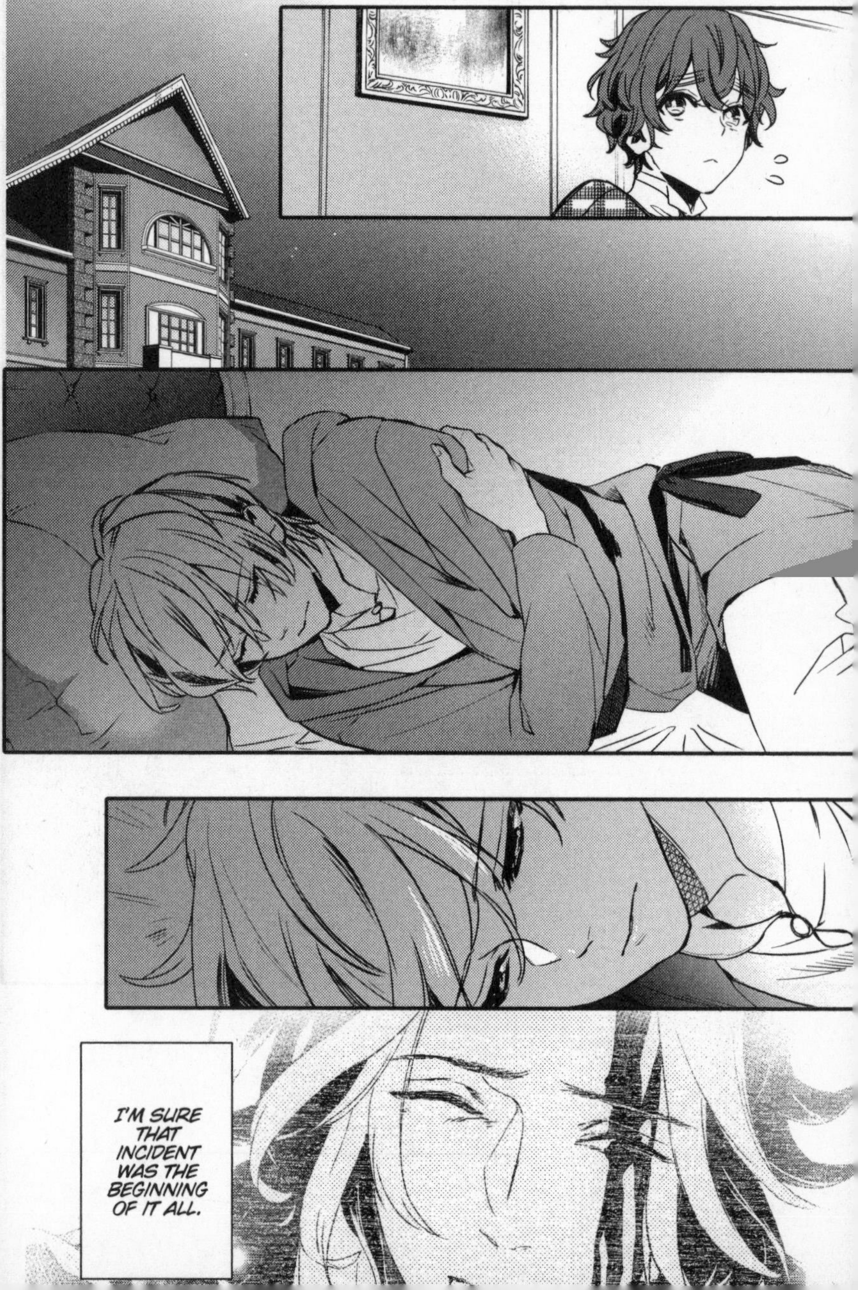
I'M SURE THAT INCIDENT WAS THE BEGINNING OF IT ALL.

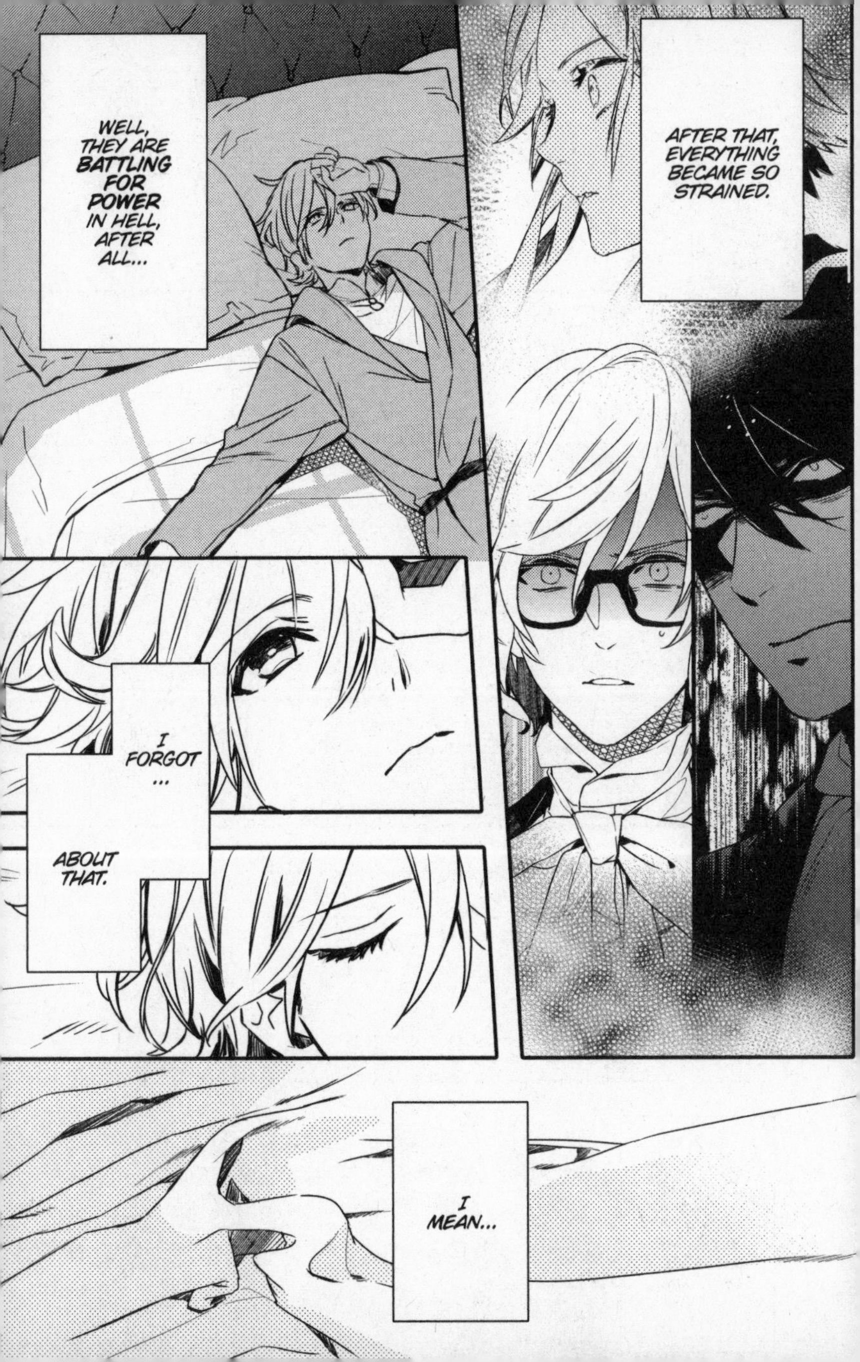
AFTER THAT, EVERYTHING BECAME SO STRAINED.
WELL, THEY ARE BATTLING FOR POWER IN HELL, AFTER ALL...
I FORGOT ...
ABOUT THAT.
I MEAN...

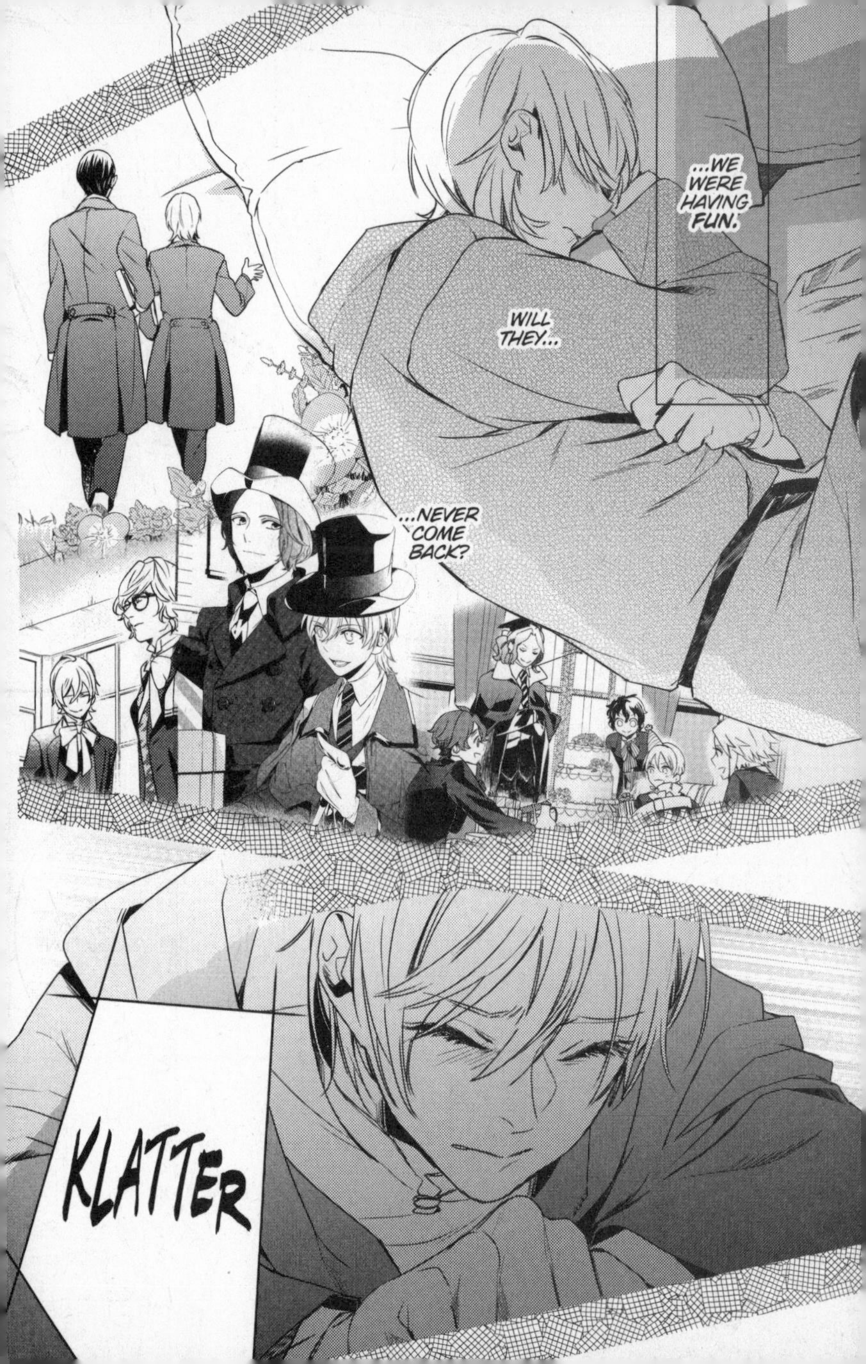
...WE WERE HAVING FUN.
WILL THEY...
...NEVER COME BACK?
KLATTER

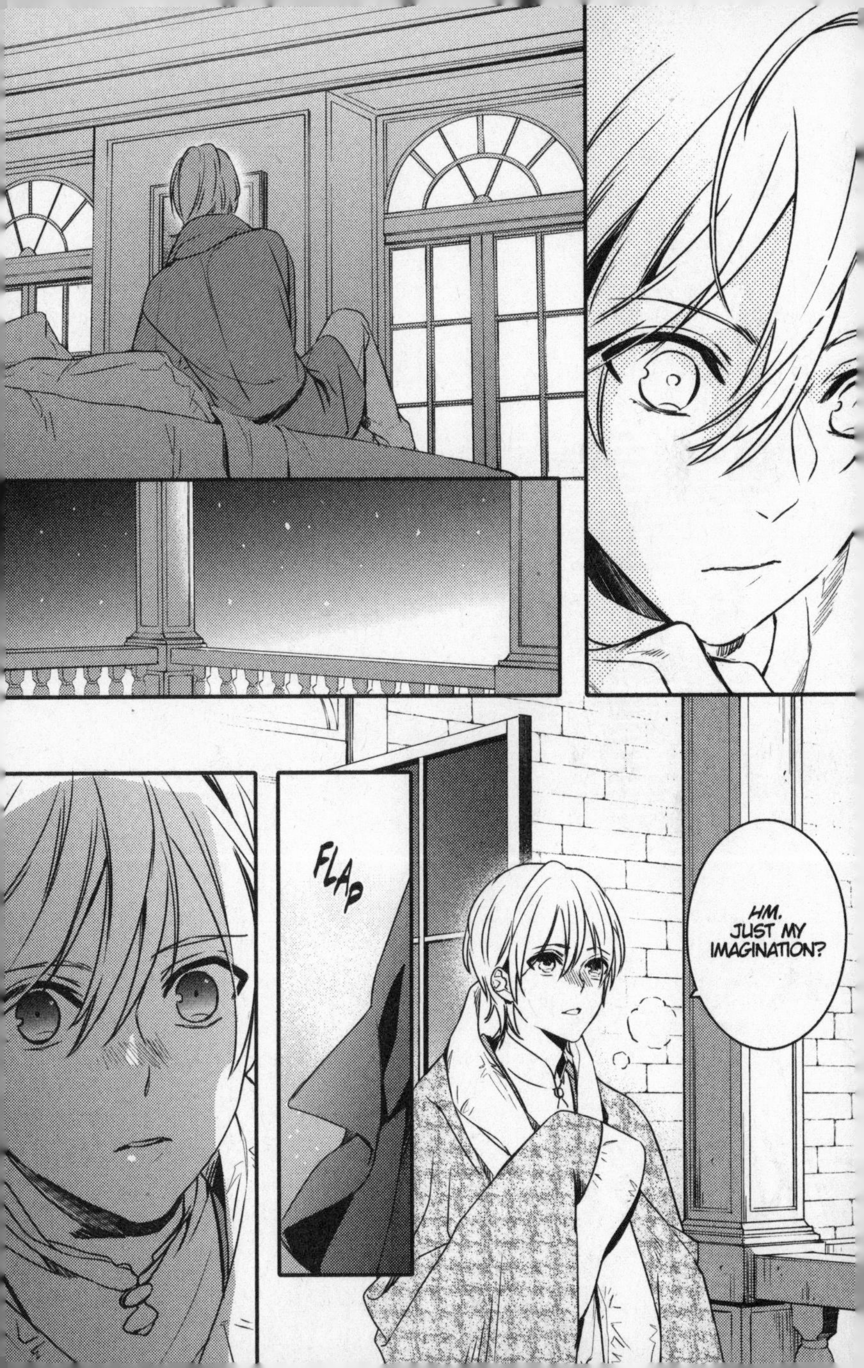
FLAP
HM. JUST MY IMAGINATION?

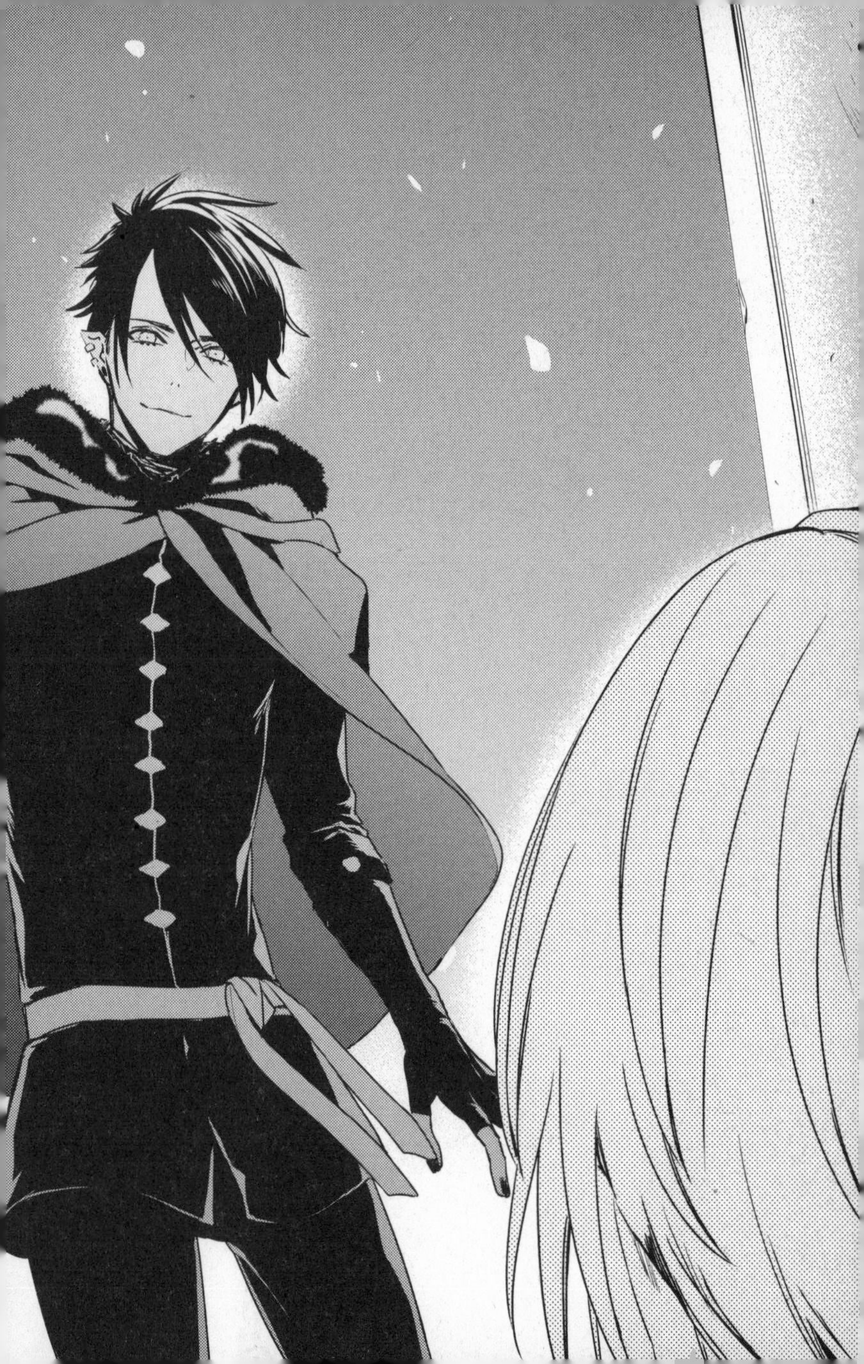

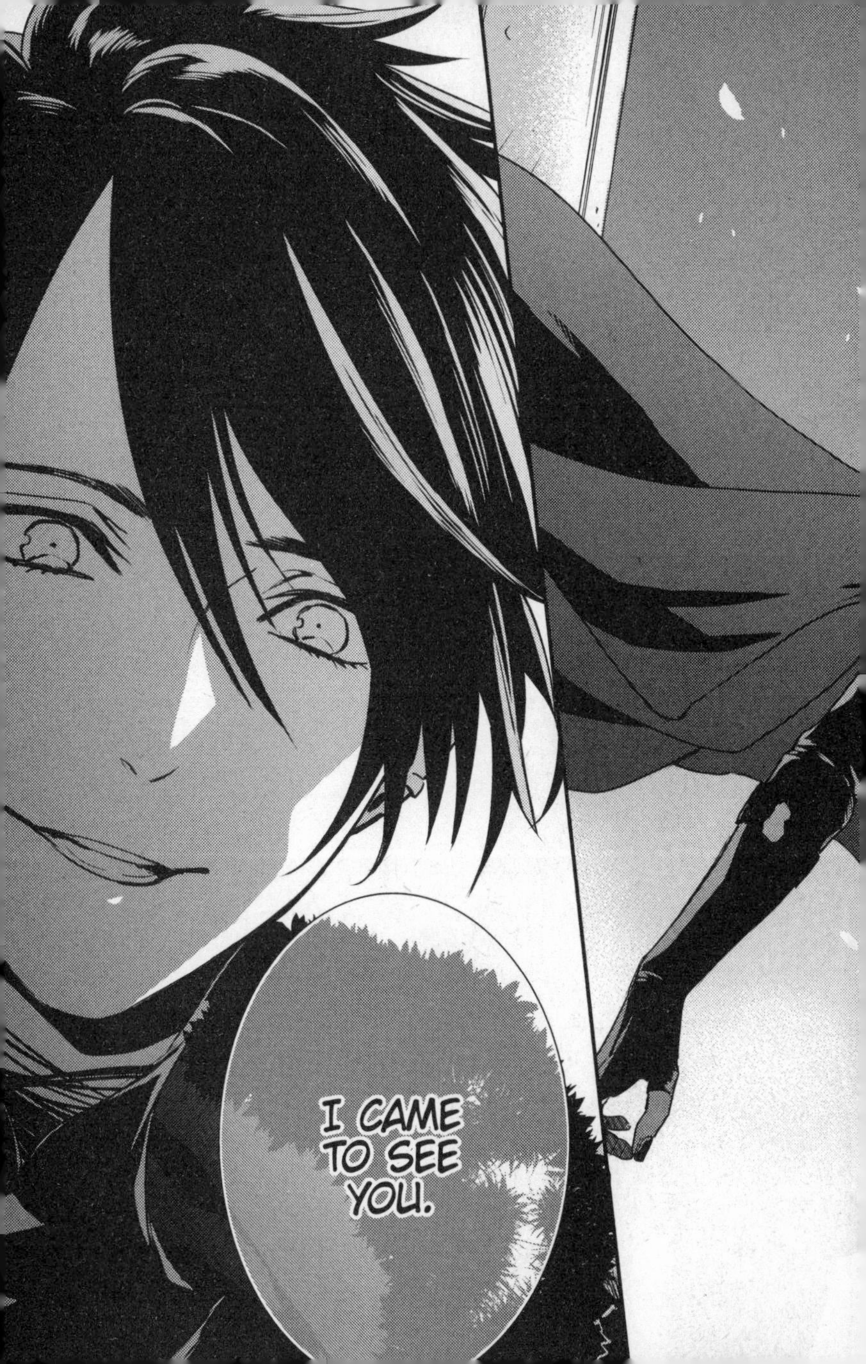
I CAME TO SEE YOU.

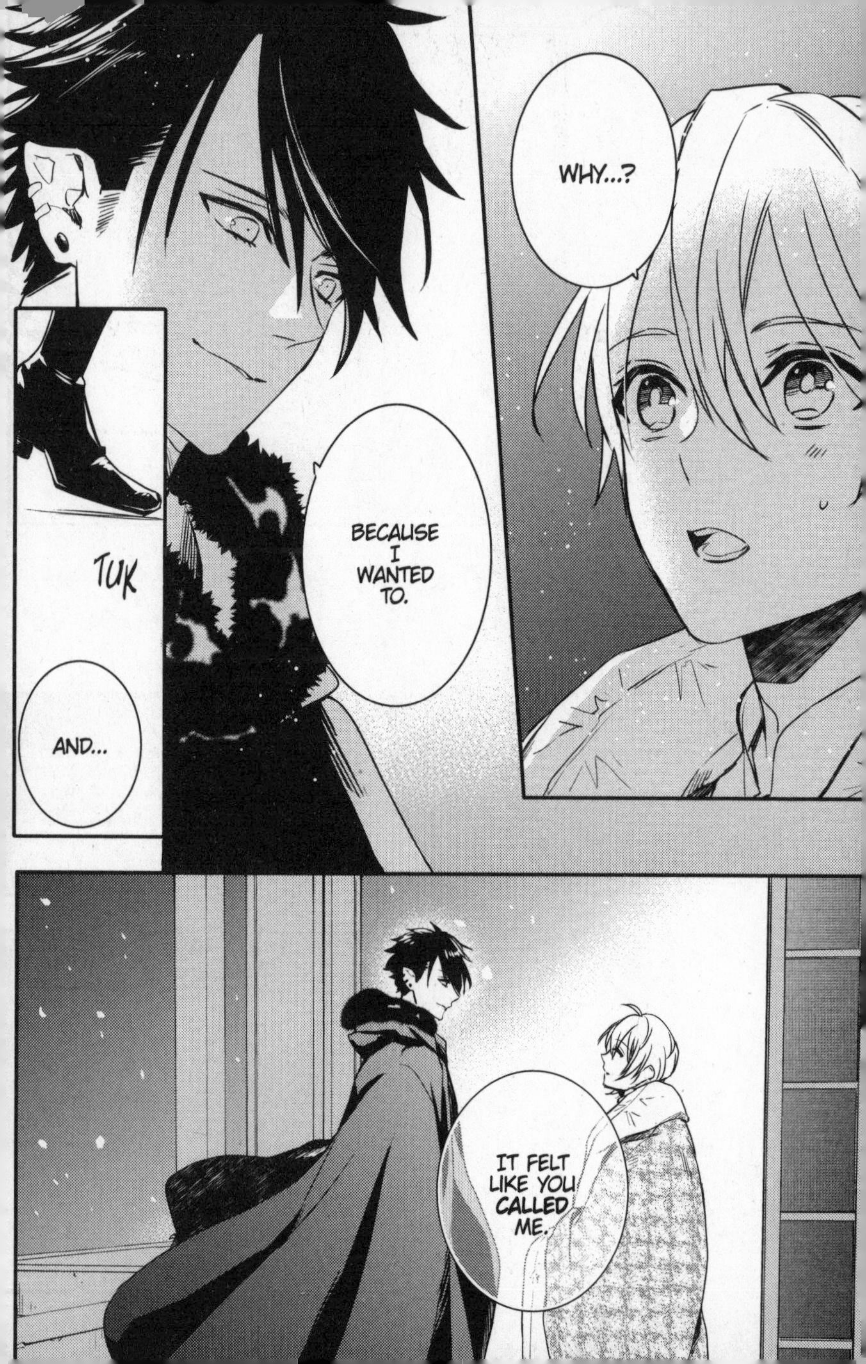
WHY...?
BECAUSE I WANTED TO.
TUK
AND...
IT FELT LIKE YOU CALLED ME.

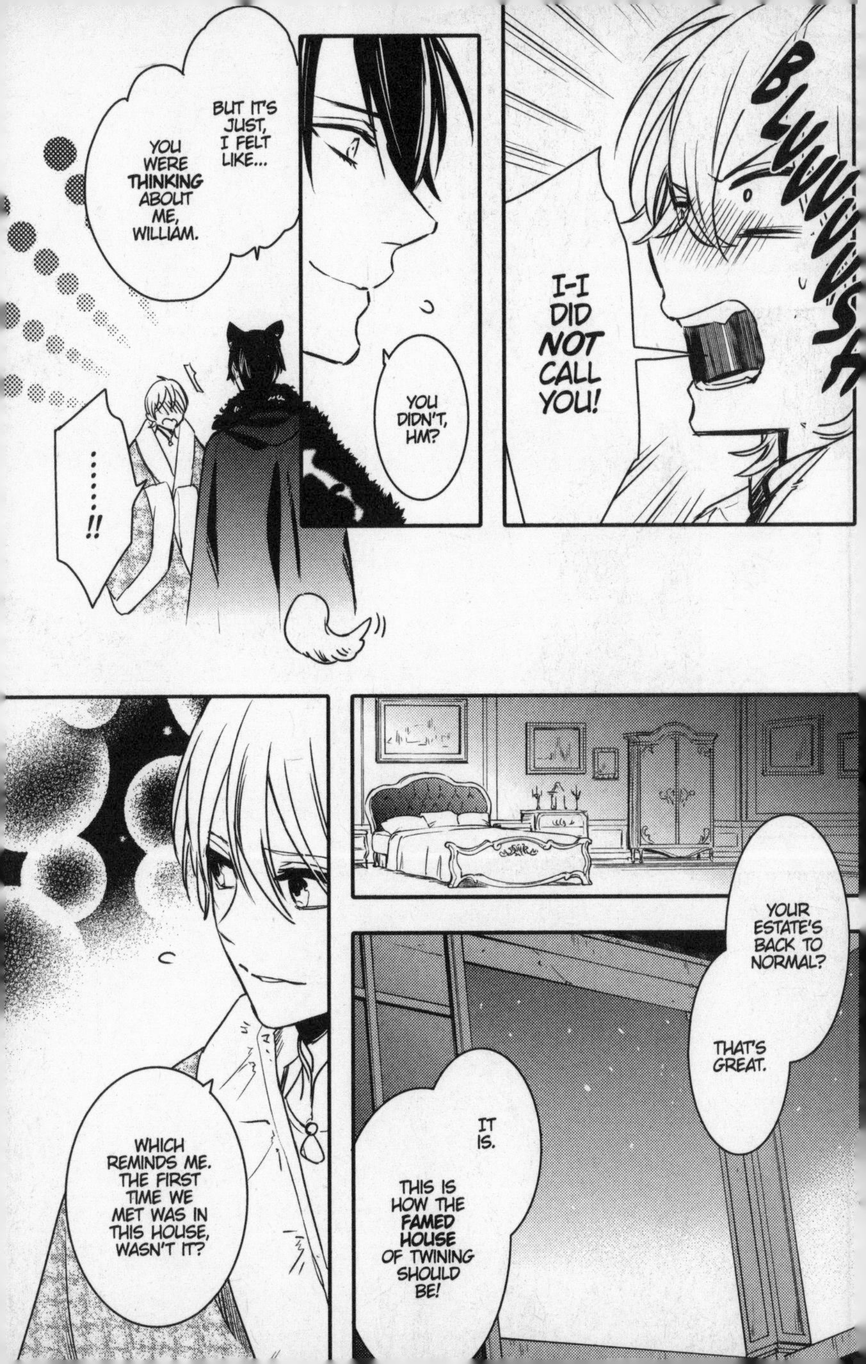
BLUUUUSH
I-I DID NOT CALL YOU!
YOU DIDN'T, HM?
BUT IT'S JUST, I FELT LIKE...
YOU WERE THINKING ABOUT ME, WILLIAM.
......!!
YOUR ESTATE'S BACK TO NORMAL?
THAT'S GREAT.
IT IS.
THIS IS HOW THE FAMED HOUSE OF TWINING SHOULD BE!
WHICH REMINDS ME. THE FIRST TIME WE MET WAS IN THIS HOUSE, WASN'T IT?

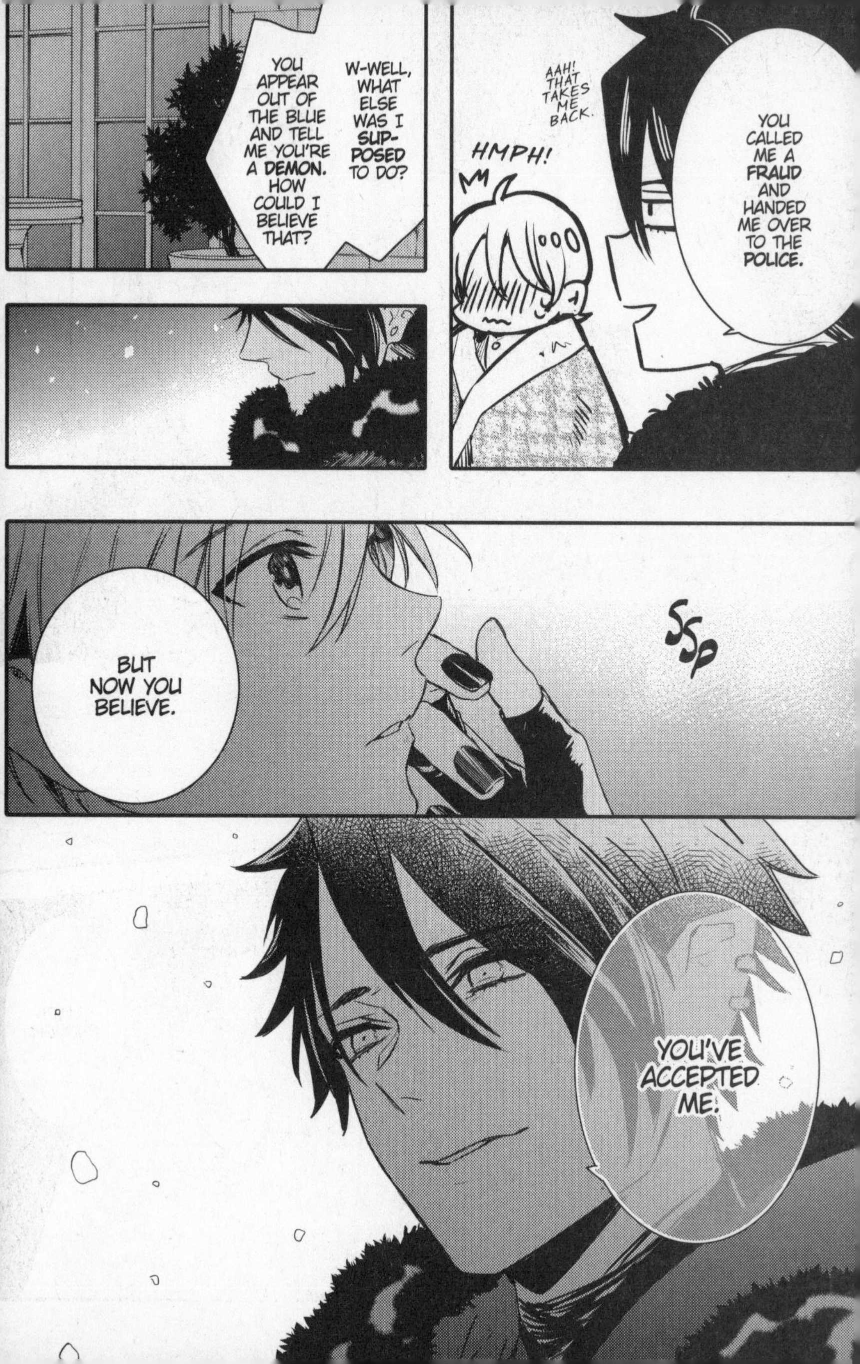
YOU CALLED ME A FRAUD AND HANDED ME OVER TO THE POLICE.
AAH! THAT TAKES ME BACK.
HMPH!
W-WELL, WHAT ELSE WAS I SUP-POSED TO DO?
YOU APPEAR OUT OF THE BLUE AND TELL ME YOU'RE A DEMON. HOW COULD I BELIEVE THAT?
SSp
BUT NOW YOU BELIEVE.
YOU'VE ACCEPTED ME.

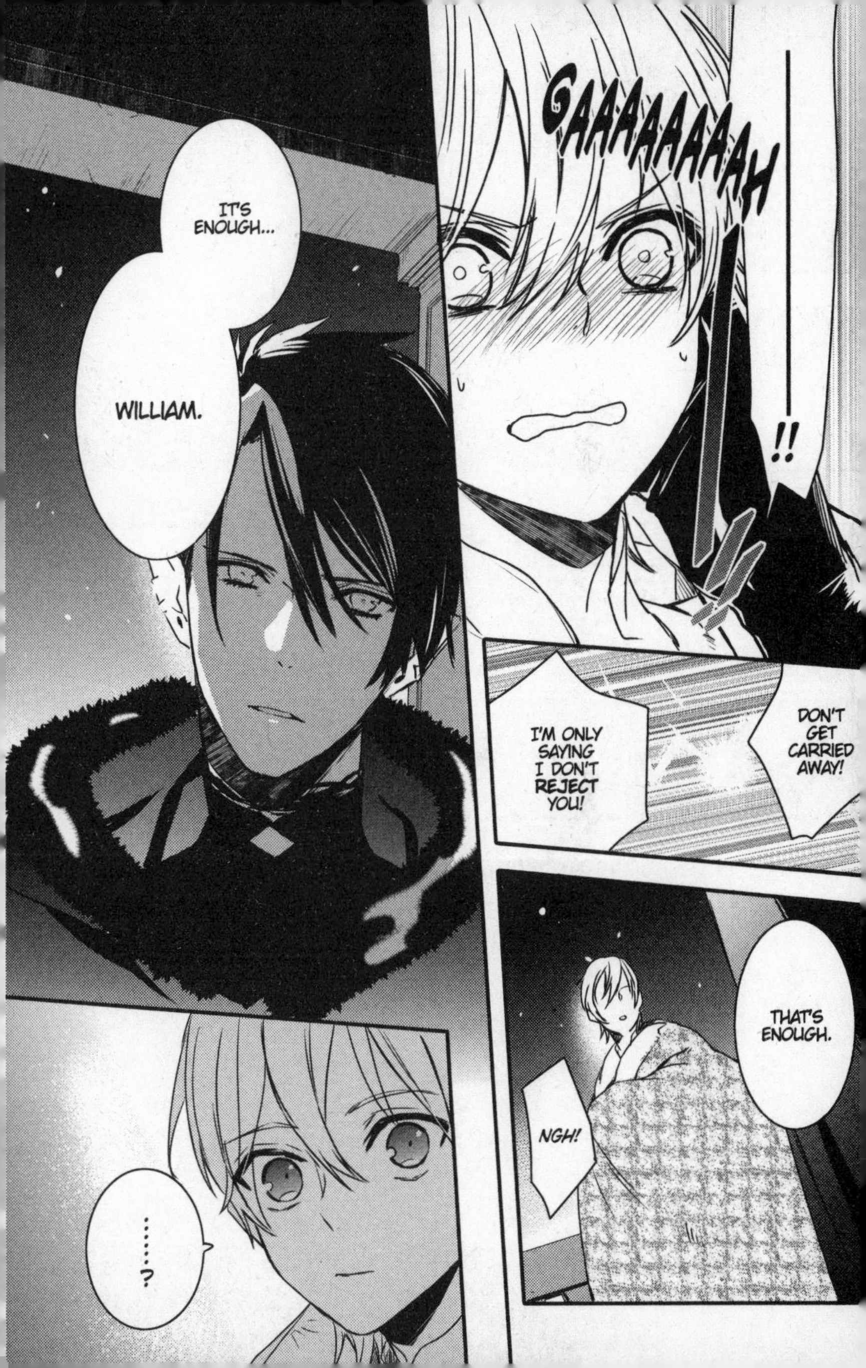
GAAAAAAAAH
!!
IT'S ENOUGH...
WILLIAM.
DON'T GET CARRIED AWAY!
I'M ONLY SAYING I DON'T REJECT YOU!
THAT'S ENOUGH.
NGH!
......?

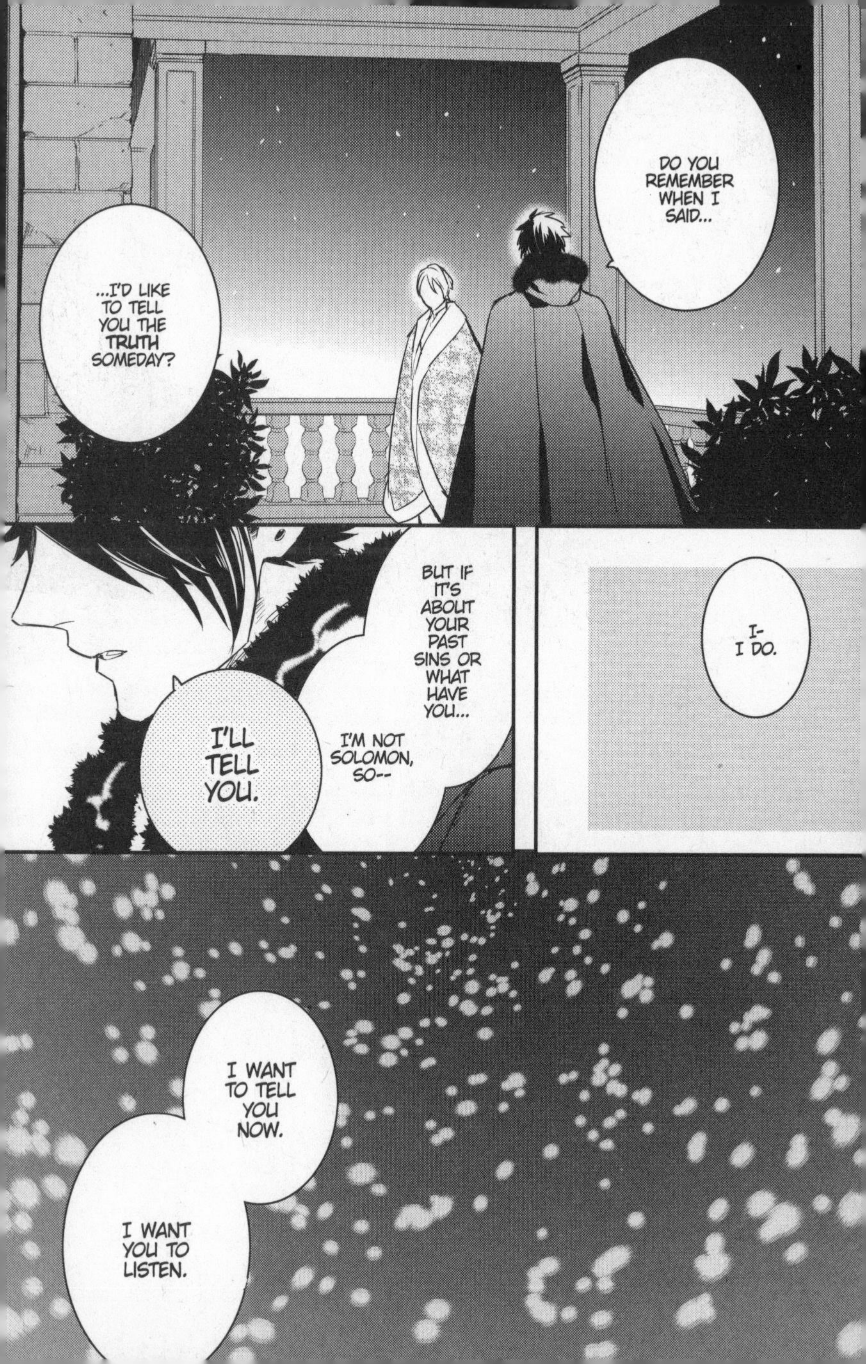
DO YOU REMEMBER WHEN I SAID...
...I'D LIKE TO TELL YOU THE TRUTH SOMEDAY?
I- I DO.
BUT IF IT'S ABOUT YOUR PAST SINS OR WHAT HAVE YOU...
I'M NOT SOLOMON, SO--
I'LL TELL YOU.
I WANT TO TELL YOU NOW.
I WANT YOU TO LISTEN.

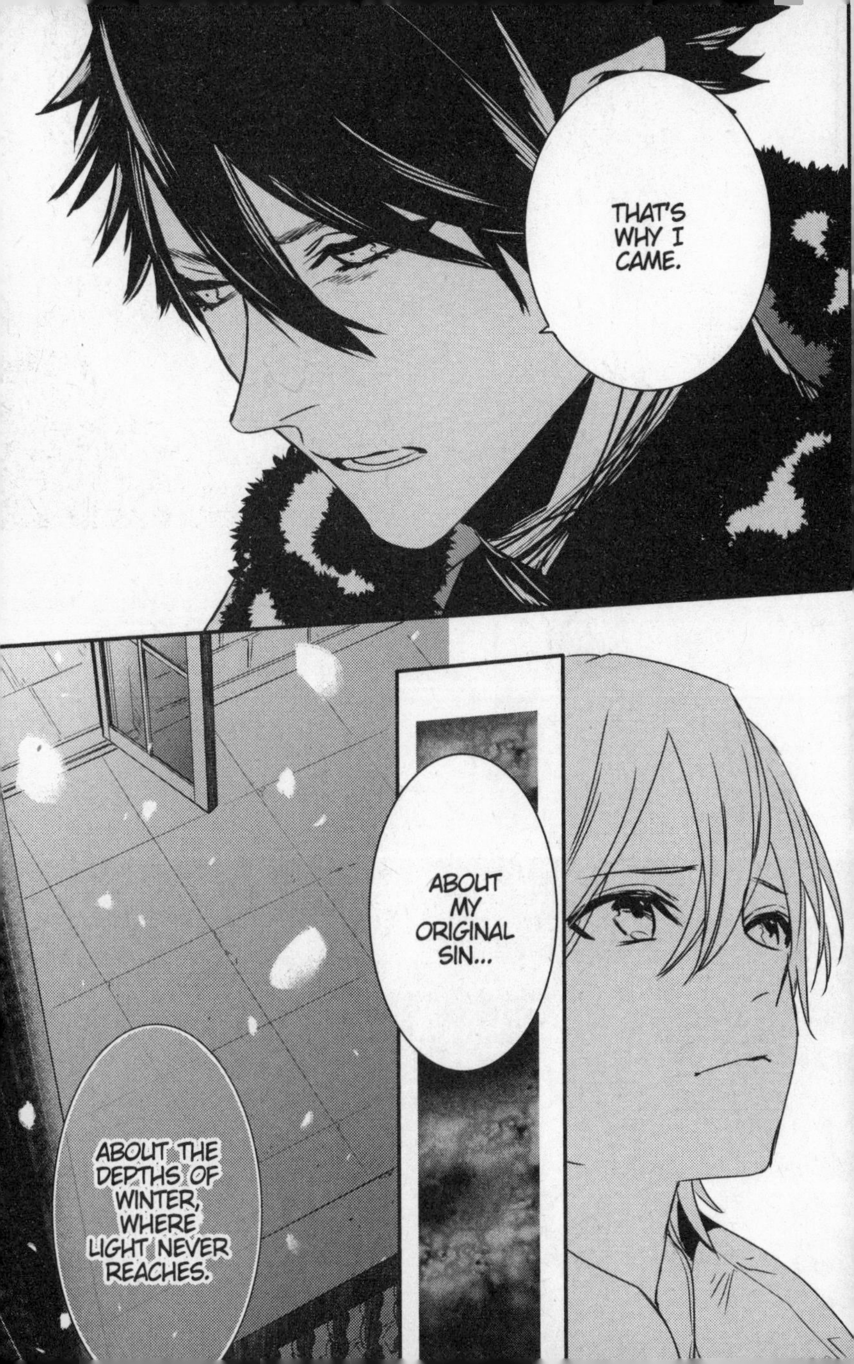
THAT'S WHY I CAME.
ABOUT MY ORIGINAL SIN...
ABOUT THE DEPTHS OF WINTER, WHERE LIGHT NEVER REACHES.

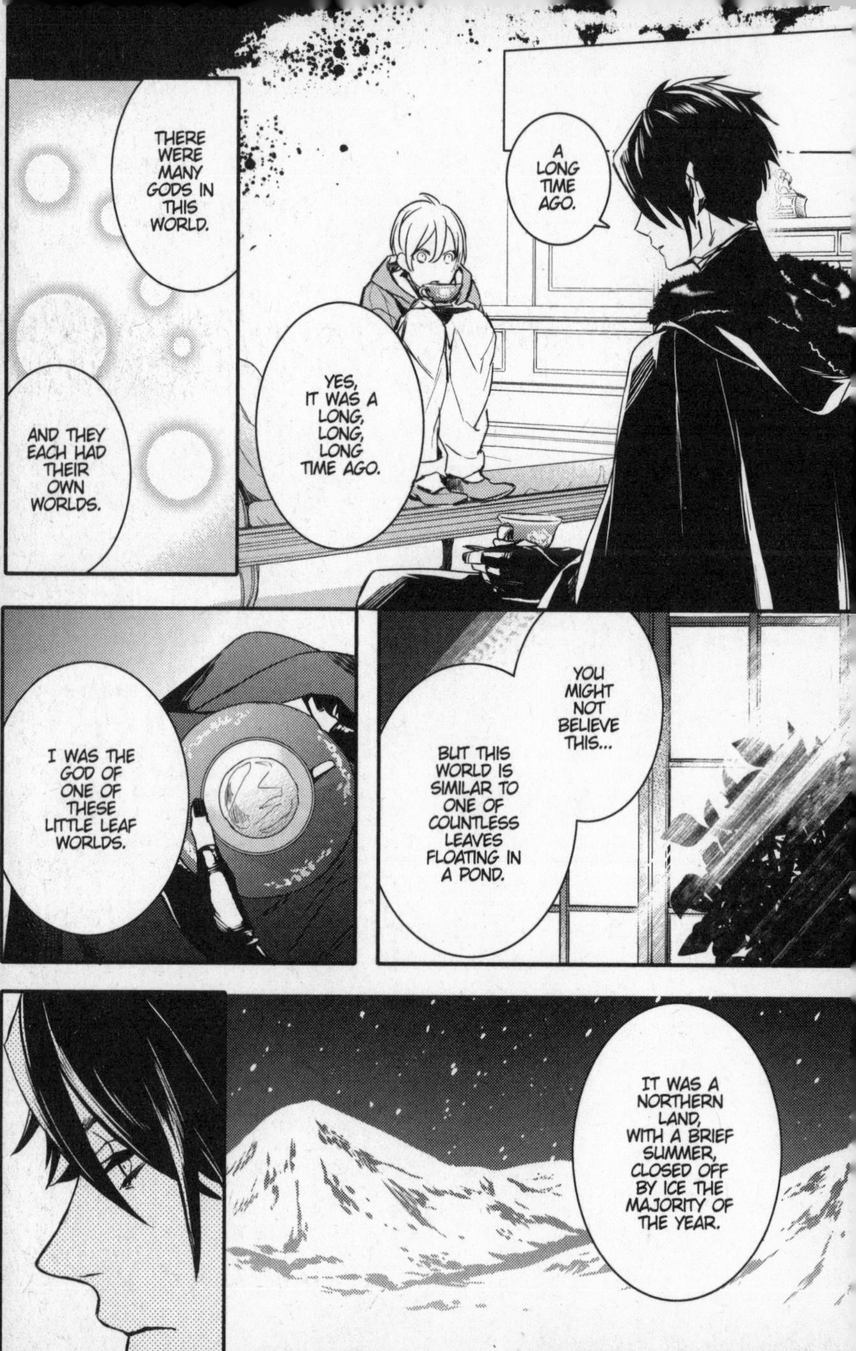
A LONG TIME AGO.
YES, IT WAS A LONG, LONG, LONG TIME AGO.
THERE WERE MANY GODS IN THIS WORLD.
AND THEY EACH HAD THEIR OWN WORLDS.
YOU MIGHT NOT BELIEVE THIS...
BUT THIS WORLD IS SIMILAR TO ONE OF COUNTLESS LEAVES FLOATING IN A POND.
I WAS THE GOD OF ONE OF THESE LITTLE LEAF WORLDS.
IT WAS A NORTHERN LAND, WITH A BRIEF SUMMER, CLOSED OFF BY ICE THE MAJORITY OF THE YEAR.

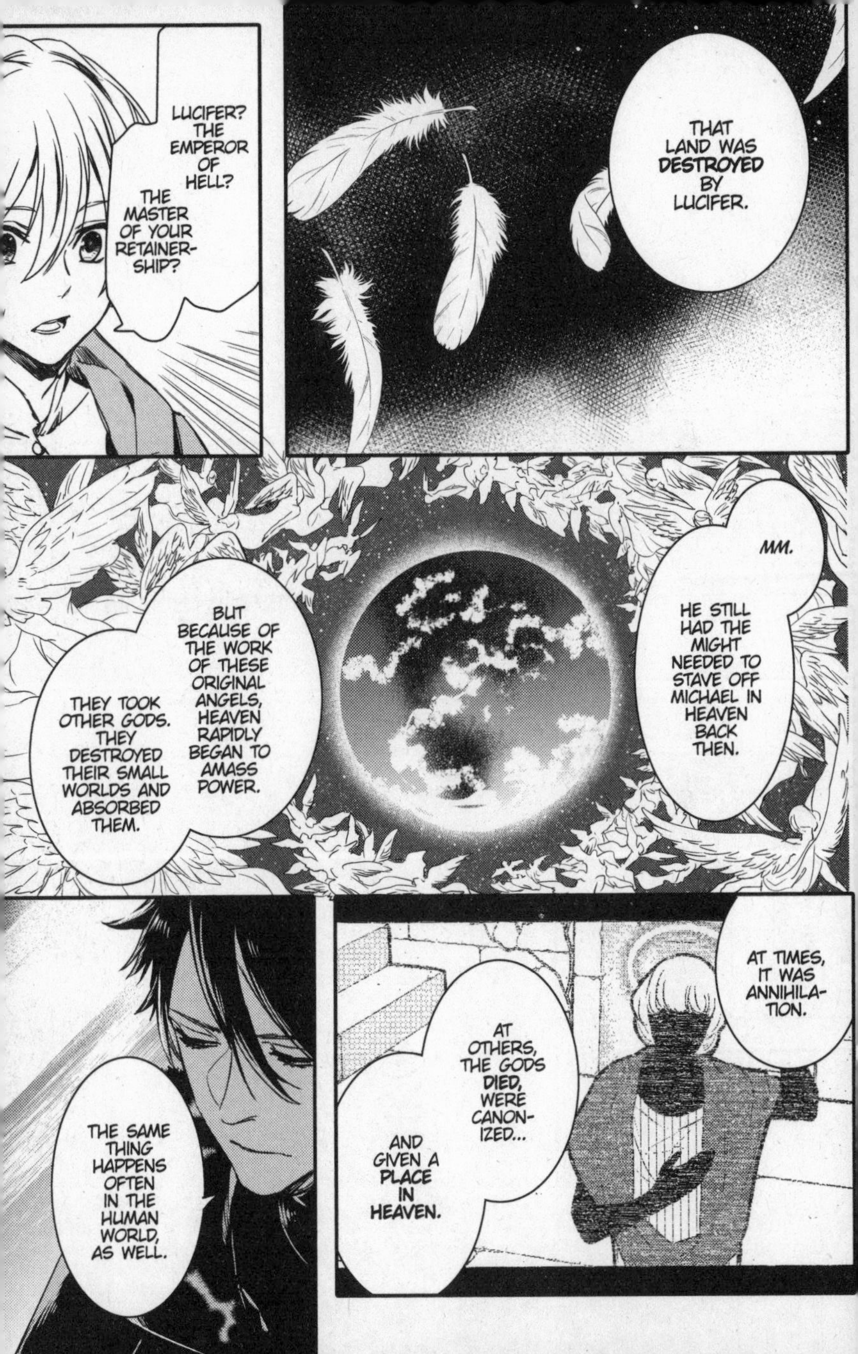
THAT LAND WAS DESTROYED BY LUCIFER.
LUCIFER? THE EMPEROR OF HELL?
THE MASTER OF YOUR RETAINER-SHIP?
MM.
HE STILL HAD THE MIGHT NEEDED TO STAVE OFF MICHAEL IN HEAVEN BACK THEN.
BUT BECAUSE OF THE WORK OF THESE ORIGINAL ANGELS, HEAVEN RAPIDLY BEGAN TO AMASS POWER.
THEY TOOK OTHER GODS. THEY DESTROYED THEIR SMALL WORLDS AND ABSORBED THEM.
AT TIMES, IT WAS ANNIHILA-TION.
AT OTHERS, THE GODS DIED, WERE CANON-IZED...
AND GIVEN A PLACE IN HEAVEN.
THE SAME THING HAPPENS OFTEN IN THE HUMAN WORLD, AS WELL.

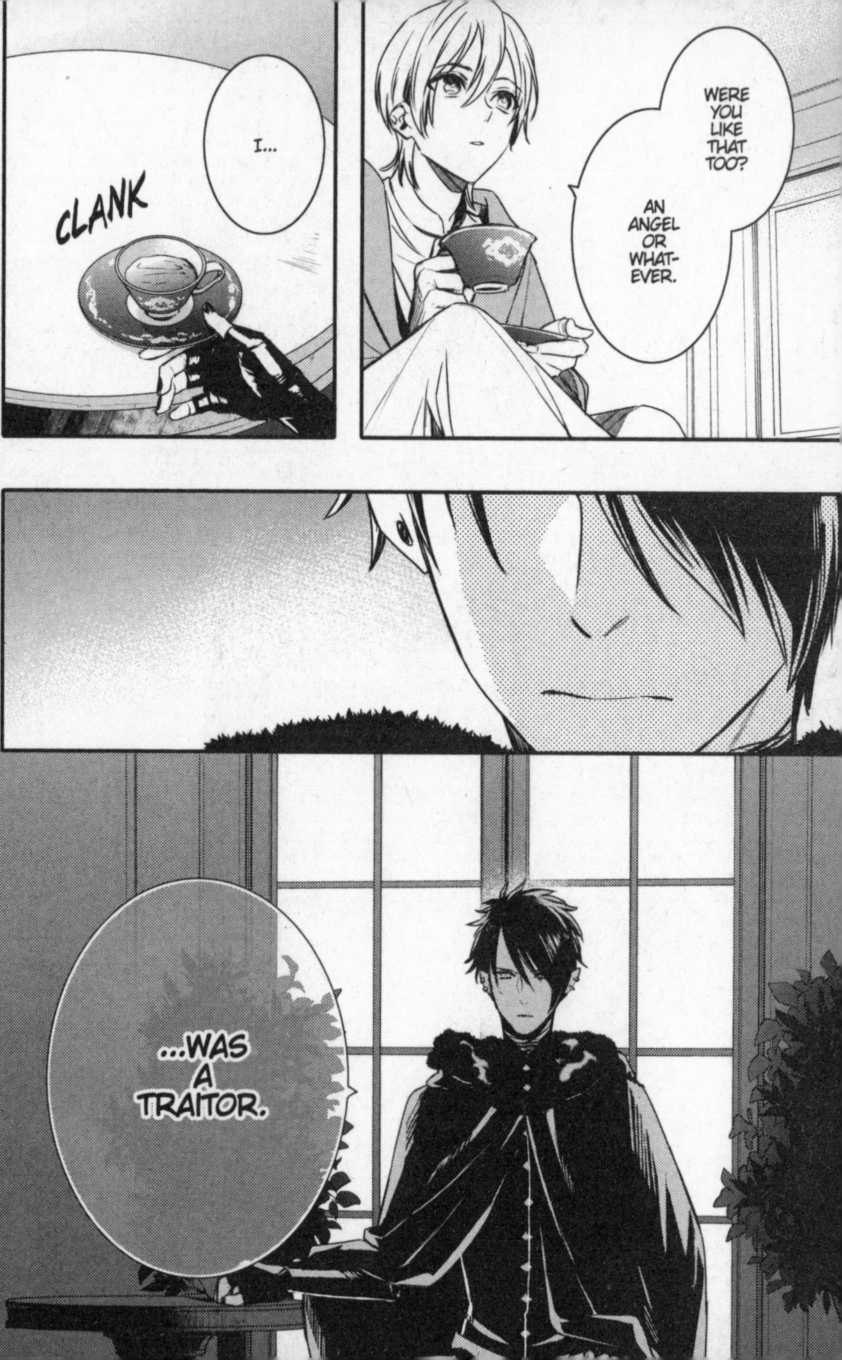
WERE YOU LIKE THAT TOO?
AN ANGEL OR WHAT-EVER.
CLANK
I...
...WAS A TRAITOR.

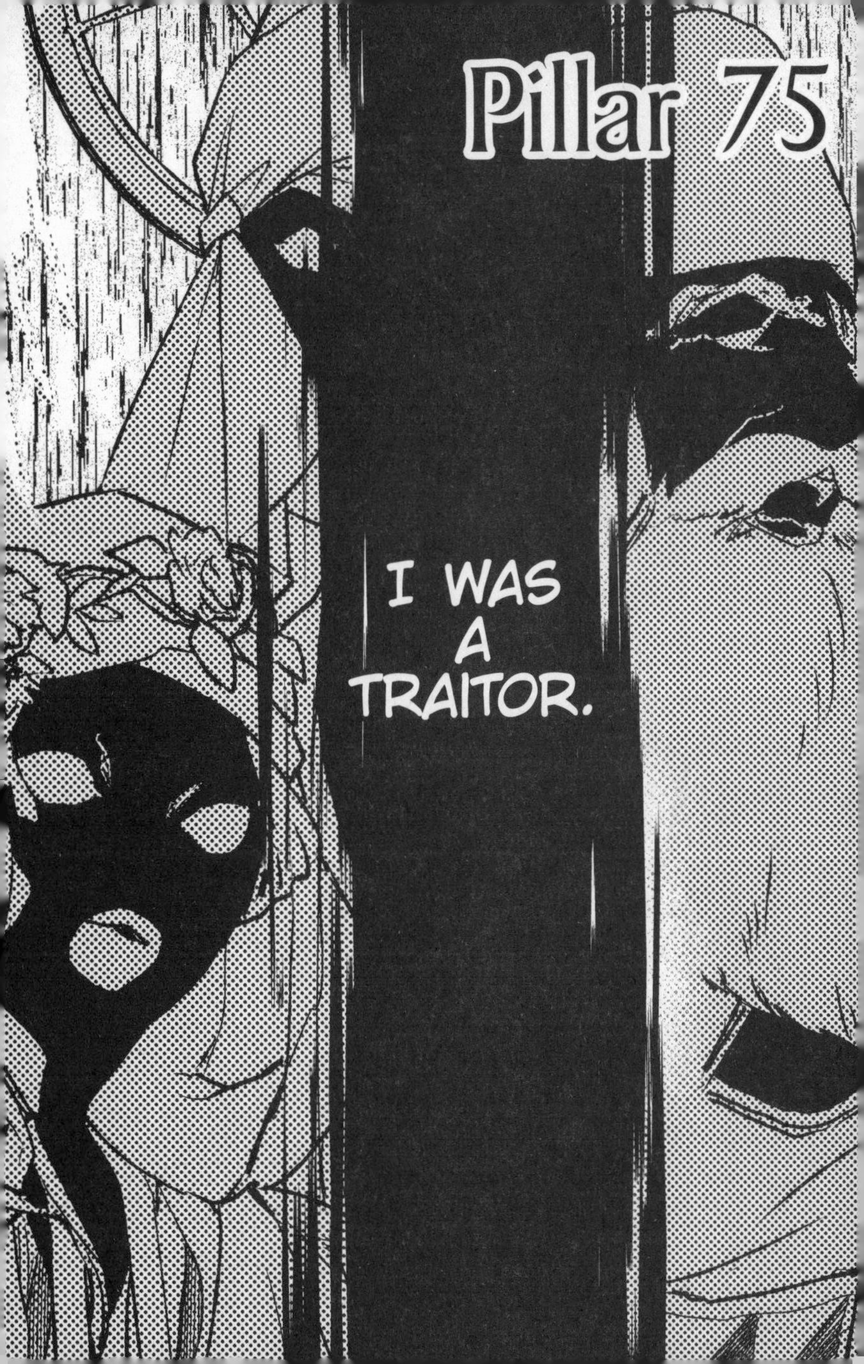
Pillar 75
I WAS A TRAITOR.

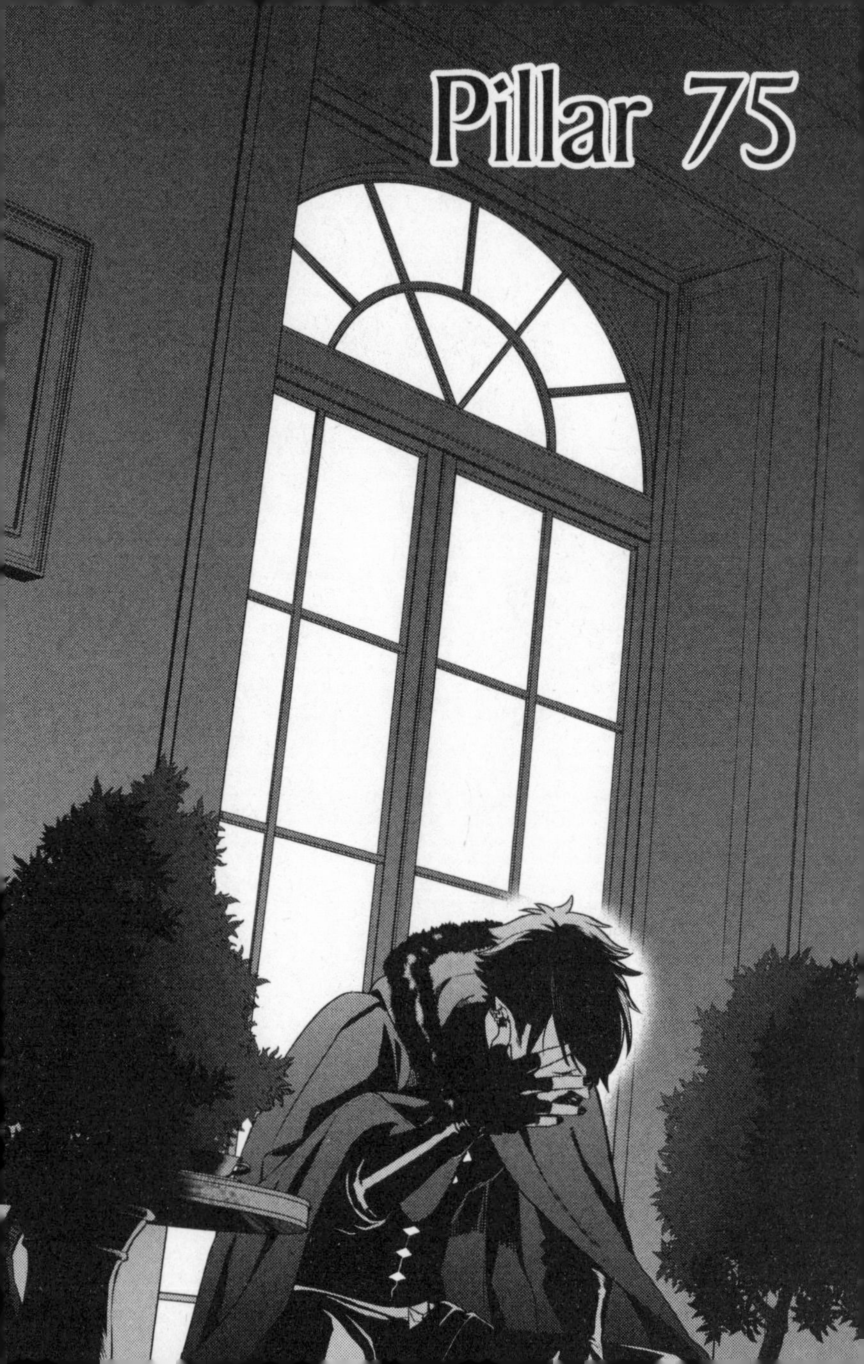
Pillar 75

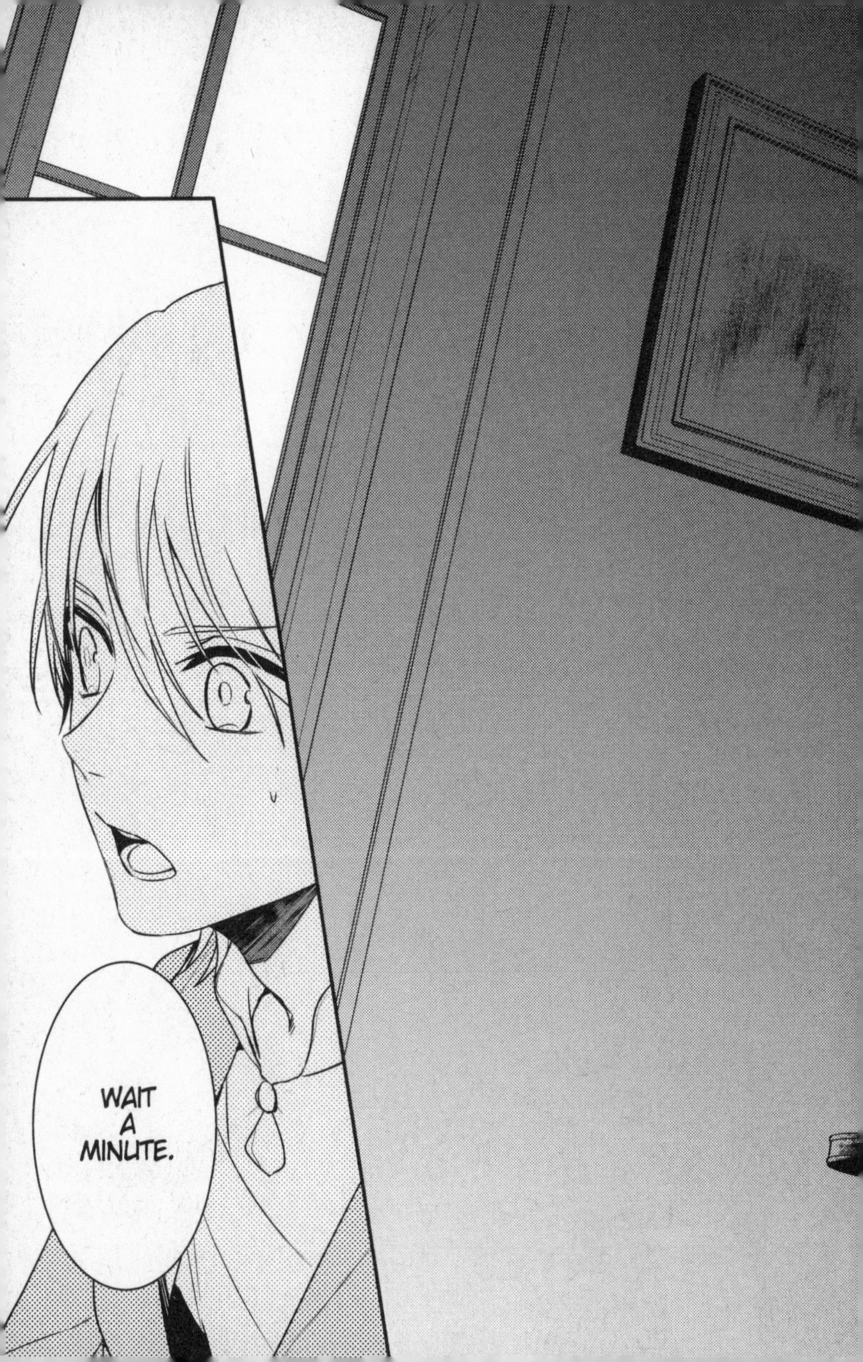
WAIT A MINUTE.

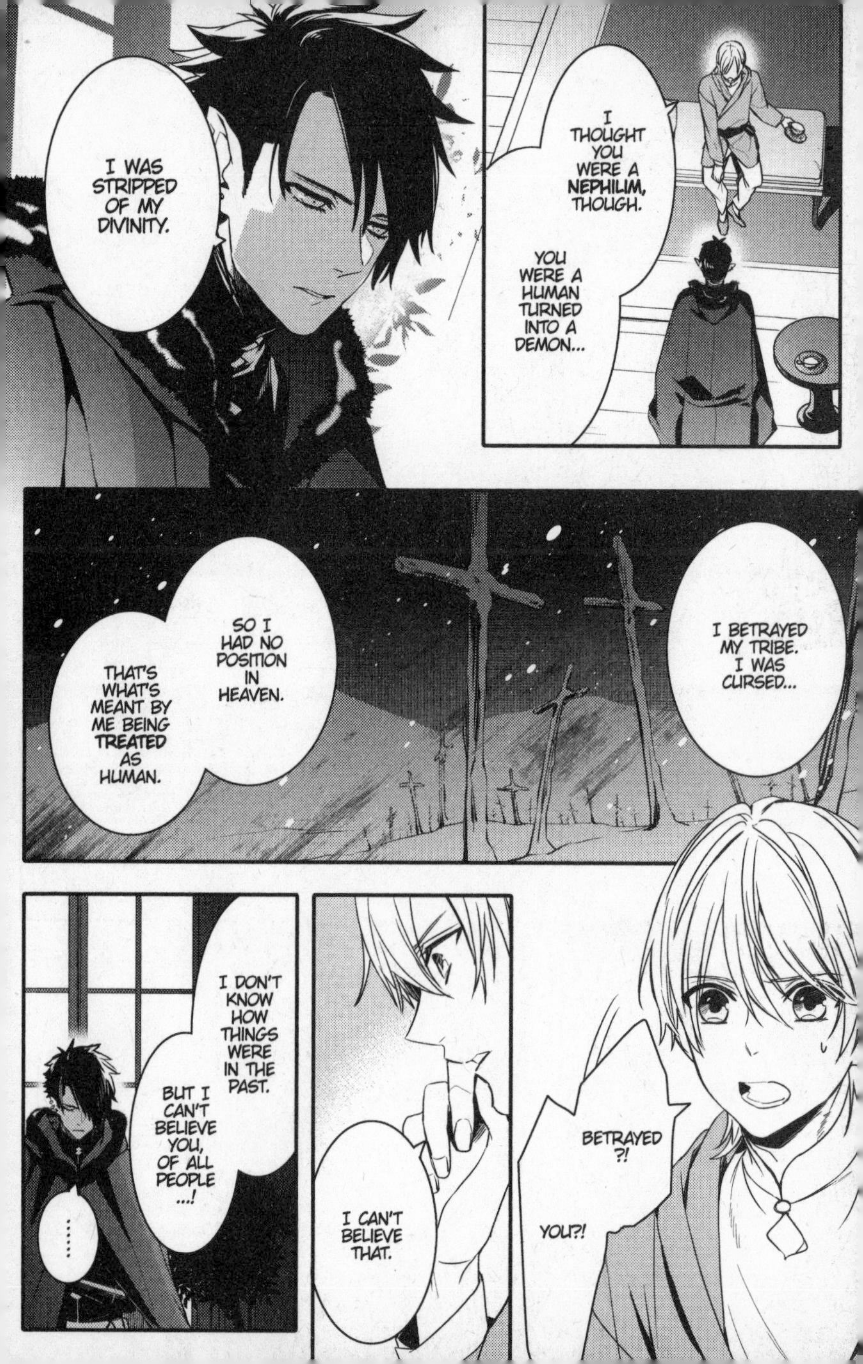
I THOUGHT YOU WERE A NEPHILIM, THOUGH.
YOU WERE A HUMAN TURNED INTO A DEMON...
I WAS STRIPPED OF MY DIVINITY.
I BETRAYED MY TRIBE. I WAS CURSED...
SO I HAD NO POSITION IN HEAVEN.
THAT'S WHAT'S MEANT BY ME BEING TREATED AS HUMAN.
BETRAYED?!
YOU?!
I CAN'T BELIEVE THAT.
I DON'T KNOW HOW THINGS WERE IN THE PAST.
BUT I CAN'T BELIEVE YOU, OF ALL PEOPLE ...!
......

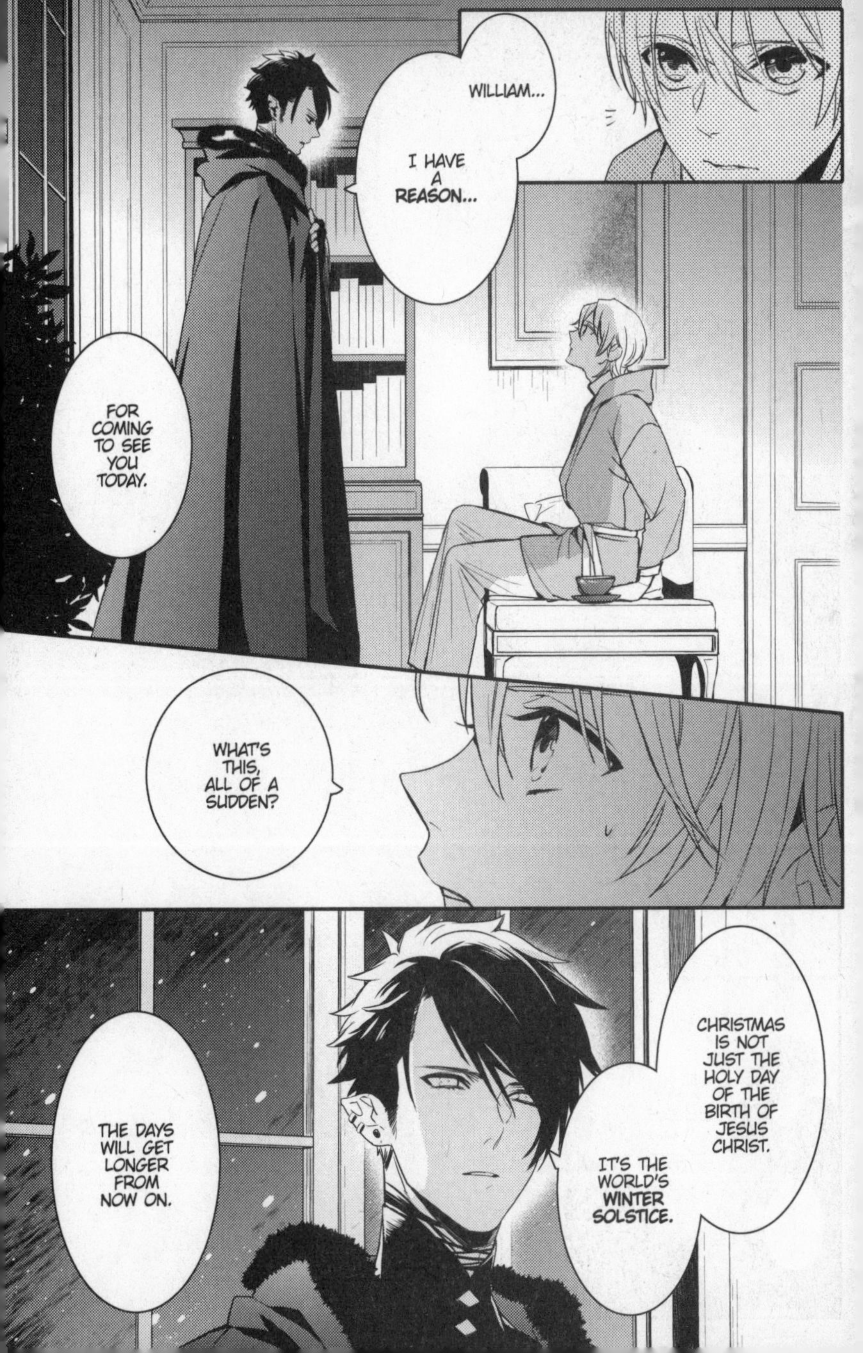

WILLIAM...
I HAVE A REASON...
FOR COMING TO SEE YOU TODAY.
WHAT'S THIS, ALL OF A SUDDEN?
CHRISTMAS IS NOT JUST THE HOLY DAY OF THE BIRTH OF JESUS CHRIST.
IT'S THE WORLD'S WINTER SOLSTICE.
THE DAYS WILL GET LONGER FROM NOW ON.

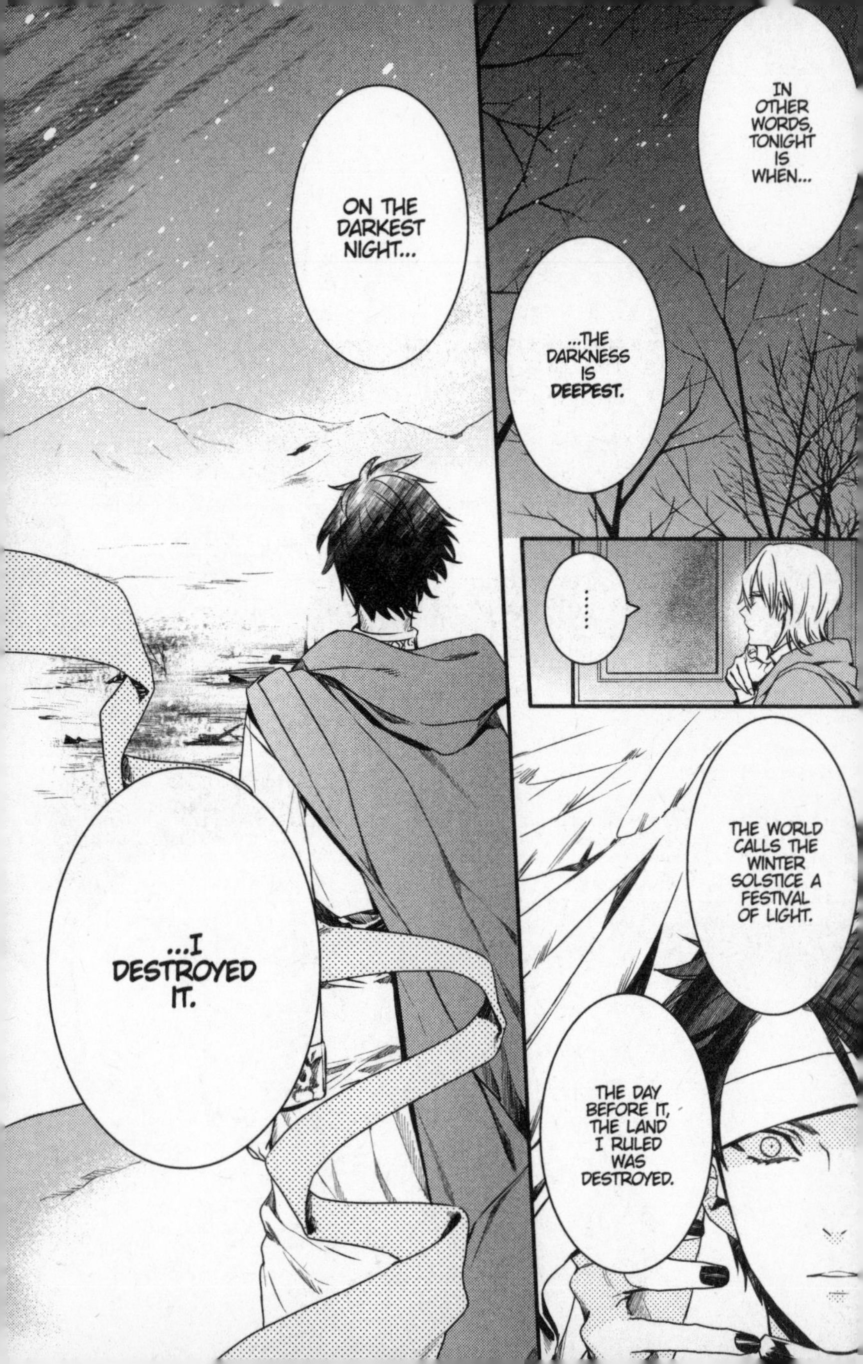
IN OTHER WORDS, TONIGHT IS WHEN...
...THE DARKNESS IS DEEPEST.
......
THE WORLD CALLS THE WINTER SOLSTICE A FESTIVAL OF LIGHT.
THE DAY BEFORE IT, THE LAND I RULED WAS DESTROYED.
ON THE DARKEST NIGHT...
...I DESTROYED IT.

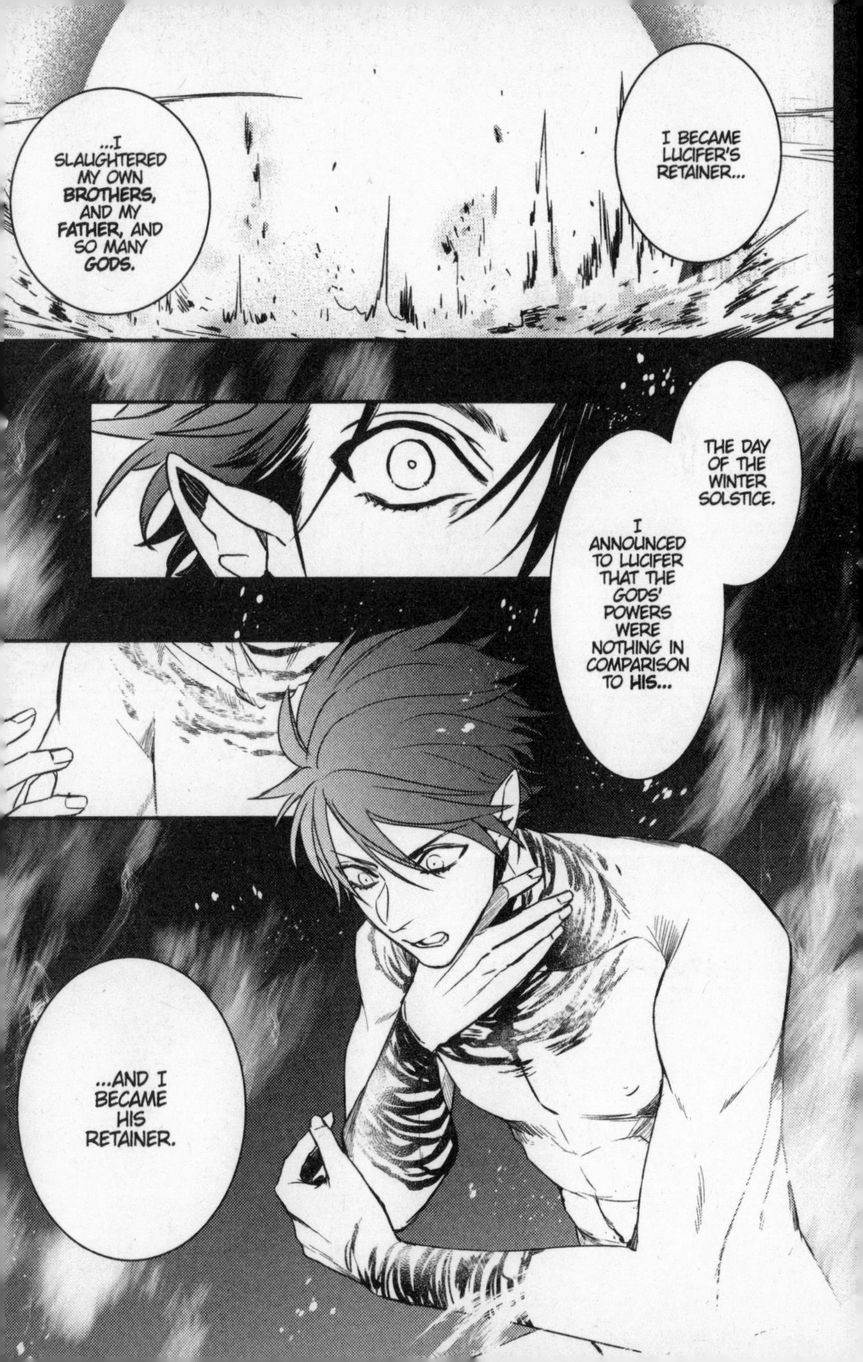
I BECAME LUCIFER'S RETAINER...
...I SLAUGHTERED MY OWN BROTHERS, AND MY FATHER, AND SO MANY GODS.
THE DAY OF THE WINTER SOLSTICE.
I ANNOUNCED TO LUCIFER THAT THE GODS' POWERS WERE NOTHING IN COMPARISON TO HIS...
...AND I BECAME HIS RETAINER.

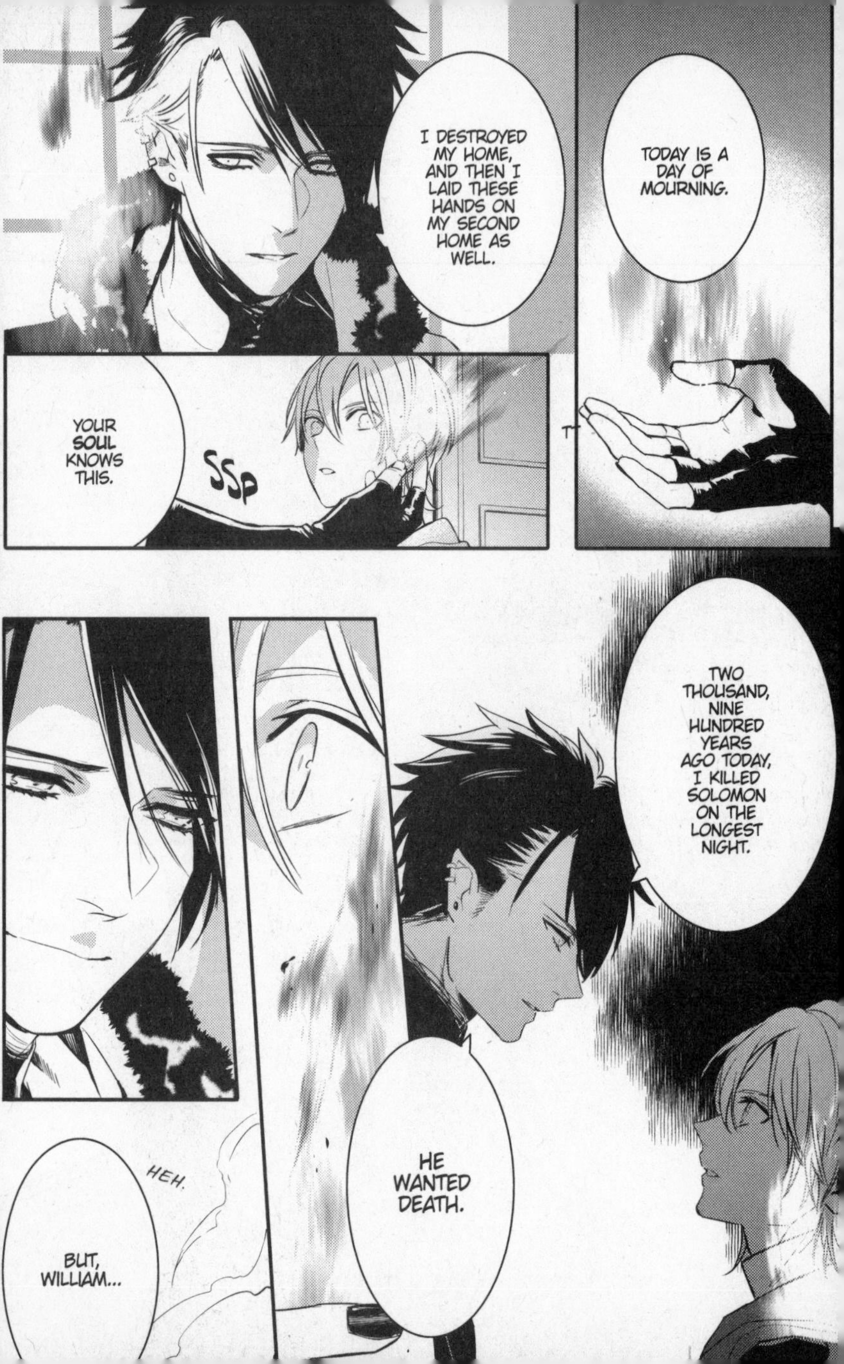
TODAY IS A DAY OF MOURNING.
I DESTROYED MY HOME, AND THEN I LAID THESE HANDS ON MY SECOND HOME AS WELL.
YOUR SOUL KNOWS THIS.
SSP
TWO THOUSAND, NINE HUNDRED YEARS AGO TODAY, I KILLED SOLOMON ON THE LONGEST NIGHT.
HE WANTED DEATH.
HEH.
BUT, WILLIAM...

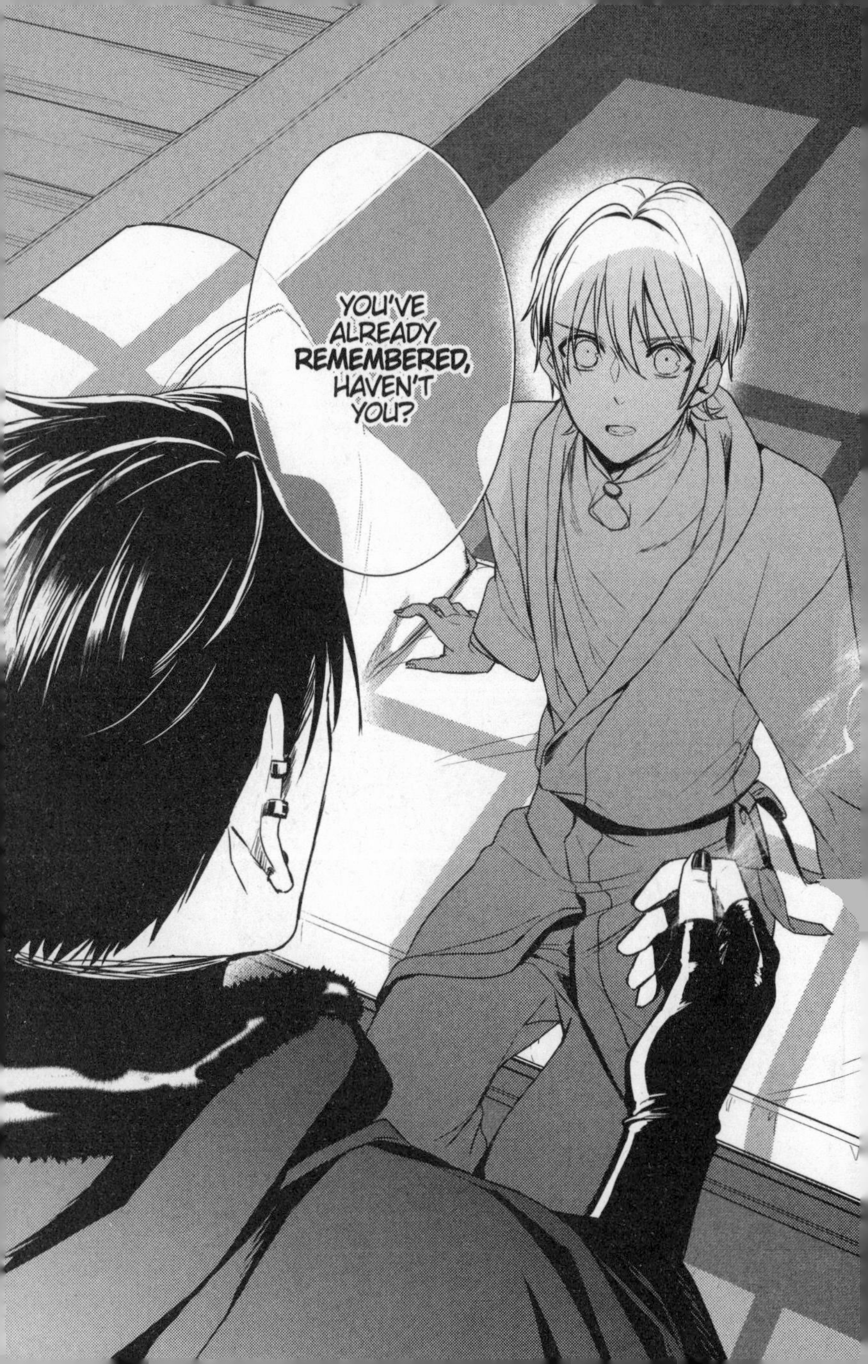
YOU'VE ALREADY REMEMBERED, HAVEN'T YOU?

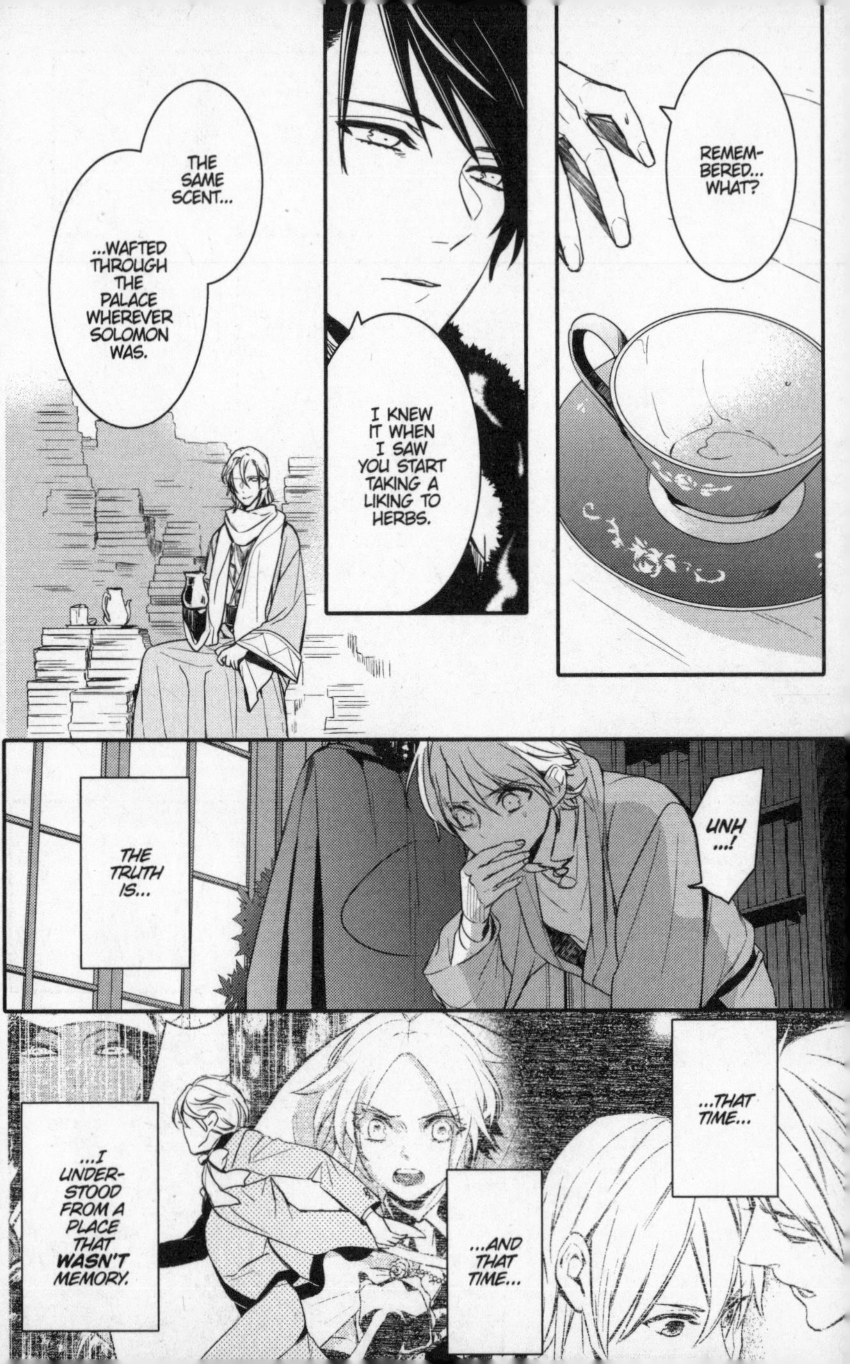
REMEMBERED... WHAT?
I KNEW IT WHEN I SAW YOU START TAKING A LIKING TO HERBS.
THE SAME SCENT...
...WAFTED THROUGH THE PALACE WHEREVER SOLOMON WAS.
UNH...!
THE TRUTH IS...
...THAT TIME...
...AND THAT TIME...
...I UNDERSTOOD FROM A PLACE THAT WASN'T MEMORY.

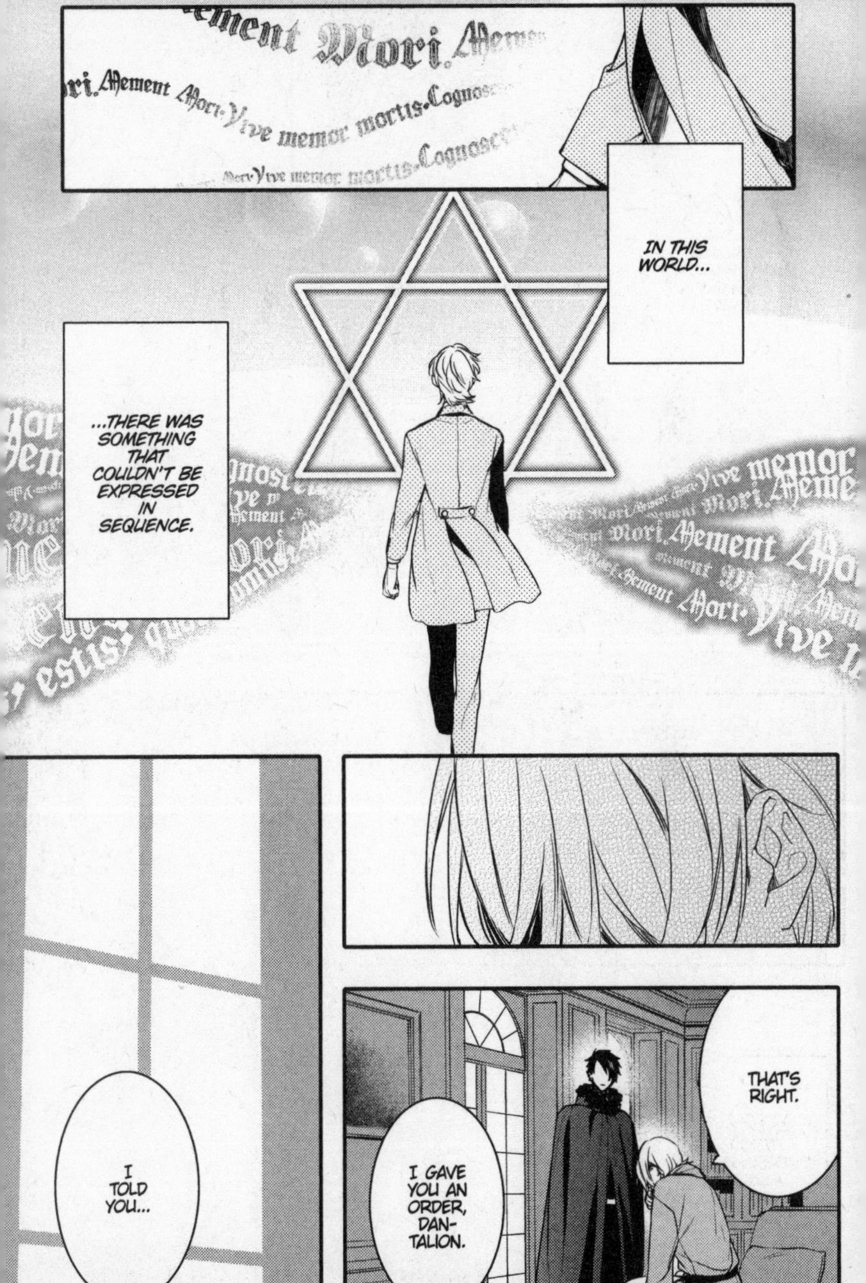
Mement Mori.
Mement Mori. Vive memor mortis.
IN THIS WORLD...
...THERE WAS SOMETHING THAT COULDN'T BE EXPRESSED IN SEQUENCE.
THAT'S RIGHT.
I GAVE YOU AN ORDER, DAN-TALION.
I TOLD YOU...

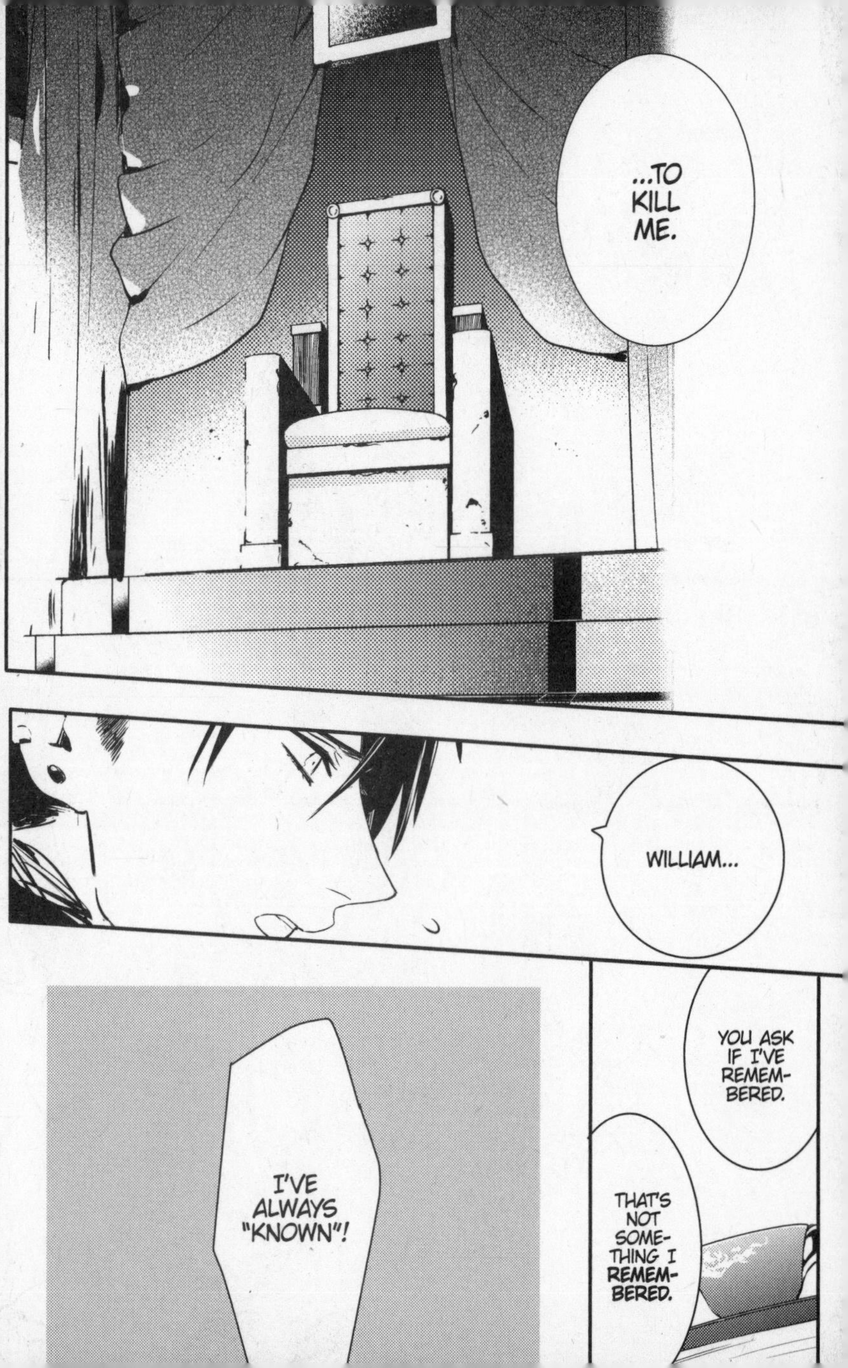
...TO KILL ME.
WILLIAM...
YOU ASK IF I'VE REMEMBERED.
THAT'S NOT SOMETHING I REMEMBERED.
I'VE ALWAYS "KNOWN"!

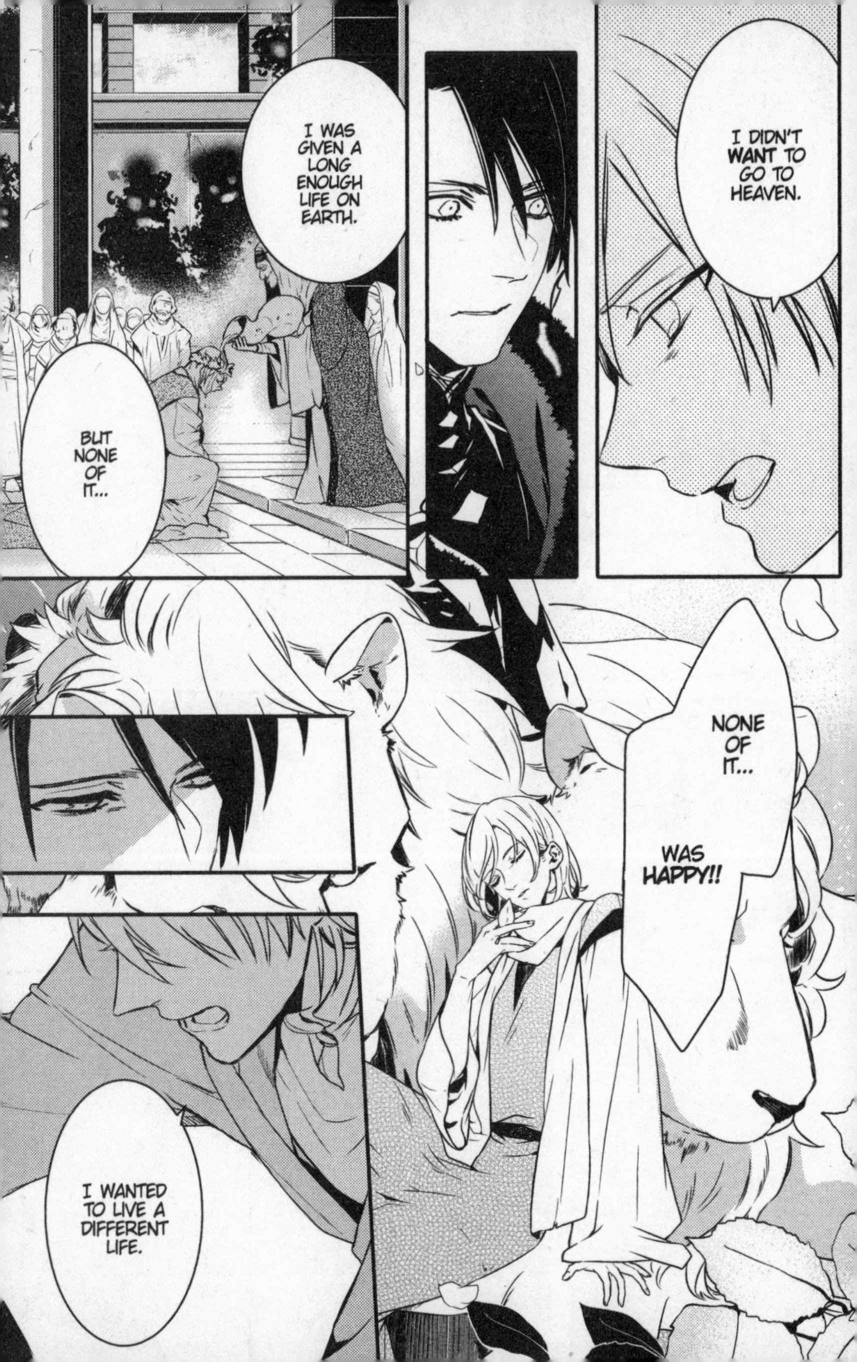
I DIDN'T WANT TO GO TO HEAVEN.
I WAS GIVEN A LONG ENOUGH LIFE ON EARTH.
BUT NONE OF IT...
NONE OF IT...
WAS HAPPY!!
I WANTED TO LIVE A DIFFERENT LIFE.

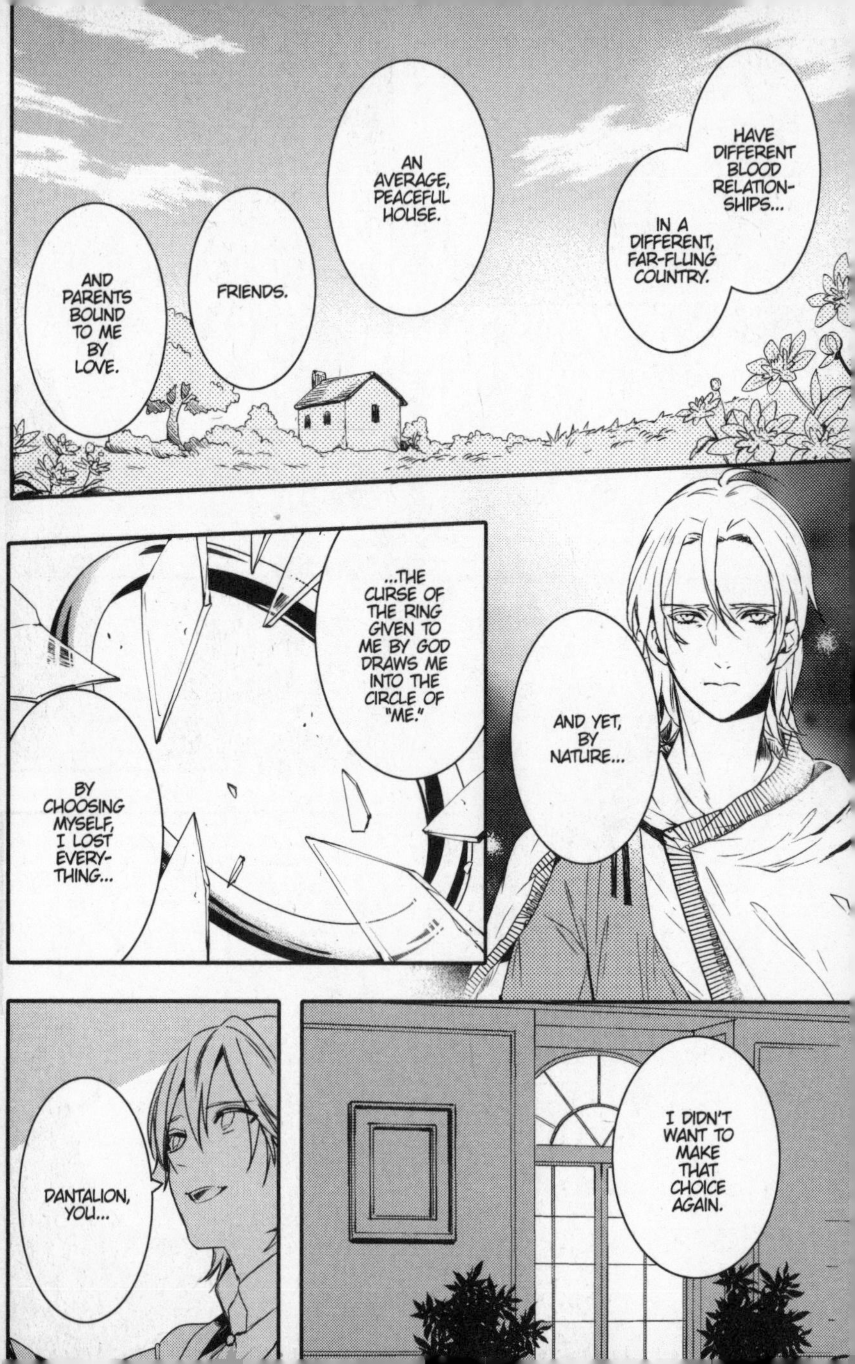
HAVE DIFFERENT BLOOD RELATION-SHIPS...
IN A DIFFERENT, FAR-FLUNG COUNTRY.
AN AVERAGE, PEACEFUL HOUSE.
FRIENDS.
AND PARENTS BOUND TO ME BY LOVE.
AND YET, BY NATURE...
...THE CURSE OF THE RING GIVEN TO ME BY GOD DRAWS ME INTO THE CIRCLE OF "ME."
BY CHOOSING MYSELF, I LOST EVERY-THING...
I DIDN'T WANT TO MAKE THAT CHOICE AGAIN.
DANTALION, YOU...

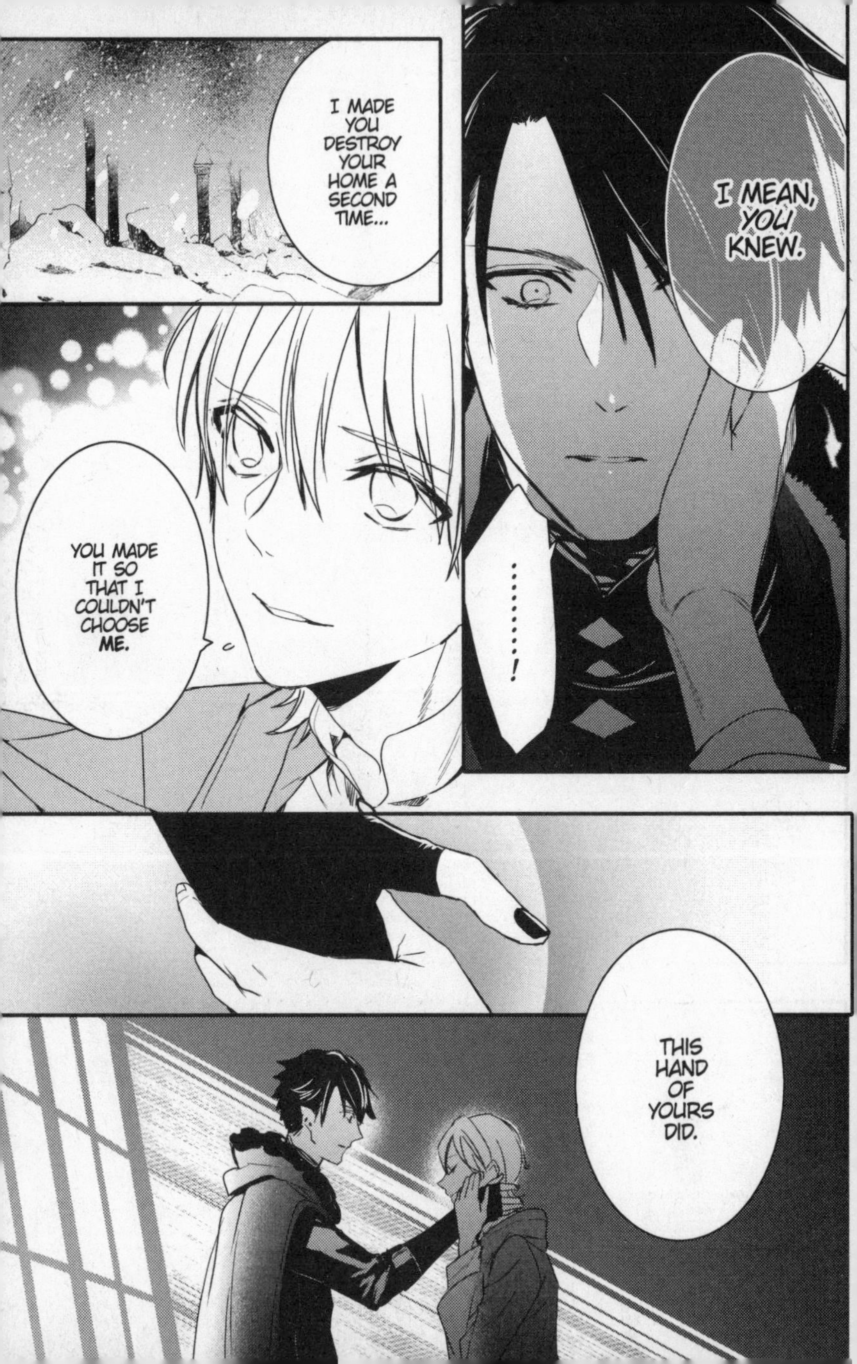
I MEAN, YOU KNEW.
......!
I MADE YOU DESTROY YOUR HOME A SECOND TIME...
YOU MADE IT SO THAT I COULDN'T CHOOSE ME.
THIS HAND OF YOURS DID.

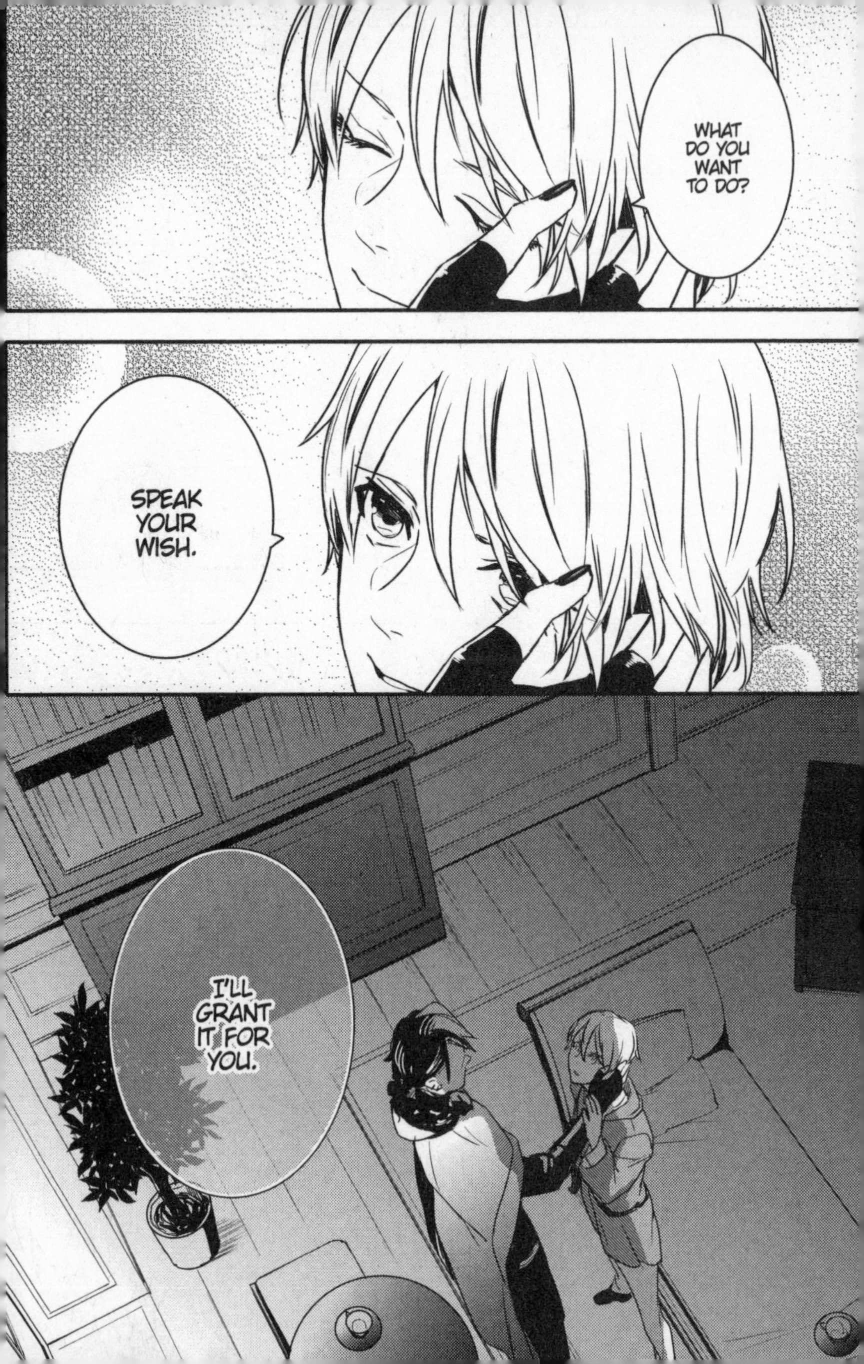
WHAT DO YOU WANT TO DO?
SPEAK YOUR WISH.
I'LL GRANT IT FOR YOU.

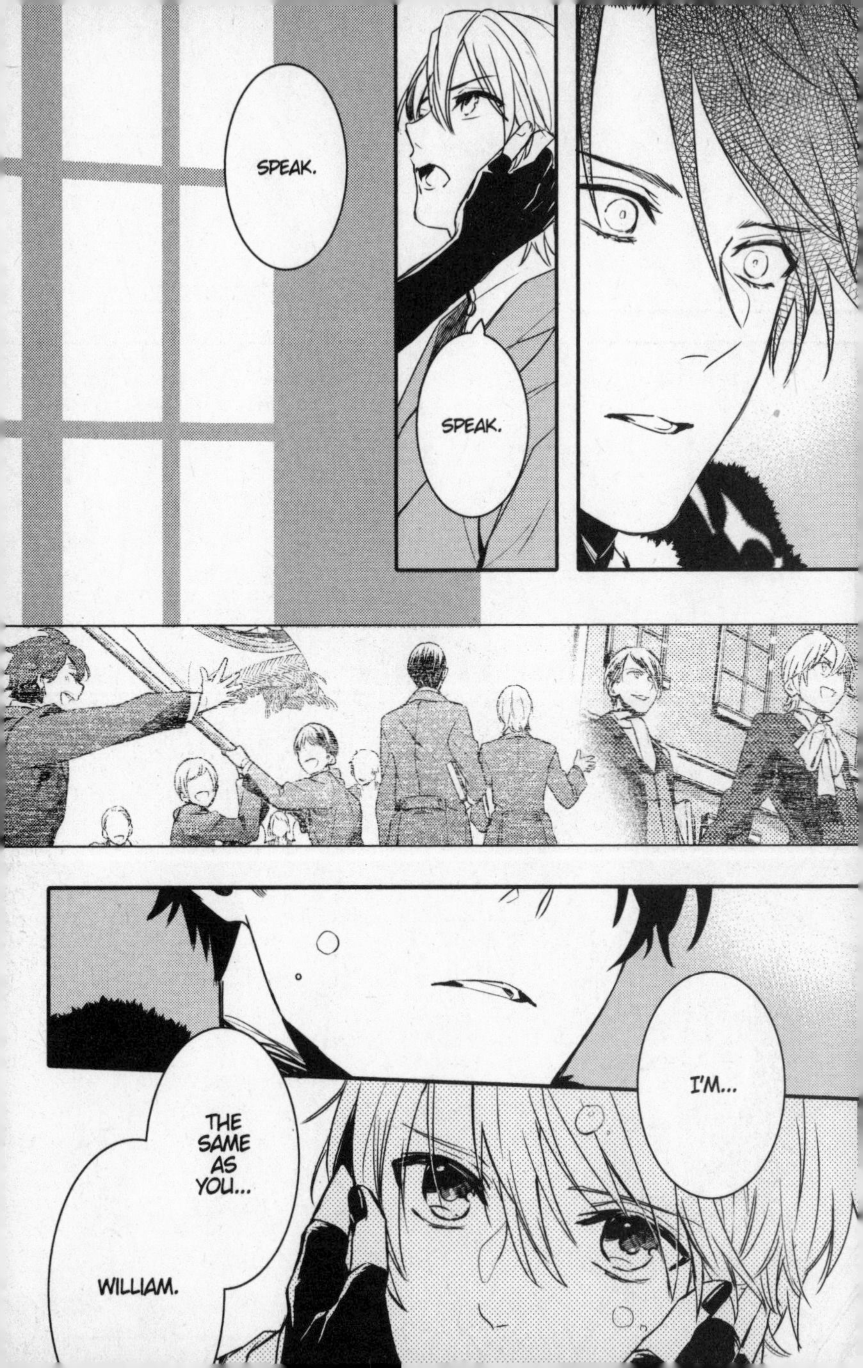
SPEAK.
SPEAK.
I'M...
THE SAME AS YOU...
WILLIAM.

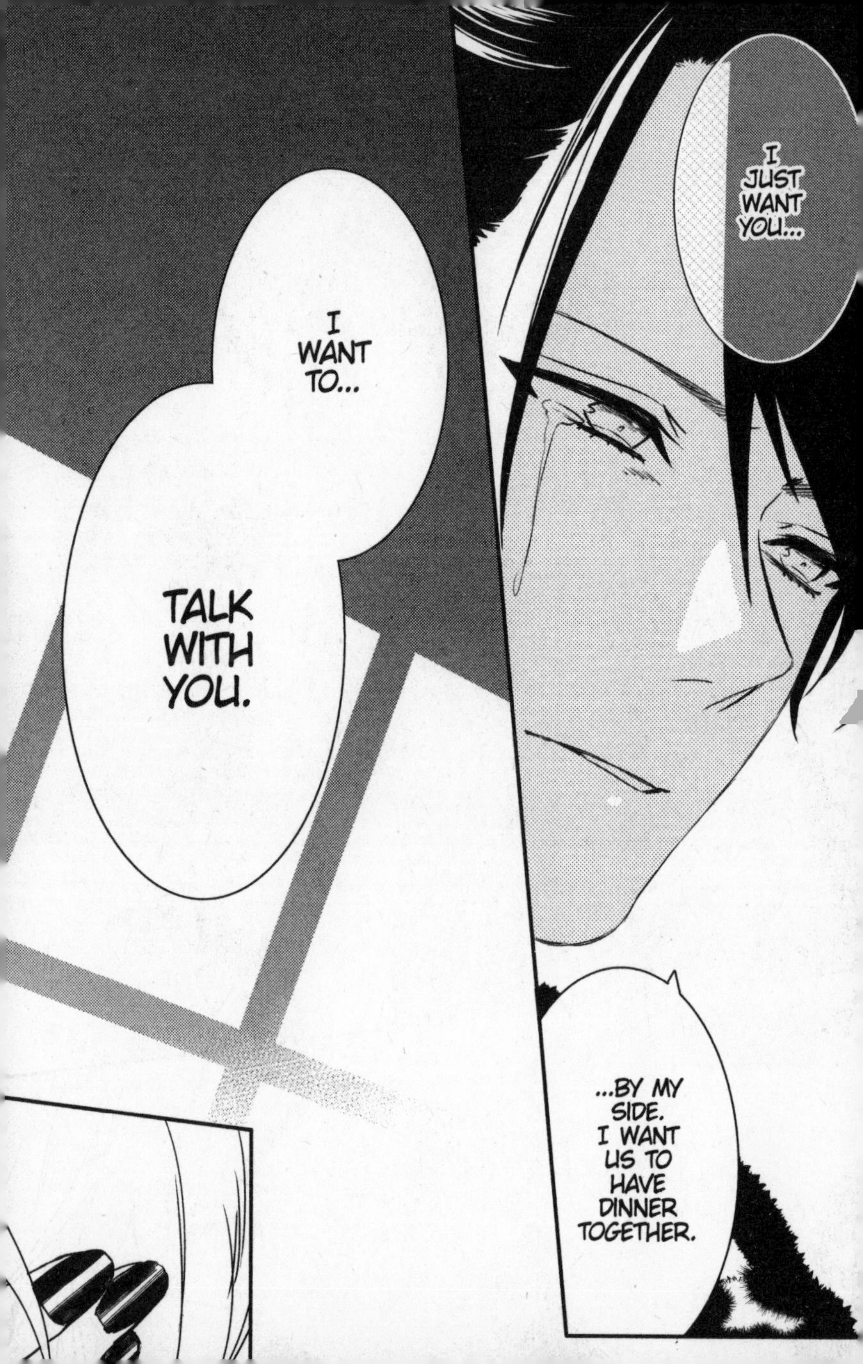
I JUST WANT YOU...
I WANT TO...
TALK WITH YOU.
...BY MY SIDE. I WANT US TO HAVE DINNER TOGETHER.

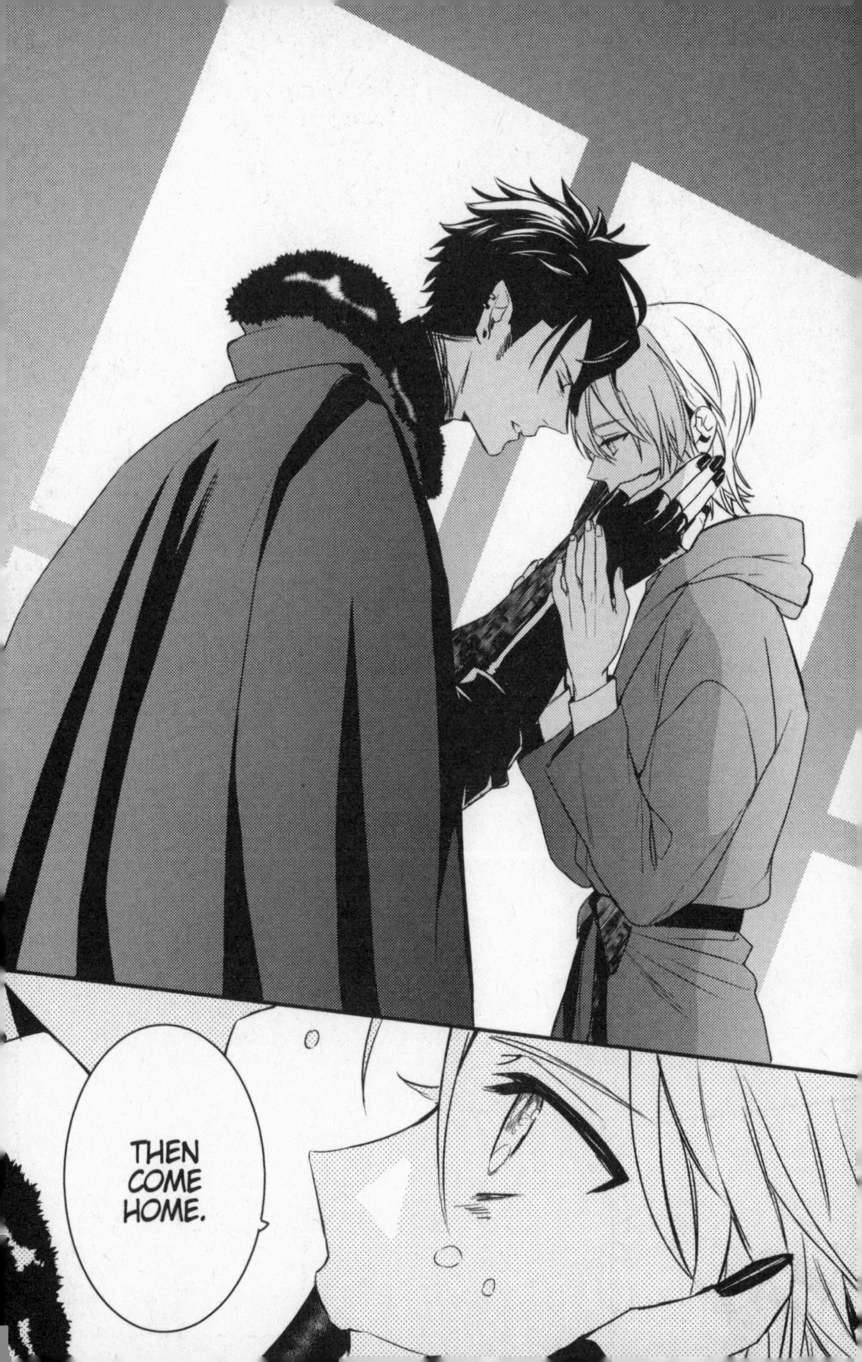
THEN COME HOME.

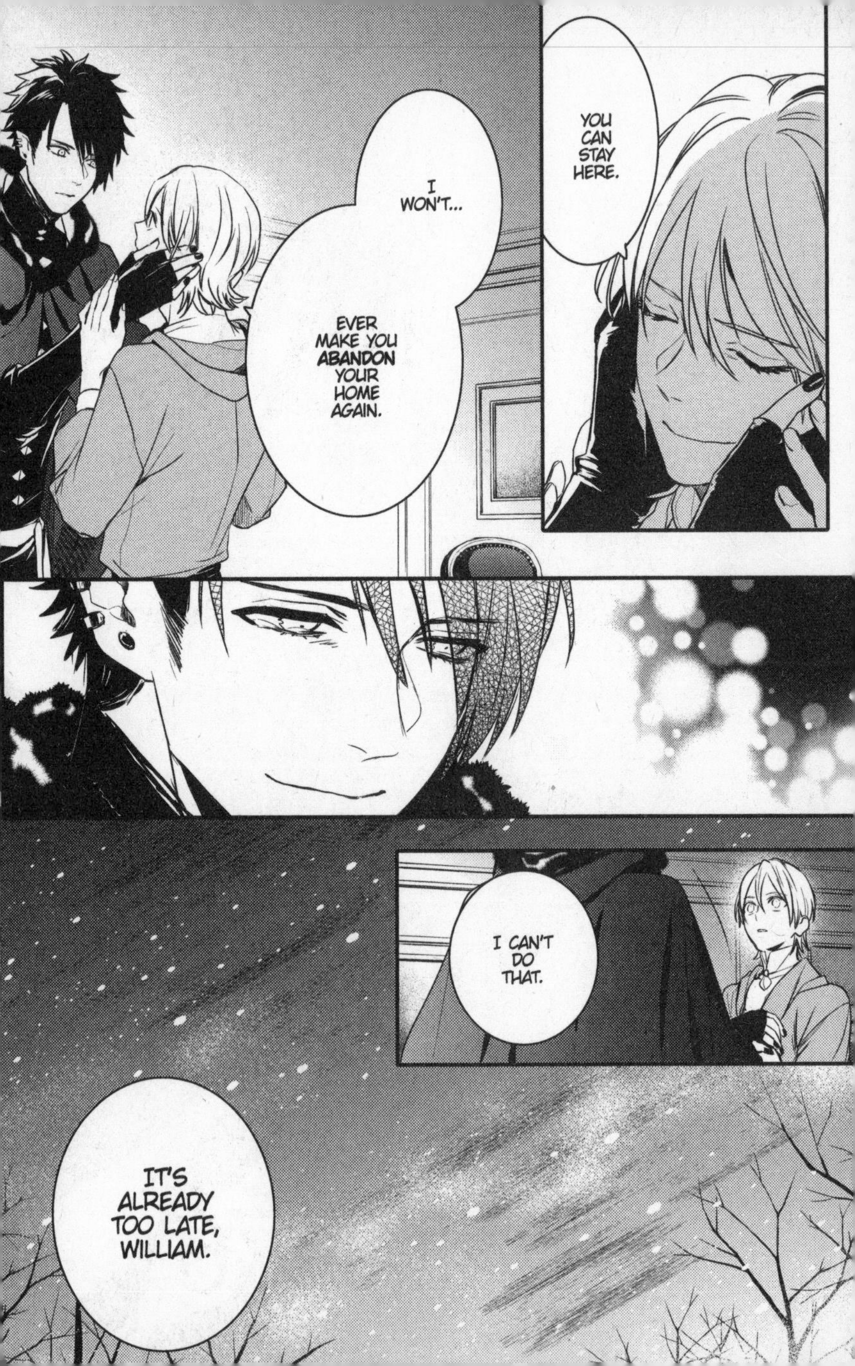
YOU CAN STAY HERE.
I WON'T...
EVER MAKE YOU ABANDON YOUR HOME AGAIN.
I CAN'T DO THAT.
IT'S ALREADY TOO LATE, WILLIAM.

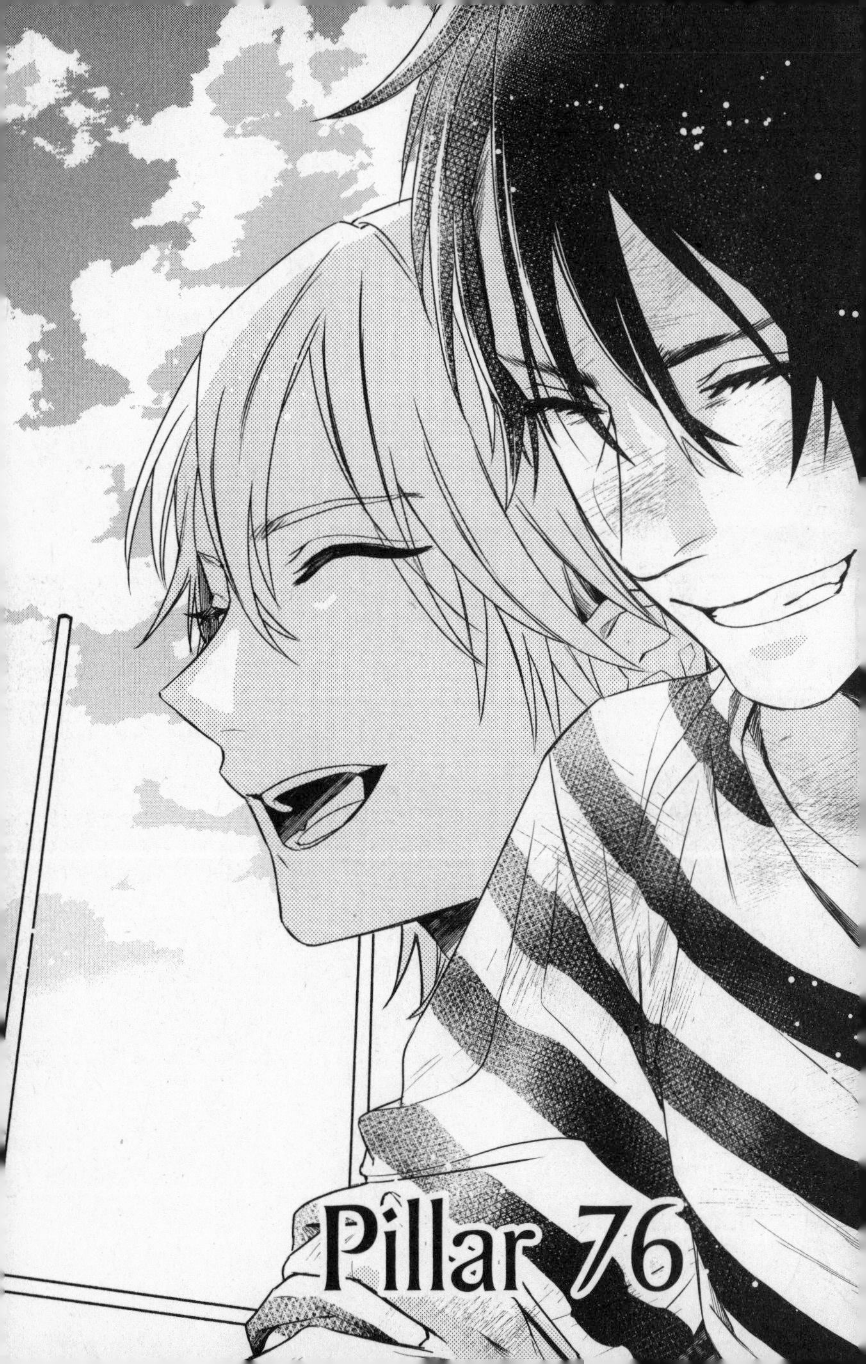
Pillar 76

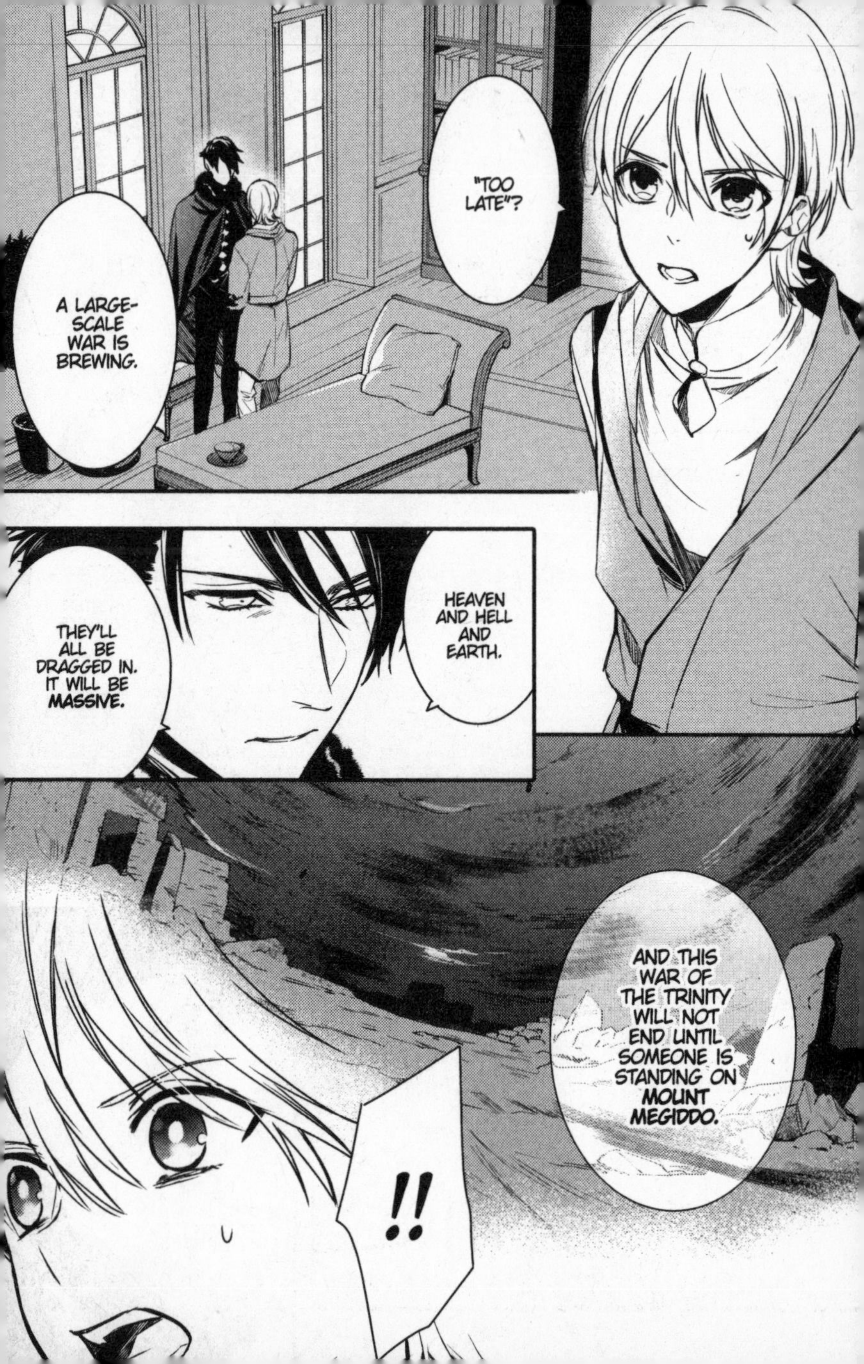
"TOO LATE"?
A LARGE-SCALE WAR IS BREWING.
HEAVEN AND HELL AND EARTH.
THEY'LL ALL BE DRAGGED IN. IT WILL BE MASSIVE.
AND THIS WAR OF THE TRINITY WILL NOT END UNTIL SOMEONE IS STANDING ON MOUNT MEGIDDO.
!!

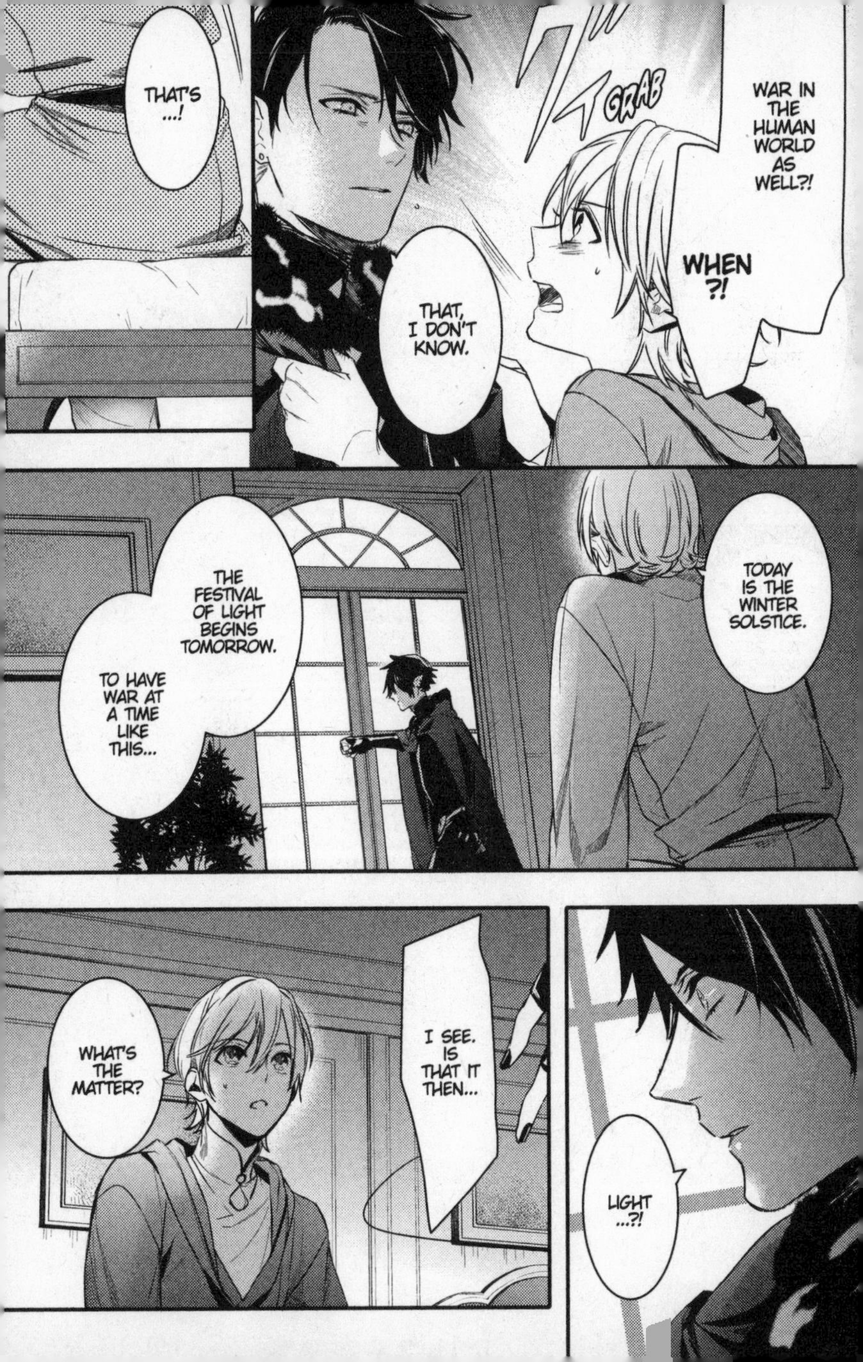
WAR IN THE HUMAN WORLD AS WELL?!
GRAB
WHEN?!
THAT, I DON'T KNOW.
THAT'S ...!
TODAY IS THE WINTER SOLSTICE.
THE FESTIVAL OF LIGHT BEGINS TOMORROW.
TO HAVE WAR AT A TIME LIKE THIS...
LIGHT ...?!
I SEE. IS THAT IT THEN...
WHAT'S THE MATTER?

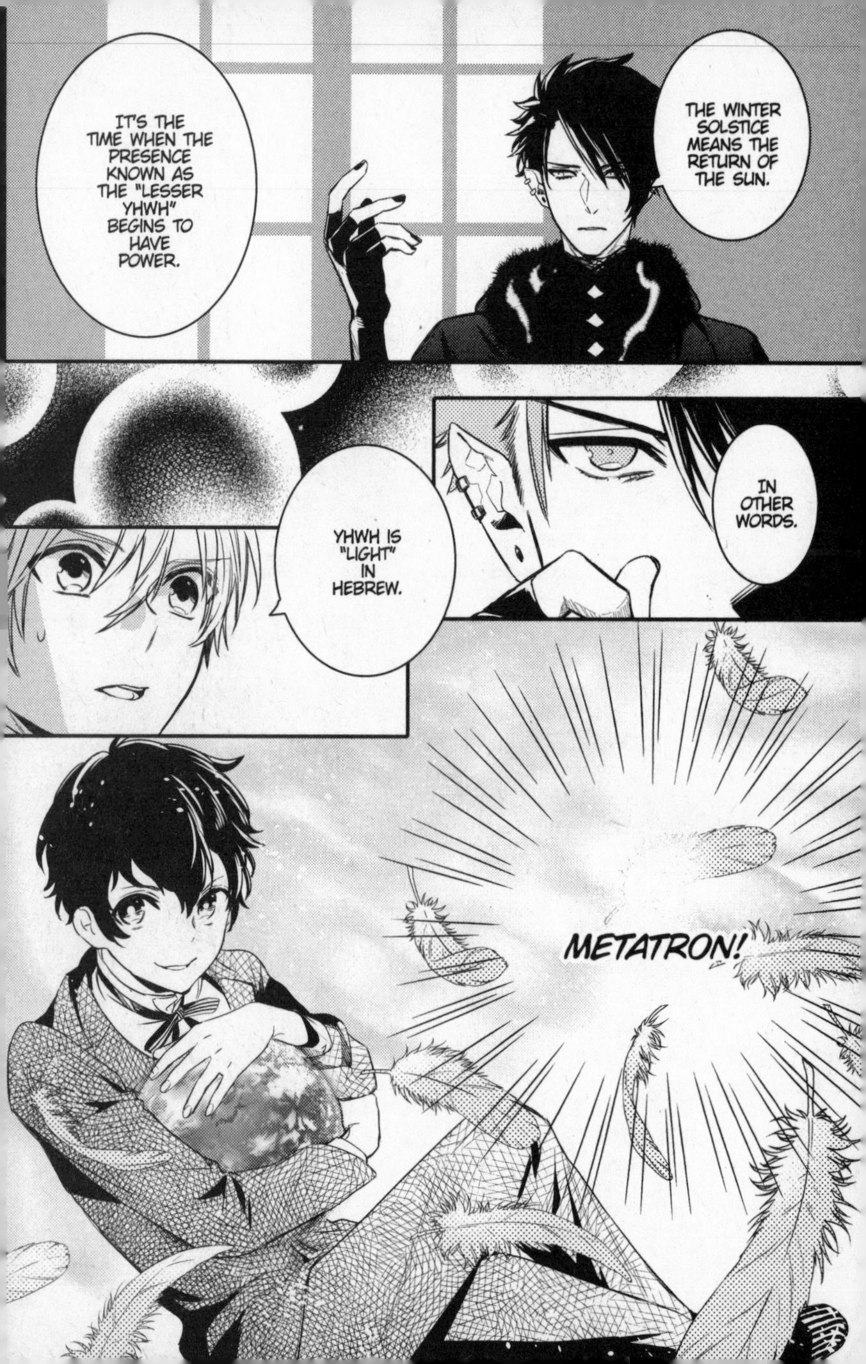
THE WINTER SOLSTICE MEANS THE RETURN OF THE SUN.
IT'S THE TIME WHEN THE PRESENCE KNOWN AS THE "LESSER YHWH" BEGINS TO HAVE POWER.
IN OTHER WORDS.
YHWH IS "LIGHT" IN HEBREW.
METATRON!

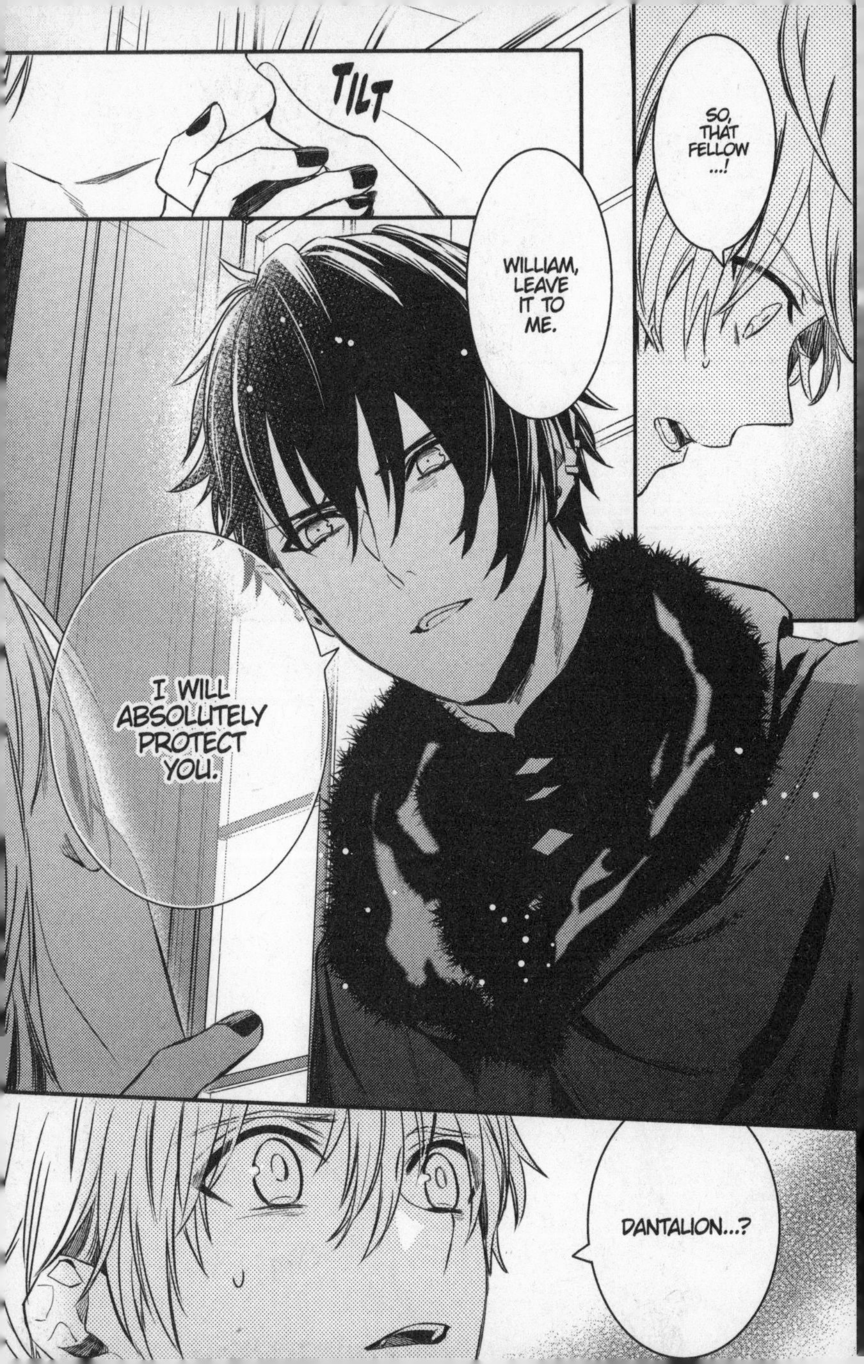
SO, THAT FELLOW ...!
TILT
WILLIAM, LEAVE IT TO ME.
I WILL ABSOLUTELY PROTECT YOU.
DANTALION...?

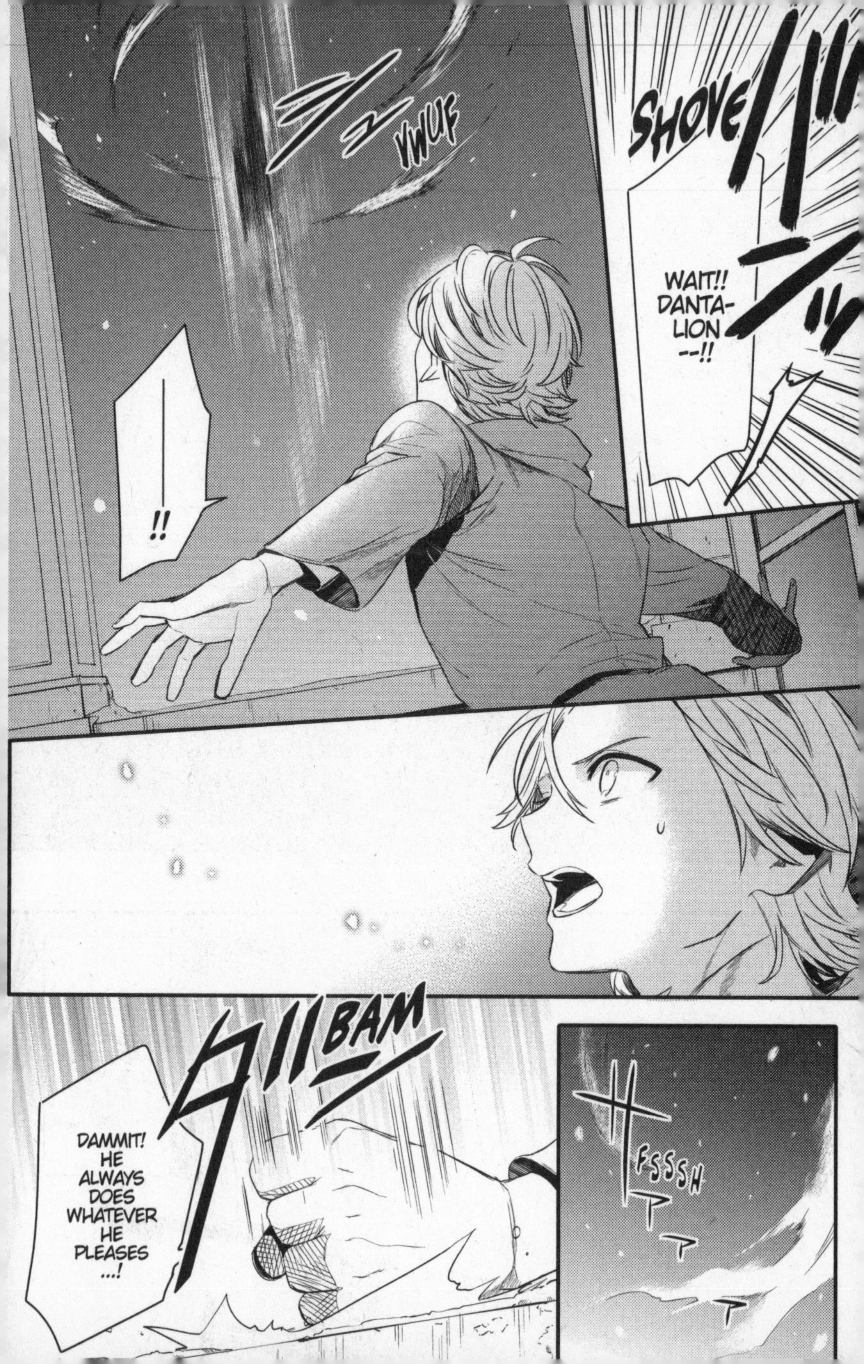
SHOVE
WAIT!! DANTALION --!!
VWUF
!!
FSSSH
BAM
DAMMIT! HE ALWAYS DOES WHATEVER HE PLEASES ...!

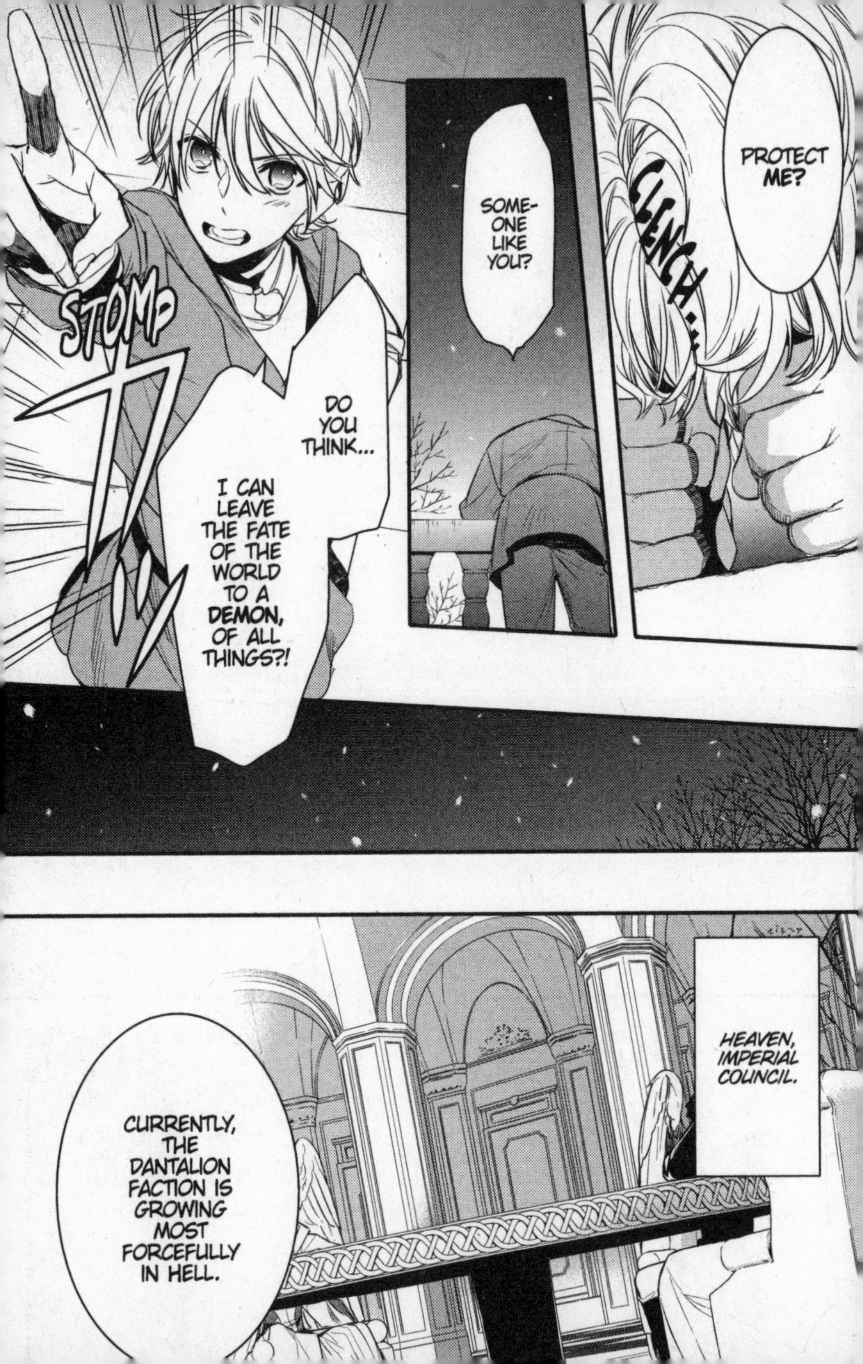
PROTECT ME?
CLENCH...
SOME-ONE LIKE YOU?
STOMP
DO YOU THINK...
I CAN LEAVE THE FATE OF THE WORLD TO A DEMON, OF ALL THINGS?!
HEAVEN, IMPERIAL COUNCIL.
CURRENTLY, THE DANTALION FACTION IS GROWING MOST FORCEFULLY IN HELL.

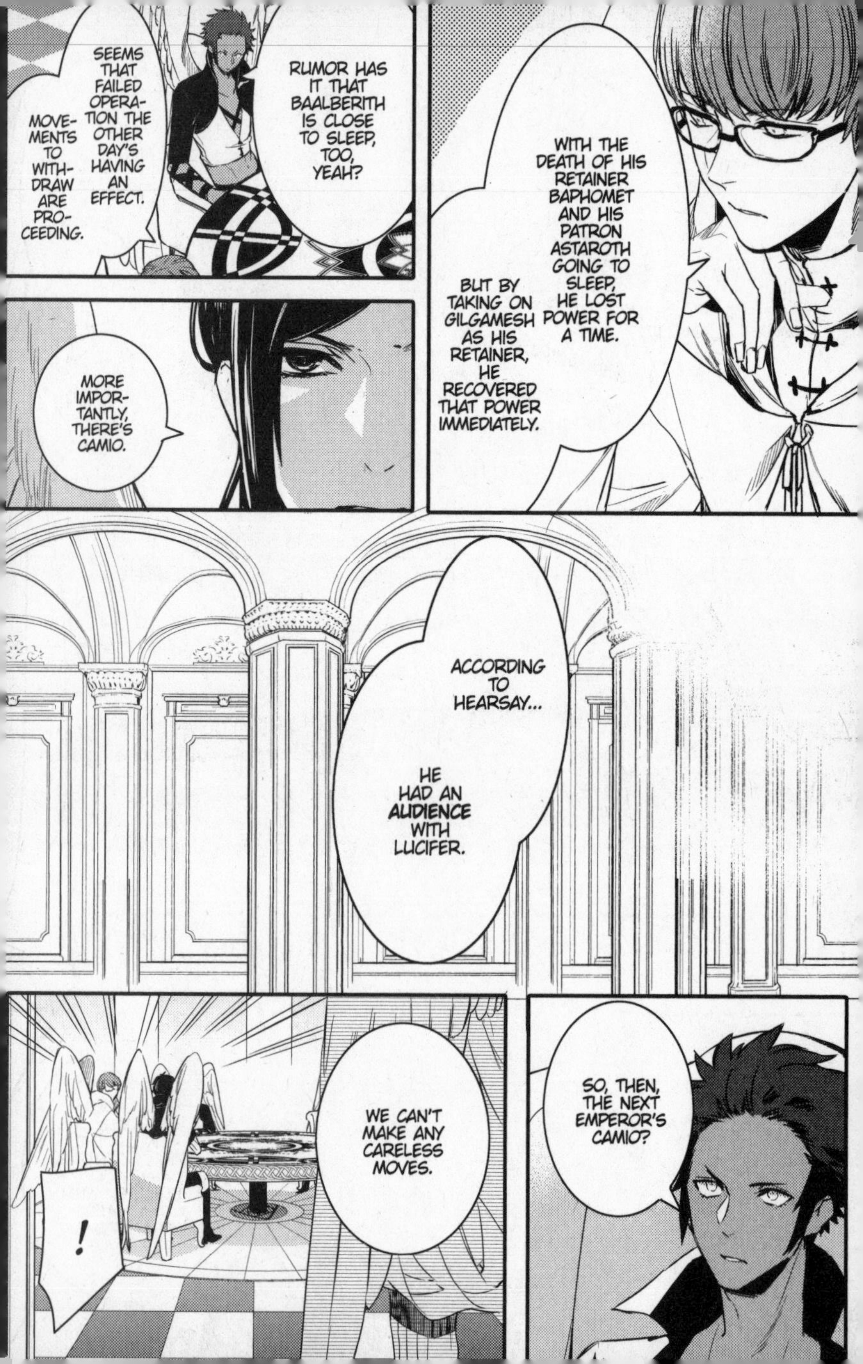
WITH THE DEATH OF HIS RETAINER BAPHOMET AND HIS PATRON ASTAROTH GOING TO SLEEP, HE LOST POWER FOR A TIME.
BUT BY TAKING ON GILGAMESH AS HIS RETAINER, HE RECOVERED THAT POWER IMMEDIATELY.
RUMOR HAS IT THAT BAALBERITH IS CLOSE TO SLEEP, TOO, YEAH?
SEEMS THAT FAILED OPERATION THE OTHER DAY'S HAVING AN EFFECT.
MOVEMENTS TO WITHDRAW ARE PROCEEDING.
MORE IMPORTANTLY, THERE'S CAMIO.
ACCORDING TO HEARSAY...
HE HAD AN **AUDIENCE** WITH LUCIFER.
SO, THEN, THE NEXT EMPEROR'S CAMIO?
WE CAN'T MAKE ANY CARELESS MOVES.
!

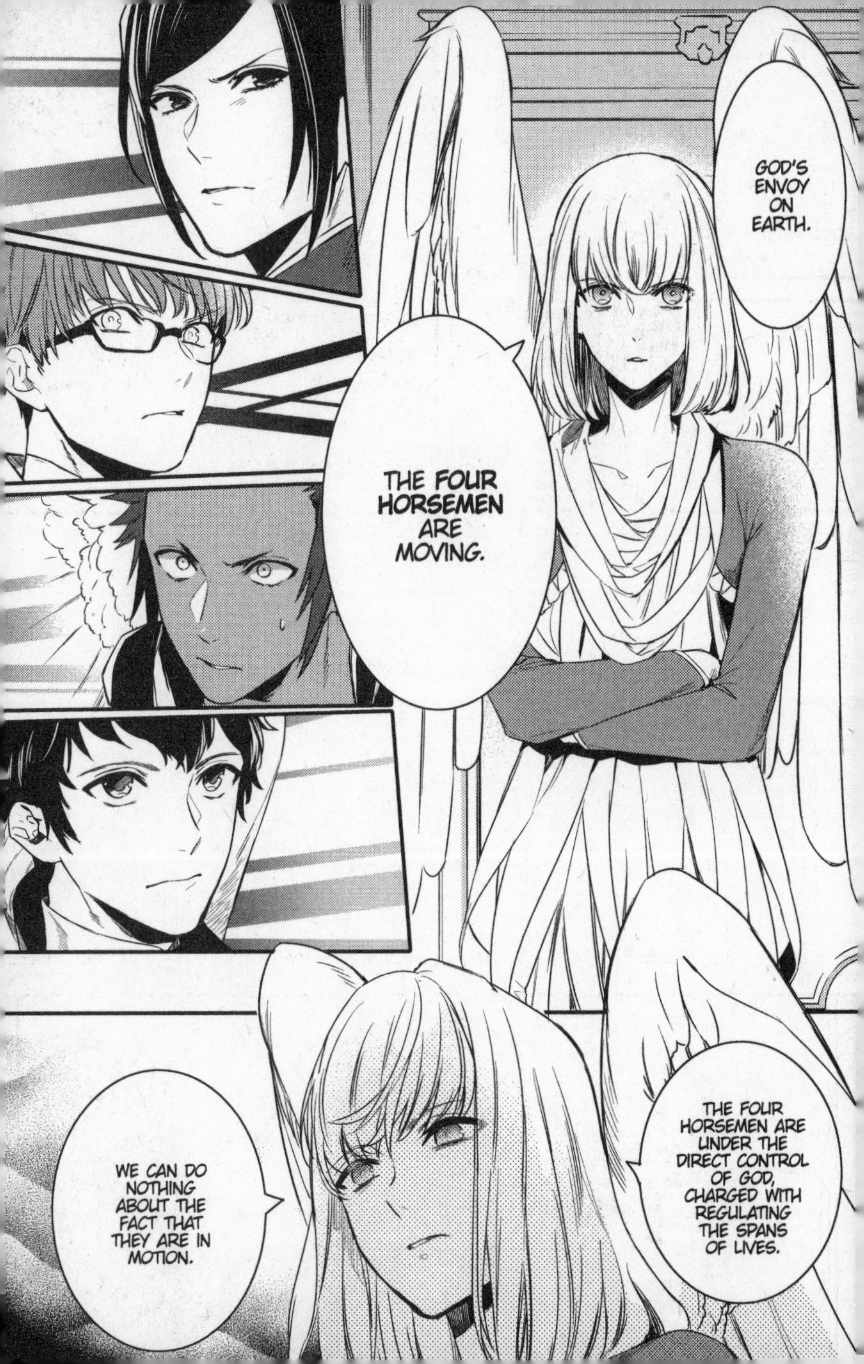
GOD'S ENVOY ON EARTH.
THE FOUR HORSEMEN ARE MOVING.
THE FOUR HORSEMEN ARE UNDER THE DIRECT CONTROL OF GOD, CHARGED WITH REGULATING THE SPANS OF LIVES.
WE CAN DO NOTHING ABOUT THE FACT THAT THEY ARE IN MOTION.

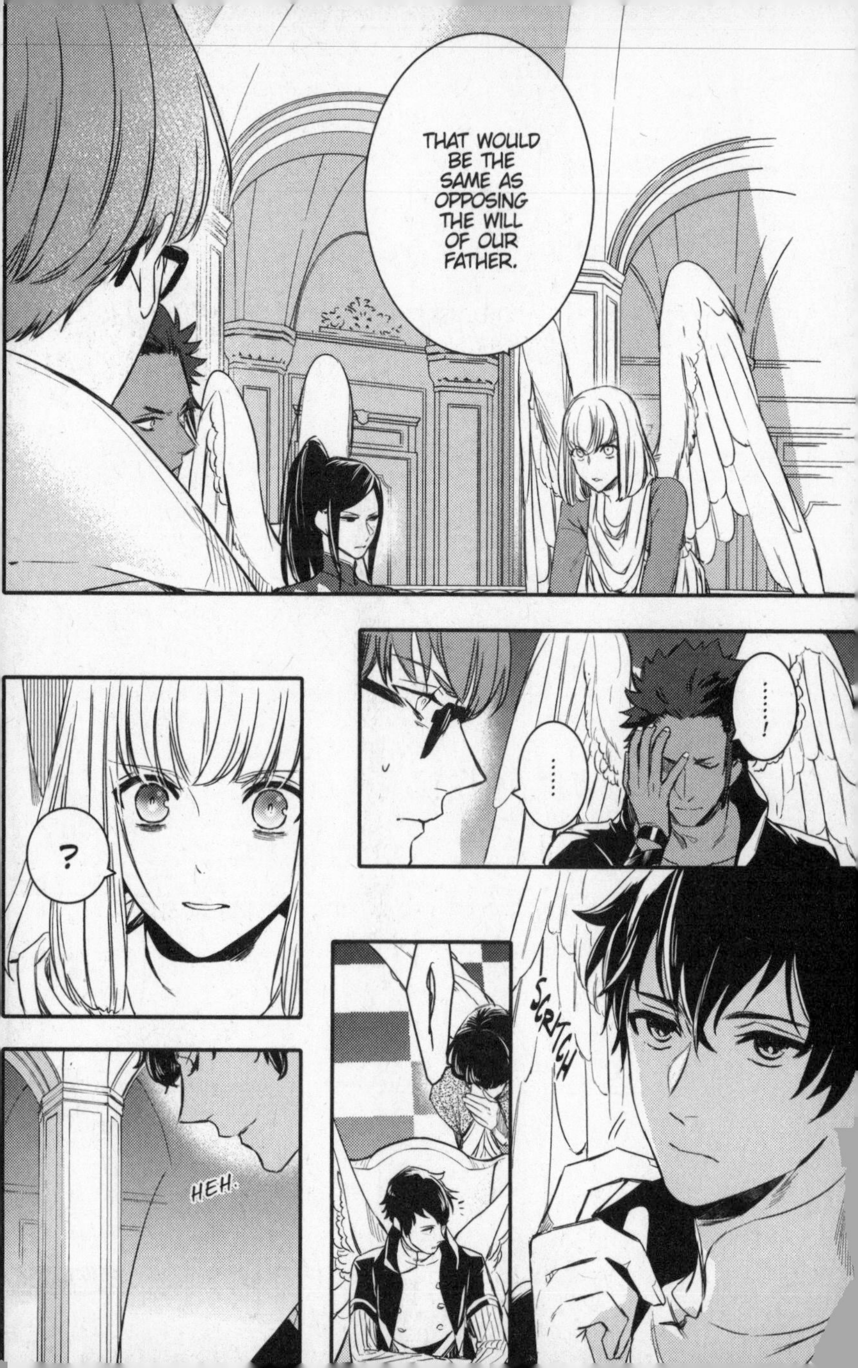
THAT WOULD BE THE SAME AS OPPOSING THE WILL OF OUR FATHER.
......!
......
?
SCRITCH
HEH.

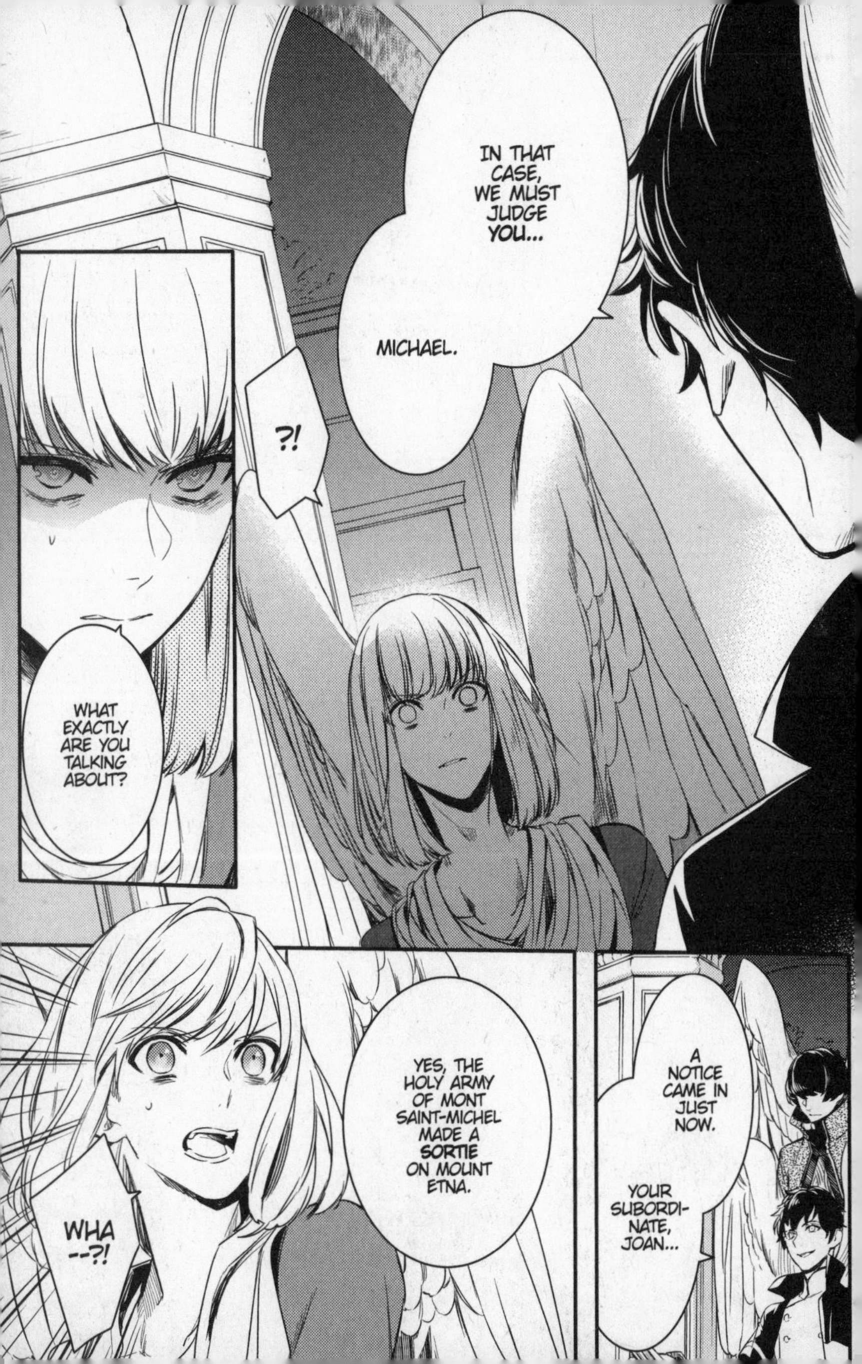
IN THAT CASE, WE MUST JUDGE YOU...
MICHAEL.
?!
WHAT EXACTLY ARE YOU TALKING ABOUT?
A NOTICE CAME IN JUST NOW.
YOUR SUBORDI-NATE, JOAN...
YES, THE HOLY ARMY OF MONT SAINT-MICHEL MADE A SORTIE ON MOUNT ETNA.
WHA--?!

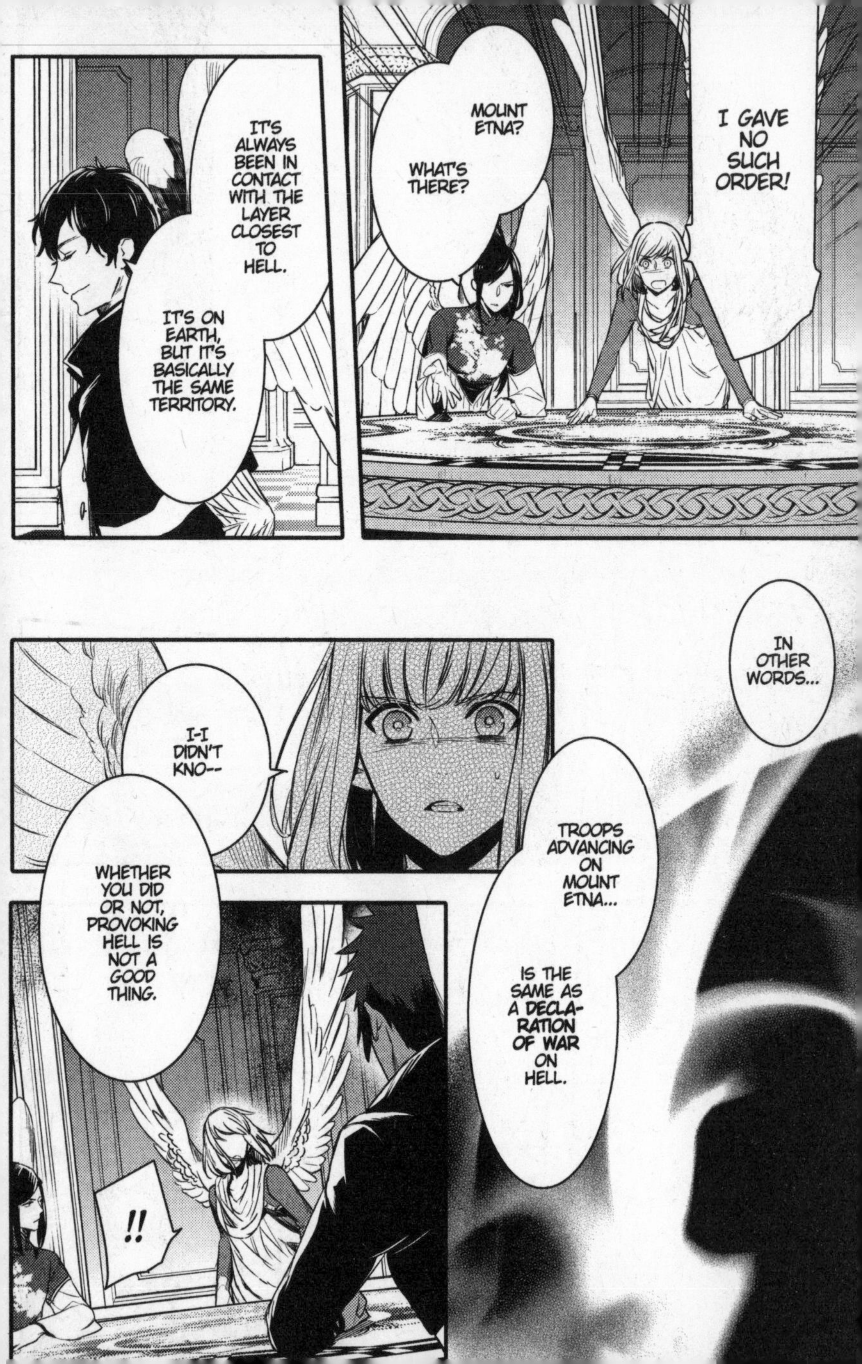
I GAVE NO SUCH ORDER!
MOUNT ETNA?
WHAT'S THERE?
IT'S ALWAYS BEEN IN CONTACT WITH THE LAYER CLOSEST TO HELL.
IT'S ON EARTH, BUT IT'S BASICALLY THE SAME TERRITORY.
IN OTHER WORDS...
TROOPS ADVANCING ON MOUNT ETNA...
IS THE SAME AS A DECLARATION OF WAR ON HELL.
I-I DIDN'T KNO--
WHETHER YOU DID OR NOT, PROVOKING HELL IS NOT A GOOD THING.
!!

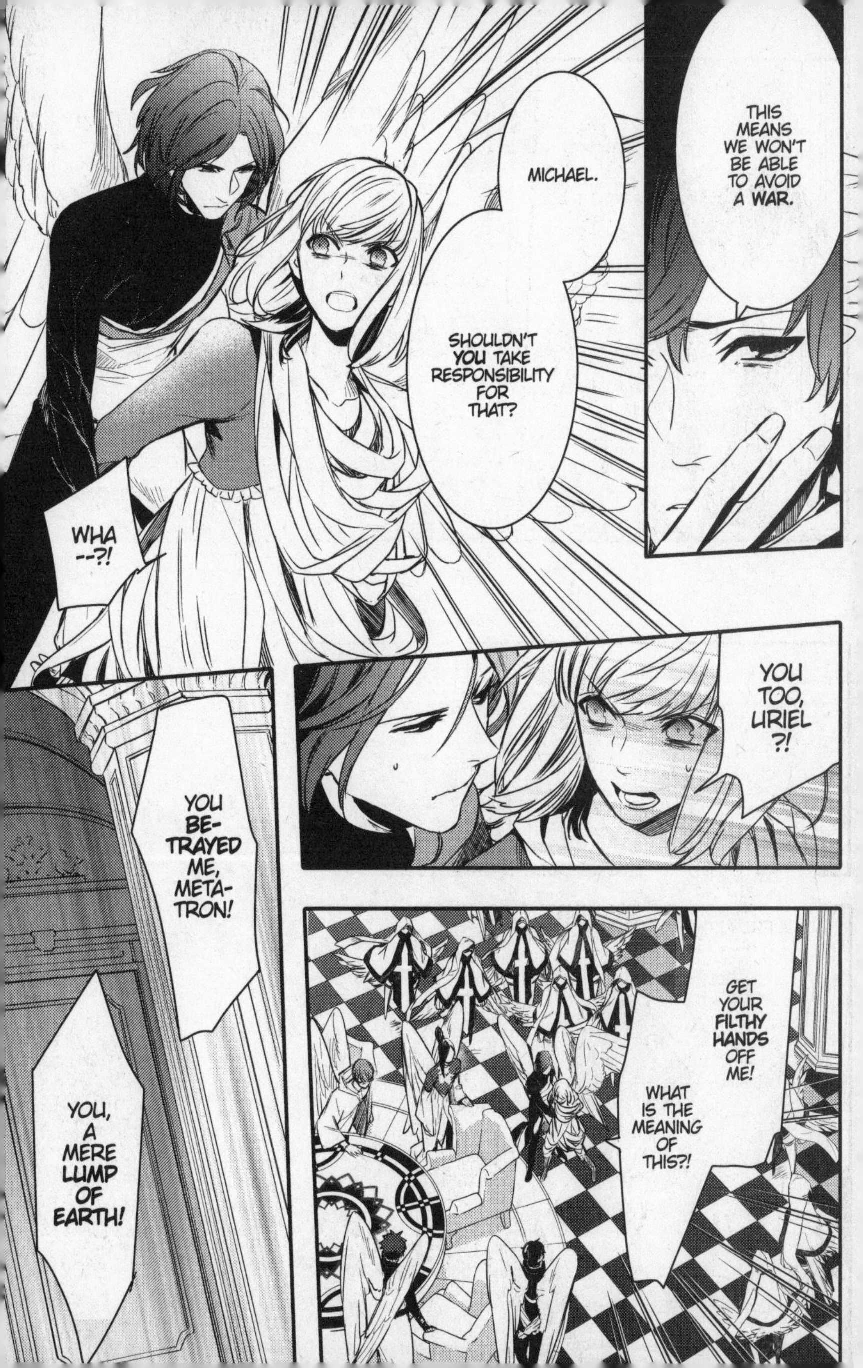
THIS MEANS WE WON'T BE ABLE TO AVOID A WAR.
MICHAEL.
SHOULDN'T YOU TAKE RESPONSIBILITY FOR THAT?
WHA--?!
YOU TOO, URIEL?!
GET YOUR FILTHY HANDS OFF ME!
WHAT IS THE MEANING OF THIS?!
YOU BE-TRAYED ME, META-TRON!
YOU, A MERE LUMP OF EARTH!

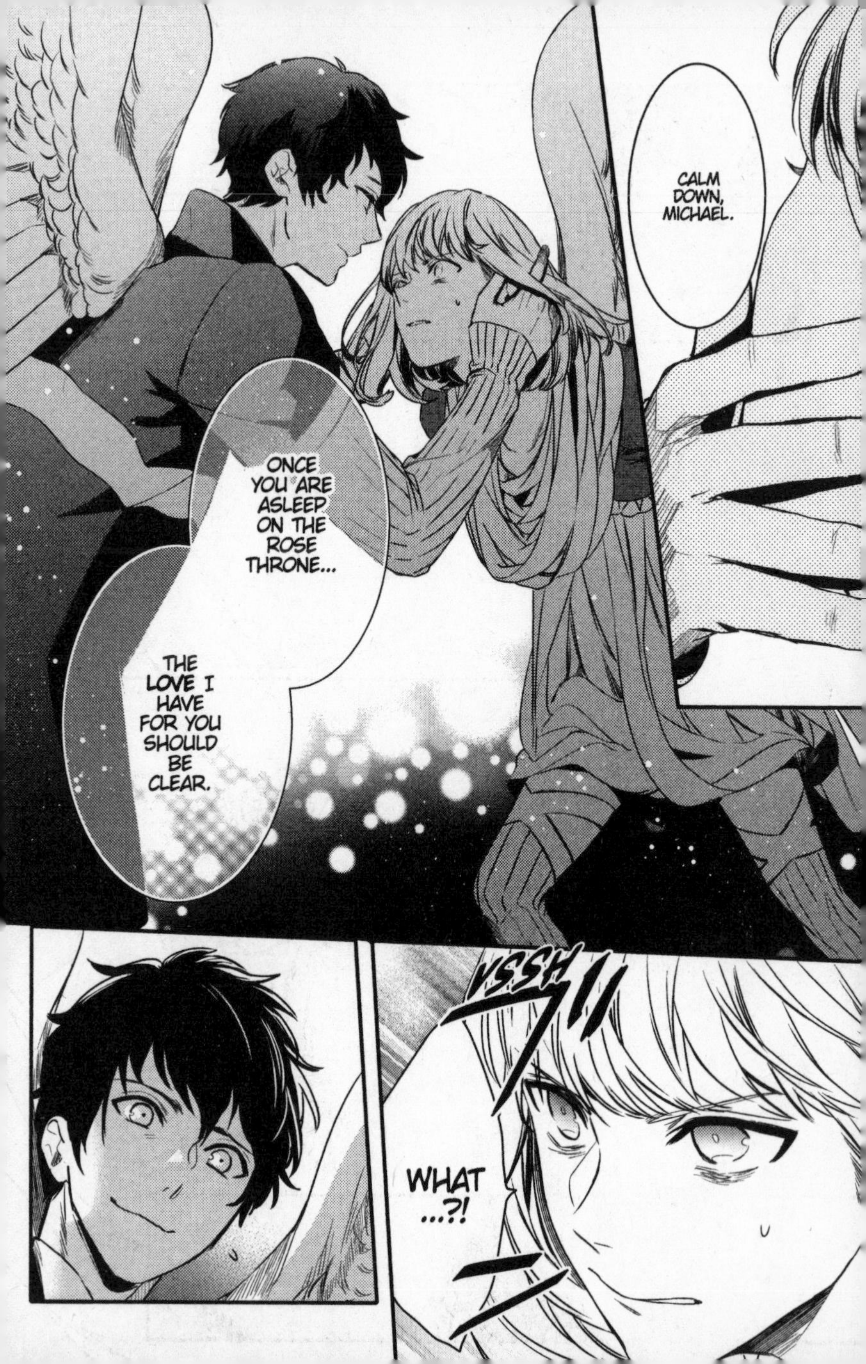
CALM DOWN, MICHAEL.
ONCE YOU ARE ASLEEP ON THE ROSE THRONE...
THE LOVE I HAVE FOR YOU SHOULD BE CLEAR.
WHAT ...?!

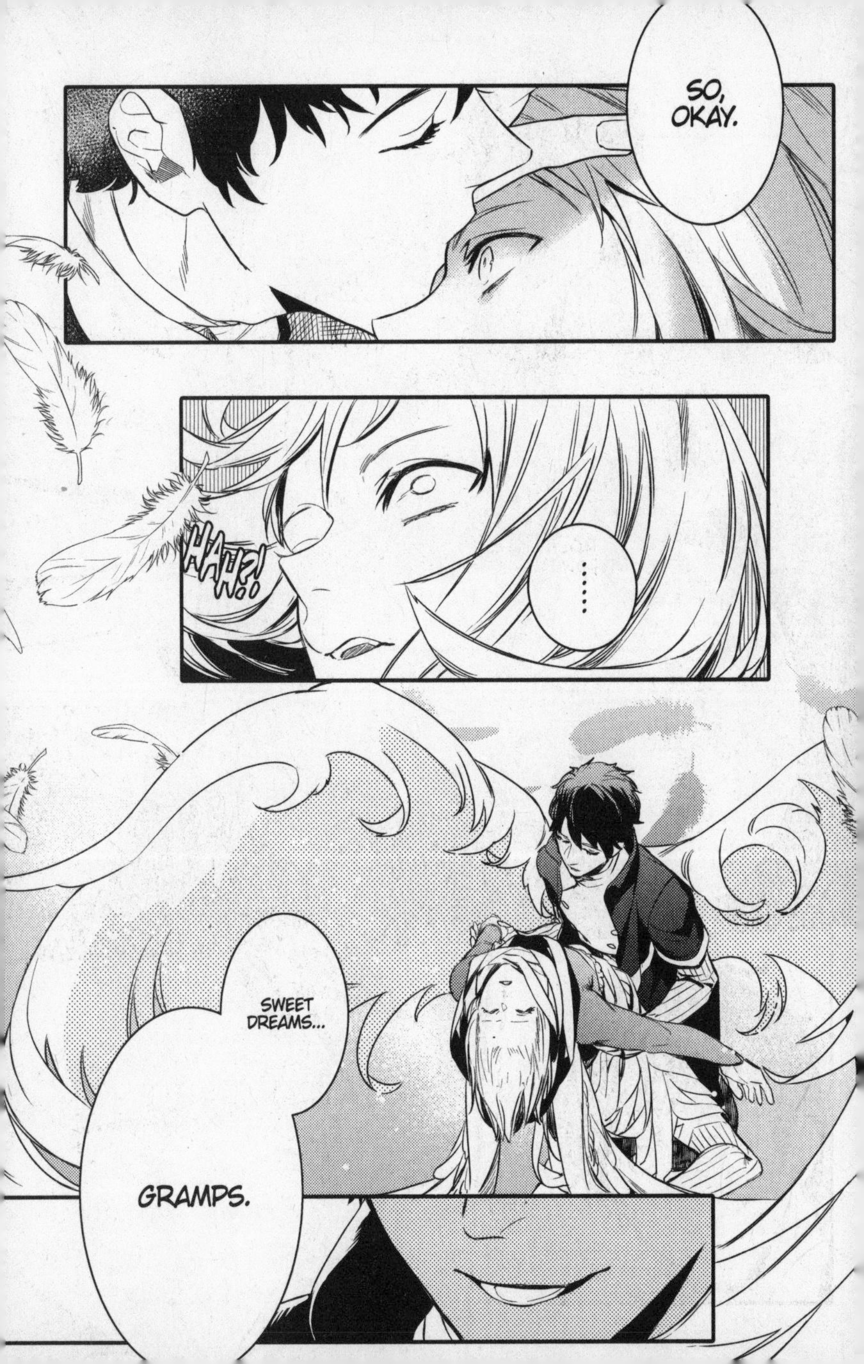
SO, OKAY.
......
HAH?!
SWEET DREAMS...
GRAMPS.

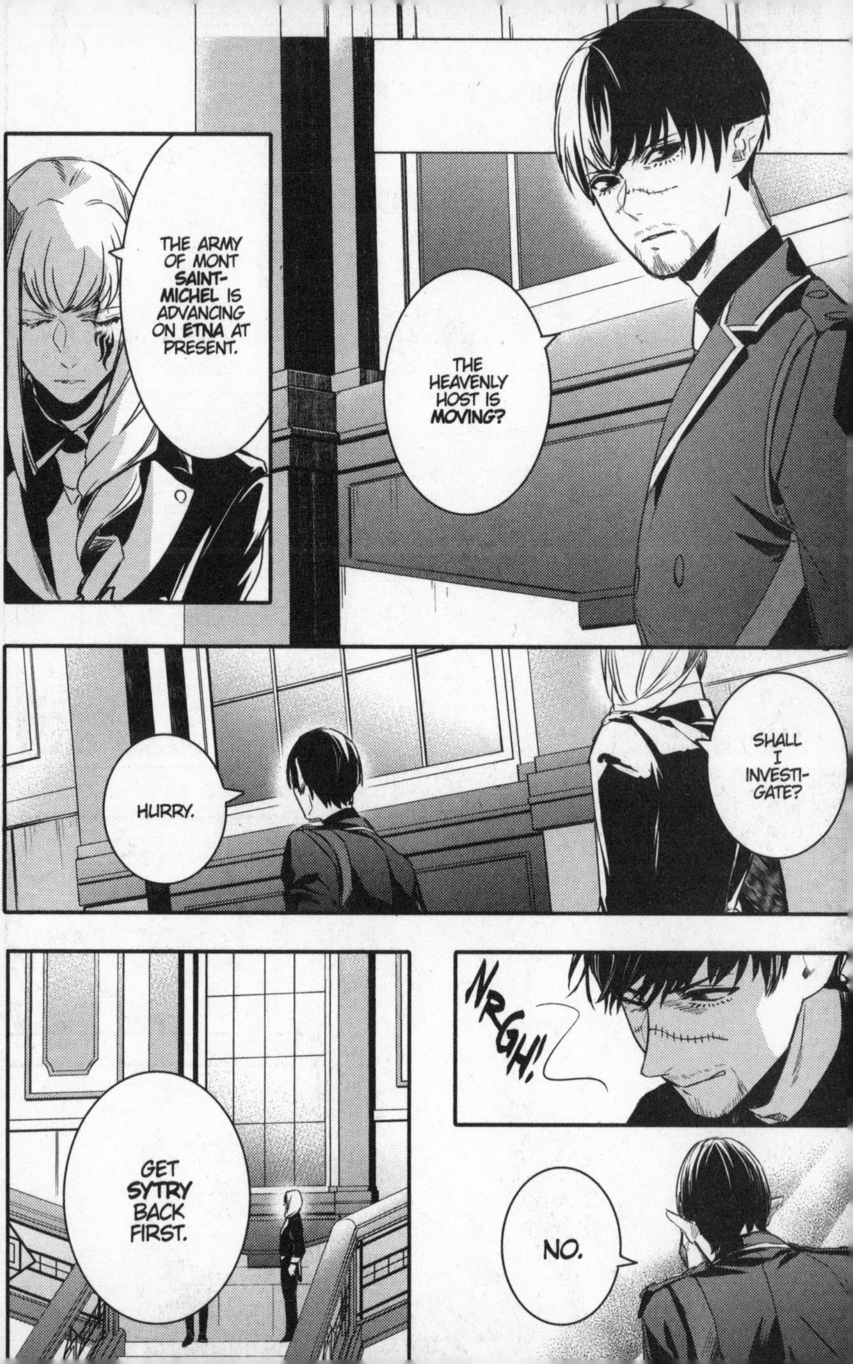
THE HEAVENLY HOST IS MOVING?
THE ARMY OF MONT SAINT-MICHEL IS ADVANCING ON ETNA AT PRESENT.
SHALL I INVESTIGATE?
HURRY.
NRGH!
NO.
GET SYTRY BACK FIRST.

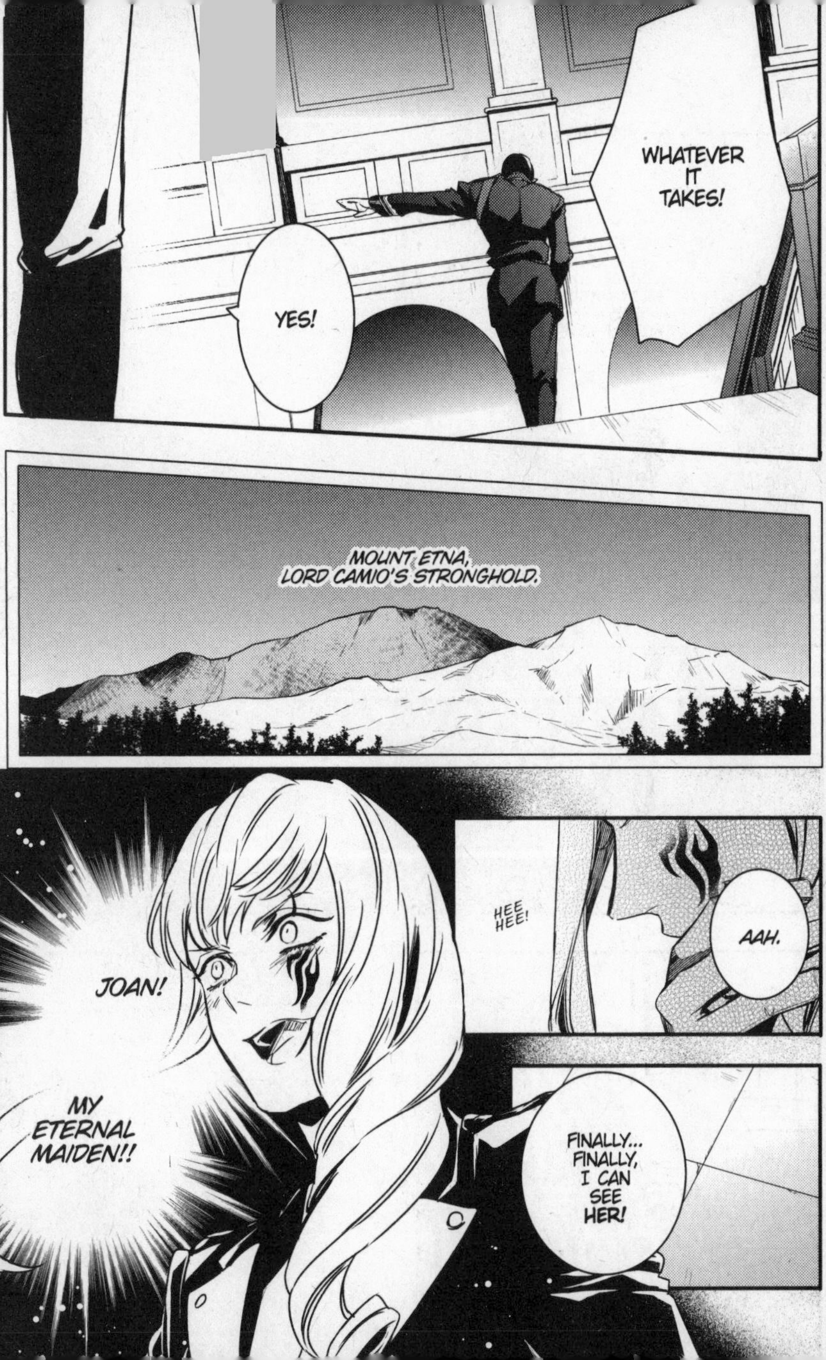
WHATEVER IT TAKES!
YES!
MOUNT ETNA, LORD CAMIO'S STRONGHOLD.
AAH.
HEE HEE!
FINALLY... FINALLY, I CAN SEE HER!
JOAN!
MY ETERNAL MAIDEN!!

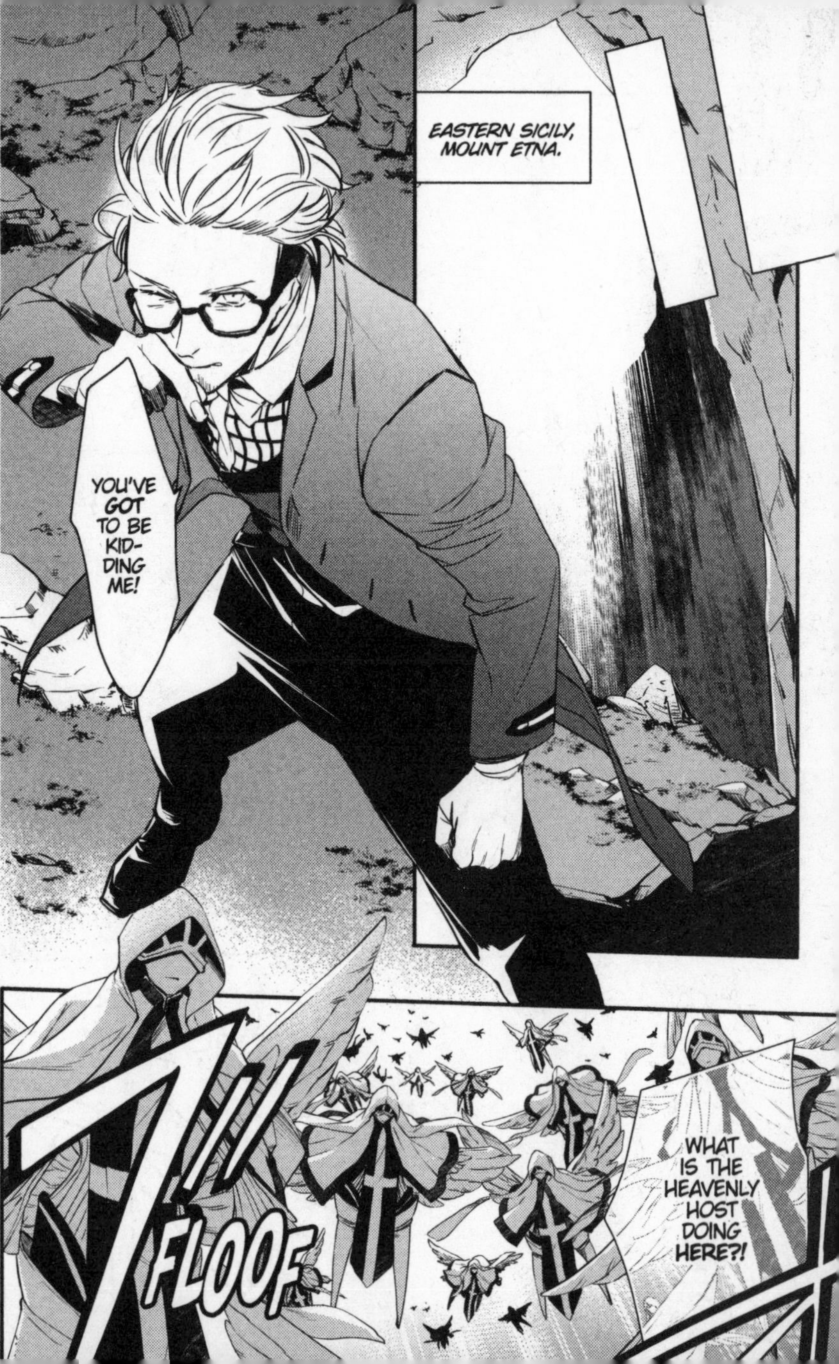
EASTERN SICILY, MOUNT ETNA.
YOU'VE GOT TO BE KID-DING ME!
WHAT IS THE HEAVENLY HOST DOING HERE?!
FLOOF

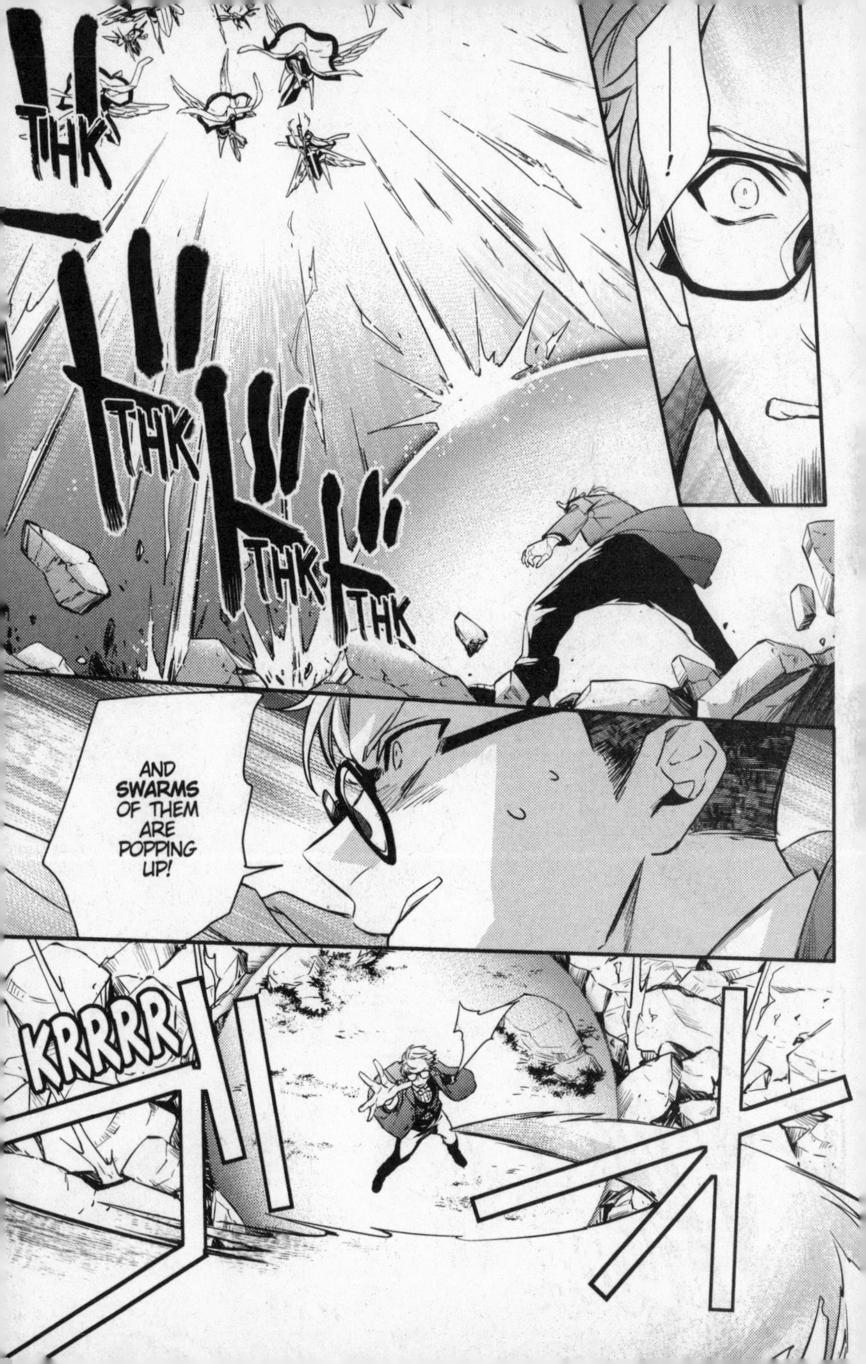
!
THK
THK
THK
THK
AND SWARMS OF THEM ARE POPPING UP!
KRRRR

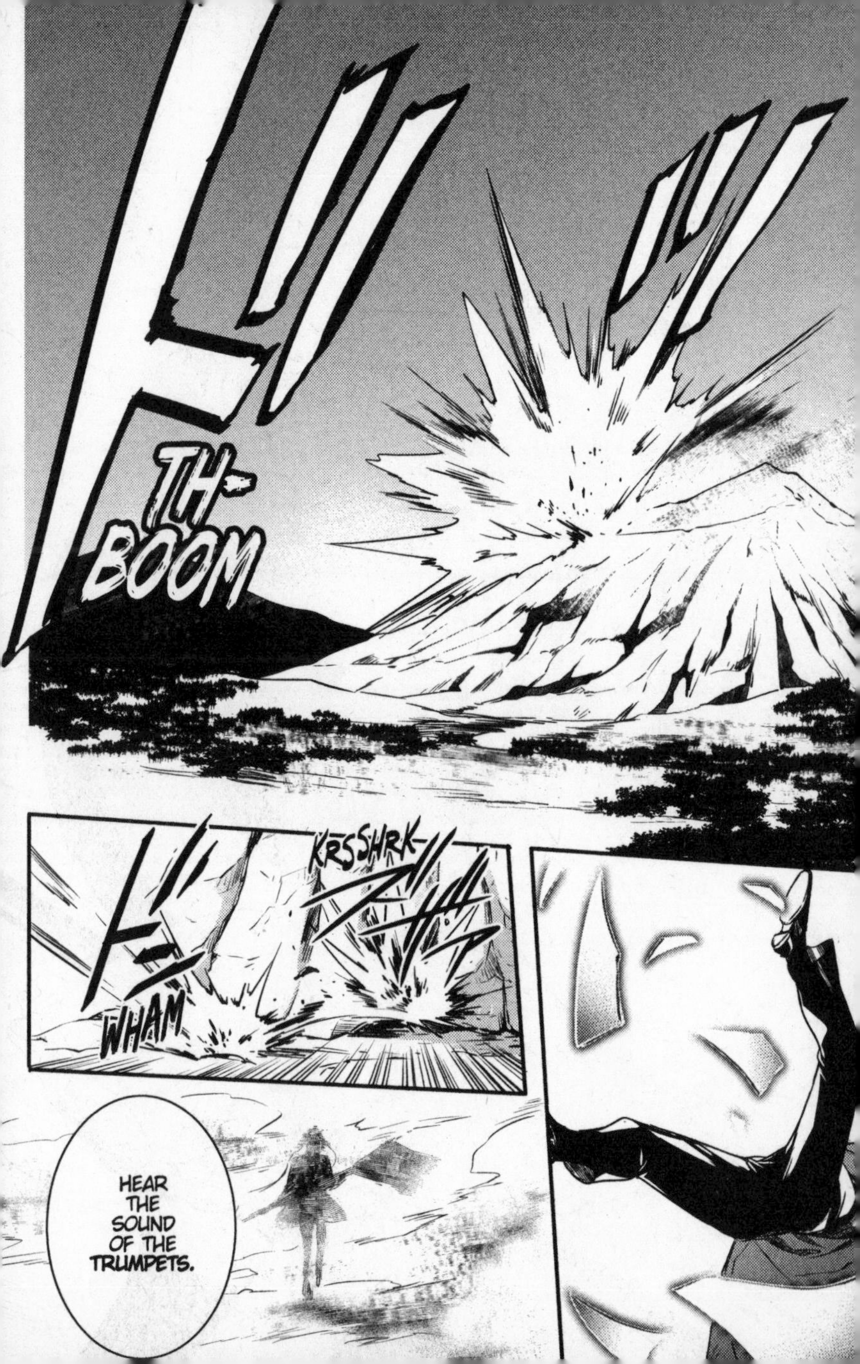
TH-BOOM
KRSSHRK
WHAM
HEAR THE SOUND OF THE TRUMPETS.

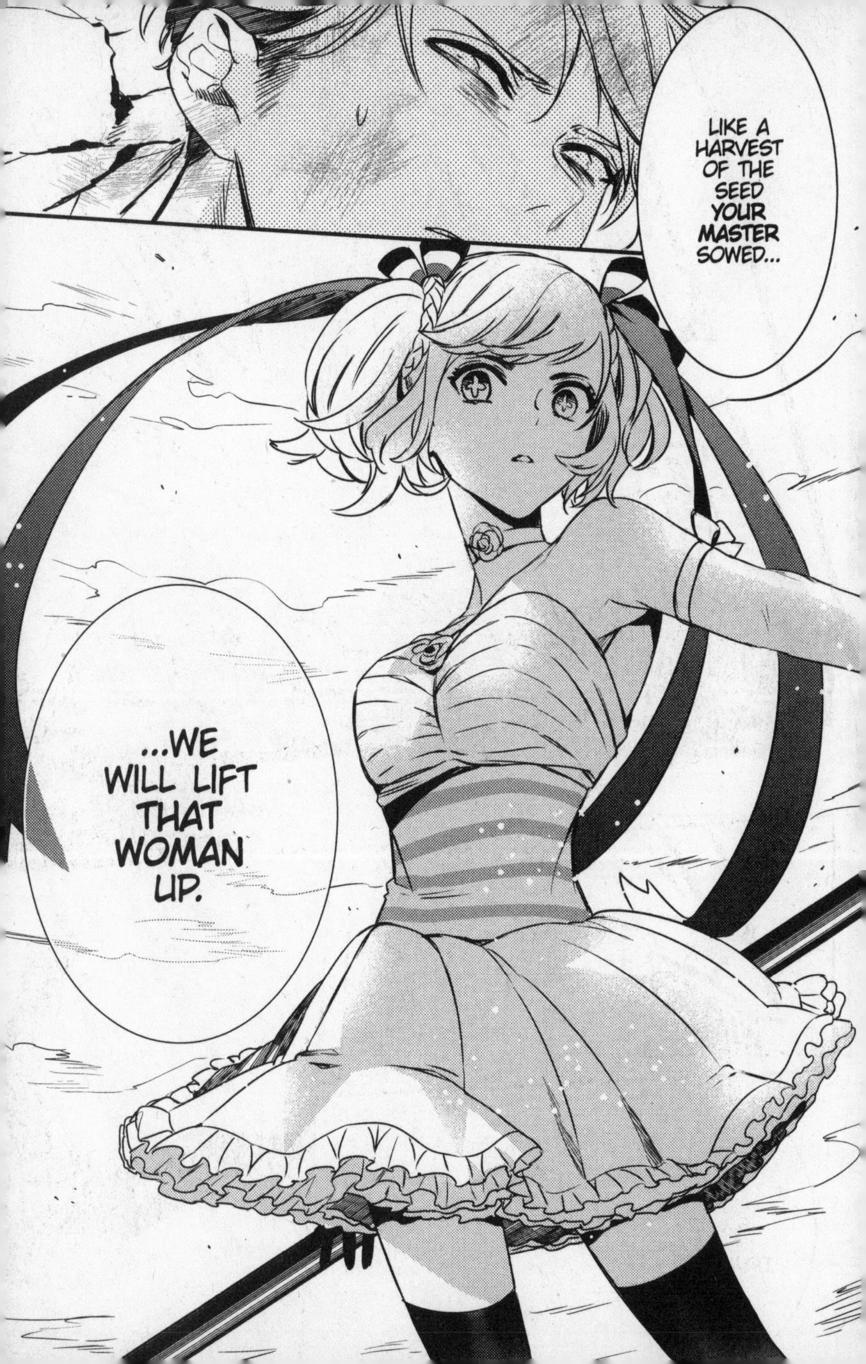
LIKE A HARVEST OF THE SEED YOUR MASTER SOWED...
...WE WILL LIFT THAT WOMAN UP.

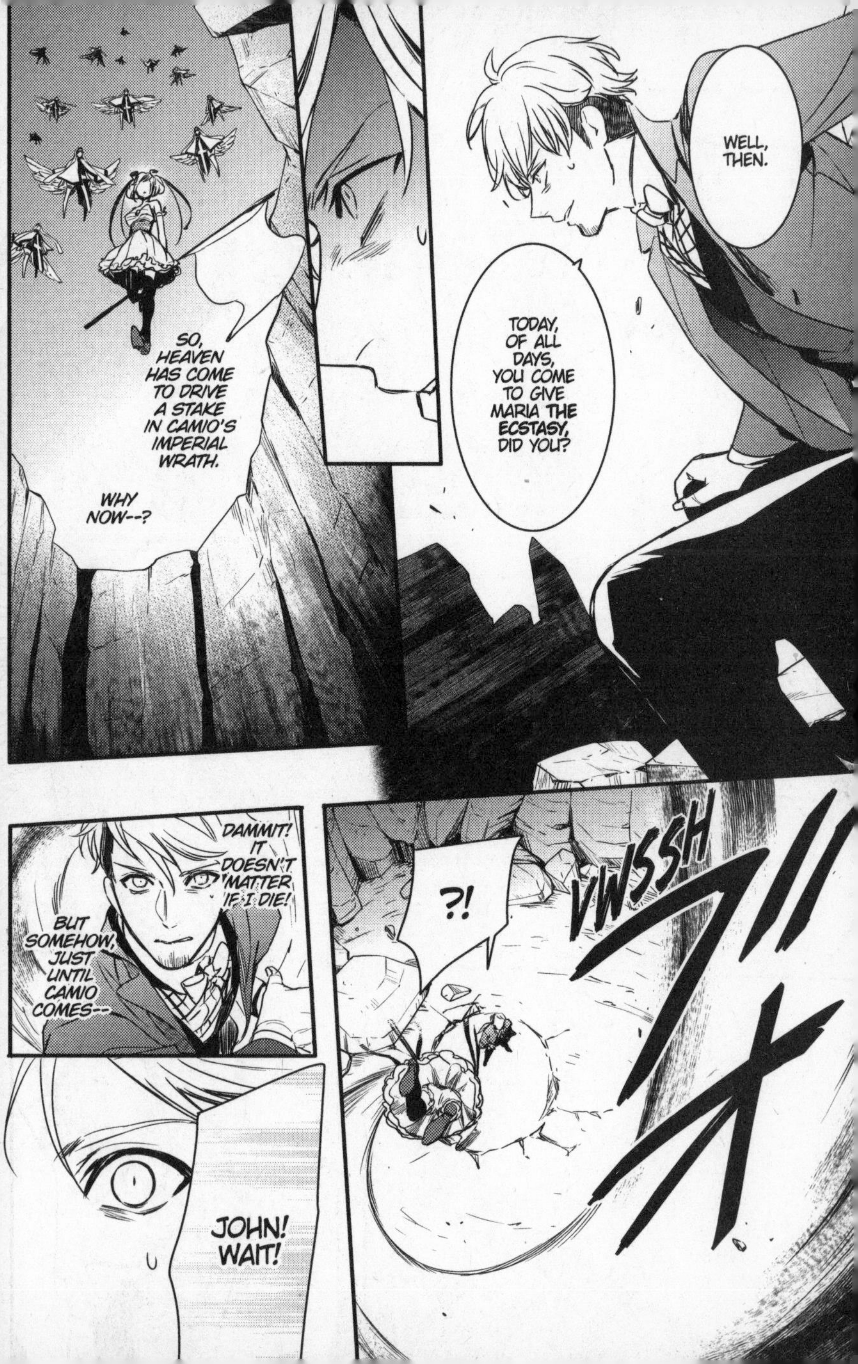
WELL, THEN.
TODAY, OF ALL DAYS, YOU COME TO GIVE MARIA THE ECSTASY, DID YOU?
SO, HEAVEN HAS COME TO DRIVE A STAKE IN CAMIO'S IMPERIAL WRATH.
WHY NOW--?
VWSSH
?!
DAMMIT! IT DOESN'T MATTER IF I DIE!
BUT SOMEHOW, JUST UNTIL CAMIO COMES--
JOHN! WAIT!

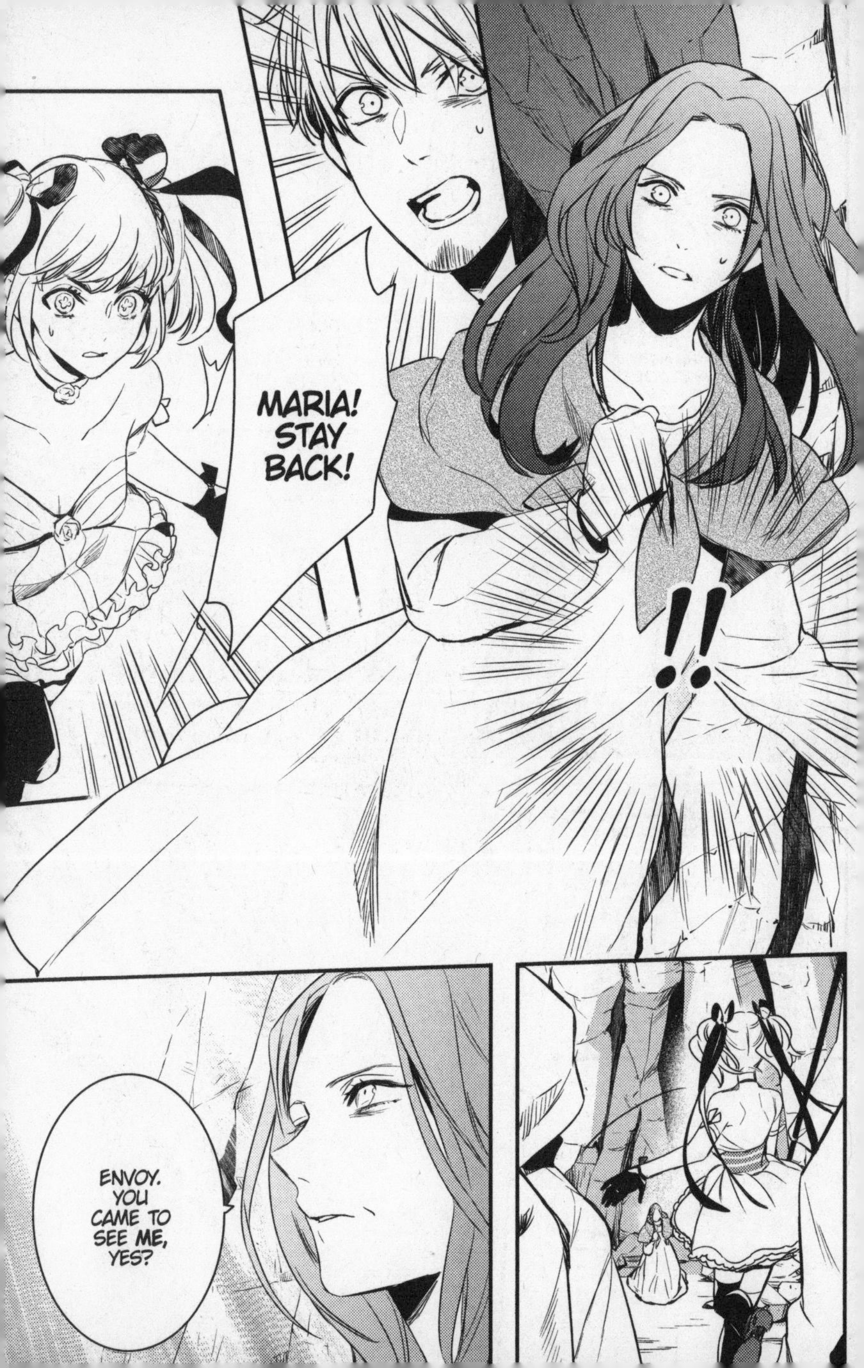
MARIA! STAY BACK!
!!
ENVOY. YOU CAME TO SEE ME, YES?

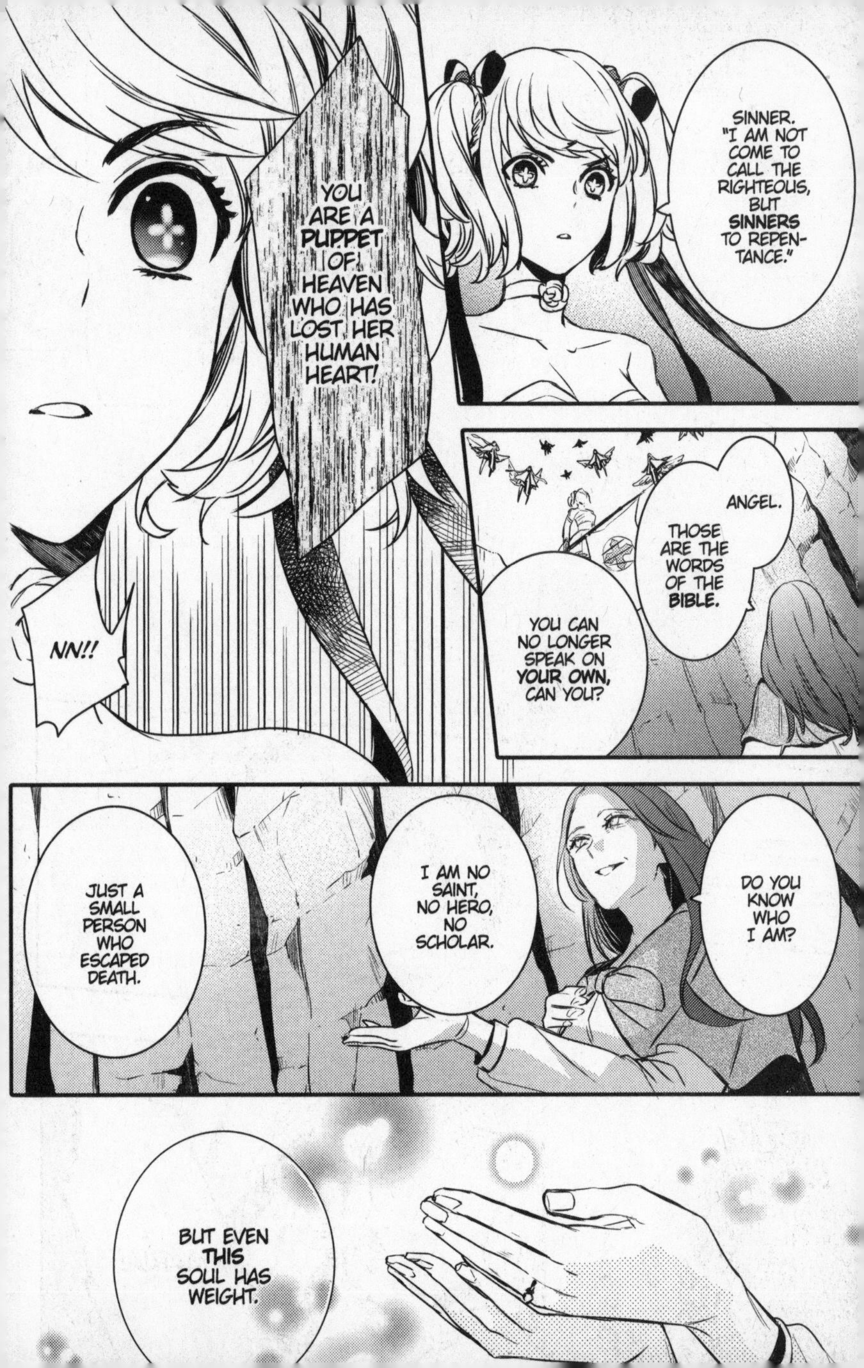
SINNER. "I AM NOT COME TO CALL THE RIGHTEOUS, BUT SINNERS TO REPENTANCE."
ANGEL.
THOSE ARE THE WORDS OF THE BIBLE.
YOU CAN NO LONGER SPEAK ON YOUR OWN, CAN YOU?
YOU ARE A PUPPET OF HEAVEN WHO HAS LOST HER HUMAN HEART!
NN!!
DO YOU KNOW WHO I AM?
I AM NO SAINT, NO HERO, NO SCHOLAR.
JUST A SMALL PERSON WHO ESCAPED DEATH.
BUT EVEN THIS SOUL HAS WEIGHT.

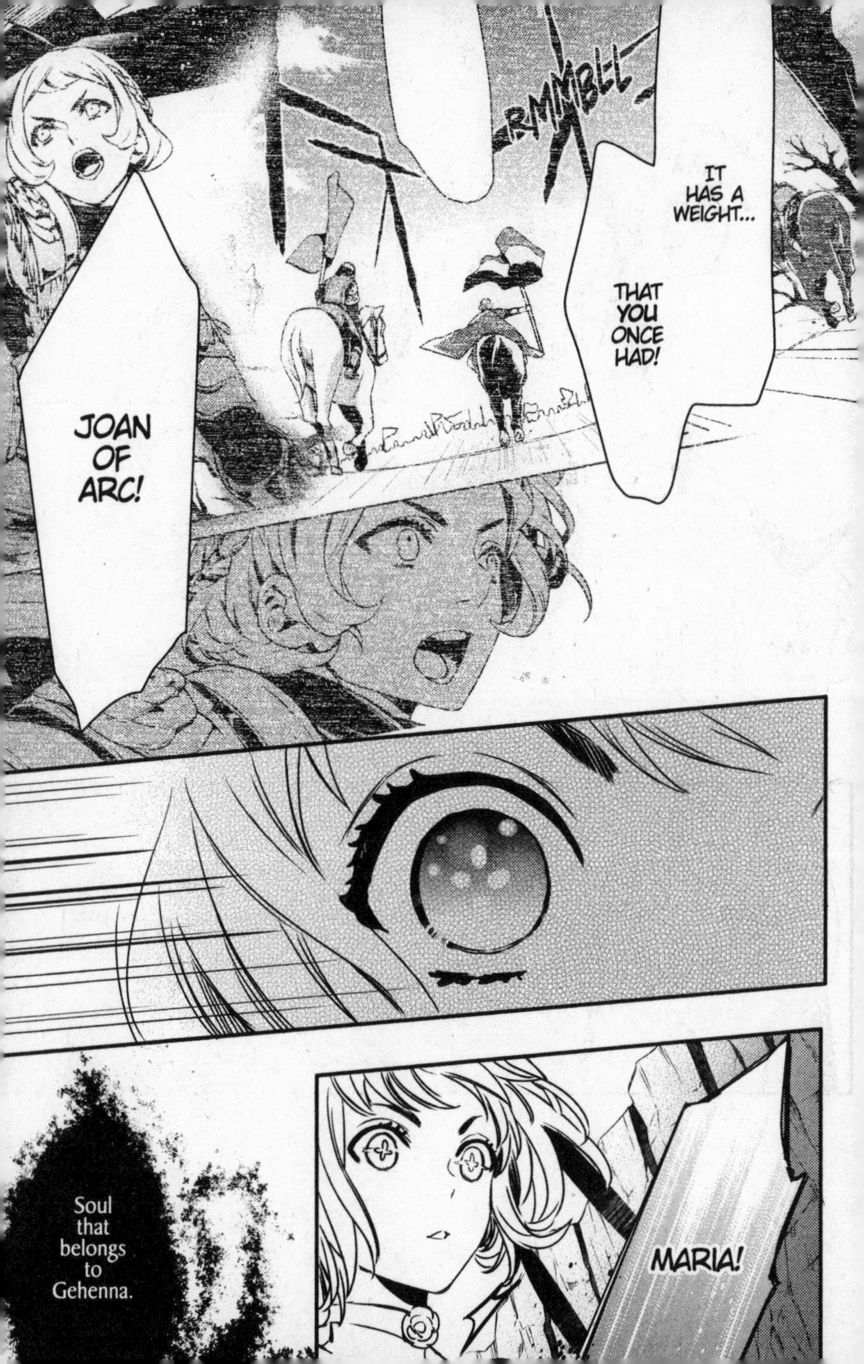
RMMBLE
IT HAS A WEIGHT...
THAT YOU ONCE HAD!
JOAN OF ARC!
MARIA!
Soul that belongs to Gehenna.

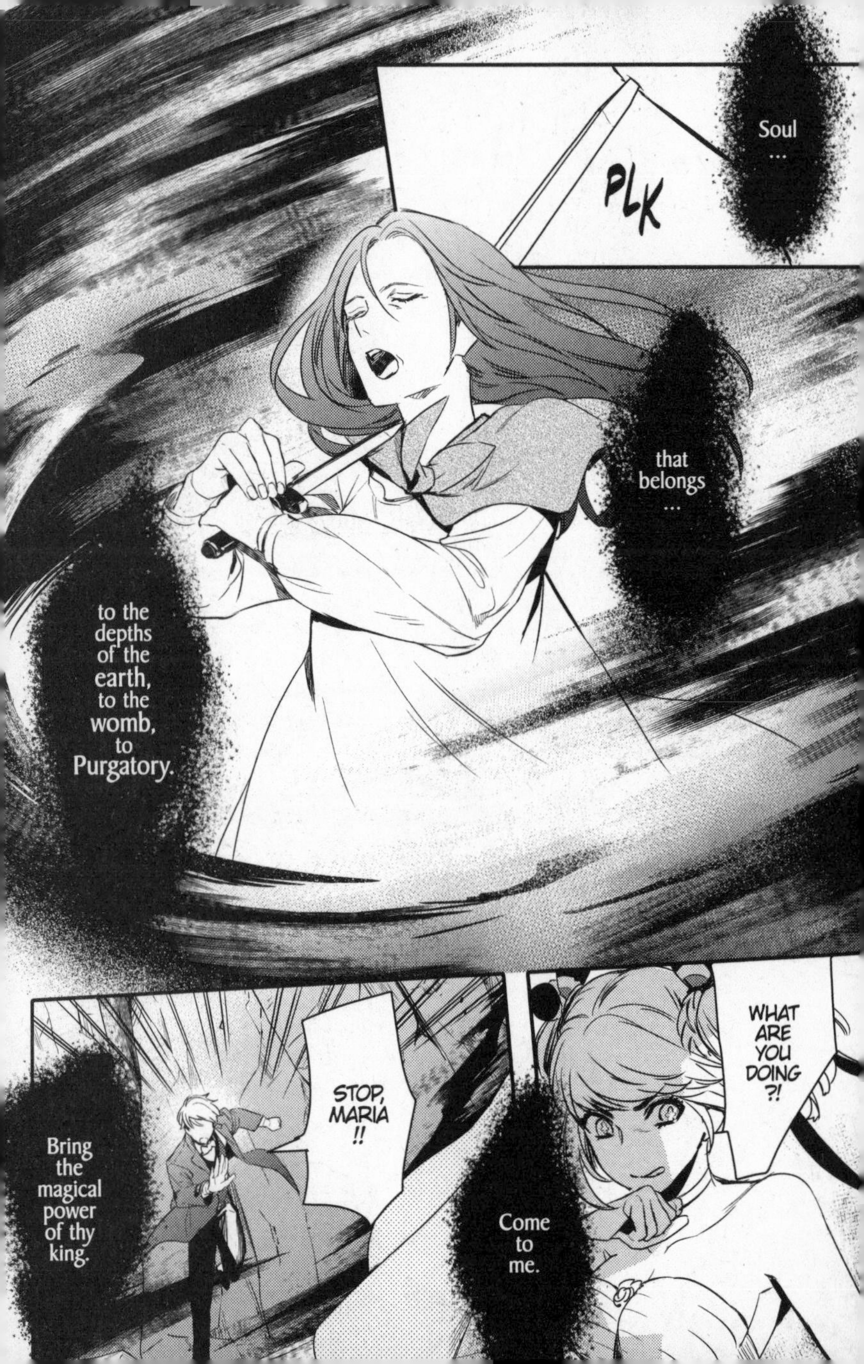
Soul ...
PLK
that belongs ...
to the depths of the earth, to the womb, to Purgatory.
WHAT ARE YOU DOING ?!
Come to me.
STOP, MARIA !!
Bring the magical power of thy king.

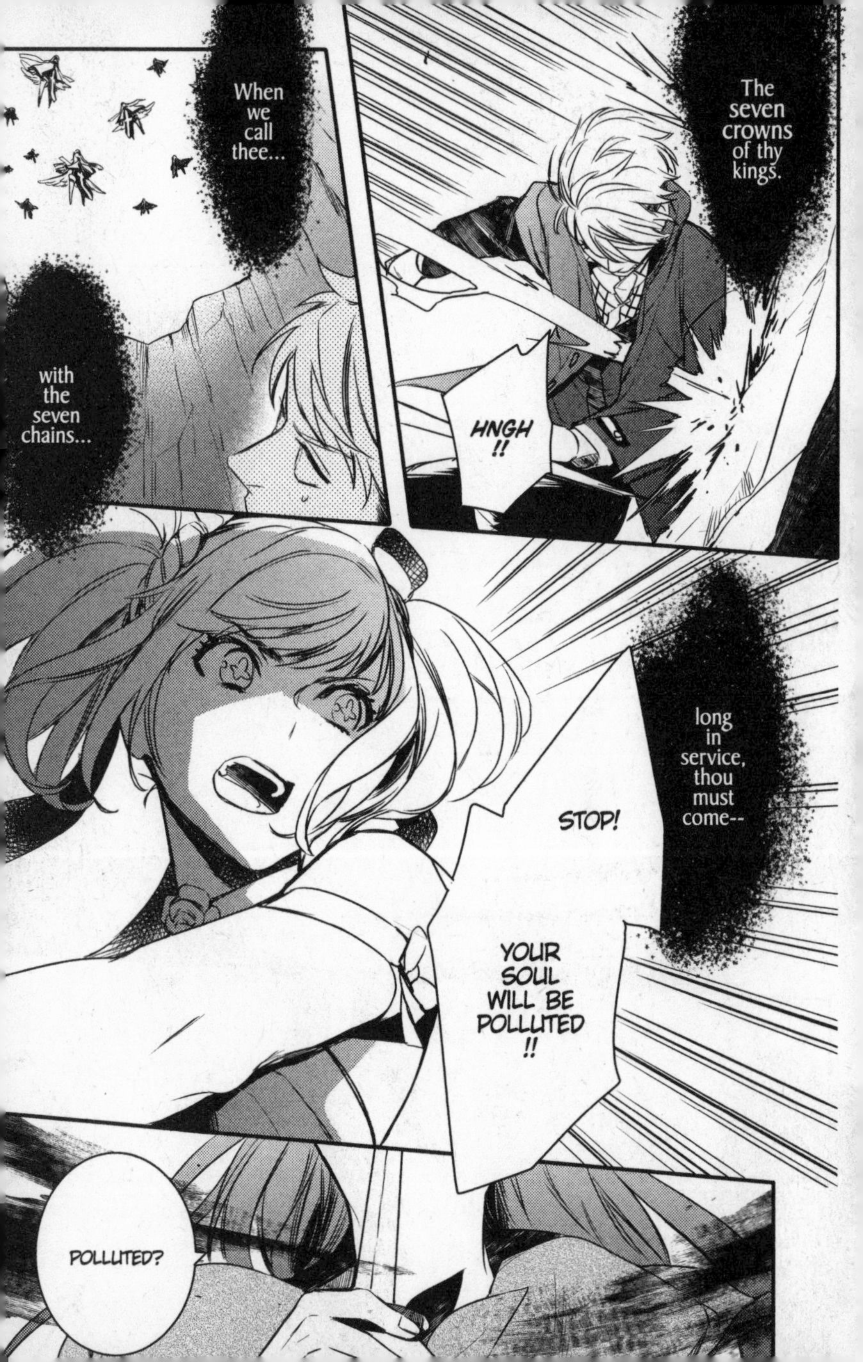
The seven crowns of thy kings.
HNGH !!
When we call thee...
with the seven chains...
long in service, thou must come--
STOP!
YOUR SOUL WILL BE POLLUTED !!
POLLUTED?

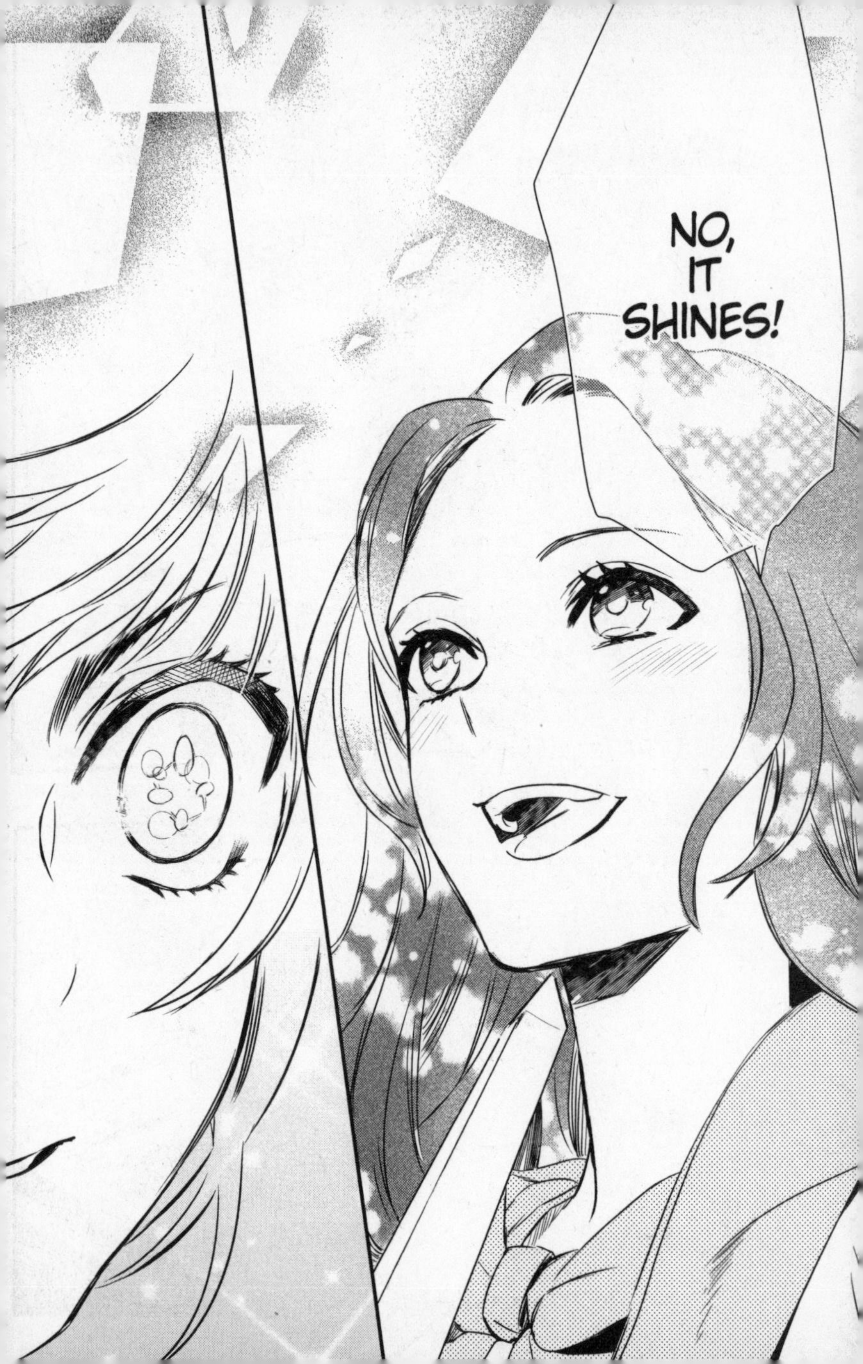
NO, IT SHINES!

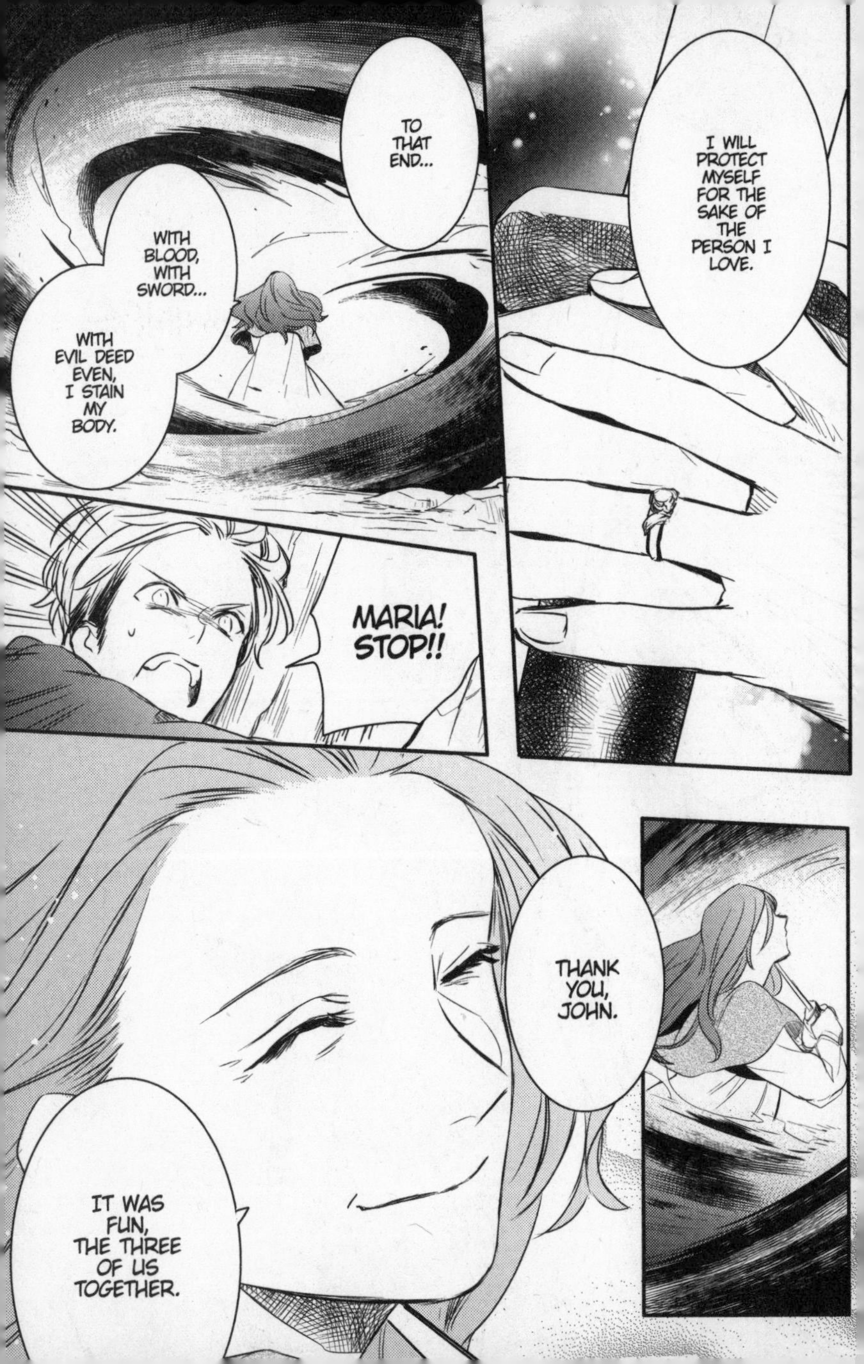
I WILL PROTECT MYSELF FOR THE SAKE OF THE PERSON I LOVE.
TO THAT END...
WITH BLOOD, WITH SWORD...
WITH EVIL DEED EVEN, I STAIN MY BODY.
MARIA! STOP!!
THANK YOU, JOHN.
IT WAS FUN, THE THREE OF US TOGETHER.

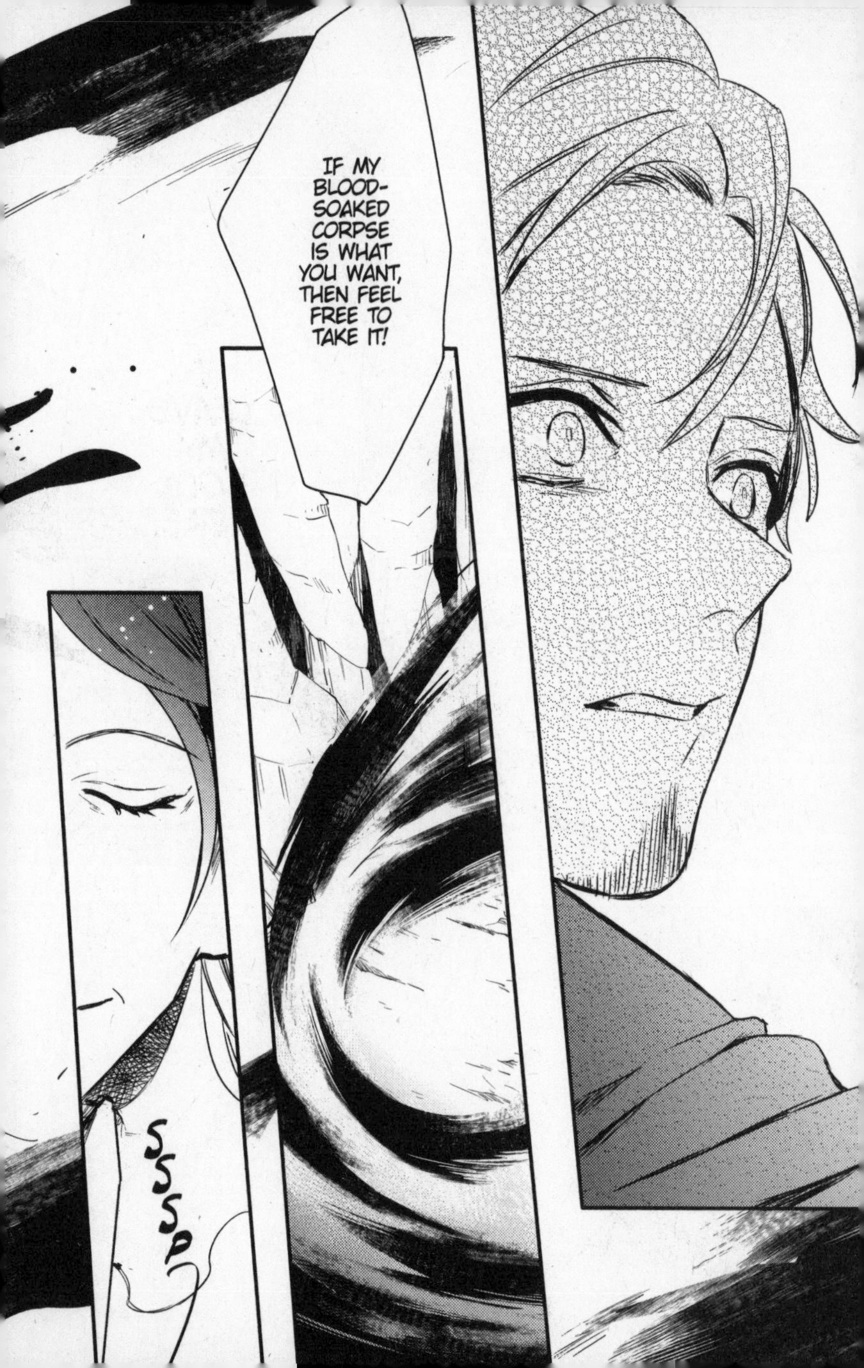
IF MY BLOOD-SOAKED CORPSE IS WHAT YOU WANT, THEN FEEL FREE TO TAKE IT!

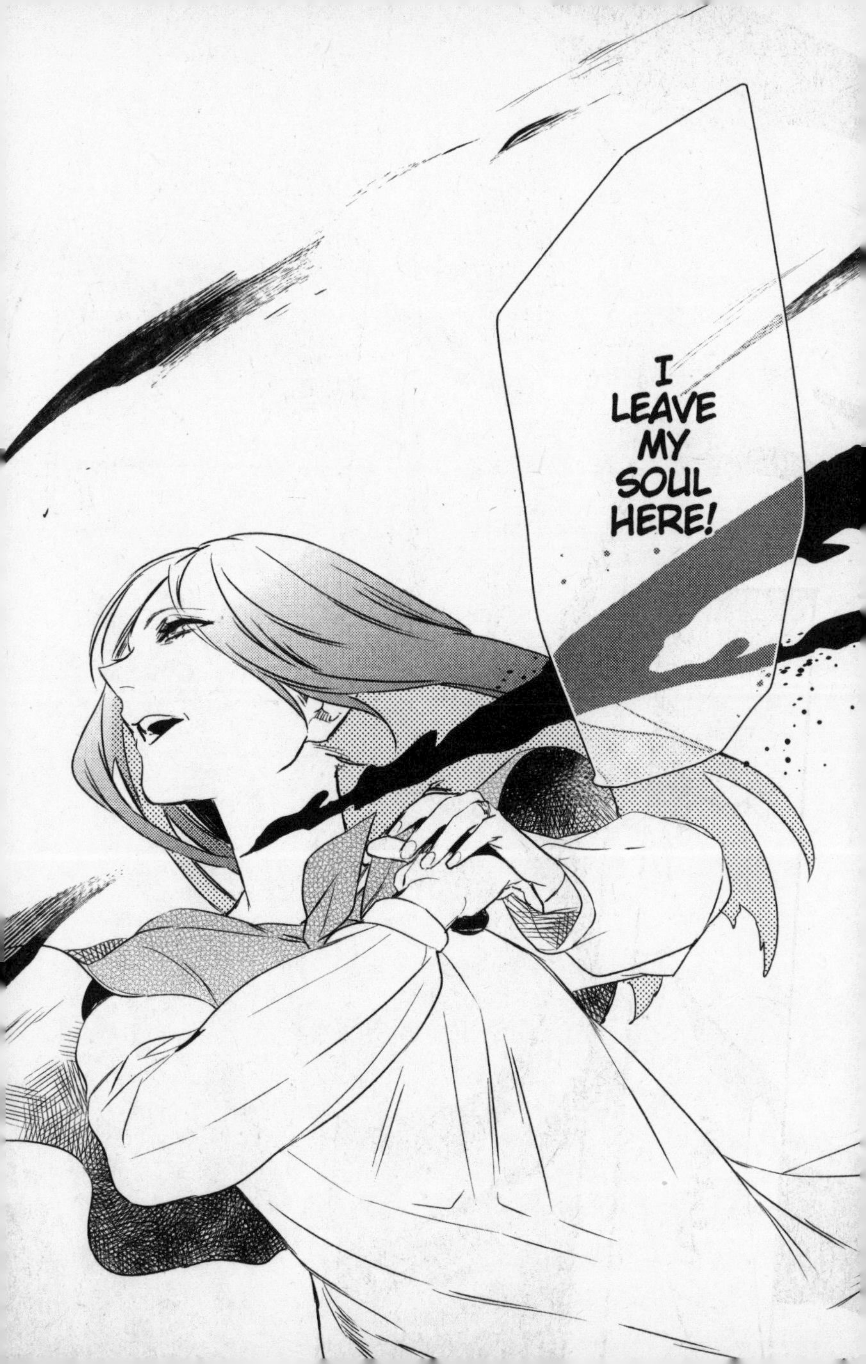
I LEAVE MY SOUL HERE!

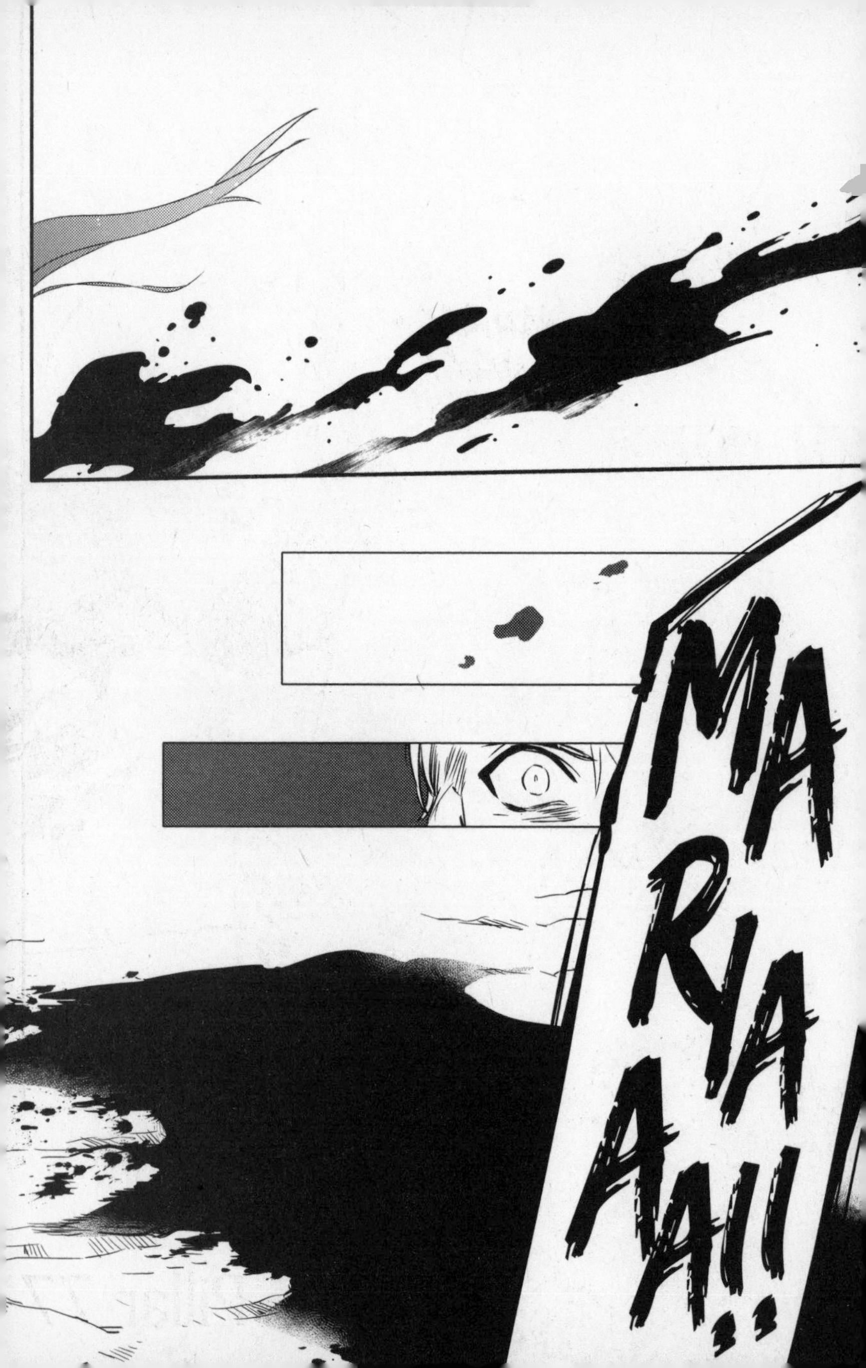
MARIAA!!

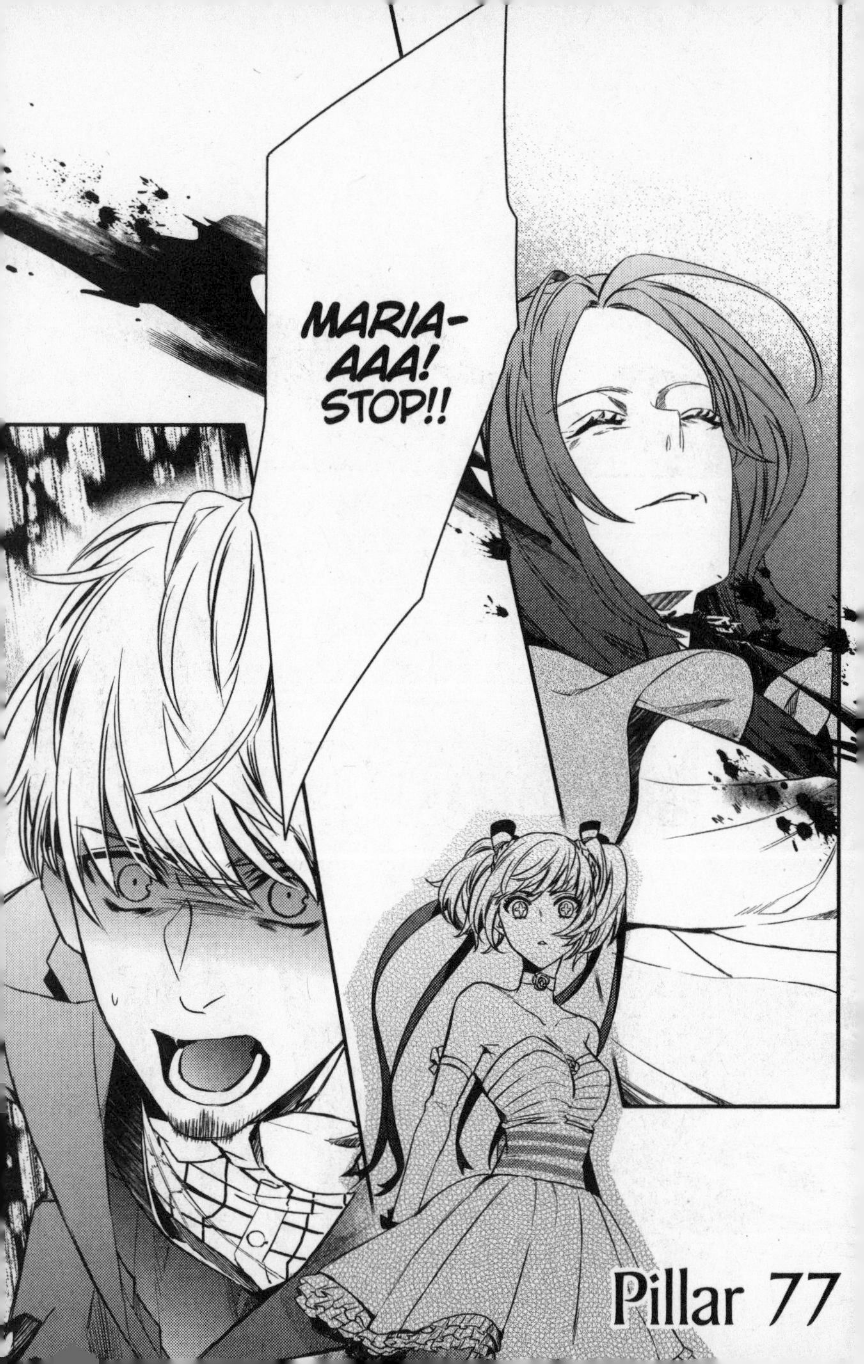
MARIA-AAA! STOP!!

Pillar 77

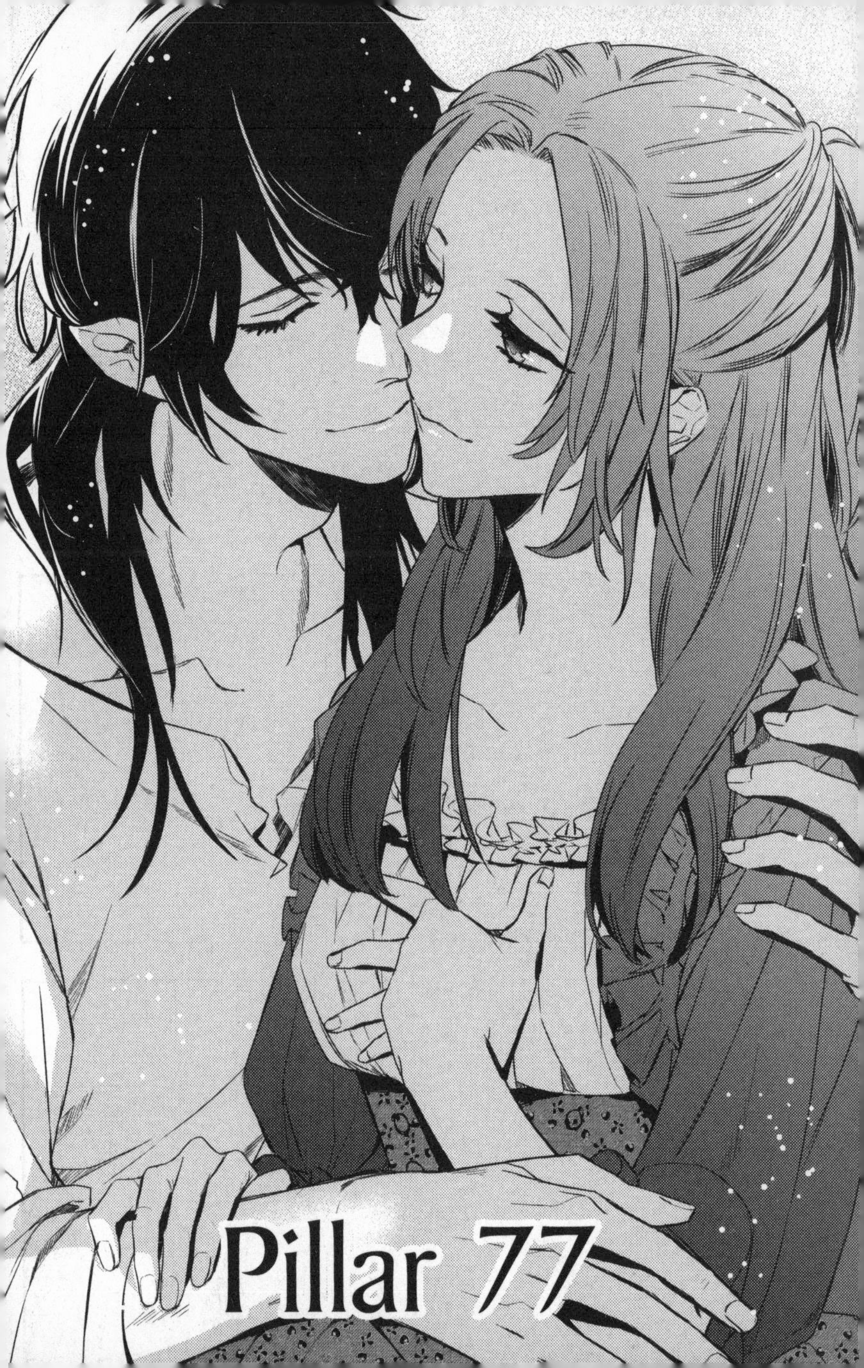
Pillar 77

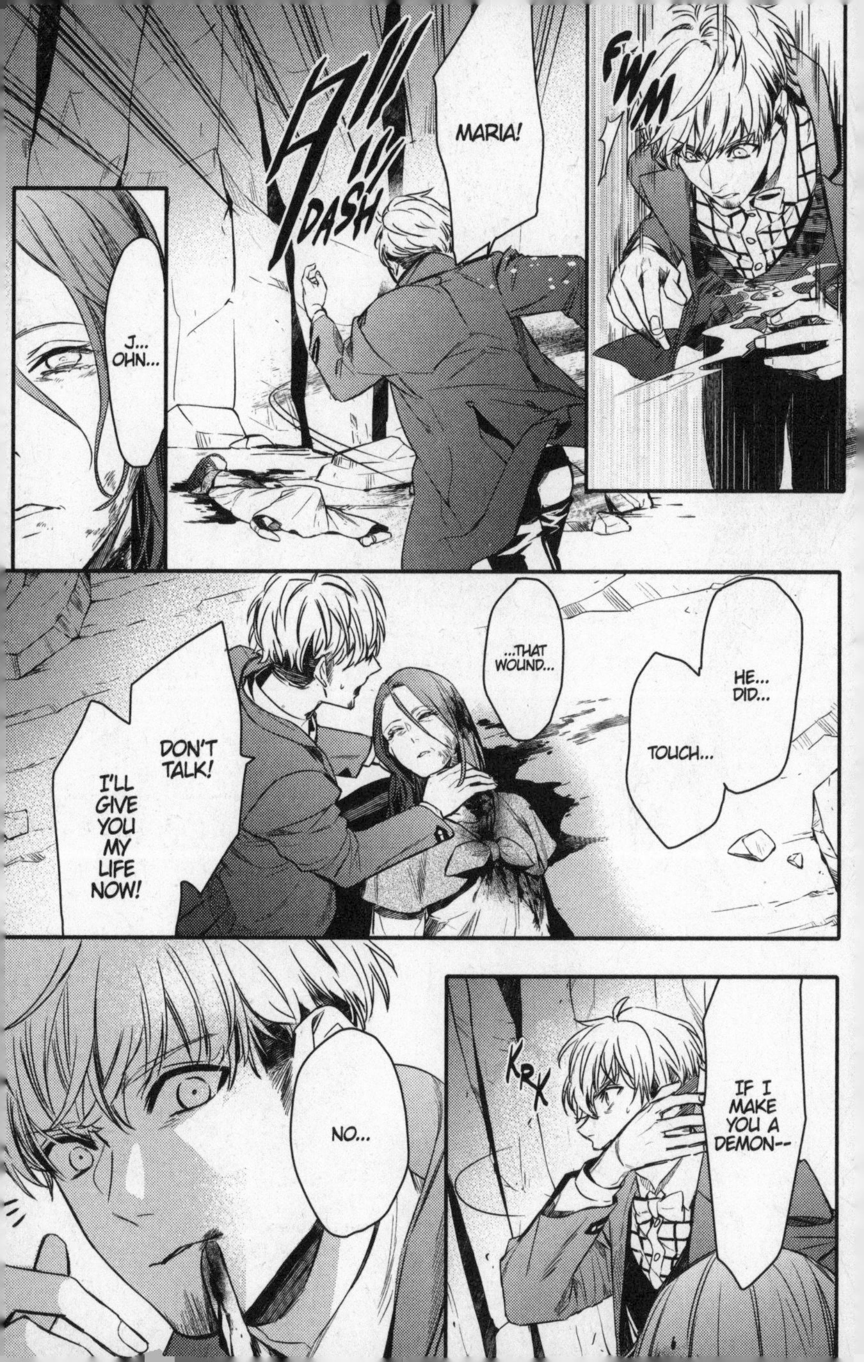
FWM
MARIA!
DASH
J... OHN...
HE... DID... TOUCH...
...THAT WOUND...
DON'T TALK!
I'LL GIVE YOU MY LIFE NOW!
KRK
IF I MAKE YOU A DEMON--
NO...

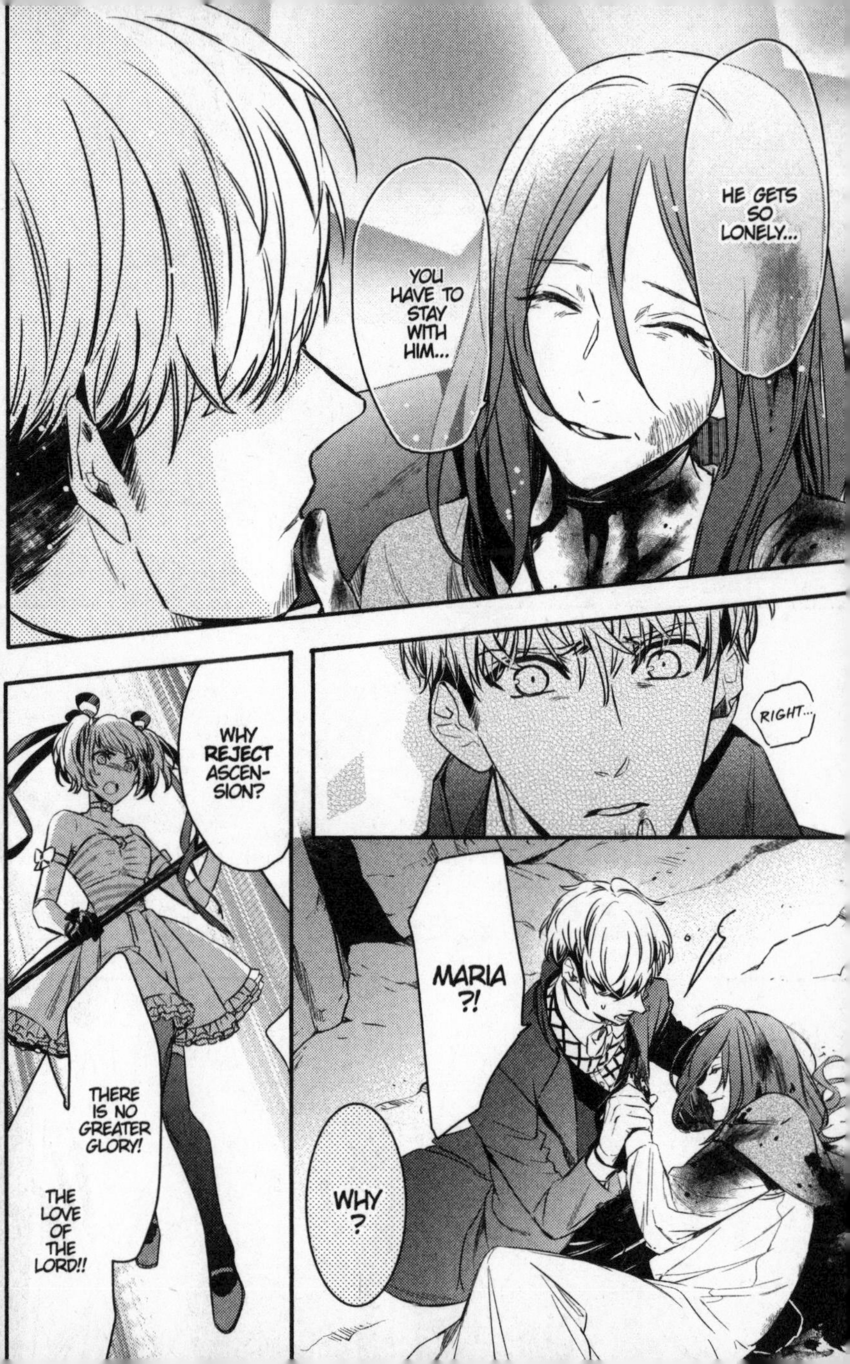
HE GETS SO LONELY...
YOU HAVE TO STAY WITH HIM...
RIGHT...
MARIA?!
WHY?
WHY REJECT ASCENSION?
THERE IS NO GREATER GLORY!
THE LOVE OF THE LORD!!

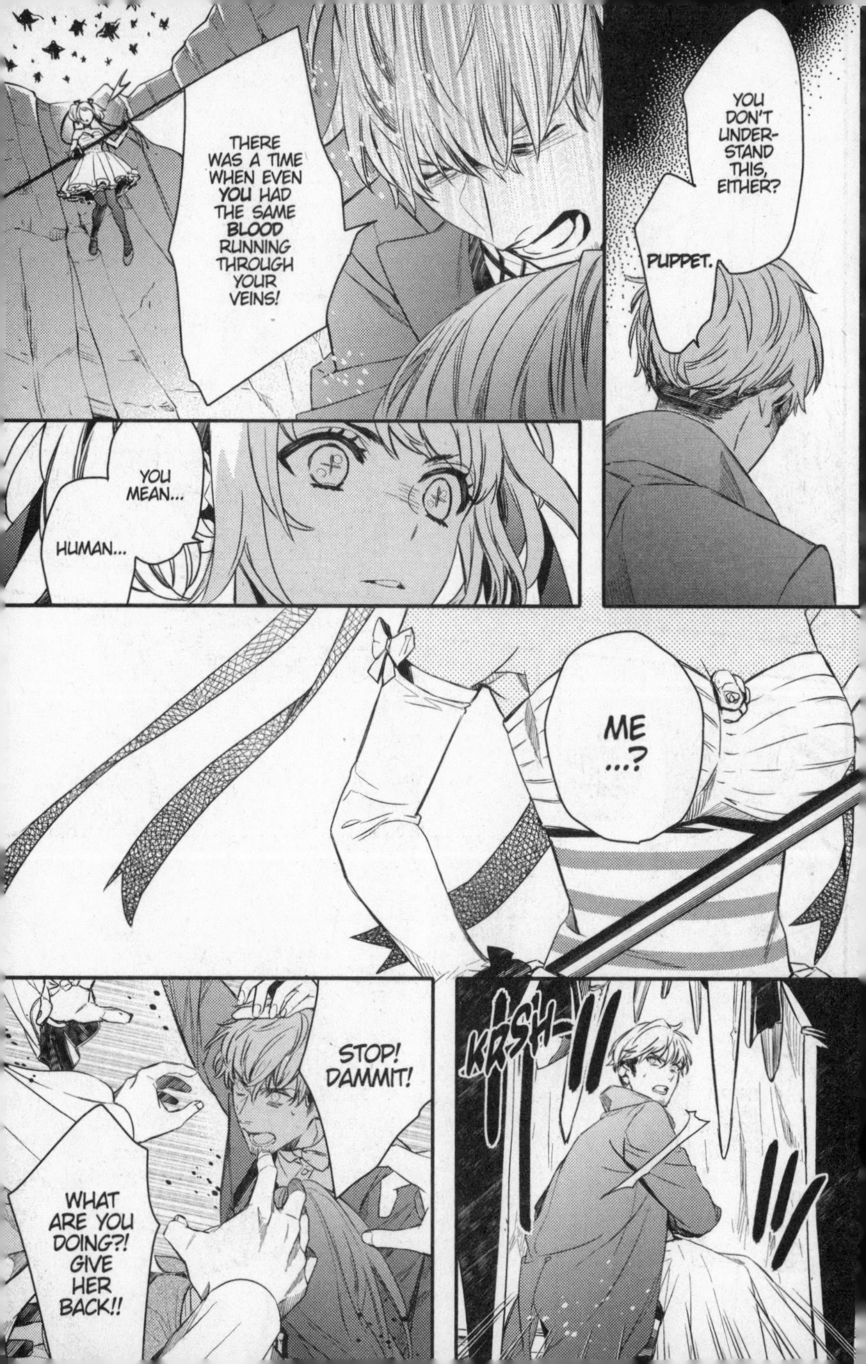
YOU DON'T UNDER-STAND THIS, EITHER?
PUPPET.
THERE WAS A TIME WHEN EVEN YOU HAD THE SAME BLOOD RUNNING THROUGH YOUR VEINS!
YOU MEAN...
HUMAN...
ME ...?
KRSH
STOP! DAMMIT!
WHAT ARE YOU DOING?! GIVE HER BACK!!

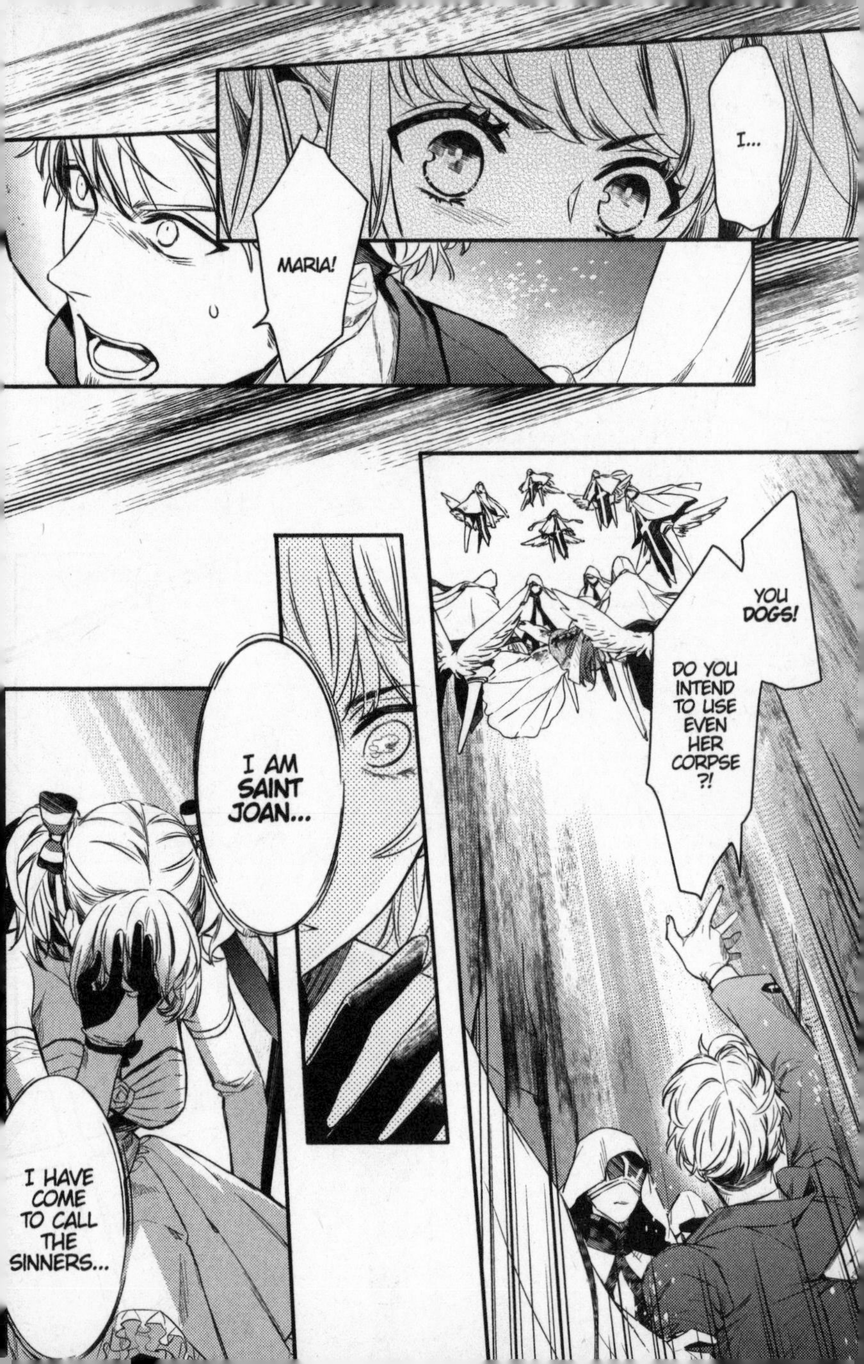
I...
MARIA!
YOU DOGS!
DO YOU INTEND TO USE EVEN HER CORPSE?!
I AM SAINT JOAN...
I HAVE COME TO CALL THE SINNERS...

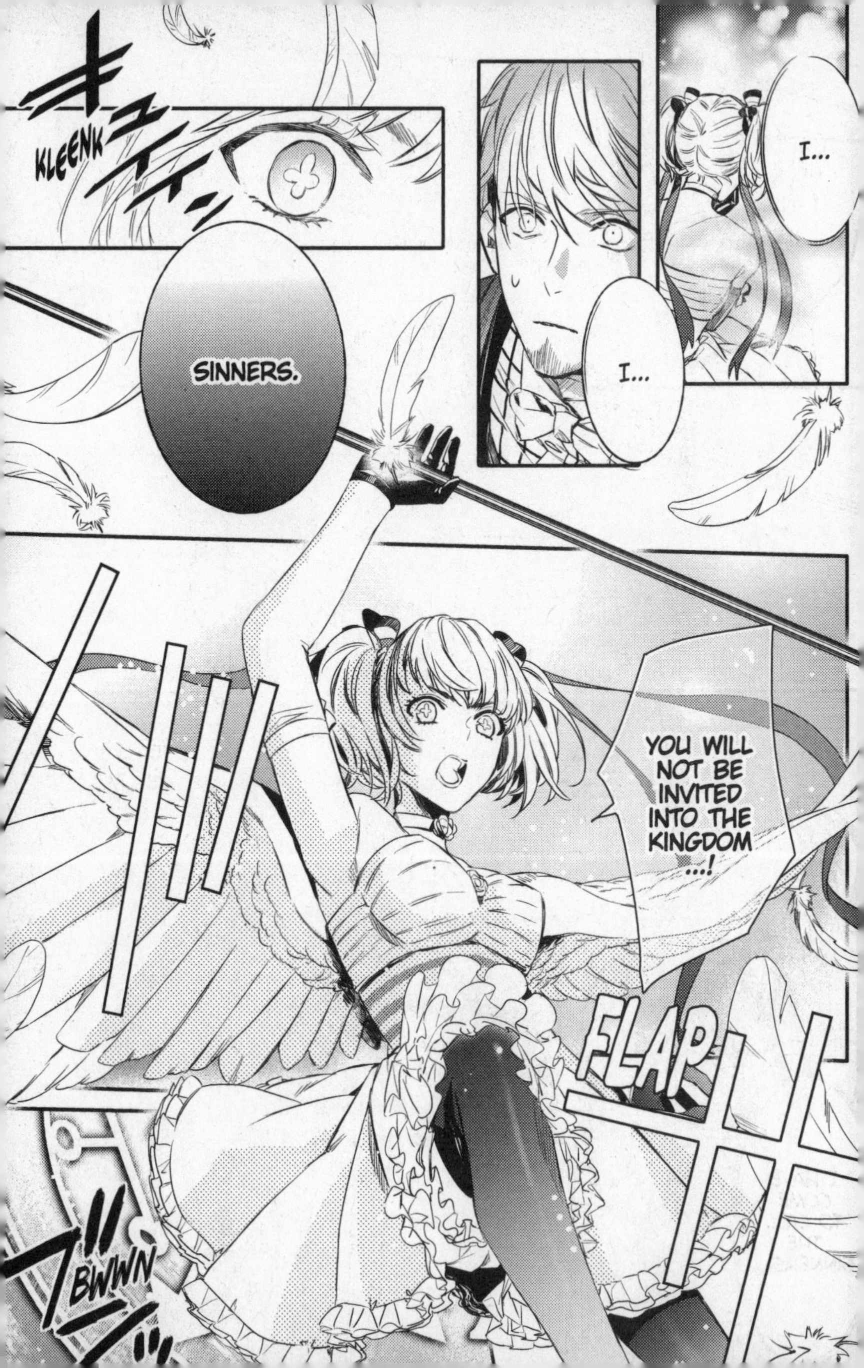
I...
I...
KLEENK
SINNERS.
YOU WILL NOT BE INVITED INTO THE KINGDOM ...!
FLAP
BWWN

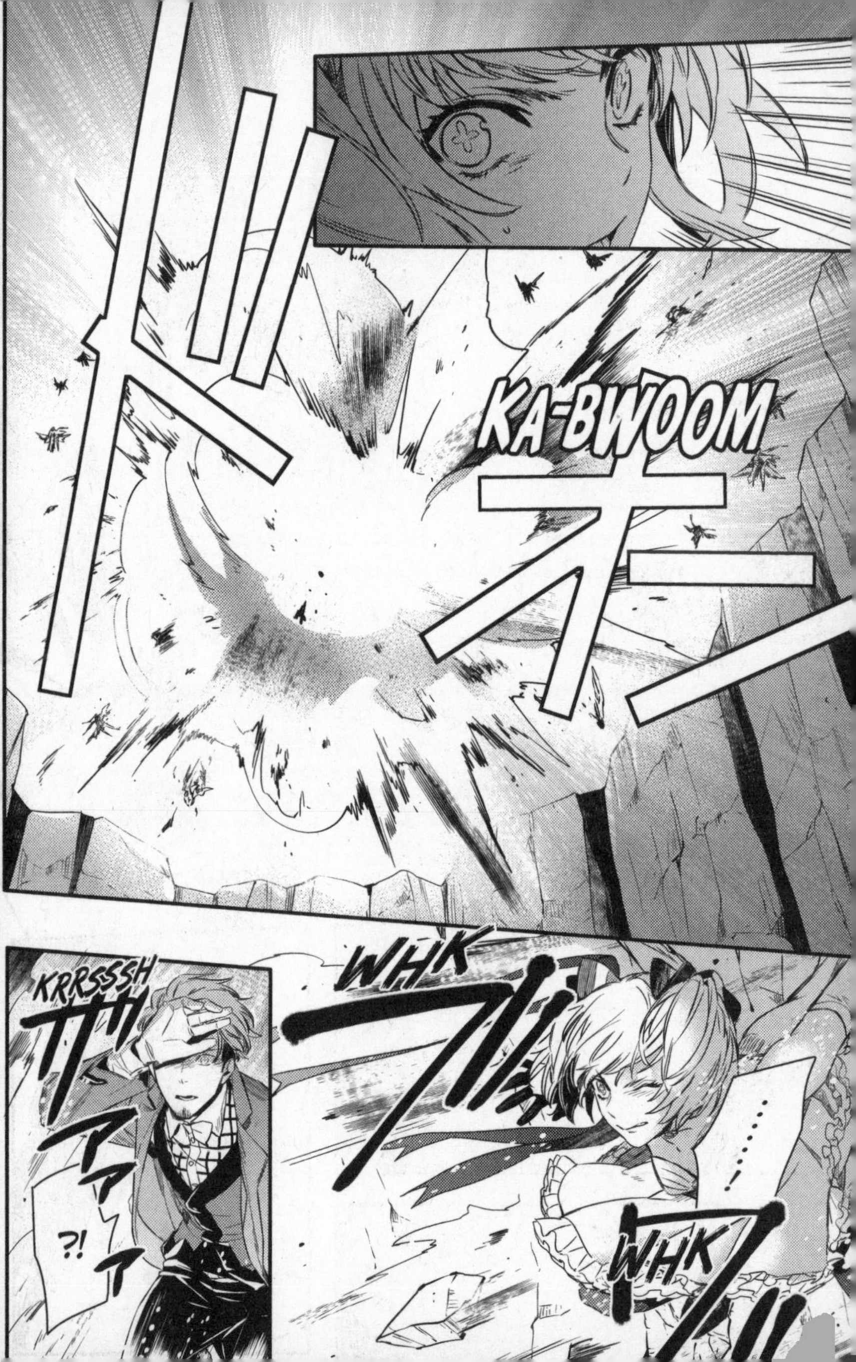
KA-BWOOM
WHK
......!
WHK
KRRSSSH
?!

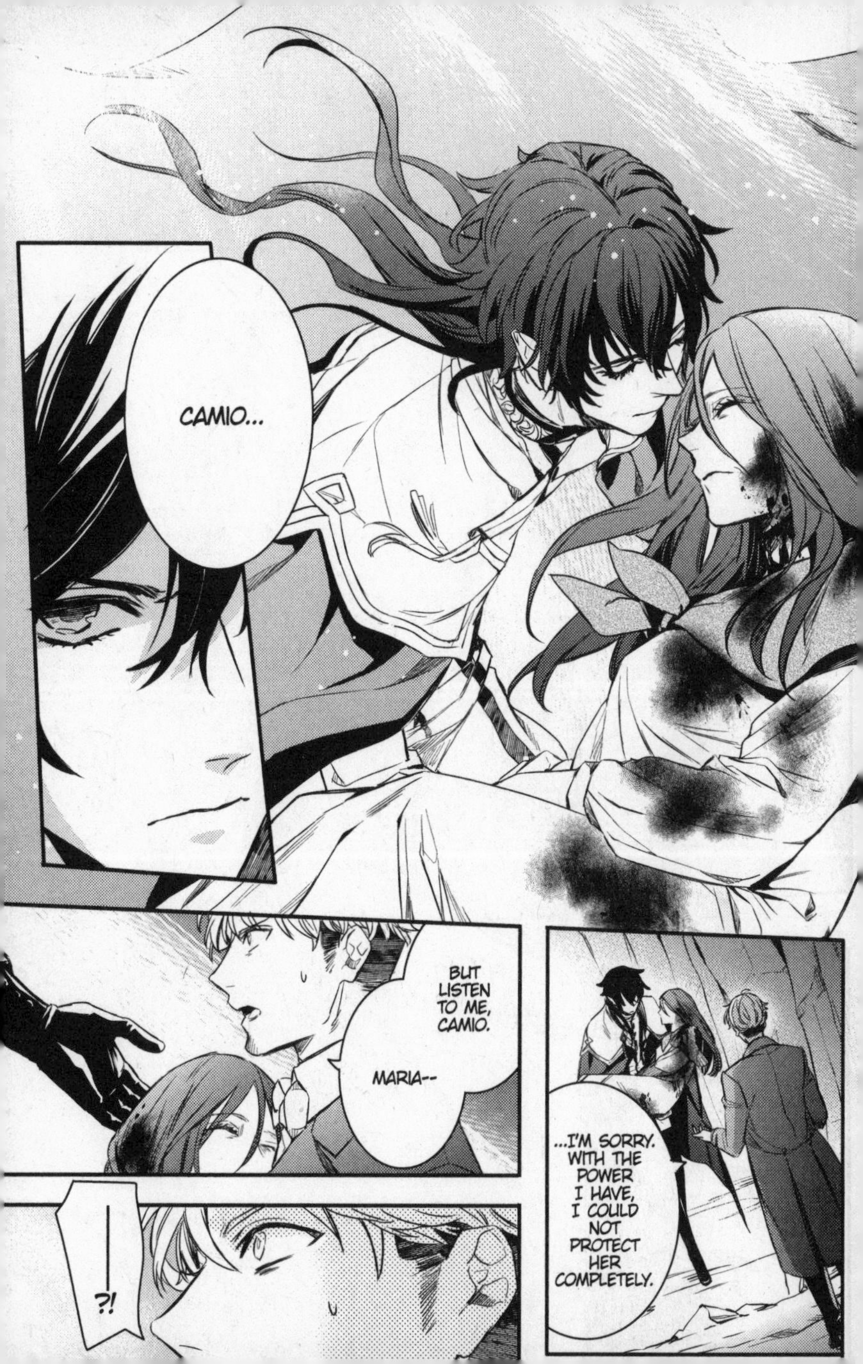
CAMIO...
...I'M SORRY. WITH THE POWER I HAVE, I COULD NOT PROTECT HER COMPLETELY.
BUT LISTEN TO ME, CAMIO.
MARIA--
—?!

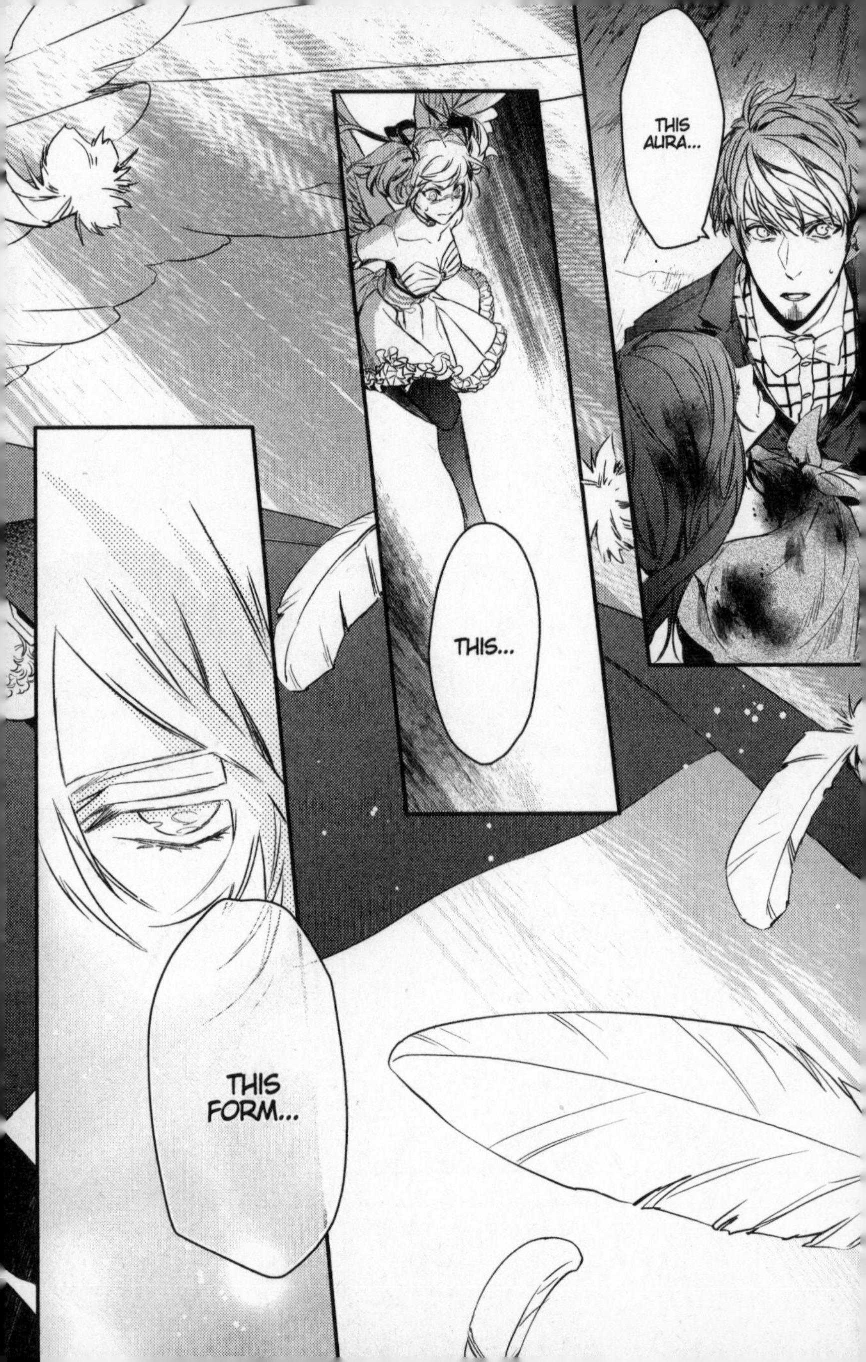
THIS AURA...
THIS...
THIS FORM...

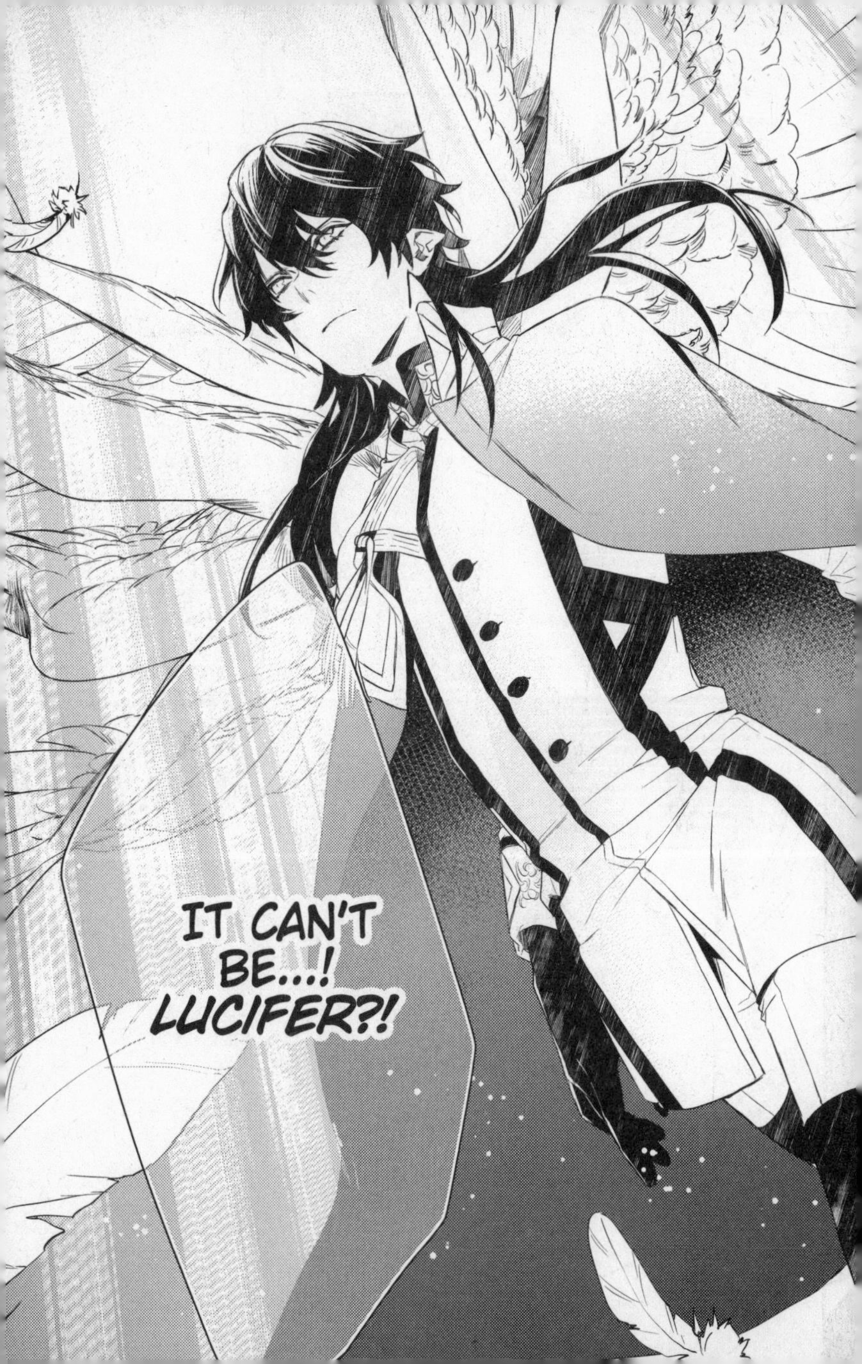
IT CAN'T BE...! LUCIFER?!

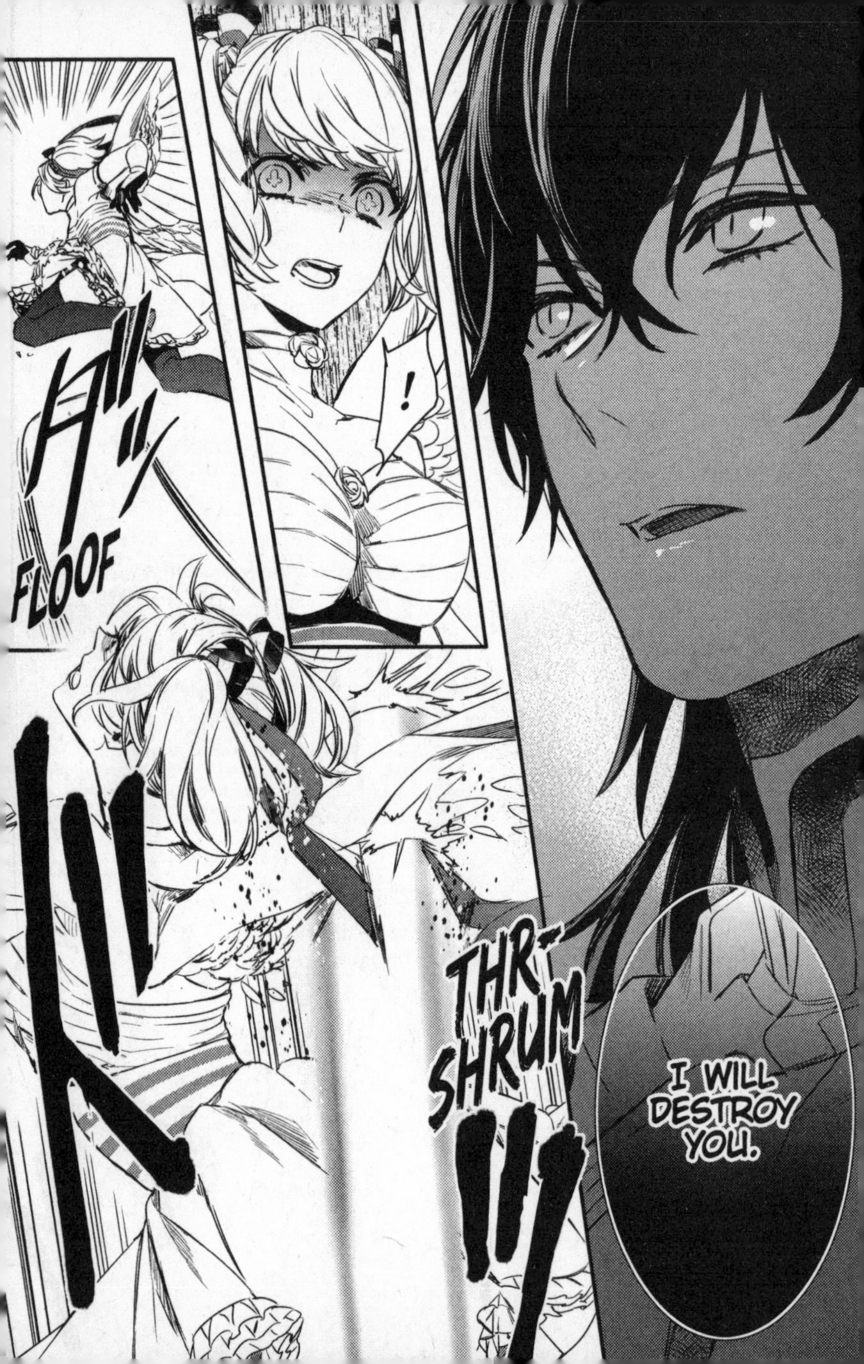
I WILL DESTROY YOU.
!
FLOOF
THR-SHRUM

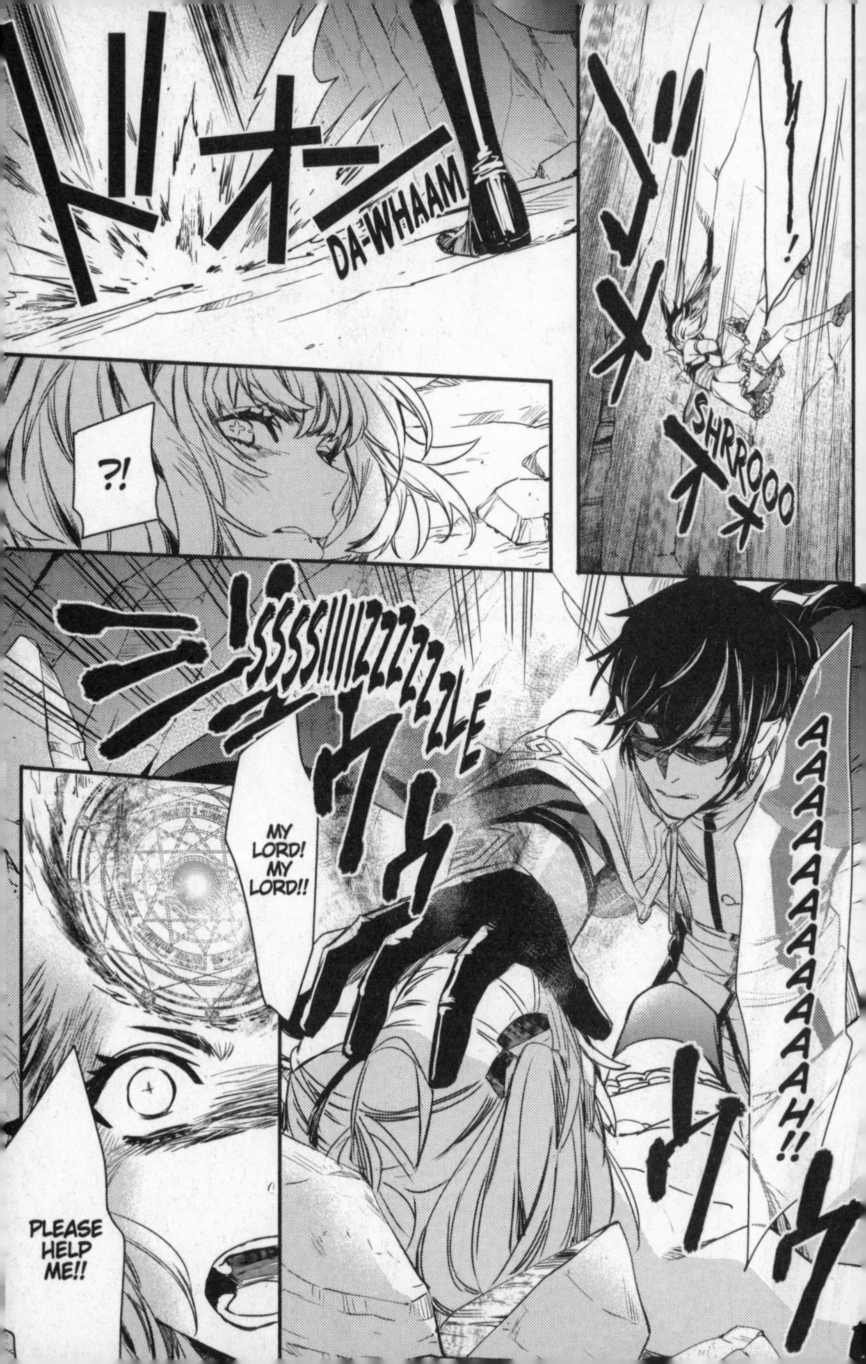
SHRROOO
DA-WHAAM
?!
AAAAAAAAAAAAAAH!!
SSSSIIIIZZZZZZLE
MY LORD! MY LORD!!
PLEASE HELP ME!!

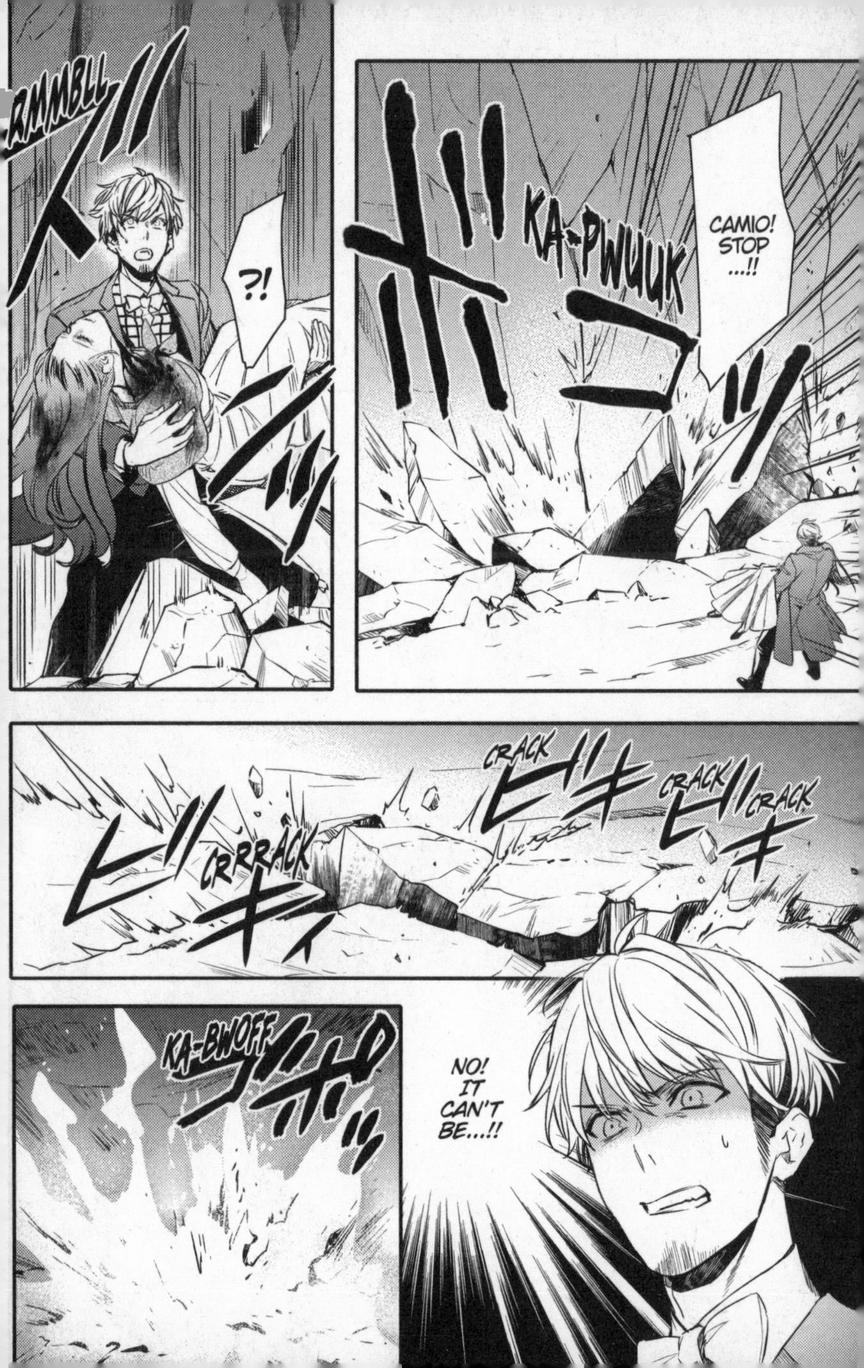

KA-PWUUK
CAMIO! STOP ...!!
RMMBLL
?!
CRACK
CRACK
CRACK
CRRRACK
NO! IT CAN'T BE...!!
KA-BWOFF

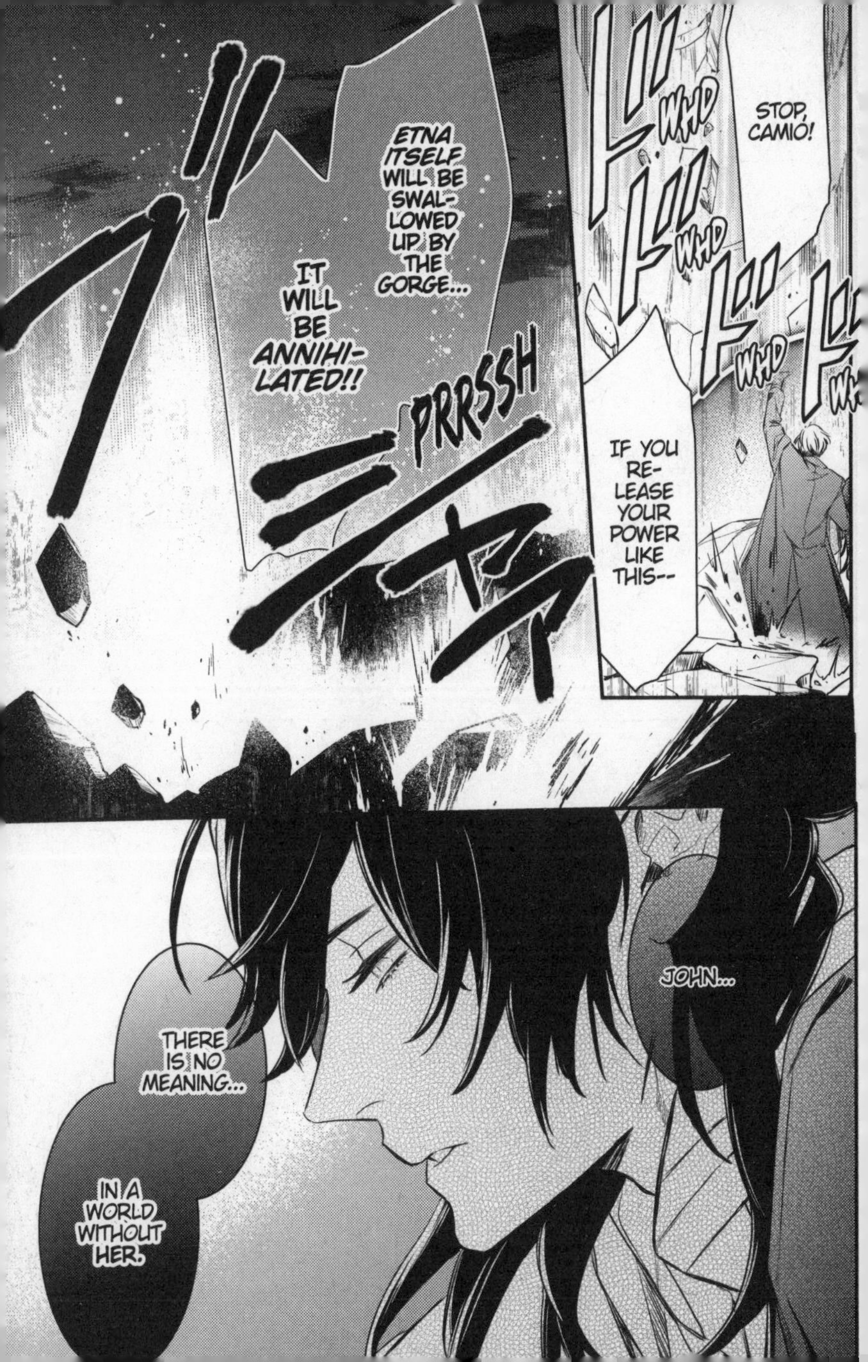
STOP, CAMIO!
WHD
WHD
WHD
IF YOU RE-LEASE YOUR POWER LIKE THIS--
ETNA ITSELF WILL BE SWAL-LOWED UP BY THE GORGE...
IT WILL BE ANNIHI-LATED!!
PRRSSH
JOHN...
THERE IS NO MEANING...
IN A WORLD WITHOUT HER.

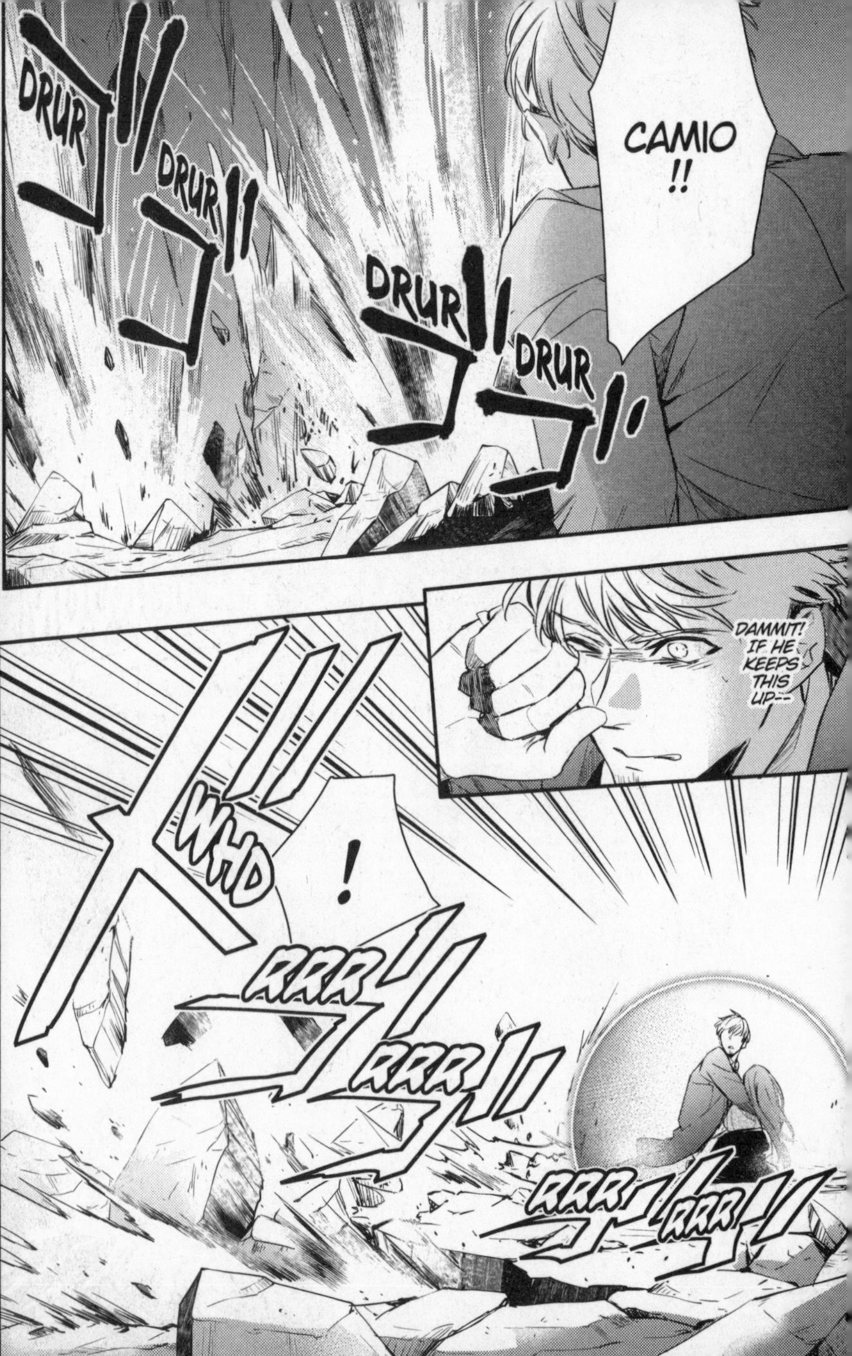
CAMIO !!
DRUR
DRUR
DRUR
DRUR
DAMMIT! IF HE KEEPS THIS UP--
WHD
!
RRR
RRR
RRR
RRR

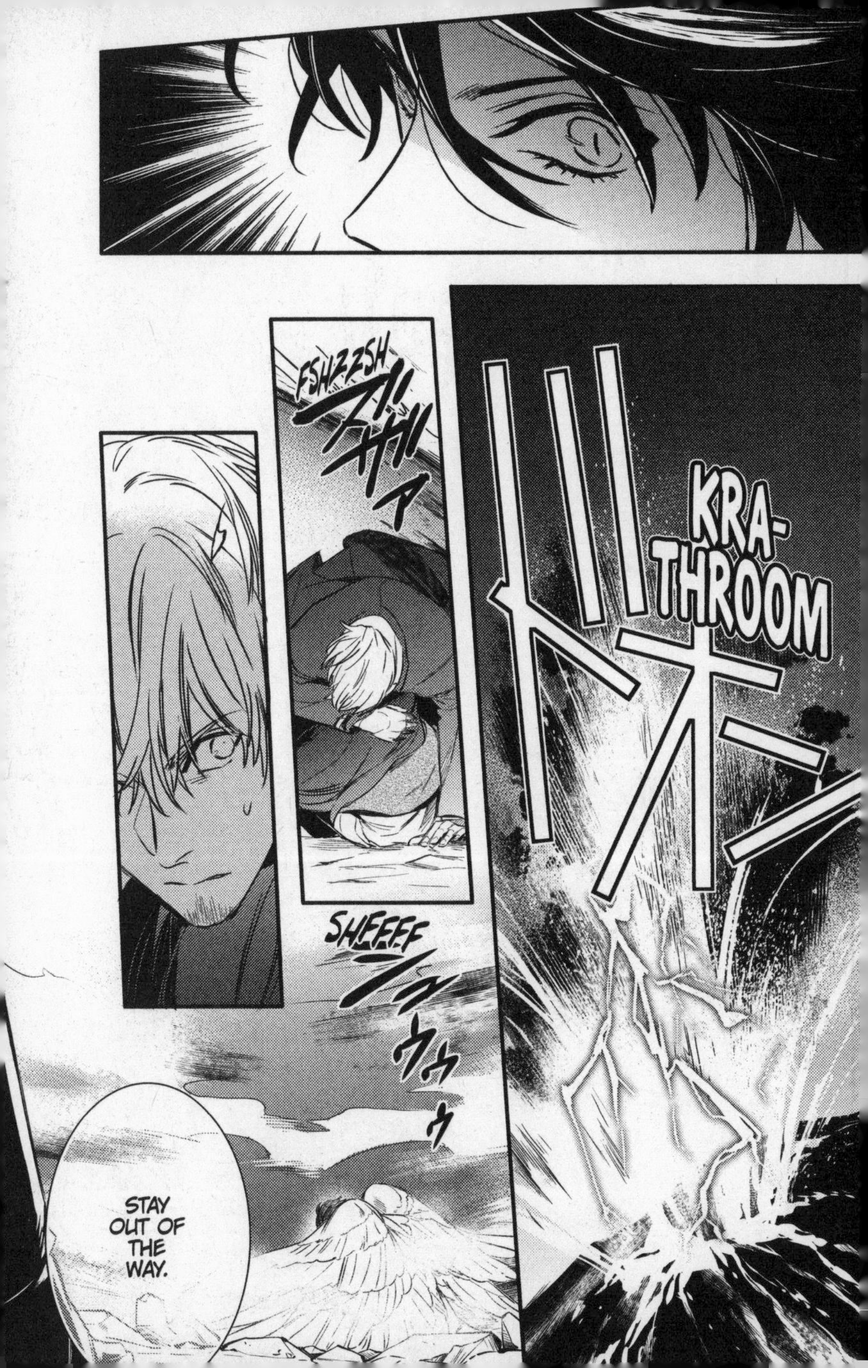
KRA-THROOM
FSHZZSH
SHEEEF
STAY OUT OF THE WAY.

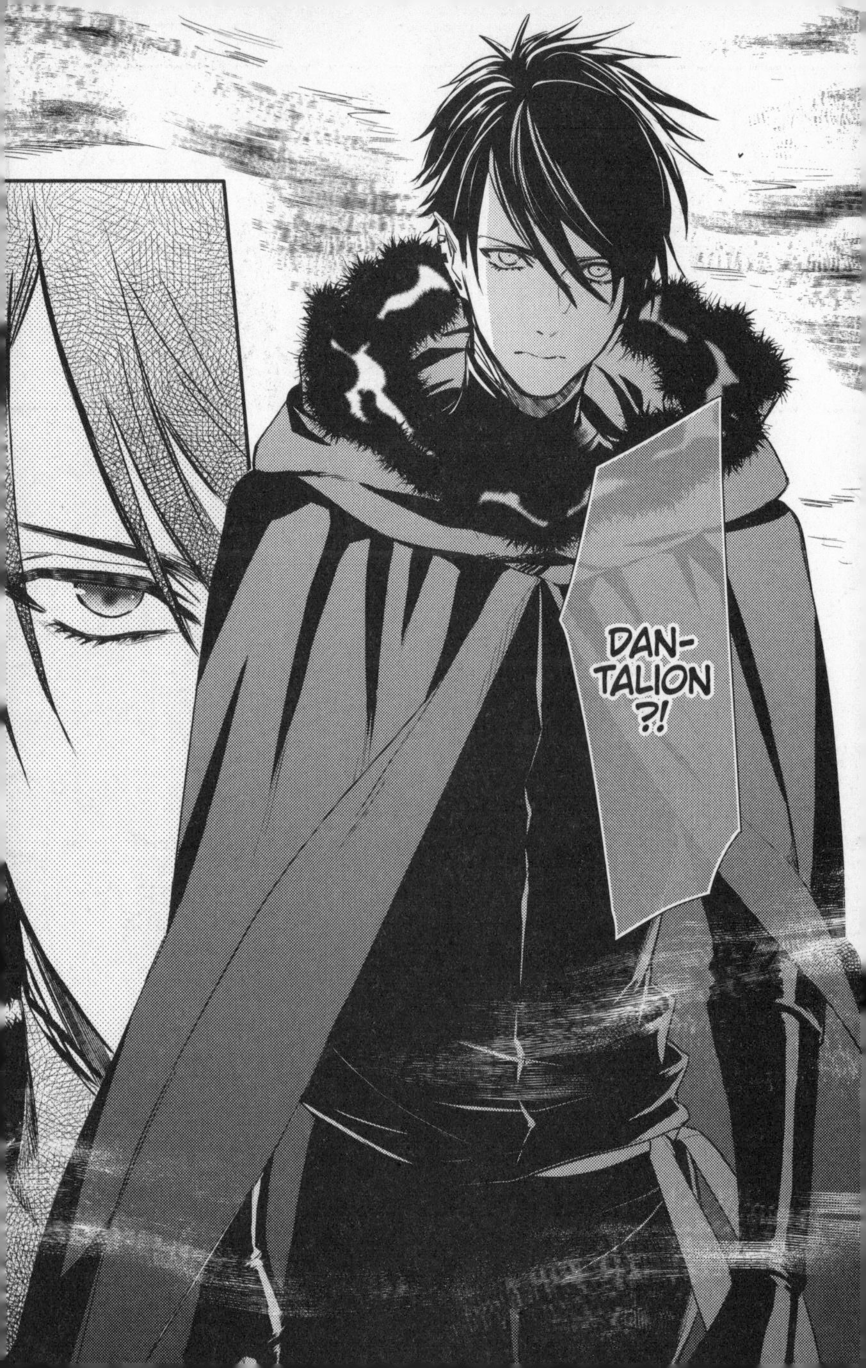
DAN-
TALION
?!

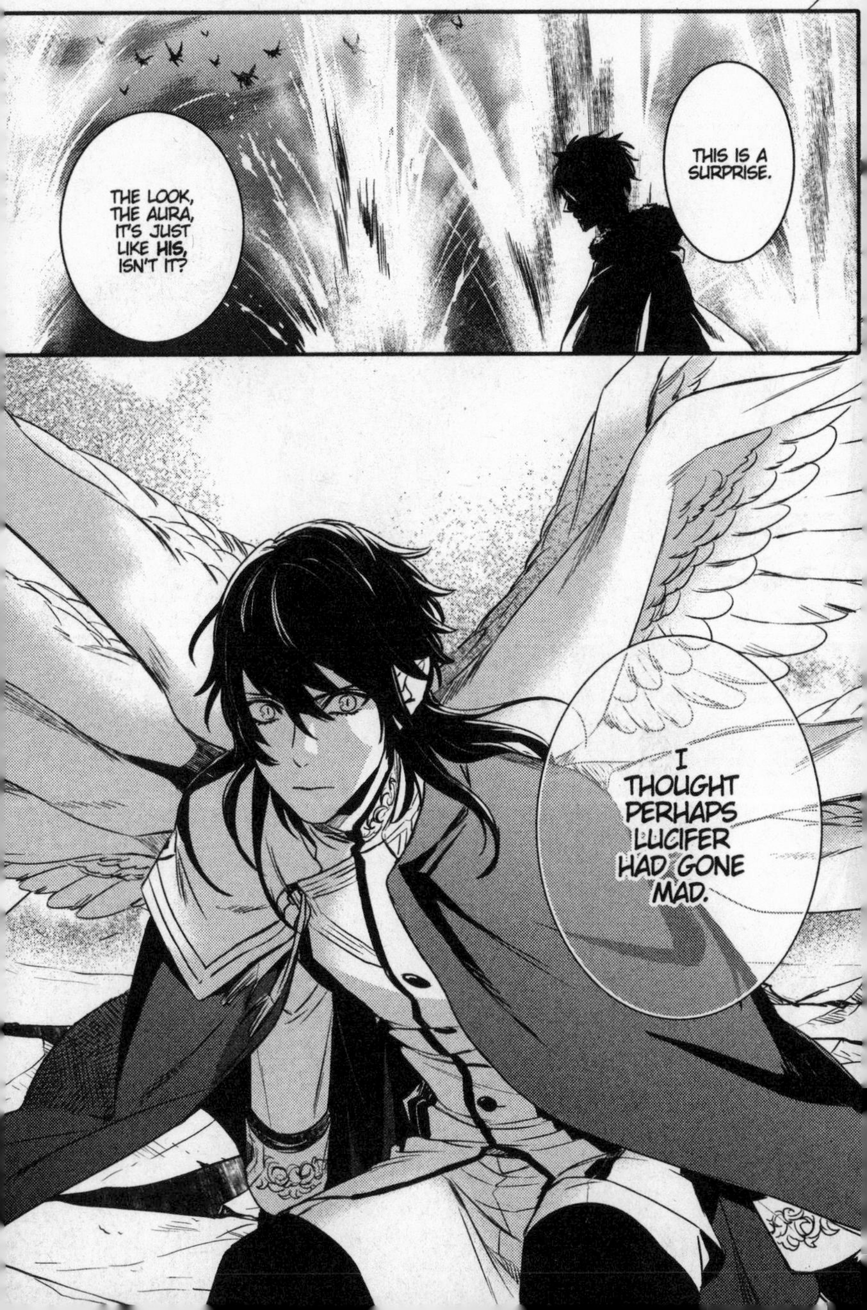
THIS IS A SURPRISE.
THE LOOK, THE AURA, IT'S JUST LIKE HIS, ISN'T IT?
I THOUGHT PERHAPS LUCIFER HAD GONE MAD.

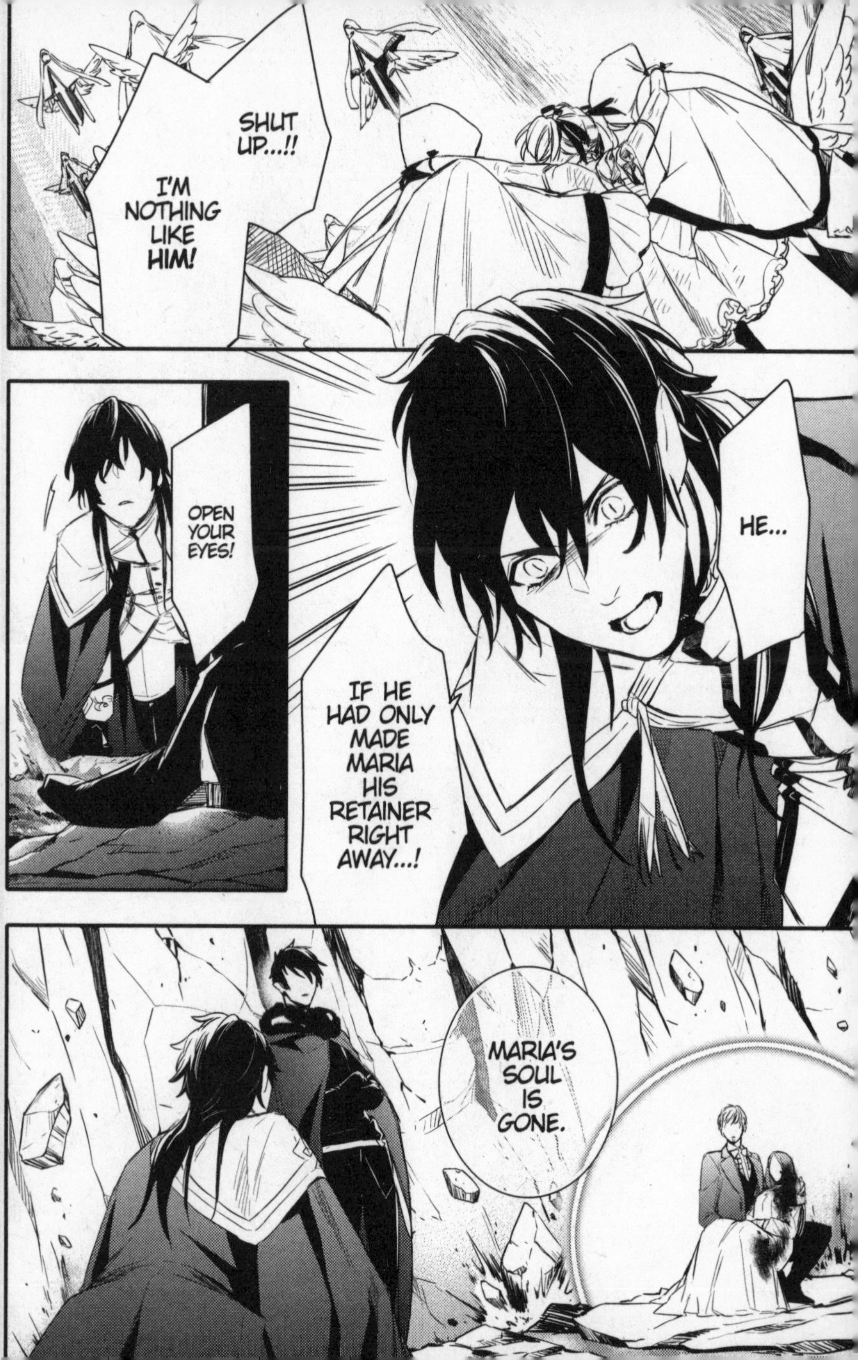
SHUT UP...!!
I'M NOTHING LIKE HIM!
HE...
IF HE HAD ONLY MADE MARIA HIS RETAINER RIGHT AWAY...!
OPEN YOUR EYES!
MARIA'S SOUL IS GONE.

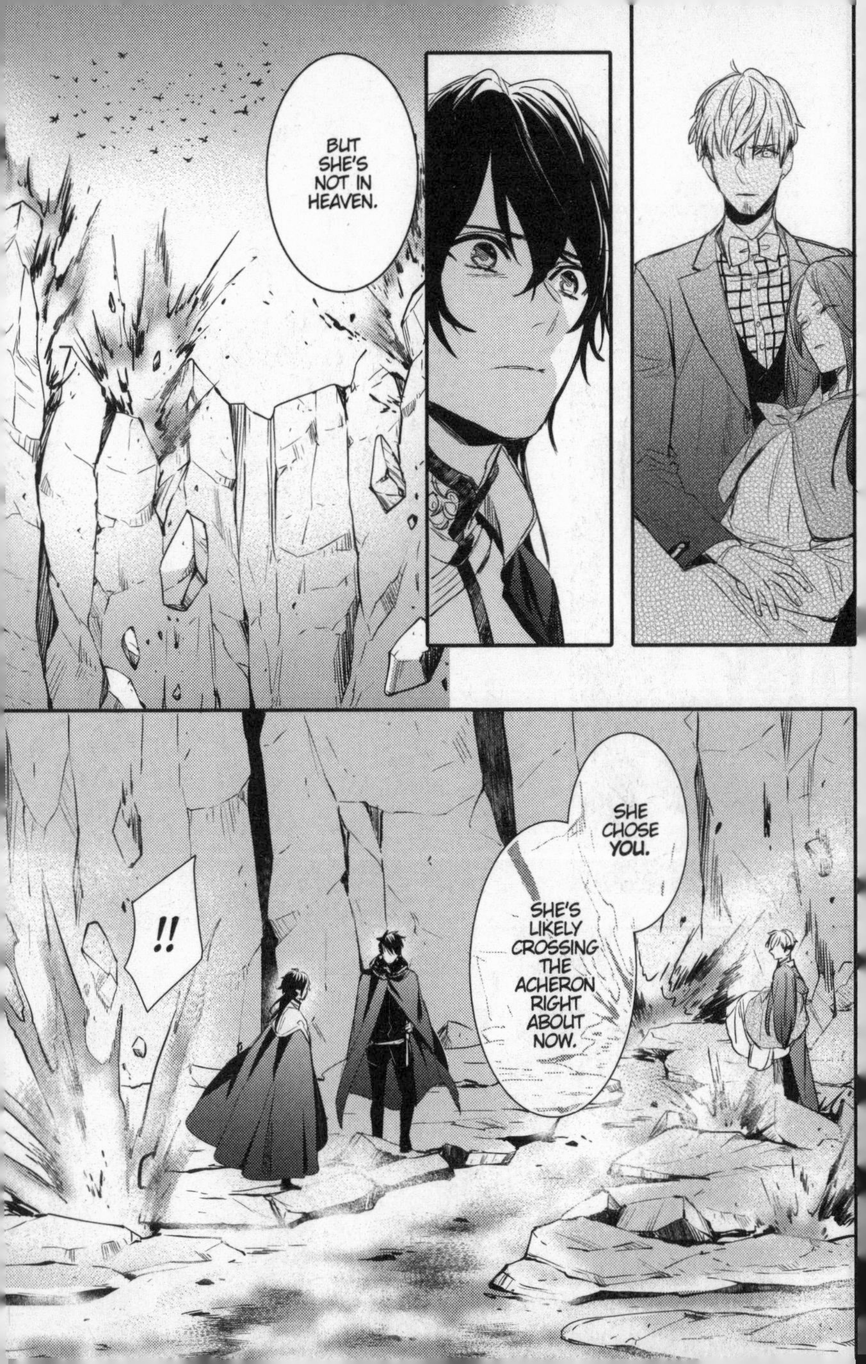
BUT SHE'S NOT IN HEAVEN.
SHE CHOSE YOU.
SHE'S LIKELY CROSSING THE ACHERON RIGHT ABOUT NOW.
!!

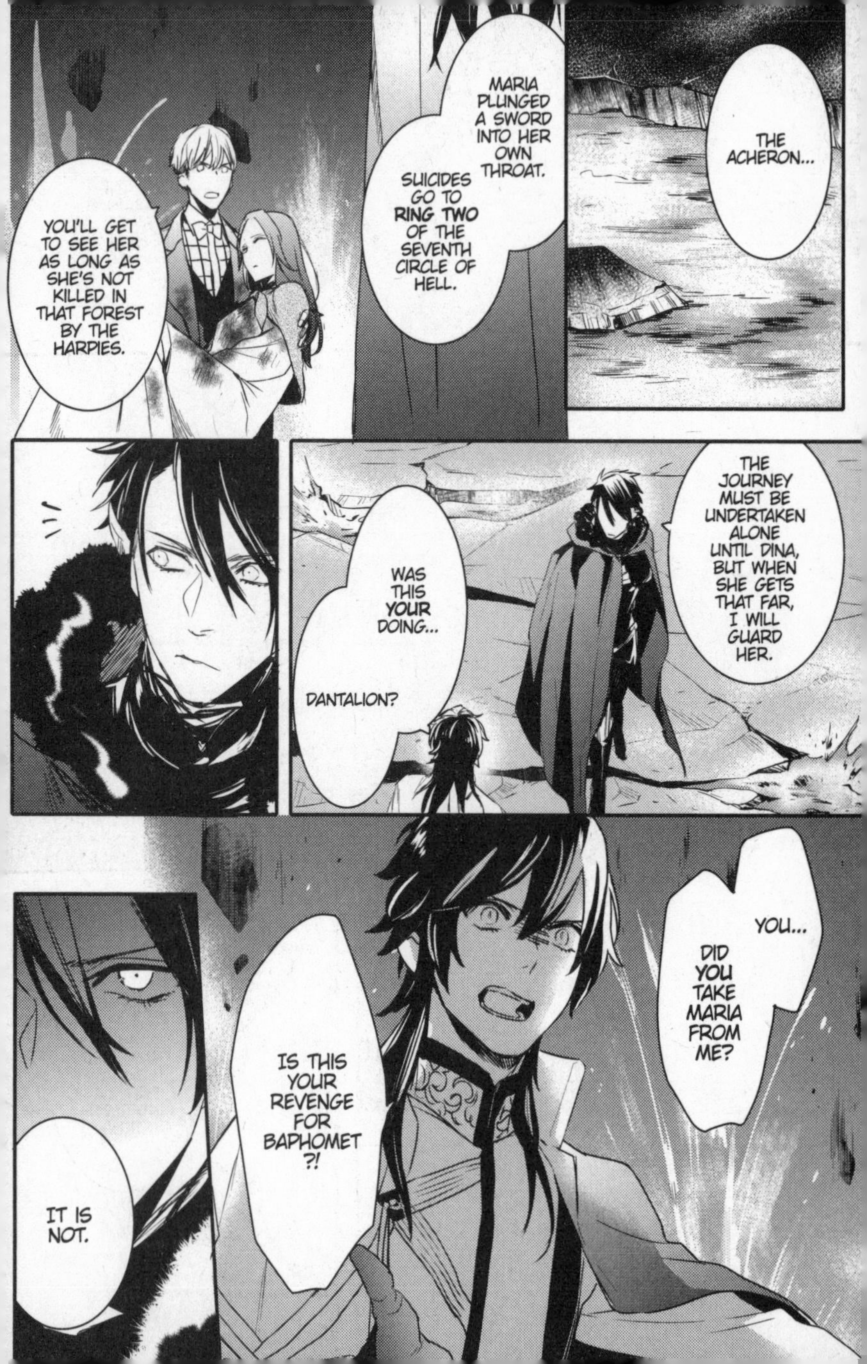
THE ACHERON...
MARIA PLUNGED A SWORD INTO HER OWN THROAT.
SUICIDES GO TO **RING TWO** OF THE SEVENTH CIRCLE OF HELL.
YOU'LL GET TO SEE HER AS LONG AS SHE'S NOT KILLED IN THAT FOREST BY THE HARPIES.
THE JOURNEY MUST BE UNDERTAKEN ALONE UNTIL DINA, BUT WHEN SHE GETS THAT FAR, I WILL GUARD HER.
WAS THIS **YOUR** DOING...
DANTALION?
YOU...
DID **YOU** TAKE MARIA FROM ME?
IS THIS YOUR REVENGE FOR BAPHOMET?!
IT IS NOT.

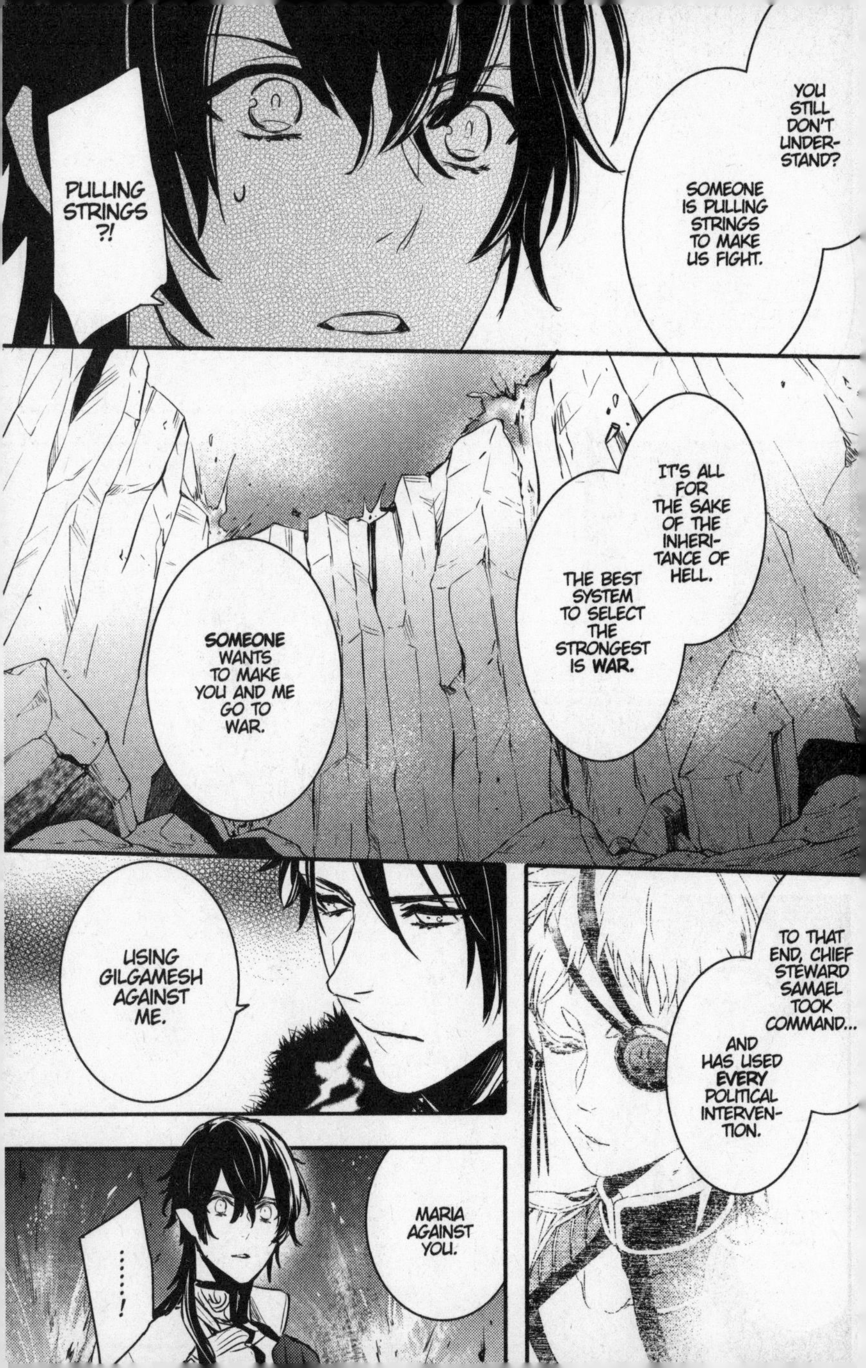
YOU STILL DON'T UNDER-STAND?
SOMEONE IS PULLING STRINGS TO MAKE US FIGHT.
PULLING STRINGS ?!
IT'S ALL FOR THE SAKE OF THE INHERI-TANCE OF HELL.
THE BEST SYSTEM TO SELECT THE STRONGEST IS WAR.
SOMEONE WANTS TO MAKE YOU AND ME GO TO WAR.
TO THAT END, CHIEF STEWARD SAMAEL TOOK COMMAND...
AND HAS USED EVERY POLITICAL INTERVEN-TION.
USING GILGAMESH AGAINST ME.
MARIA AGAINST YOU.
......!

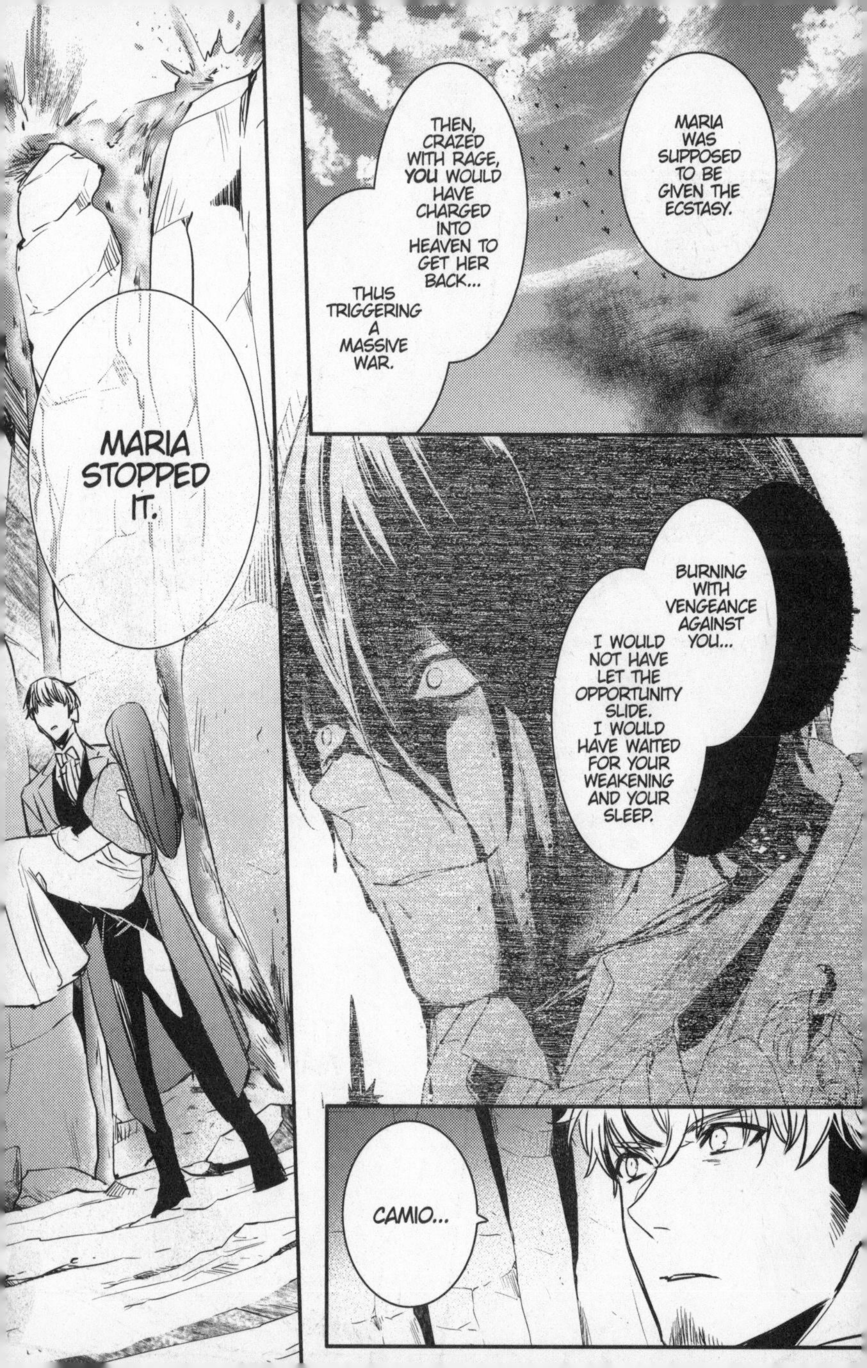
MARIA WAS SUPPOSED TO BE GIVEN THE ECSTASY.
THEN, CRAZED WITH RAGE, YOU WOULD HAVE CHARGED INTO HEAVEN TO GET HER BACK...
THUS TRIGGERING A MASSIVE WAR.
BURNING WITH VENGEANCE AGAINST YOU...
I WOULD NOT HAVE LET THE OPPORTUNITY SLIDE. I WOULD HAVE WAITED FOR YOUR WEAKENING AND YOUR SLEEP.
CAMIO...
MARIA STOPPED IT.

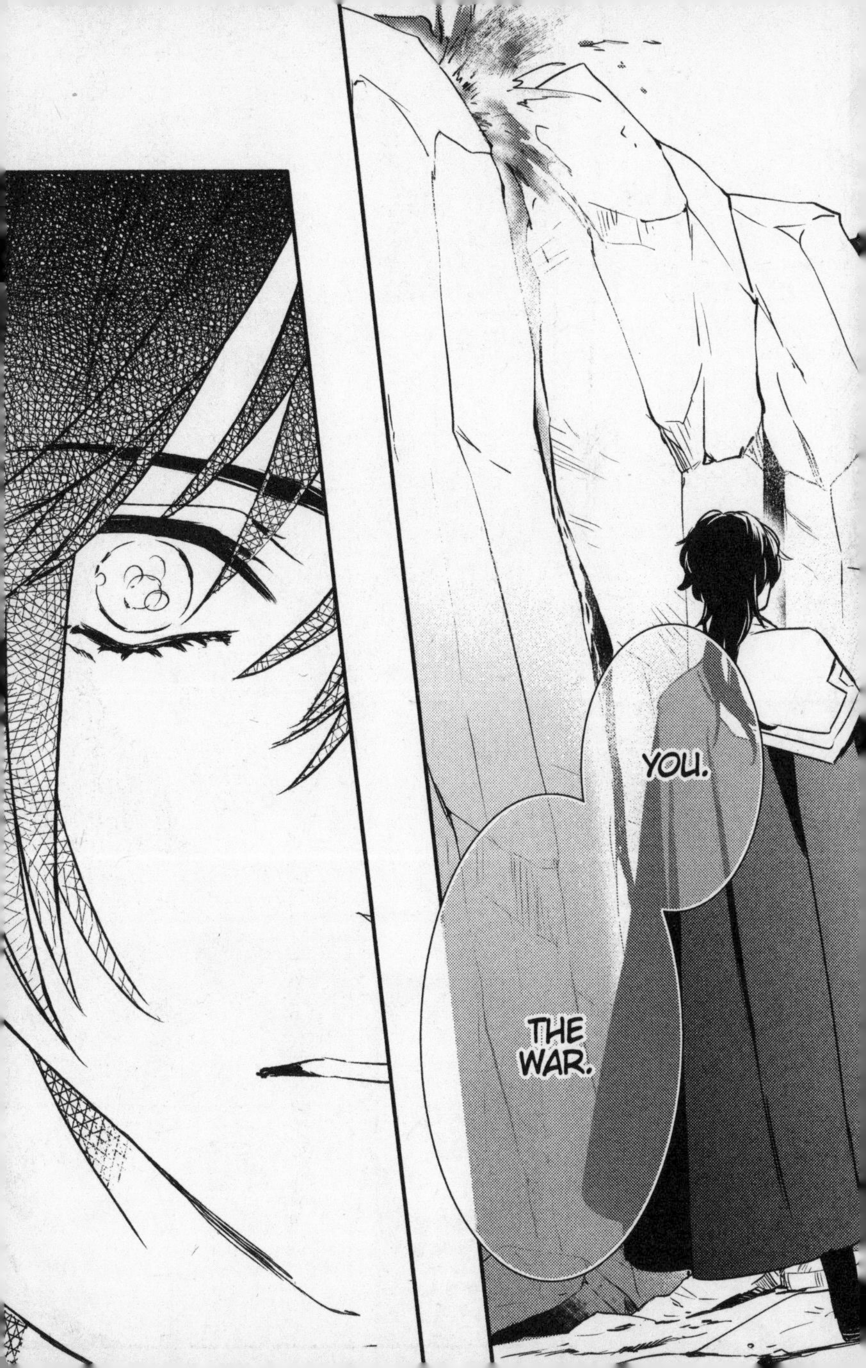
YOU.
THE WAR.

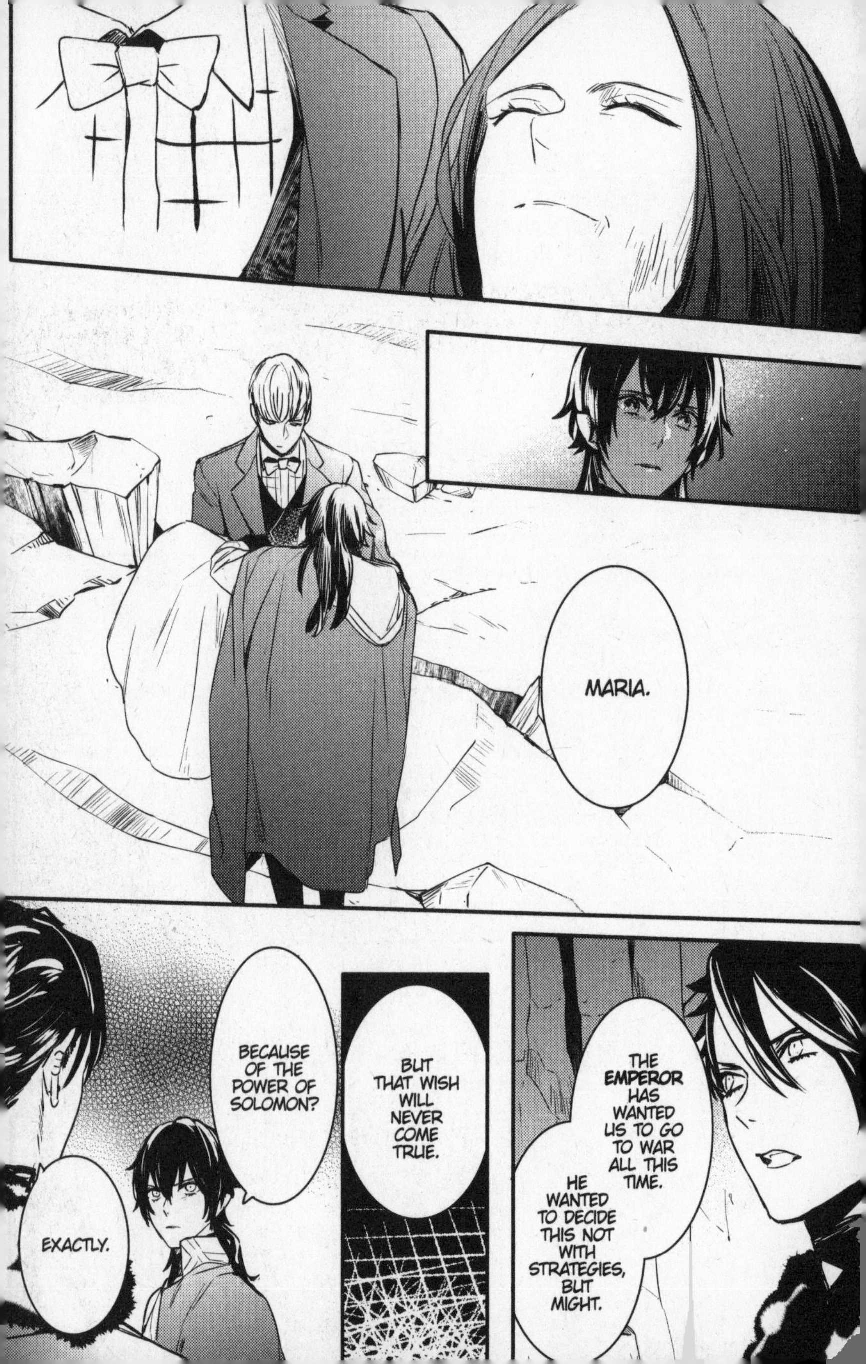
MARIA.
THE EMPEROR HAS WANTED US TO GO TO WAR ALL THIS TIME.
HE WANTED TO DECIDE THIS NOT WITH STRATEGIES, BUT MIGHT.
BUT THAT WISH WILL NEVER COME TRUE.
BECAUSE OF THE POWER OF SOLOMON?
EXACTLY.

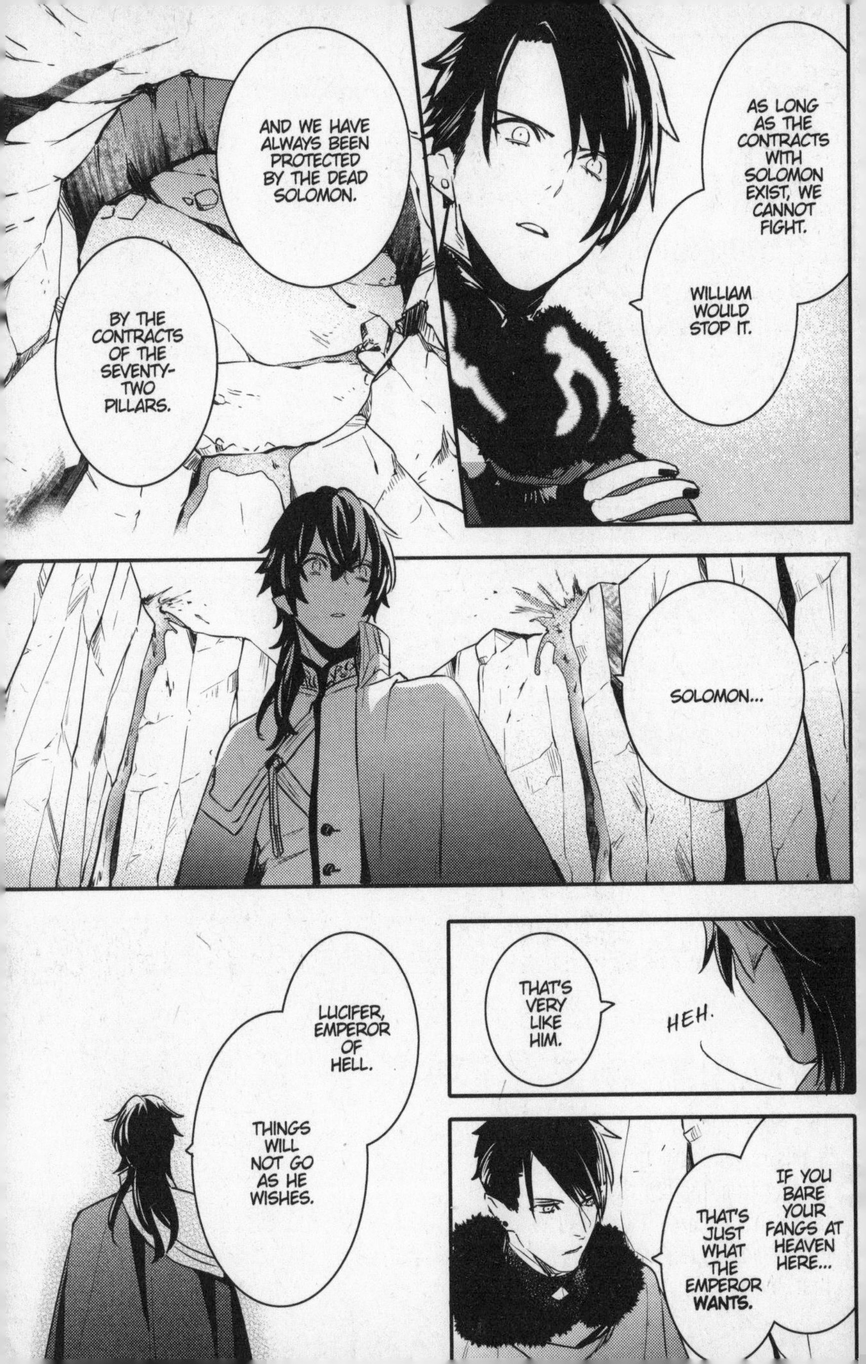
AS LONG AS THE CONTRACTS WITH SOLOMON EXIST, WE CANNOT FIGHT.
WILLIAM WOULD STOP IT.
AND WE HAVE ALWAYS BEEN PROTECTED BY THE DEAD SOLOMON.
BY THE CONTRACTS OF THE SEVENTY-TWO PILLARS.
SOLOMON...
HEH.
THAT'S VERY LIKE HIM.
IF YOU BARE YOUR FANGS AT HEAVEN HERE...
THAT'S JUST WHAT THE EMPEROR WANTS.
LUCIFER, EMPEROR OF HELL.
THINGS WILL NOT GO AS HE WISHES.

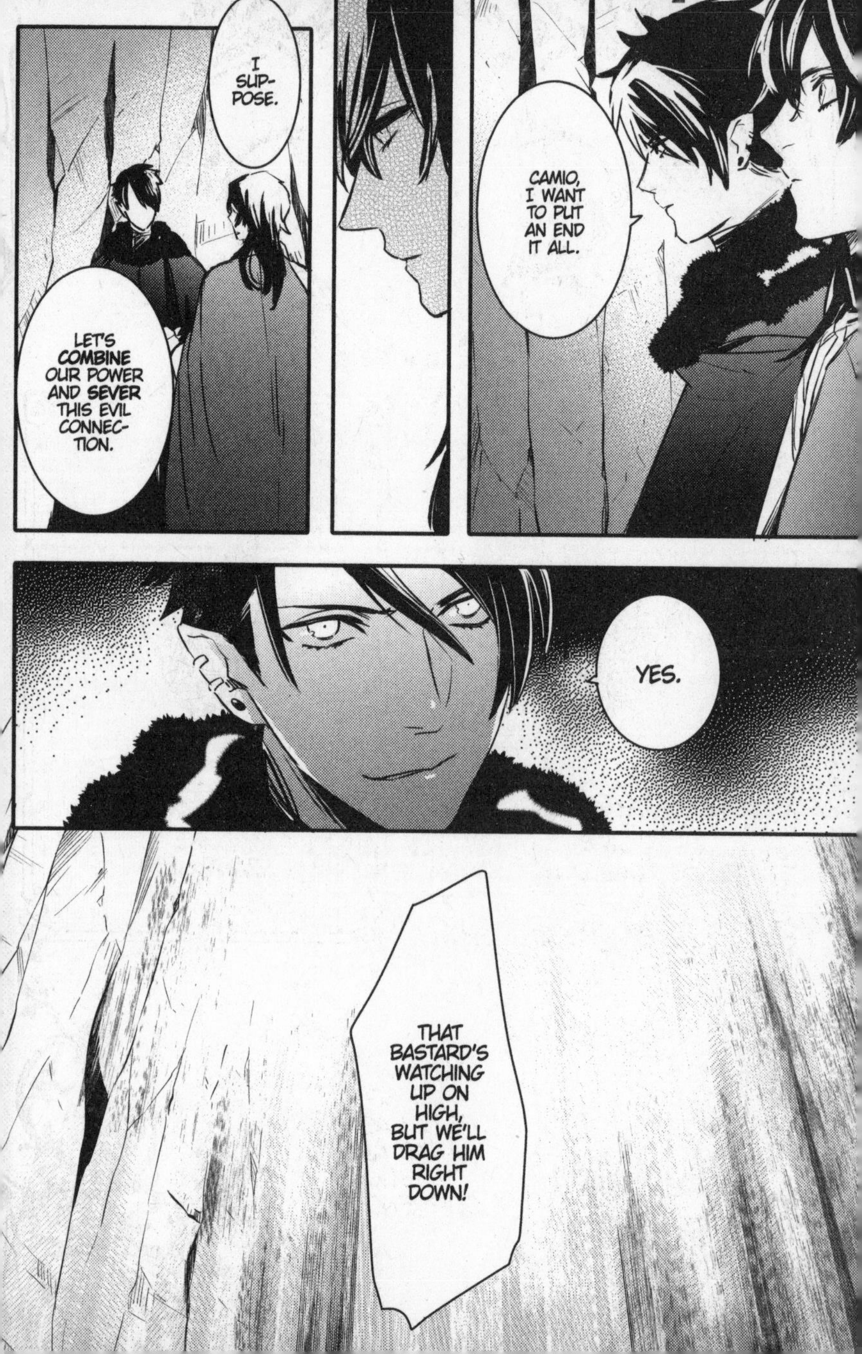
CAMIO, I WANT TO PUT AN END IT ALL.
I SUP-POSE.
LET'S COMBINE OUR POWER AND SEVER THIS EVIL CONNEC-TION.
YES.
THAT BASTARD'S WATCHING UP ON HIGH, BUT WE'LL DRAG HIM RIGHT DOWN!

Pillar 78

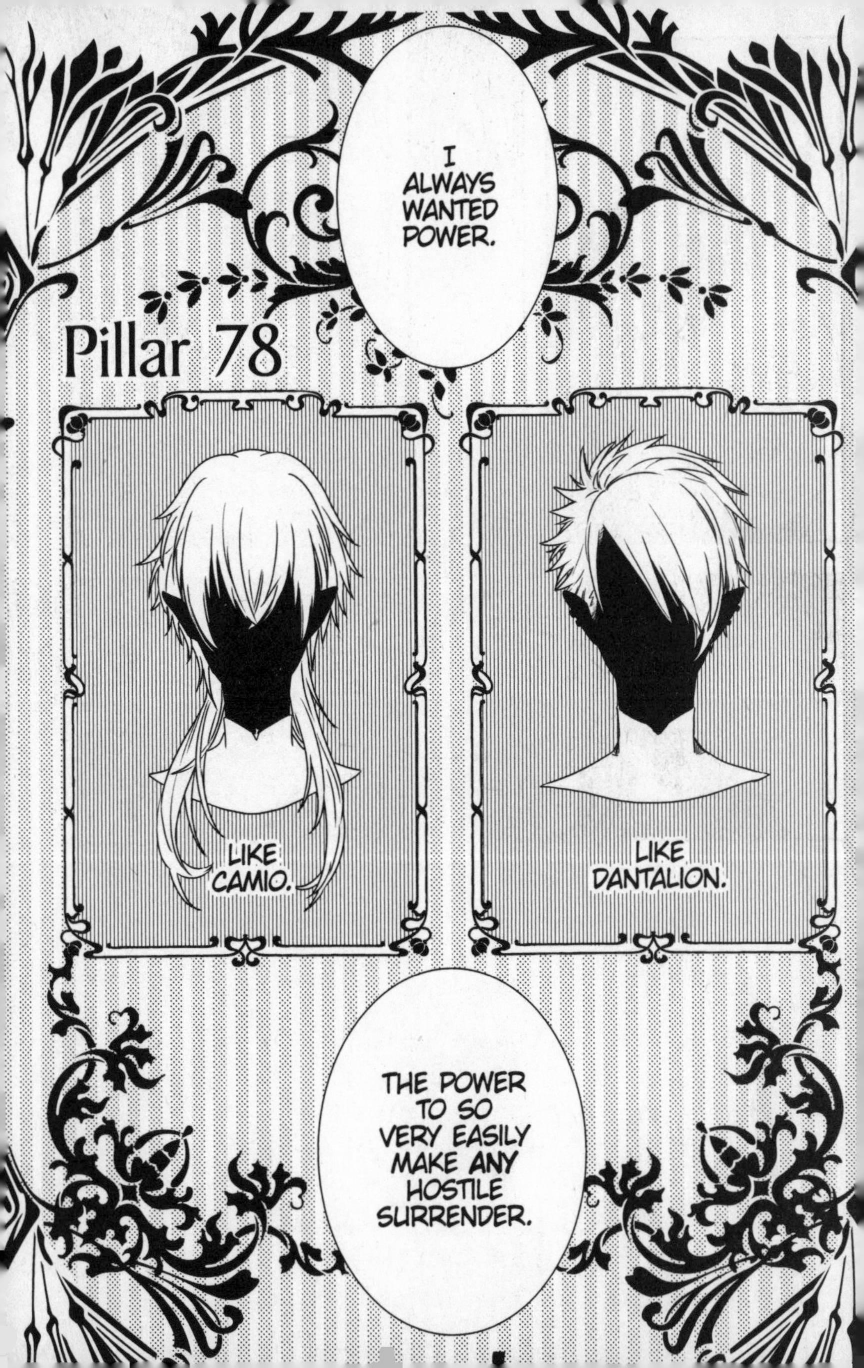
I ALWAYS WANTED POWER.
LIKE DANTALION.
LIKE CAMIO.
THE POWER TO SO VERY EASILY MAKE ANY HOSTILE SURRENDER.

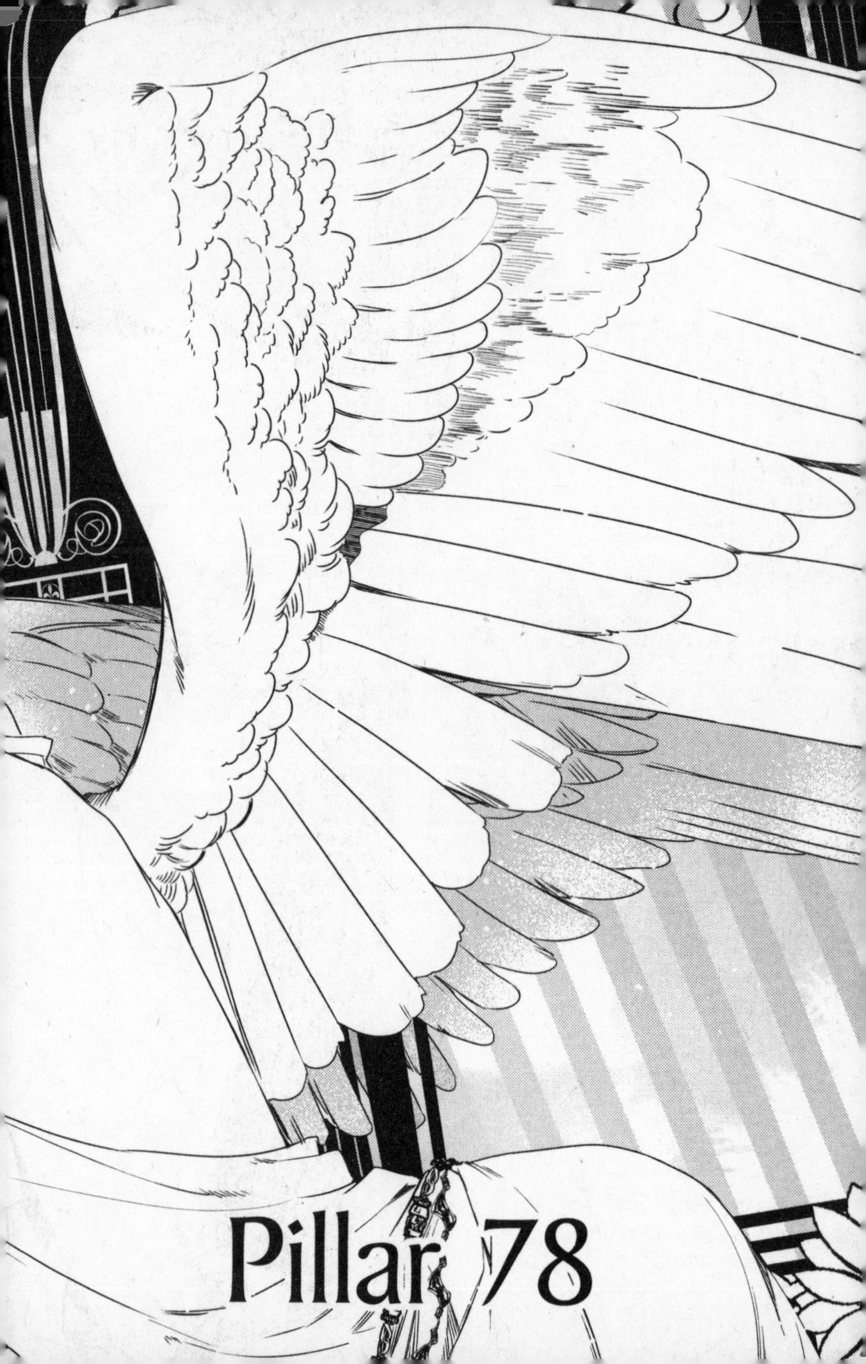

Pillar 78

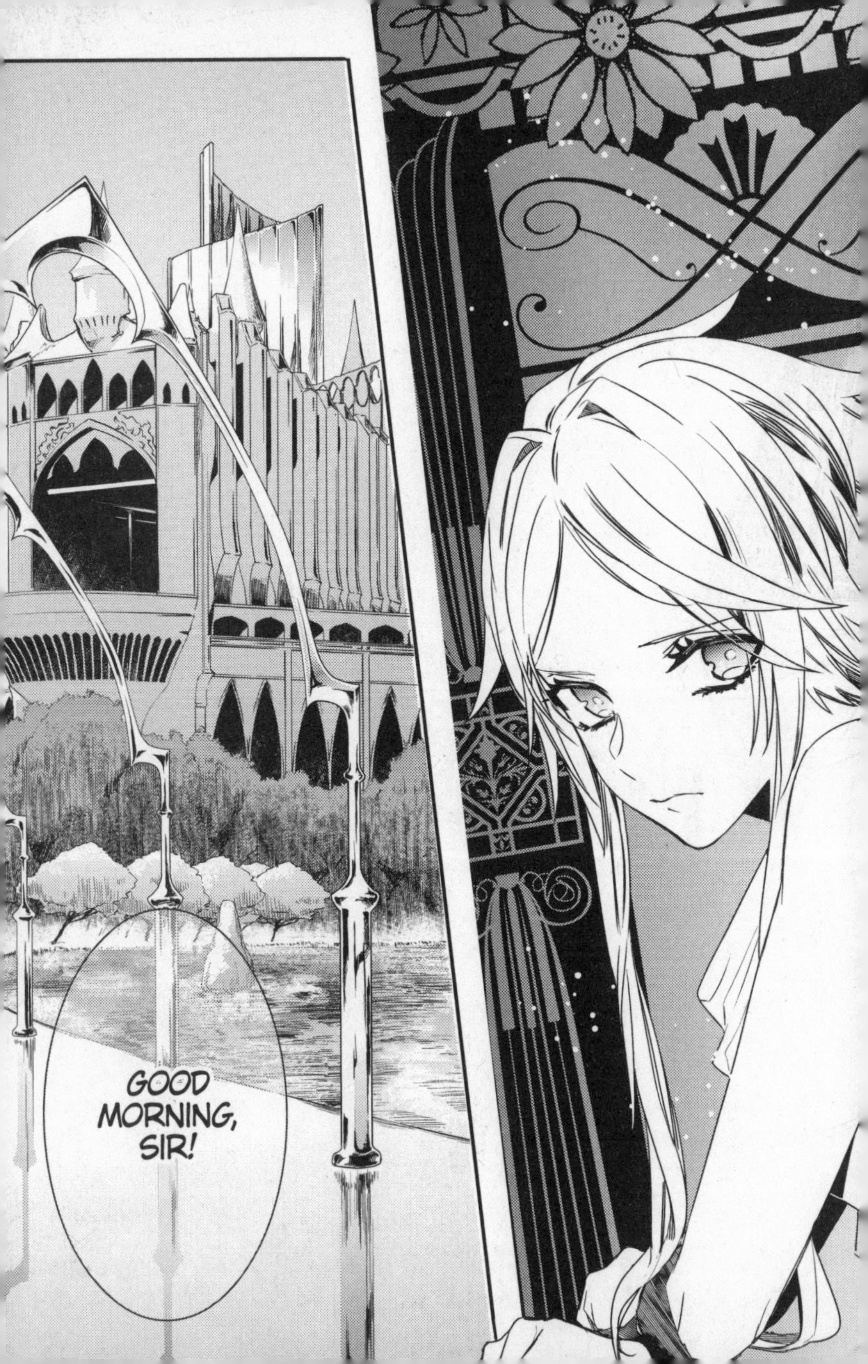
GOOD MORNING, SIR!

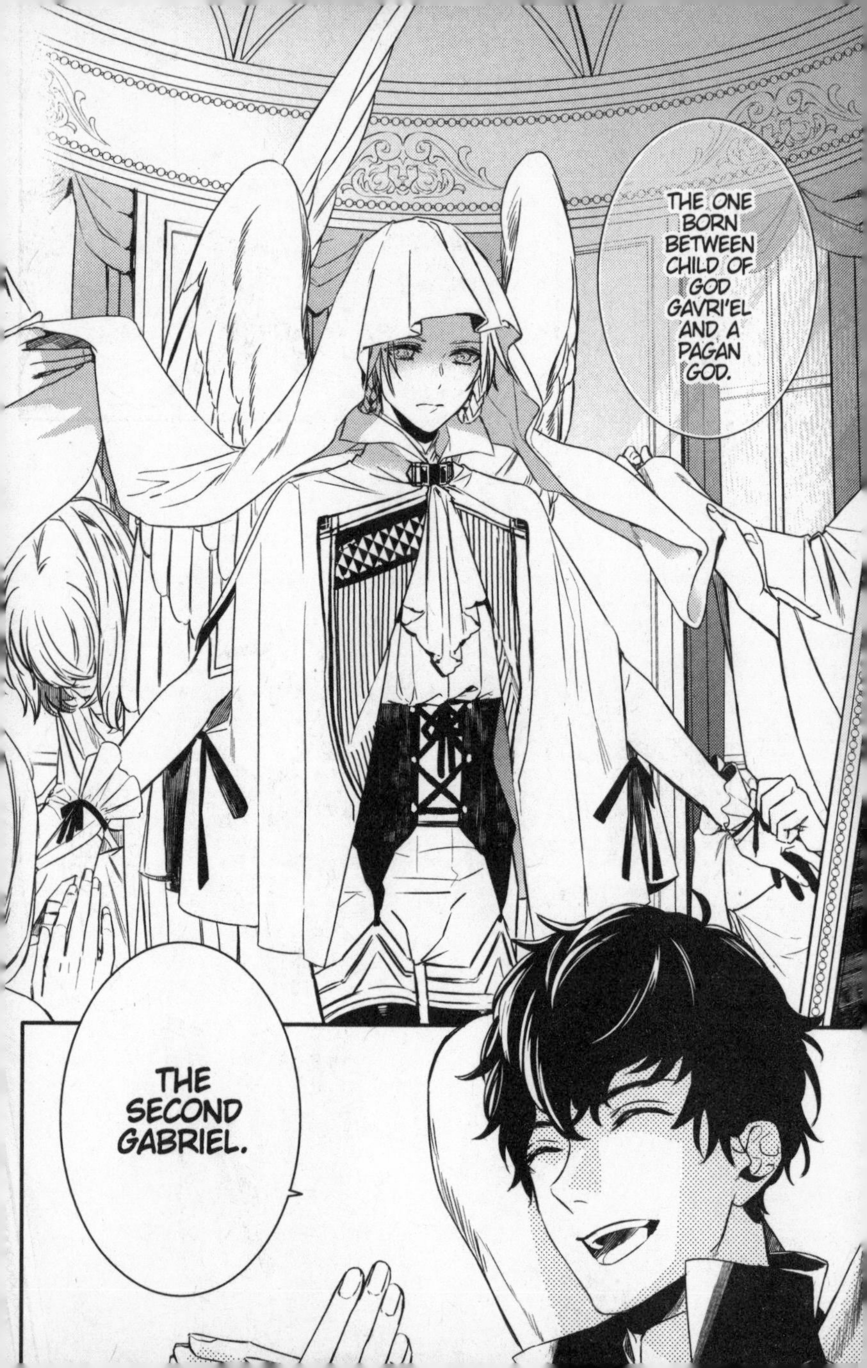
THE ONE BORN BETWEEN CHILD OF GOD GAVRI'EL AND A PAGAN GOD.
THE SECOND GABRIEL.

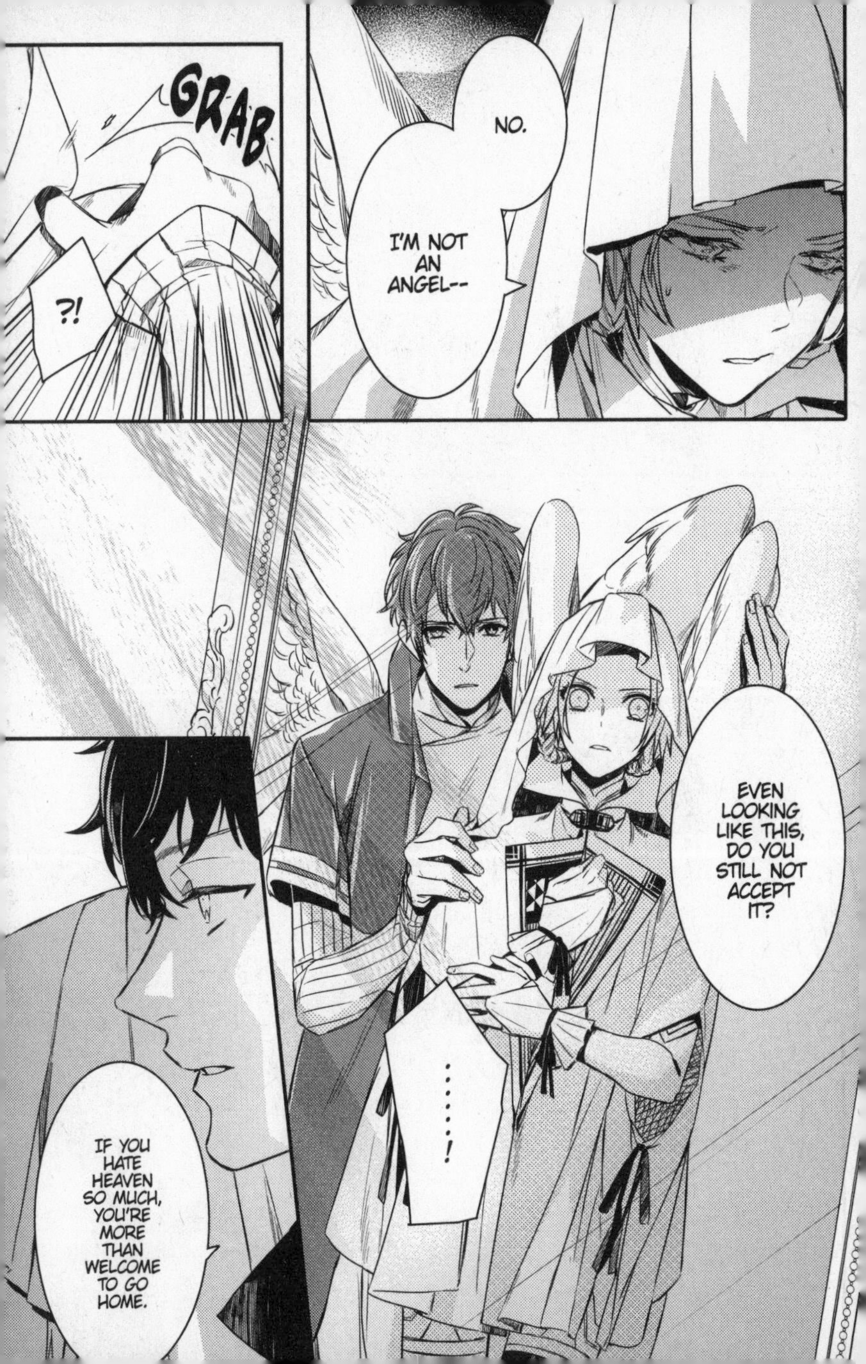
NO.
I'M NOT AN ANGEL--
GRAB
?!
EVEN LOOKING LIKE THIS, DO YOU STILL NOT ACCEPT IT?
......!
IF YOU HATE HEAVEN SO MUCH, YOU'RE MORE THAN WELCOME TO GO HOME.

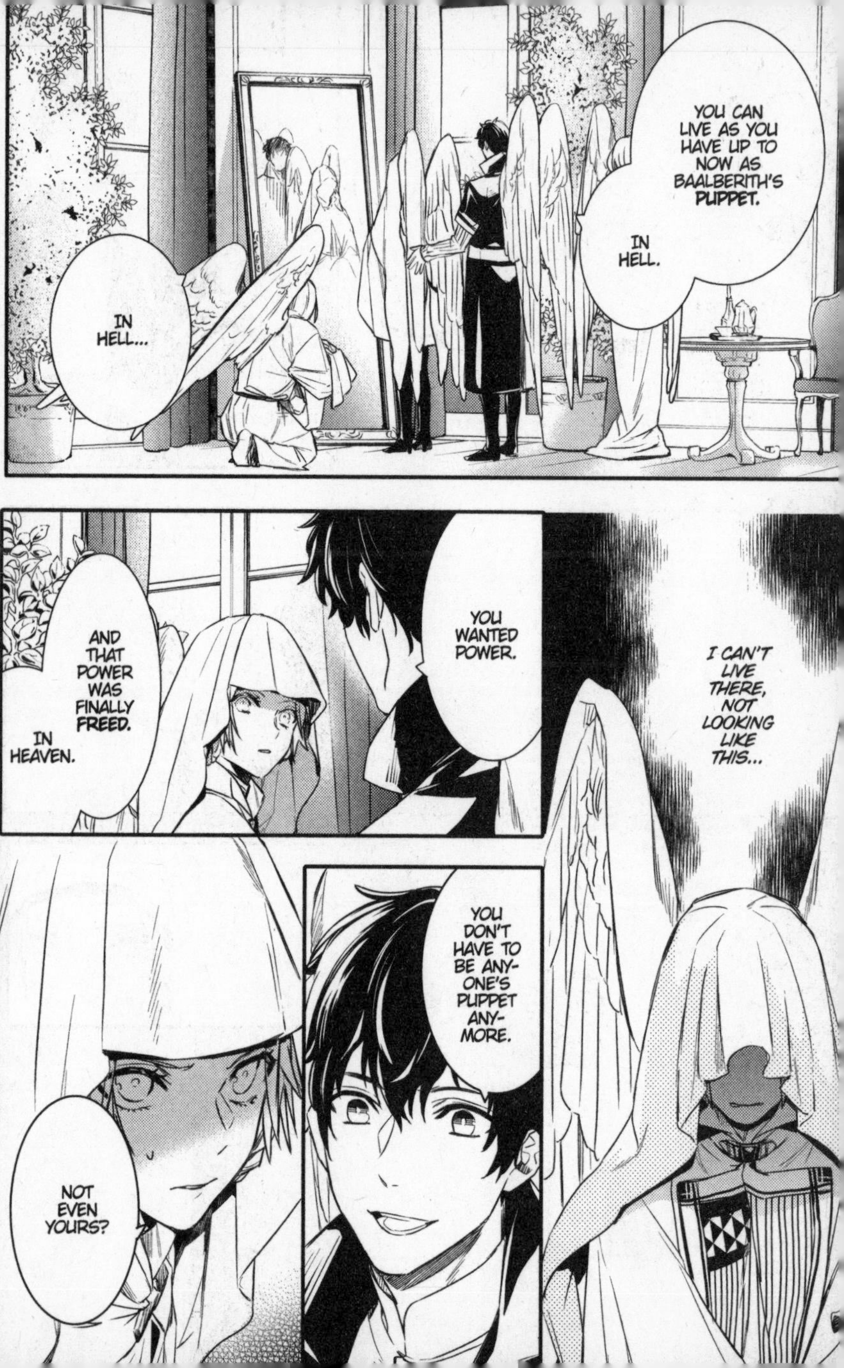
YOU CAN LIVE AS YOU HAVE UP TO NOW AS BAALBERITH'S PUPPET.
IN HELL.
IN HELL...
I CAN'T LIVE THERE, NOT LOOKING LIKE THIS...
YOU WANTED POWER.
AND THAT POWER WAS FINALLY FREED.
IN HEAVEN.
YOU DON'T HAVE TO BE ANYONE'S PUPPET ANYMORE.
NOT EVEN YOURS?

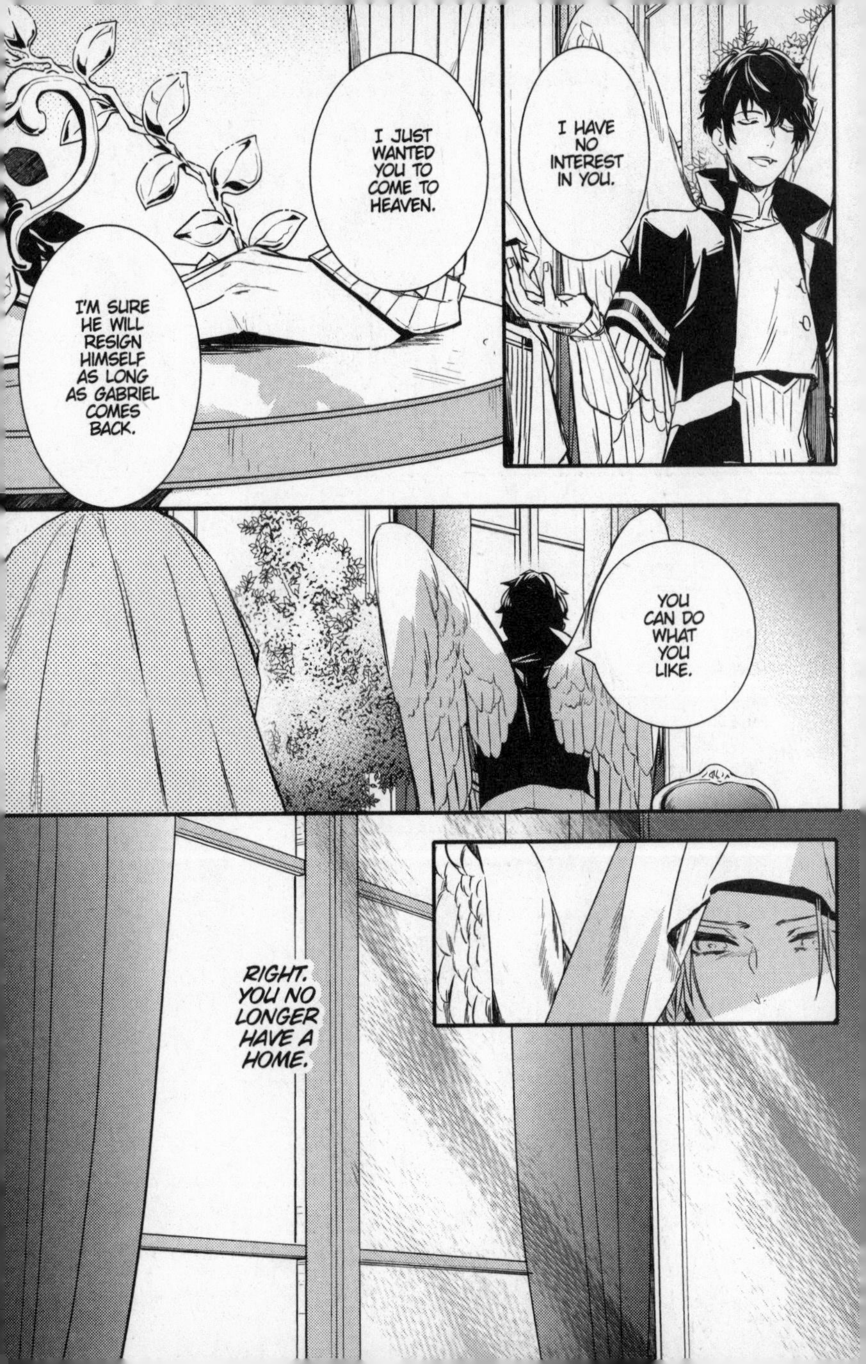
I HAVE NO INTEREST IN YOU.
I JUST WANTED YOU TO COME TO HEAVEN.
I'M SURE HE WILL RESIGN HIMSELF AS LONG AS GABRIEL COMES BACK.
YOU CAN DO WHAT YOU LIKE.
RIGHT. YOU NO LONGER HAVE A HOME.

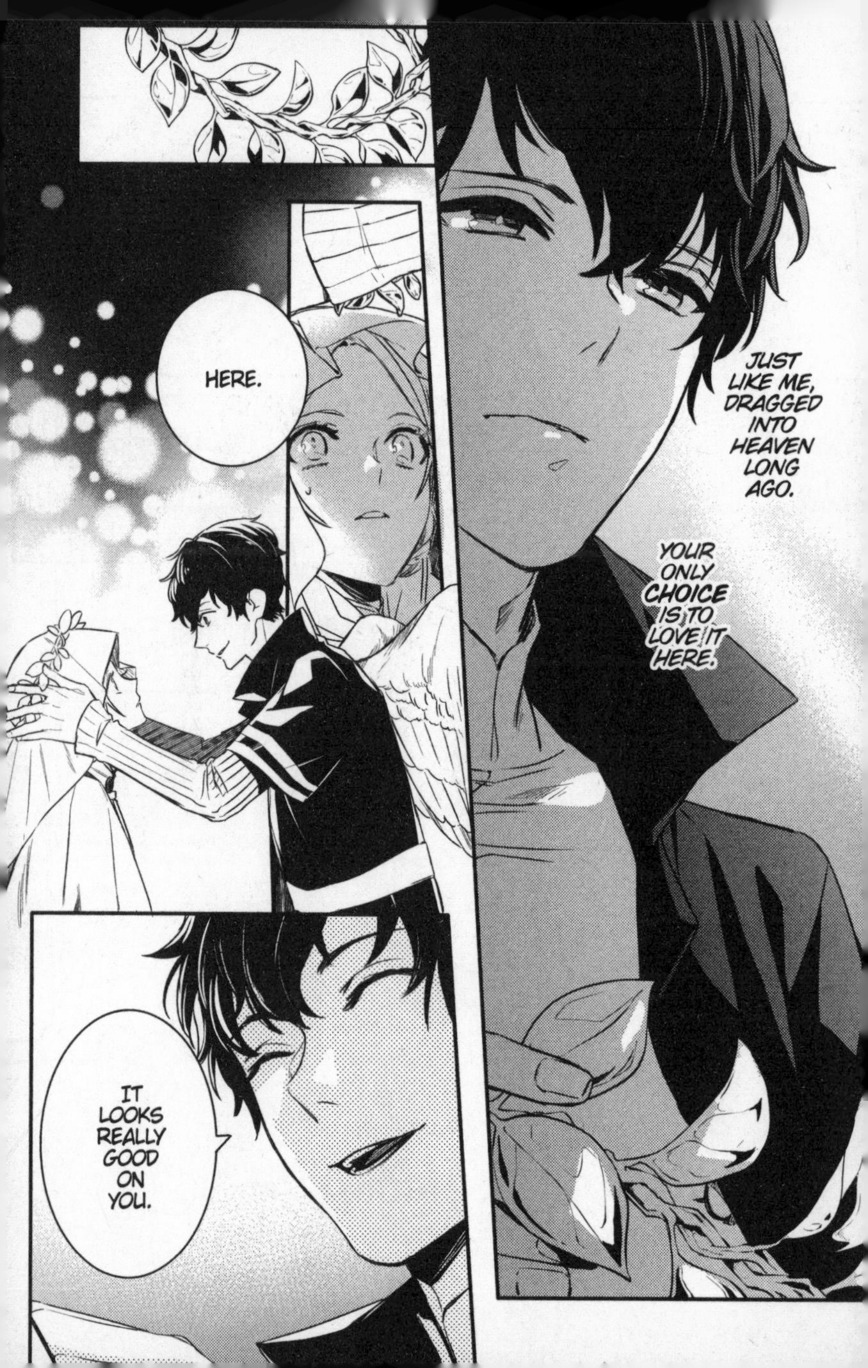
JUST LIKE ME, DRAGGED INTO HEAVEN LONG AGO.
YOUR ONLY CHOICE IS TO LOVE IT HERE.
HERE.
IT LOOKS REALLY GOOD ON YOU.

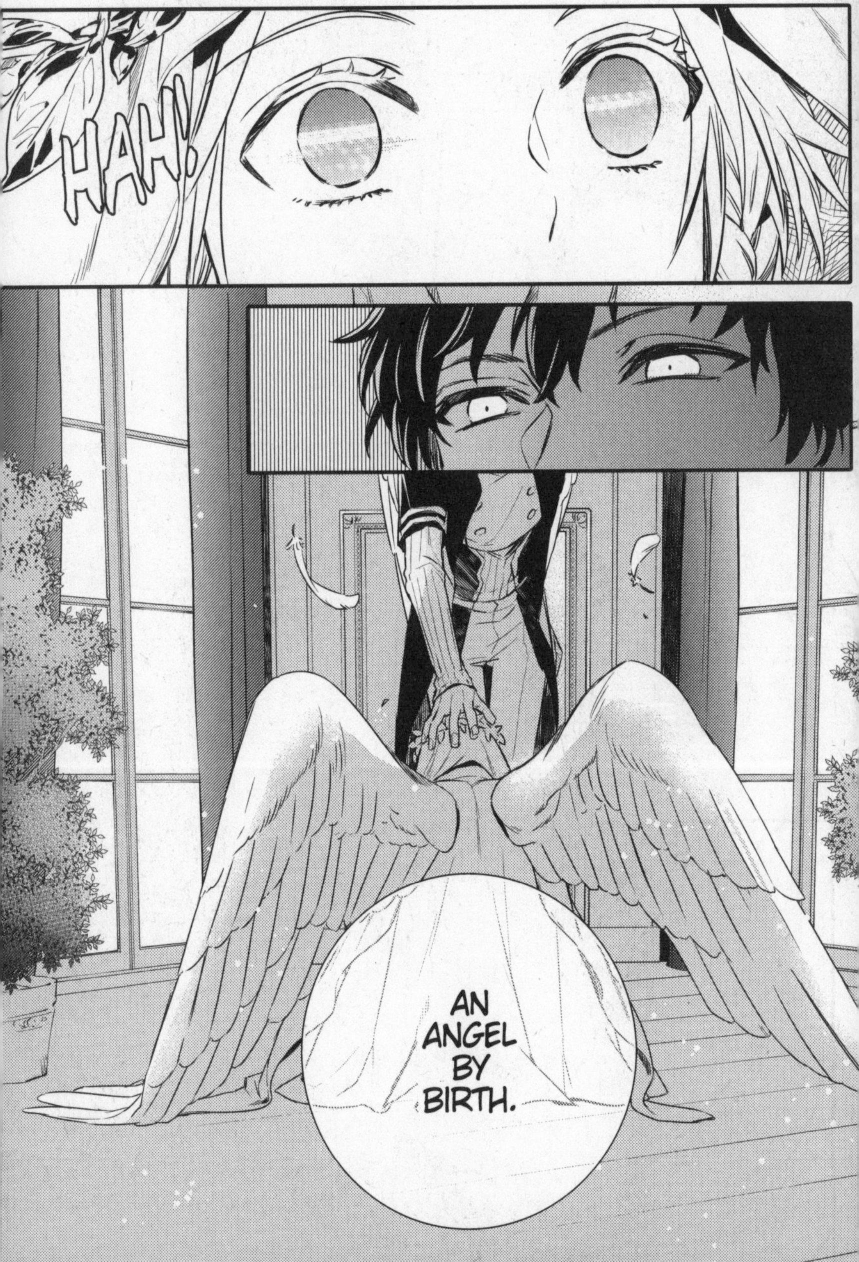
HAH!
AN ANGEL BY BIRTH.

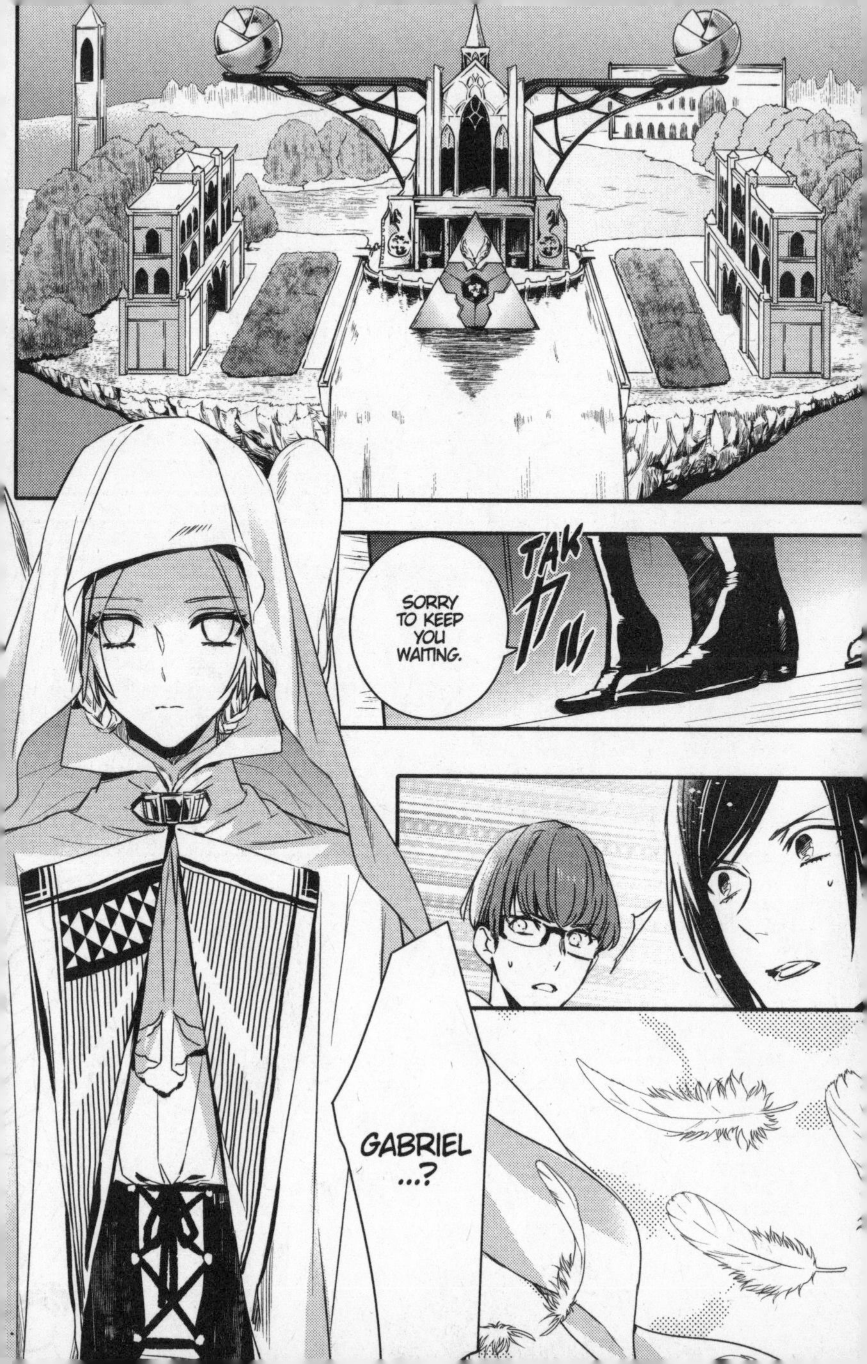
TAK
SORRY TO KEEP YOU WAITING.
GABRIEL ...?

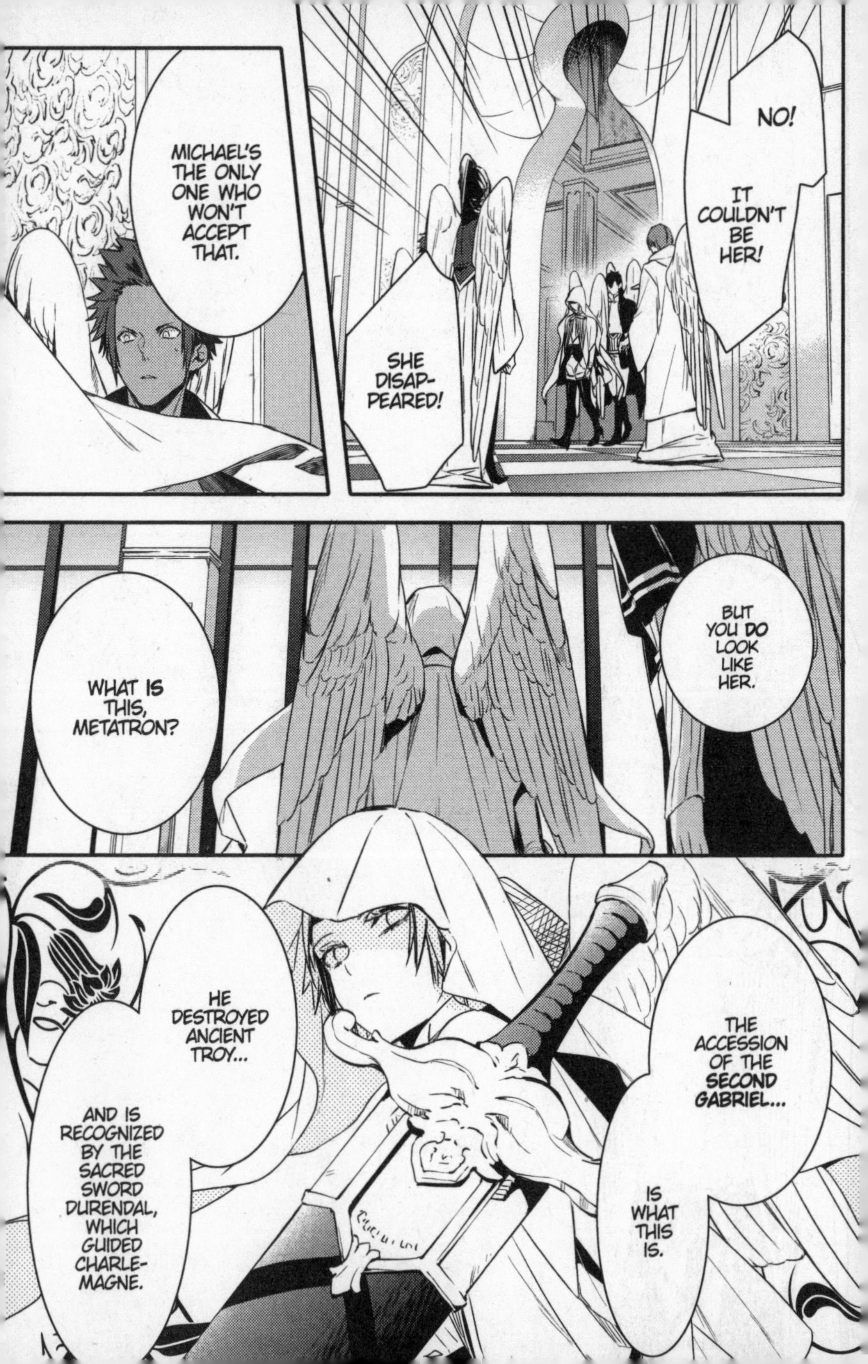
NO!
IT COULDN'T BE HER!
SHE DISAP-PEARED!
MICHAEL'S THE ONLY ONE WHO WON'T ACCEPT THAT.
BUT YOU DO LOOK LIKE HER.
WHAT IS THIS, METATRON?
THE ACCESSION OF THE SECOND GABRIEL...
IS WHAT THIS IS.
HE DESTROYED ANCIENT TROY...
AND IS RECOGNIZED BY THE SACRED SWORD DURENDAL, WHICH GUIDED CHARLE-MAGNE.

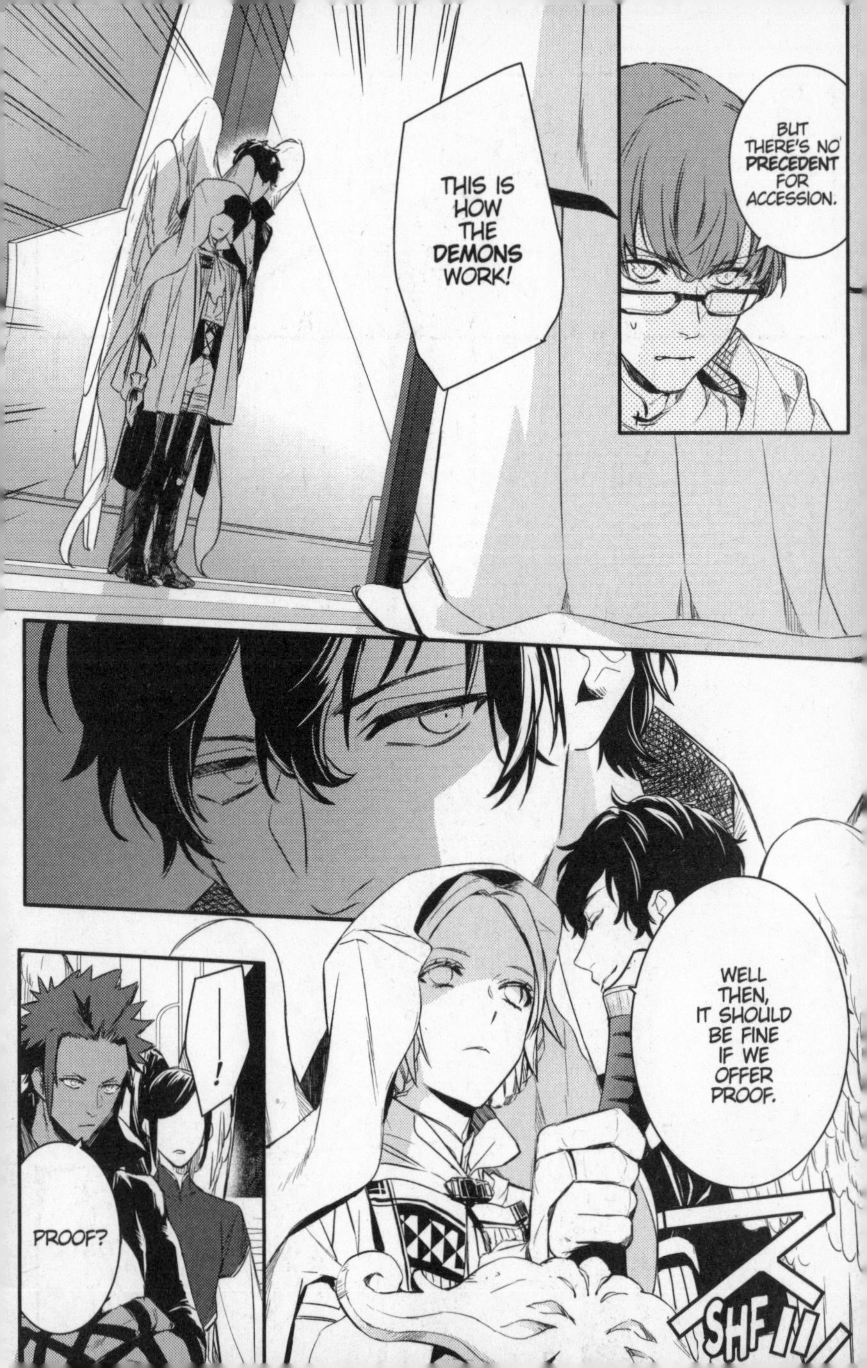
BUT THERE'S NO PRECEDENT FOR ACCESSION.
THIS IS HOW THE DEMONS WORK!
WELL THEN, IT SHOULD BE FINE IF WE OFFER PROOF.
SHF
!
PROOF?

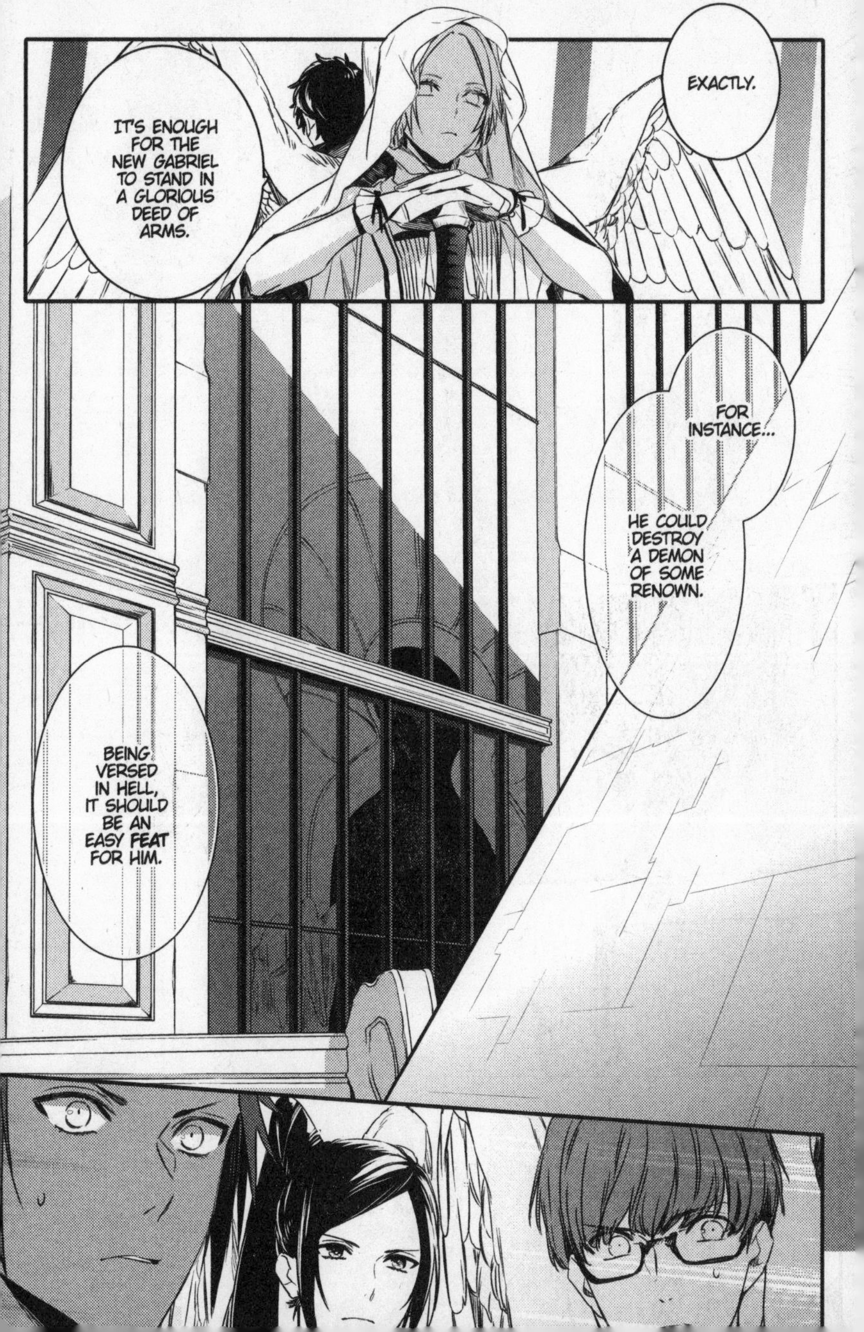
EXACTLY.
IT'S ENOUGH FOR THE NEW GABRIEL TO STAND IN A GLORIOUS DEED OF ARMS.
FOR INSTANCE...
HE COULD DESTROY A DEMON OF SOME RENOWN.
BEING VERSED IN HELL, IT SHOULD BE AN EASY FEAT FOR HIM.

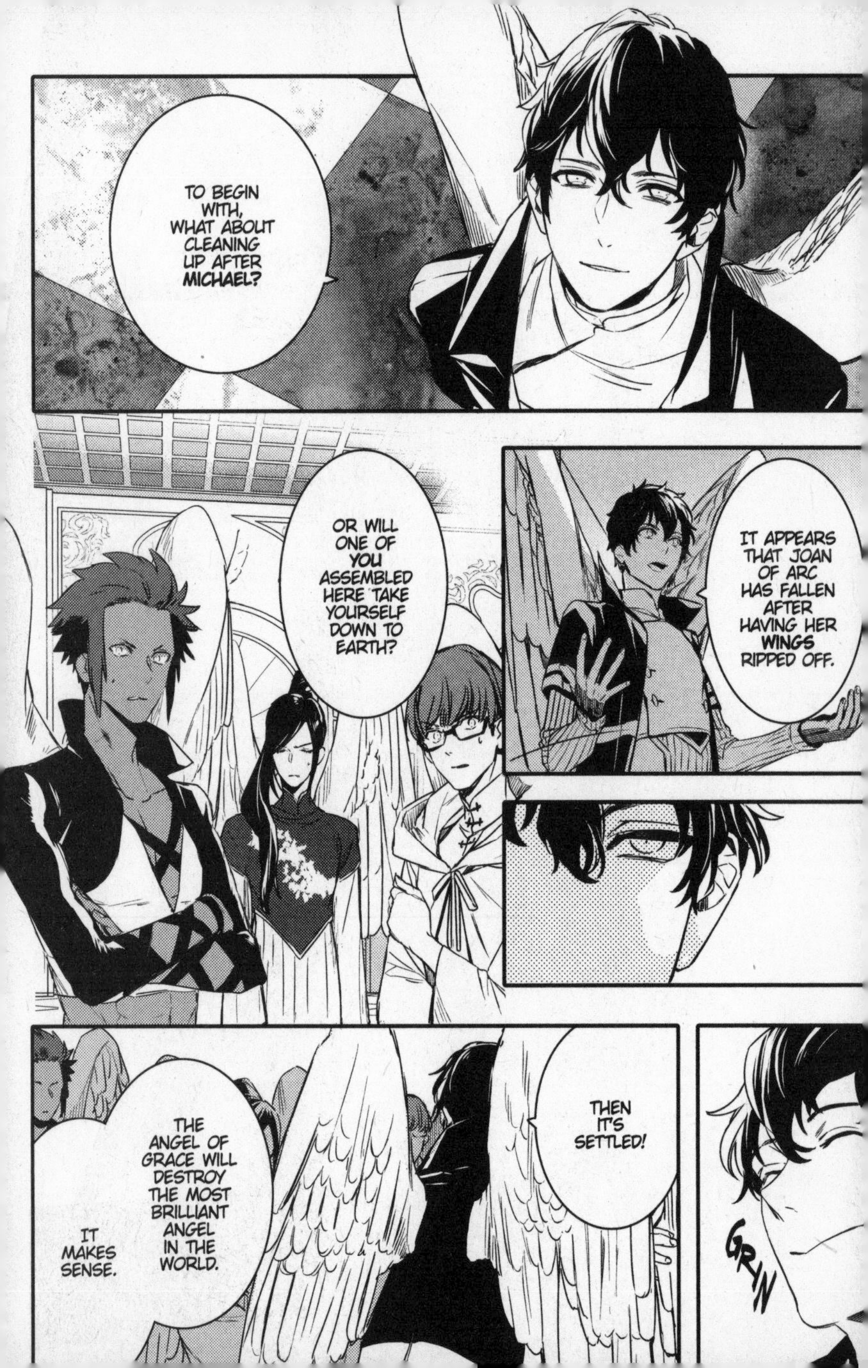
TO BEGIN WITH, WHAT ABOUT CLEANING UP AFTER MICHAEL?
IT APPEARS THAT JOAN OF ARC HAS FALLEN AFTER HAVING HER WINGS RIPPED OFF.
OR WILL ONE OF YOU ASSEMBLED HERE TAKE YOURSELF DOWN TO EARTH?
GRIN
THEN IT'S SETTLED!
THE ANGEL OF GRACE WILL DESTROY THE MOST BRILLIANT ANGEL IN THE WORLD.
IT MAKES SENSE.

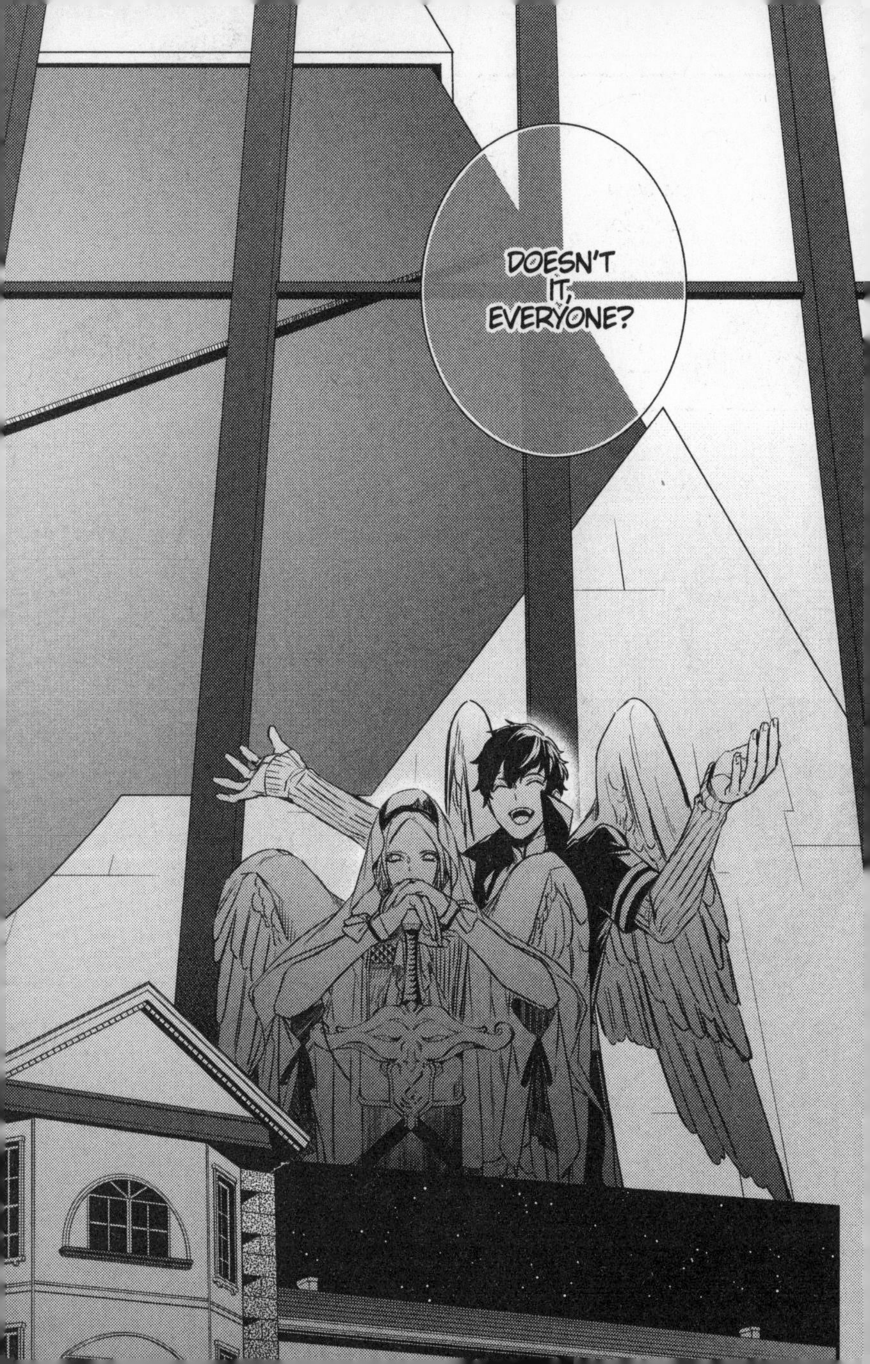
DOESN'T IT, EVERYONE?

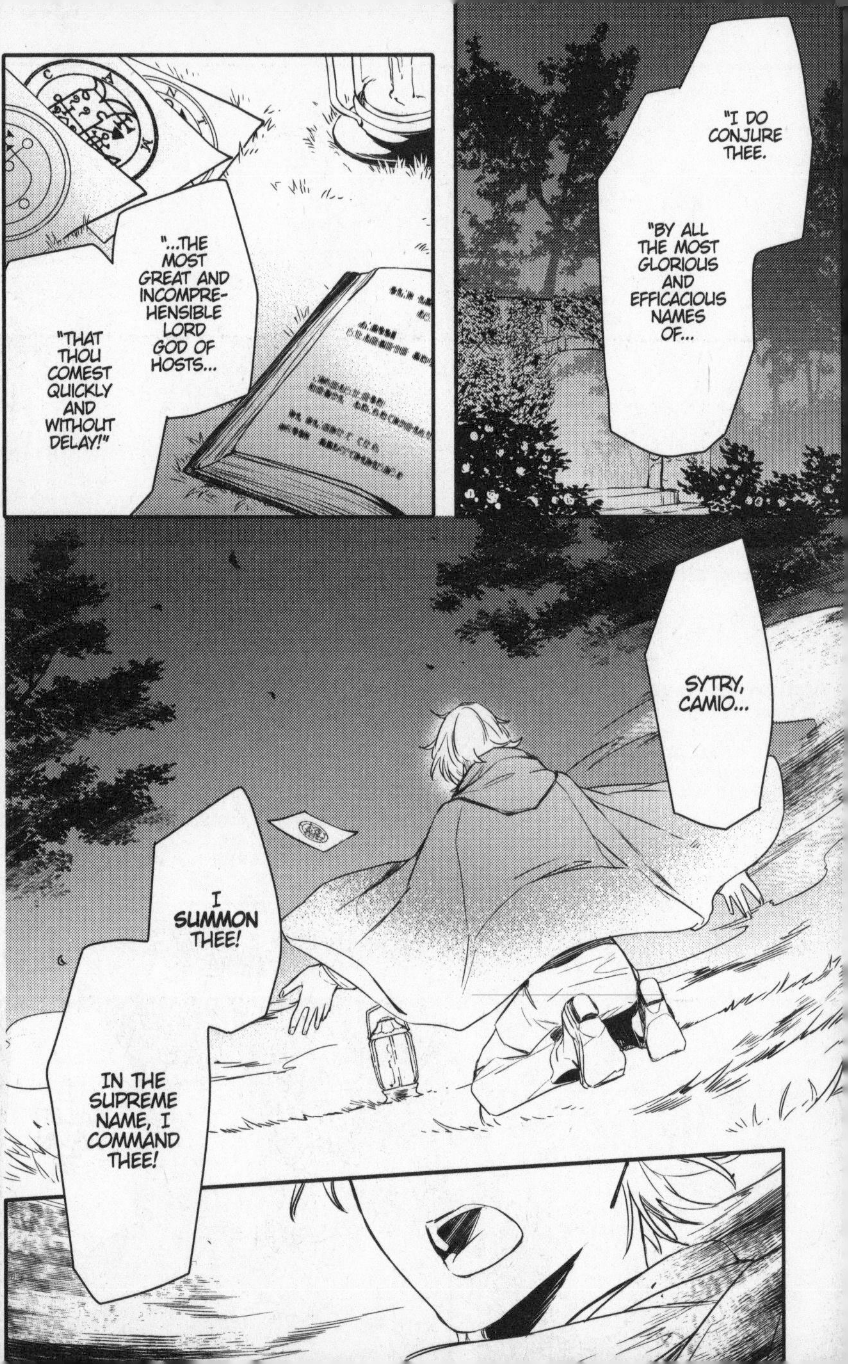
"I DO CONJURE THEE.
"BY ALL THE MOST GLORIOUS AND EFFICACIOUS NAMES OF...
"...THE MOST GREAT AND INCOMPRE-HENSIBLE LORD GOD OF HOSTS...
"THAT THOU COMEST QUICKLY AND WITHOUT DELAY!"
SYTRY, CAMIO...
I SUMMON THEE!
IN THE SUPREME NAME, I COMMAND THEE!

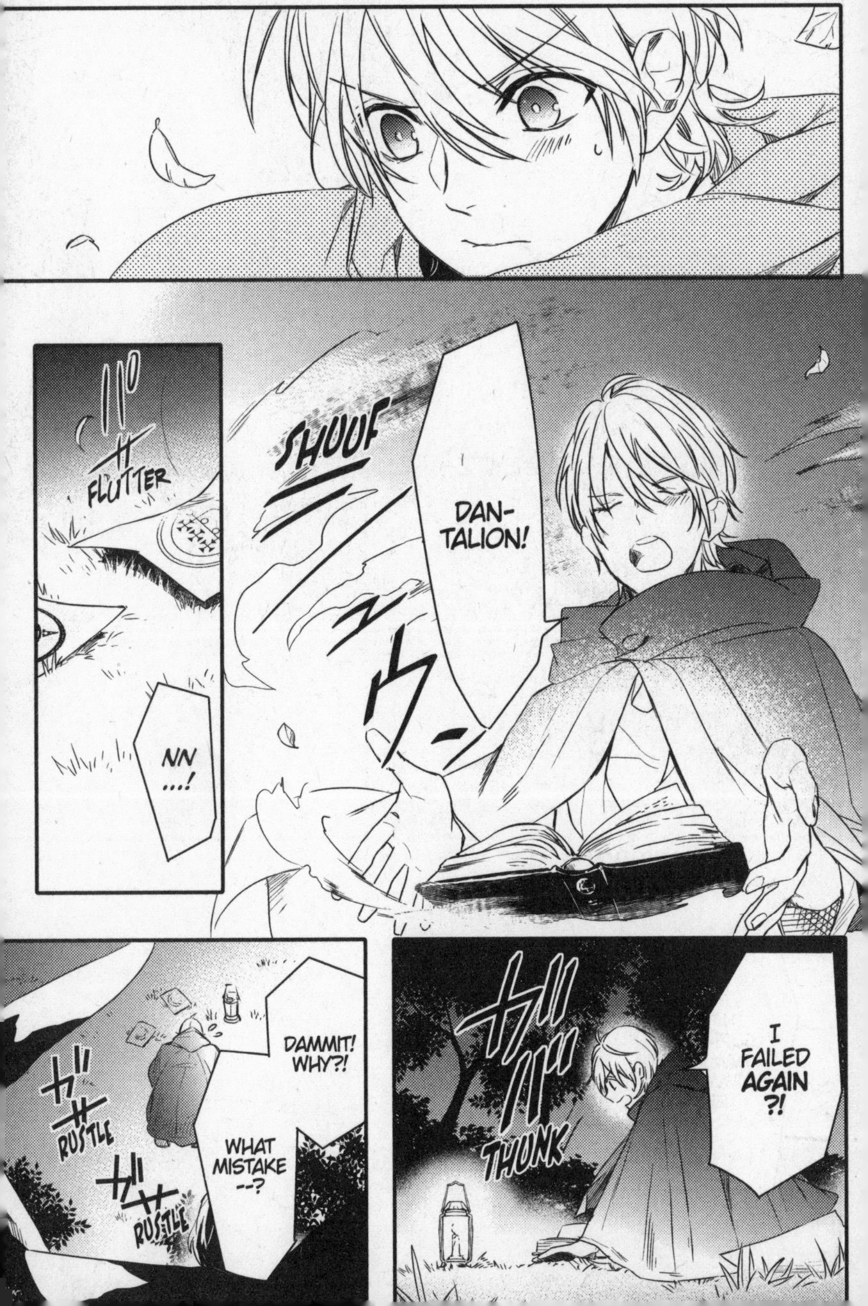
SHUUF
DAN-TALION!
FLUTTER
NN ...!
THUNK
I FAILED AGAIN ?!
DAMMIT! WHY?!
WHAT MISTAKE --?
RUSTLE
RUSTLE

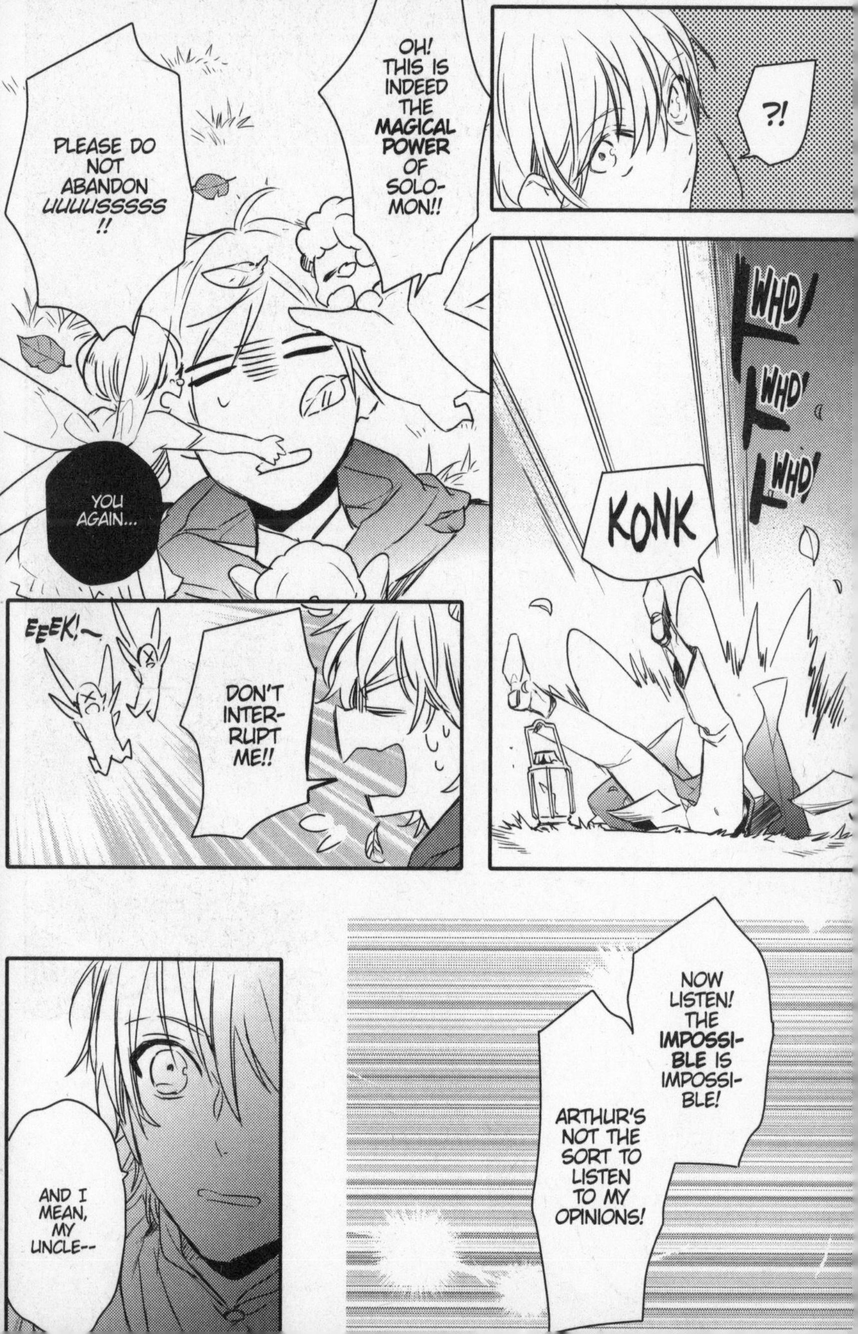
?!
WHD! WHD! WHD!
KONK
OH! THIS IS INDEED THE MAGICAL POWER OF SOLO-MON!!
PLEASE DO NOT ABANDON UUUUSSSSS!!
YOU AGAIN...
DON'T INTER-RUPT ME!!
EEEK!~
NOW LISTEN! THE IMPOSSI-BLE IS IMPOSSI-BLE!
ARTHUR'S NOT THE SORT TO LISTEN TO MY OPINIONS!
AND I MEAN, MY UNCLE--

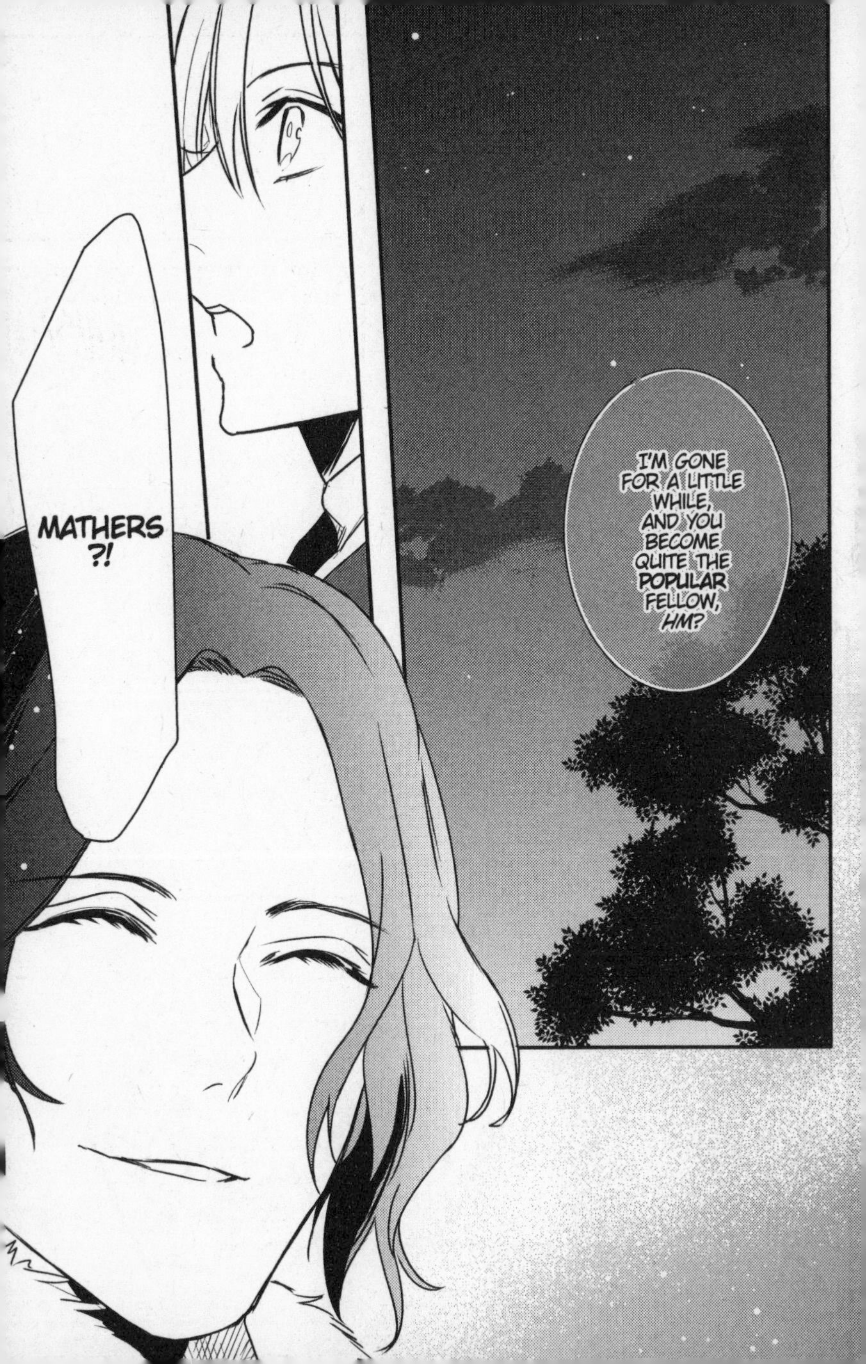
I'M GONE FOR A LITTLE WHILE, AND YOU BECOME QUITE THE POPULAR FELLOW, HM?
MATHERS ?!

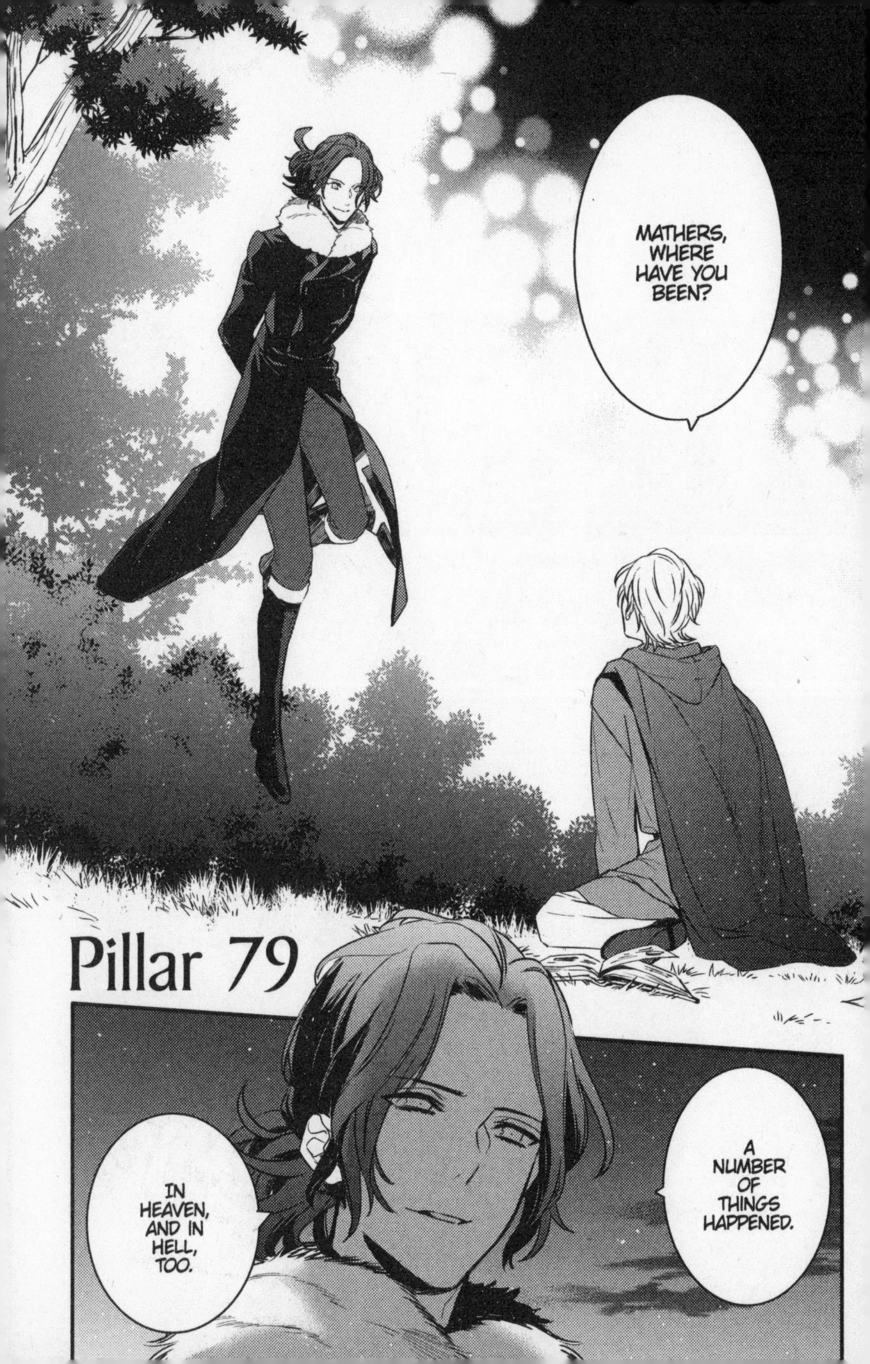
MATHERS, WHERE HAVE YOU BEEN?
Pillar 79
A NUMBER OF THINGS HAPPENED.
IN HEAVEN, AND IN HELL, TOO.

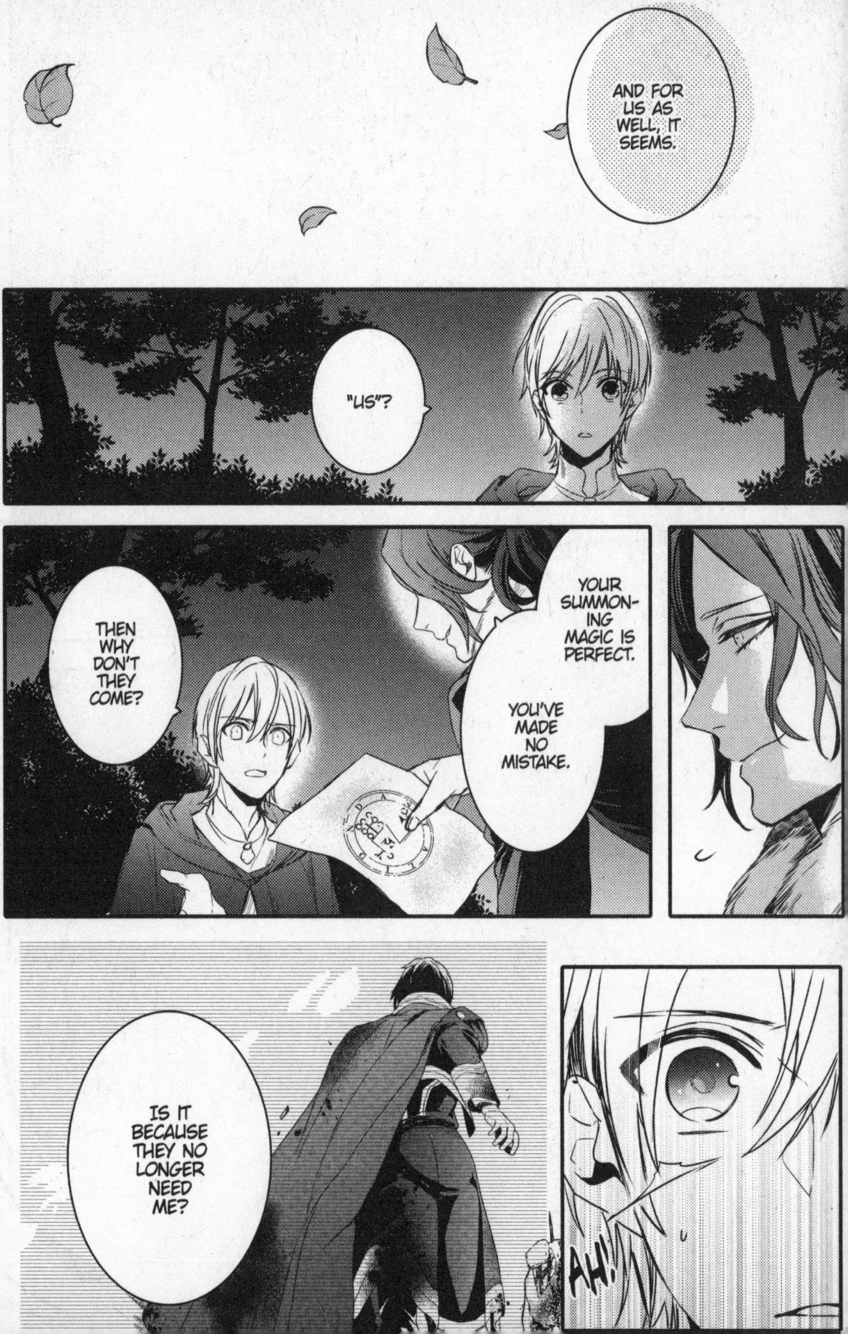
AND FOR US AS WELL, IT SEEMS.
"US"?
YOUR SUMMONING-MAGIC IS PERFECT.
YOU'VE MADE NO MISTAKE.
THEN WHY DON'T THEY COME?
AH!
IS IT BECAUSE THEY NO LONGER NEED ME?

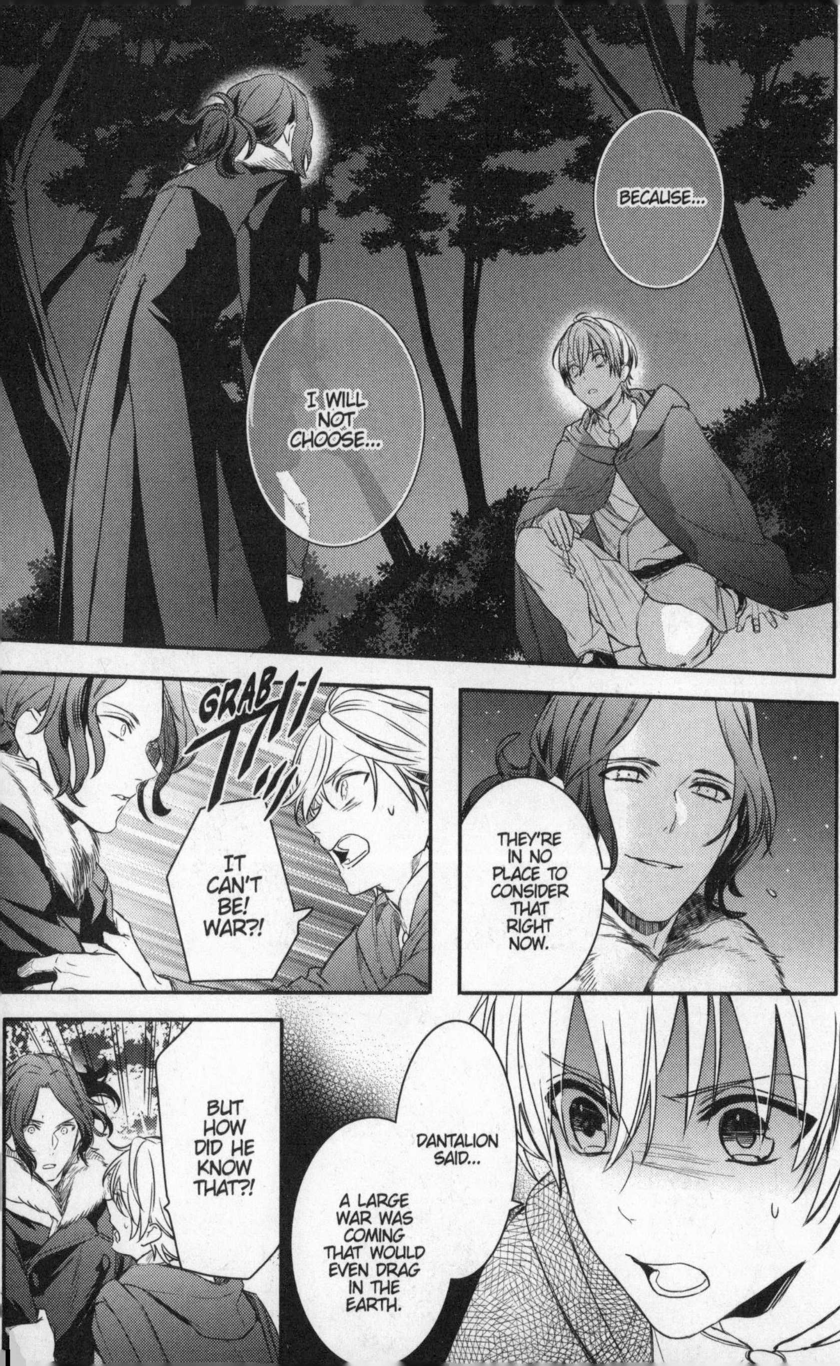
BECAUSE...
I WILL NOT CHOOSE...
THEY'RE IN NO PLACE TO CONSIDER THAT RIGHT NOW.
IT CAN'T BE! WAR?!
DANTALION SAID...
A LARGE WAR WAS COMING THAT WOULD EVEN DRAG IN THE EARTH.
BUT HOW DID HE KNOW THAT?!

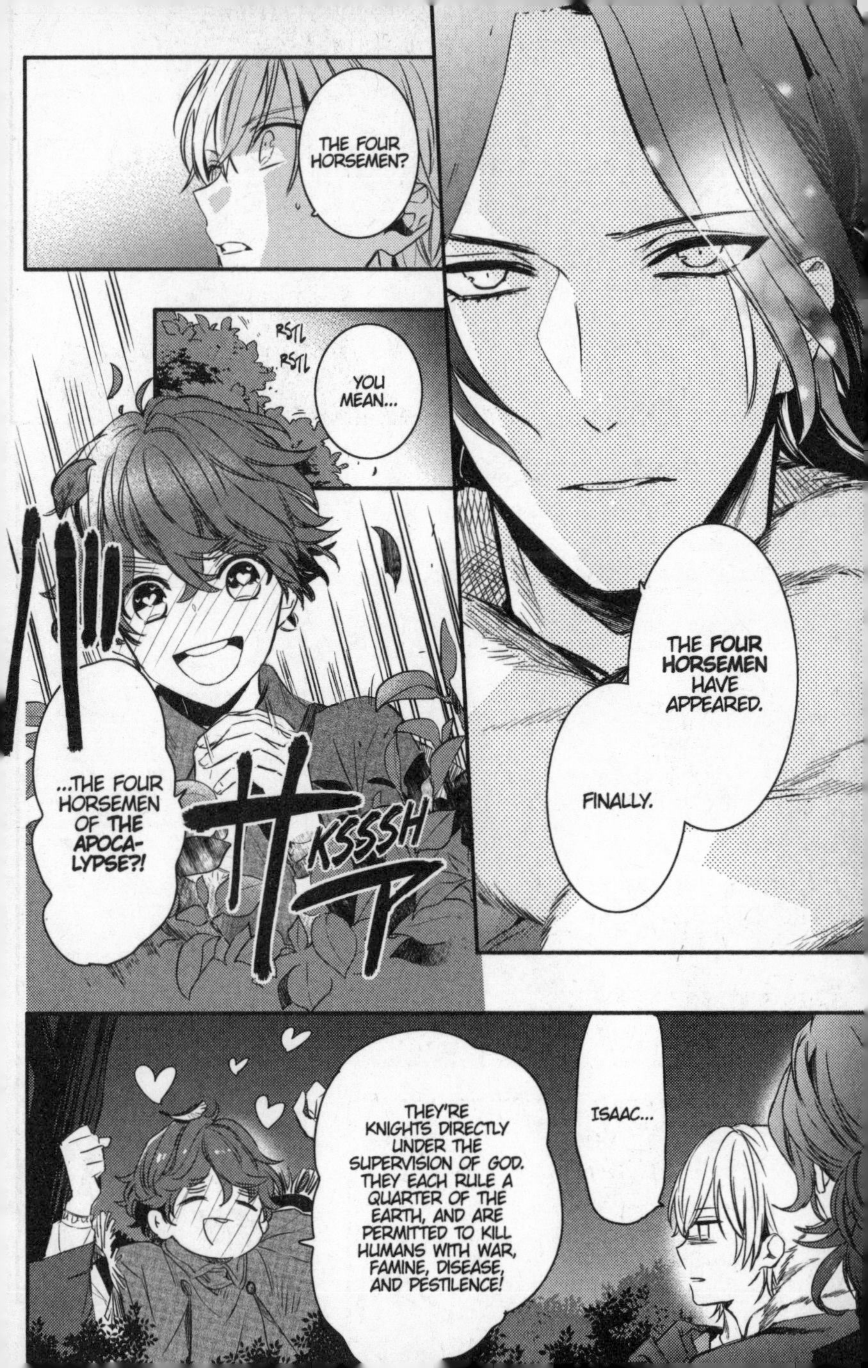
THE FOUR HORSEMEN HAVE APPEARED.
FINALLY.
THE FOUR HORSEMEN?
RSTL RSTL
YOU MEAN...
...THE FOUR HORSEMEN OF THE APOCA-LYPSE?!
KSSSH
ISAAC...
THEY'RE KNIGHTS DIRECTLY UNDER THE SUPERVISION OF GOD. THEY EACH RULE A QUARTER OF THE EARTH, AND ARE PERMITTED TO KILL HUMANS WITH WAR, FAMINE, DISEASE, AND PESTILENCE!

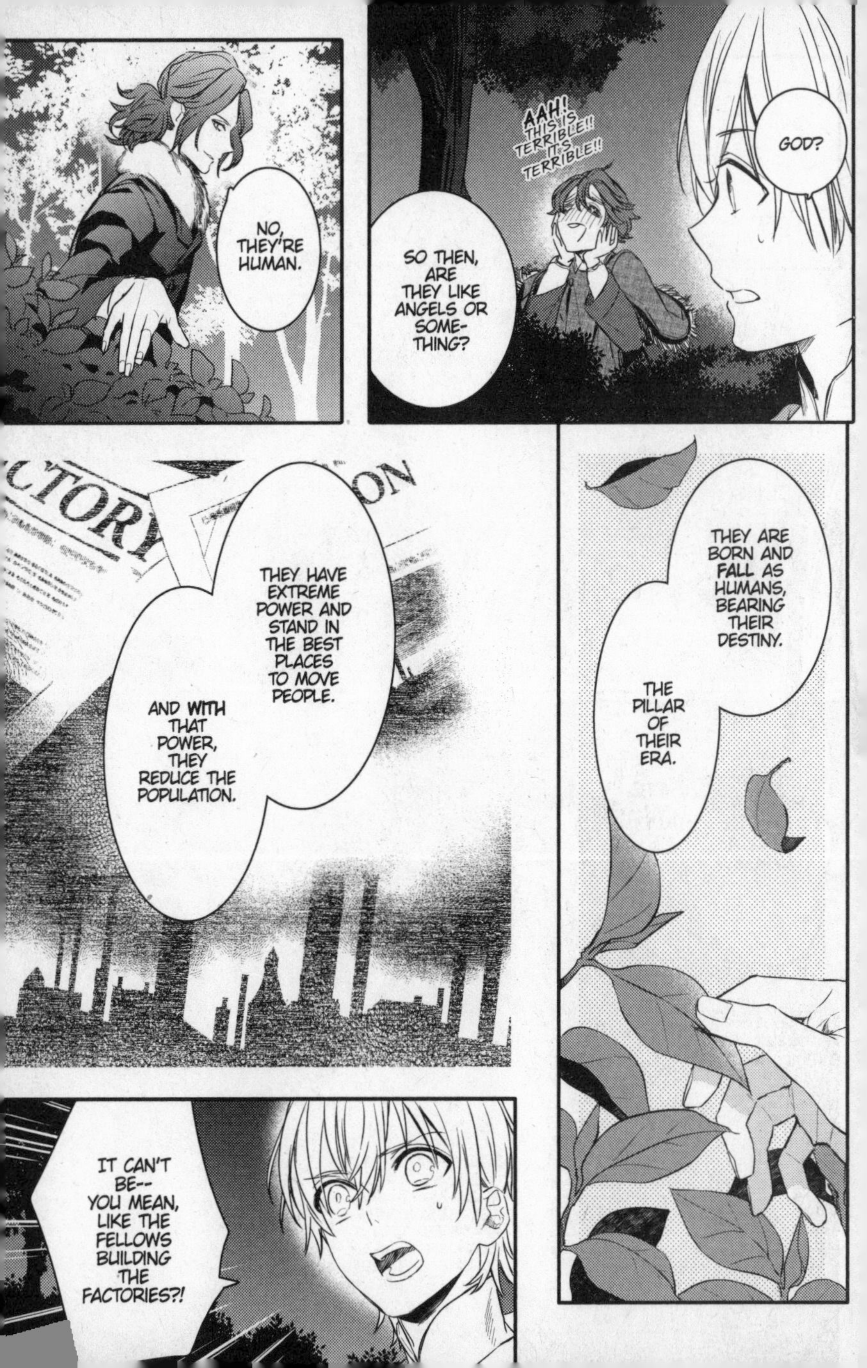
GOD?
AAH! THIS IS TERRIBLE!! IT'S TERRIBLE!!
SO THEN, ARE THEY LIKE ANGELS OR SOME-THING?
NO, THEY'RE HUMAN.
THEY ARE BORN AND FALL AS HUMANS, BEARING THEIR DESTINY.
THE PILLAR OF THEIR ERA.
THEY HAVE EXTREME POWER AND STAND IN THE BEST PLACES TO MOVE PEOPLE.
AND WITH THAT POWER, THEY REDUCE THE POPULATION.
IT CAN'T BE-- YOU MEAN, LIKE THE FELLOWS BUILDING THE FACTORIES?!

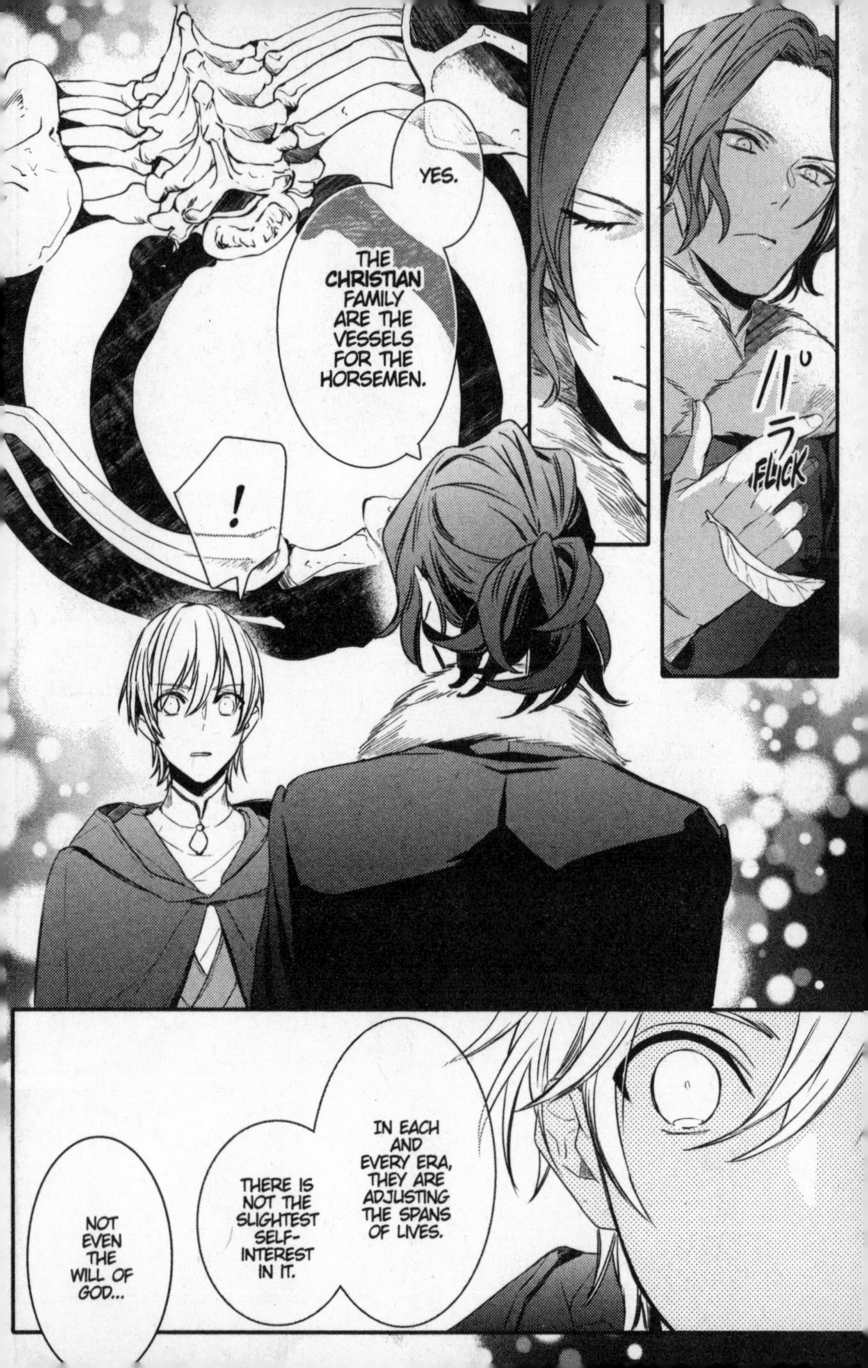
パラ
FLICK
YES.
THE CHRISTIAN FAMILY ARE THE VESSELS FOR THE HORSEMEN.
!
IN EACH AND EVERY ERA, THEY ARE ADJUSTING THE SPANS OF LIVES.
THERE IS NOT THE SLIGHTEST SELF-INTEREST IN IT.
NOT EVEN THE WILL OF GOD...

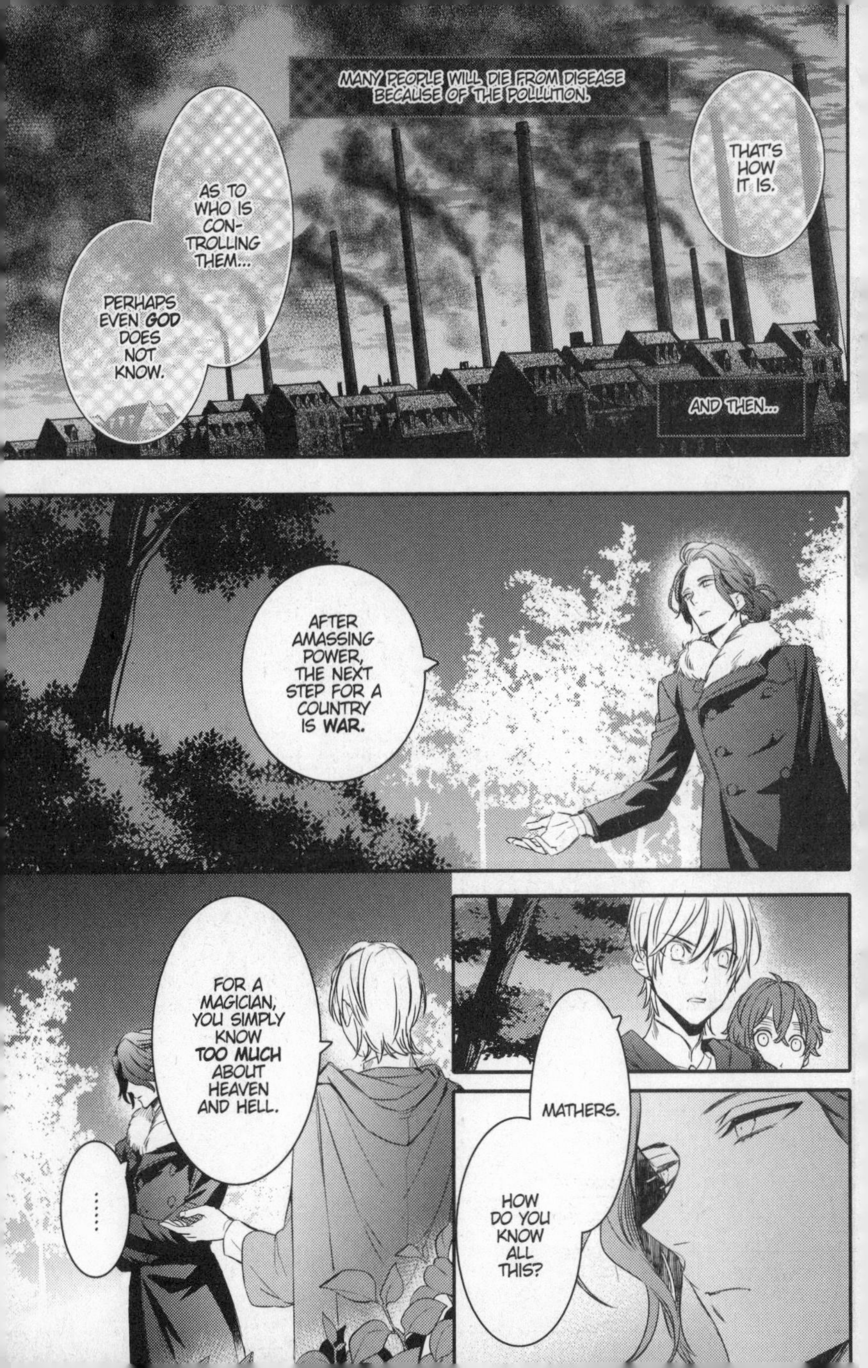
MANY PEOPLE WILL DIE FROM DISEASE BECAUSE OF THE POLLUTION.
THAT'S HOW IT IS.
AS TO WHO IS CON-TROLLING THEM...
PERHAPS EVEN GOD DOES NOT KNOW.
AND THEN...
AFTER AMASSING POWER, THE NEXT STEP FOR A COUNTRY IS WAR.
MATHERS.
HOW DO YOU KNOW ALL THIS?
FOR A MAGICIAN, YOU SIMPLY KNOW TOO MUCH ABOUT HEAVEN AND HELL.
......

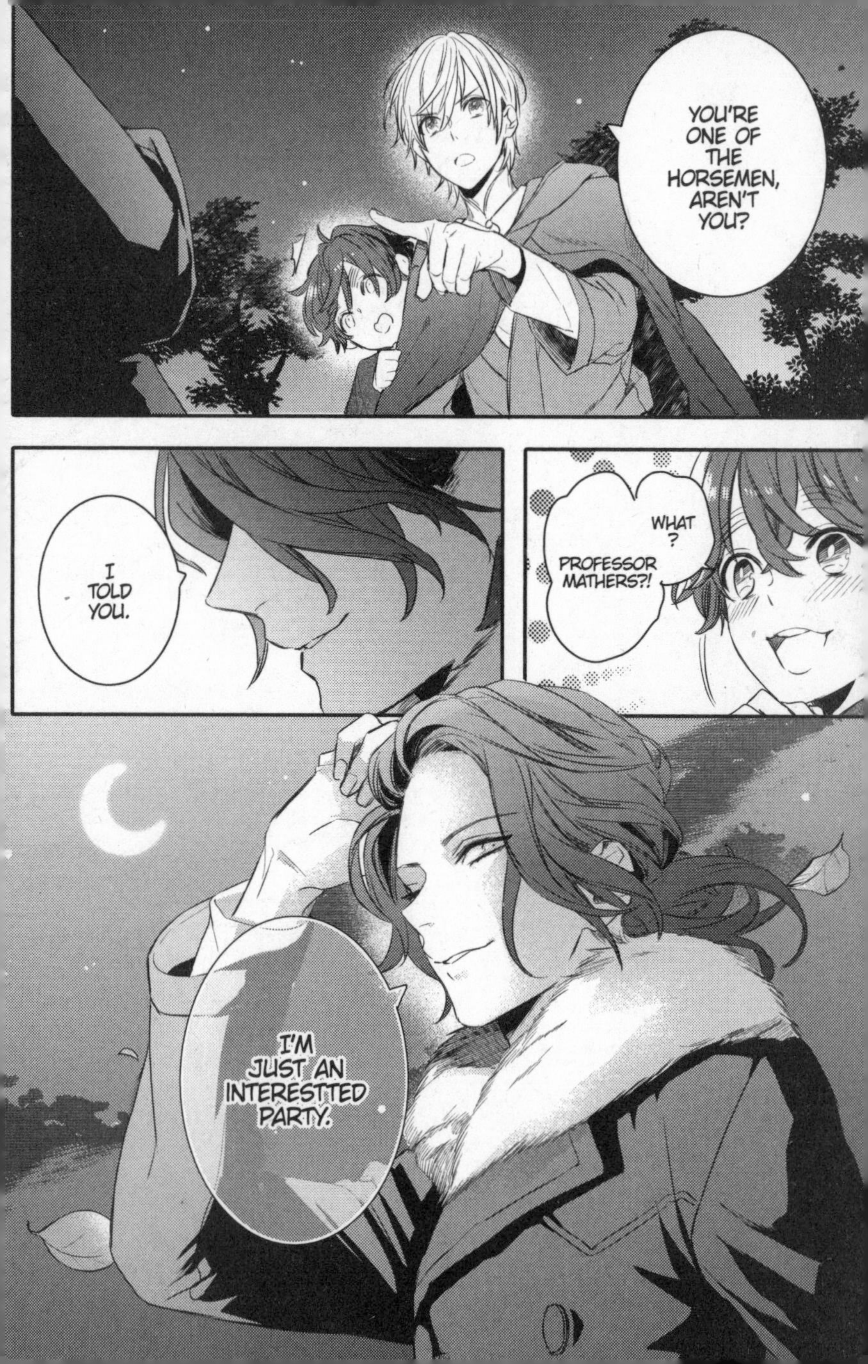
YOU'RE ONE OF THE HORSEMEN, AREN'T YOU?
WHAT? PROFESSOR MATHERS?!
I TOLD YOU.
I'M JUST AN INTERESTTED PARTY.

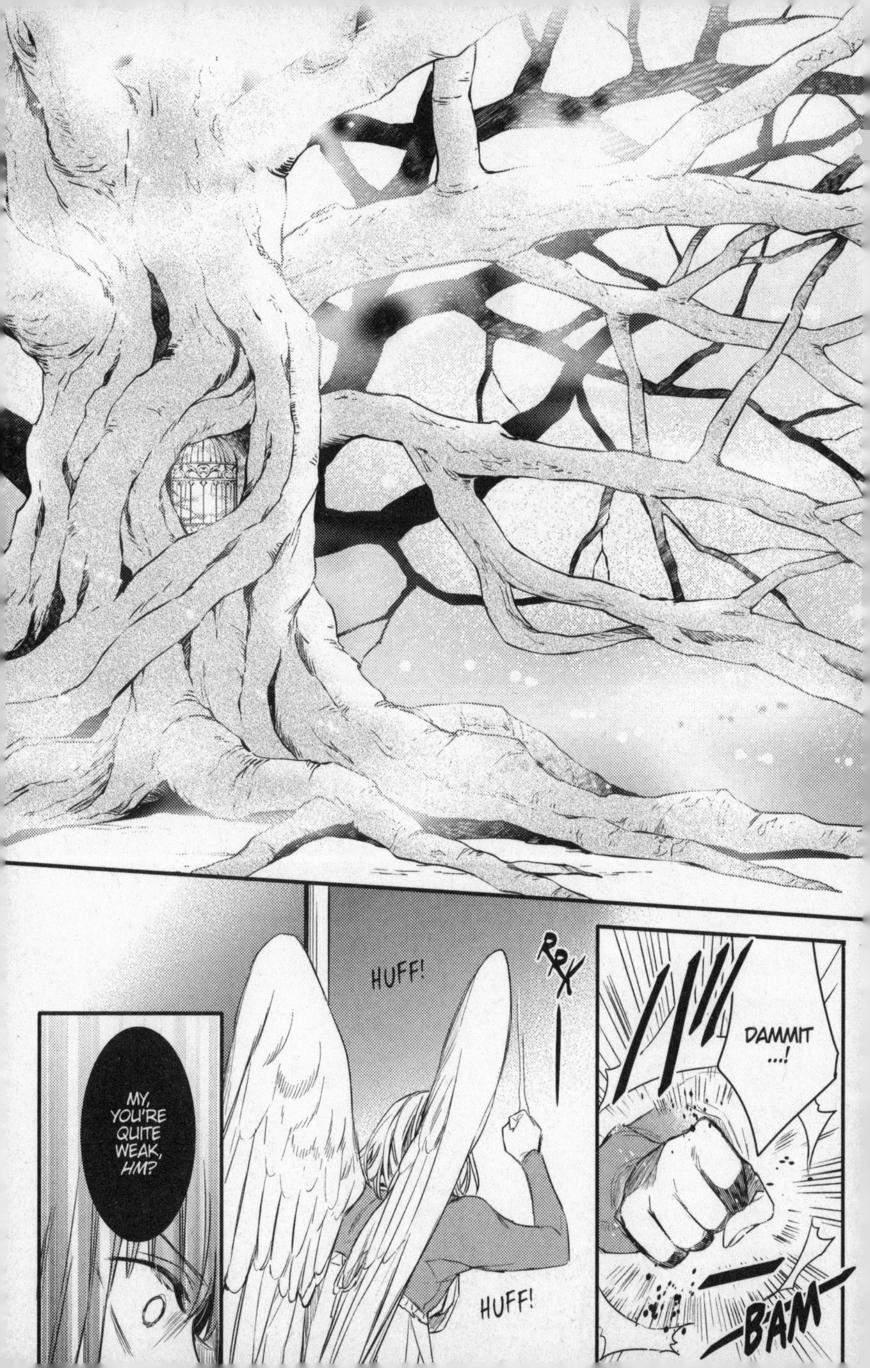
DAMMIT ...!
BAM
RRK
HUFF!
HUFF!
MY, YOU'RE QUITE WEAK, HM?

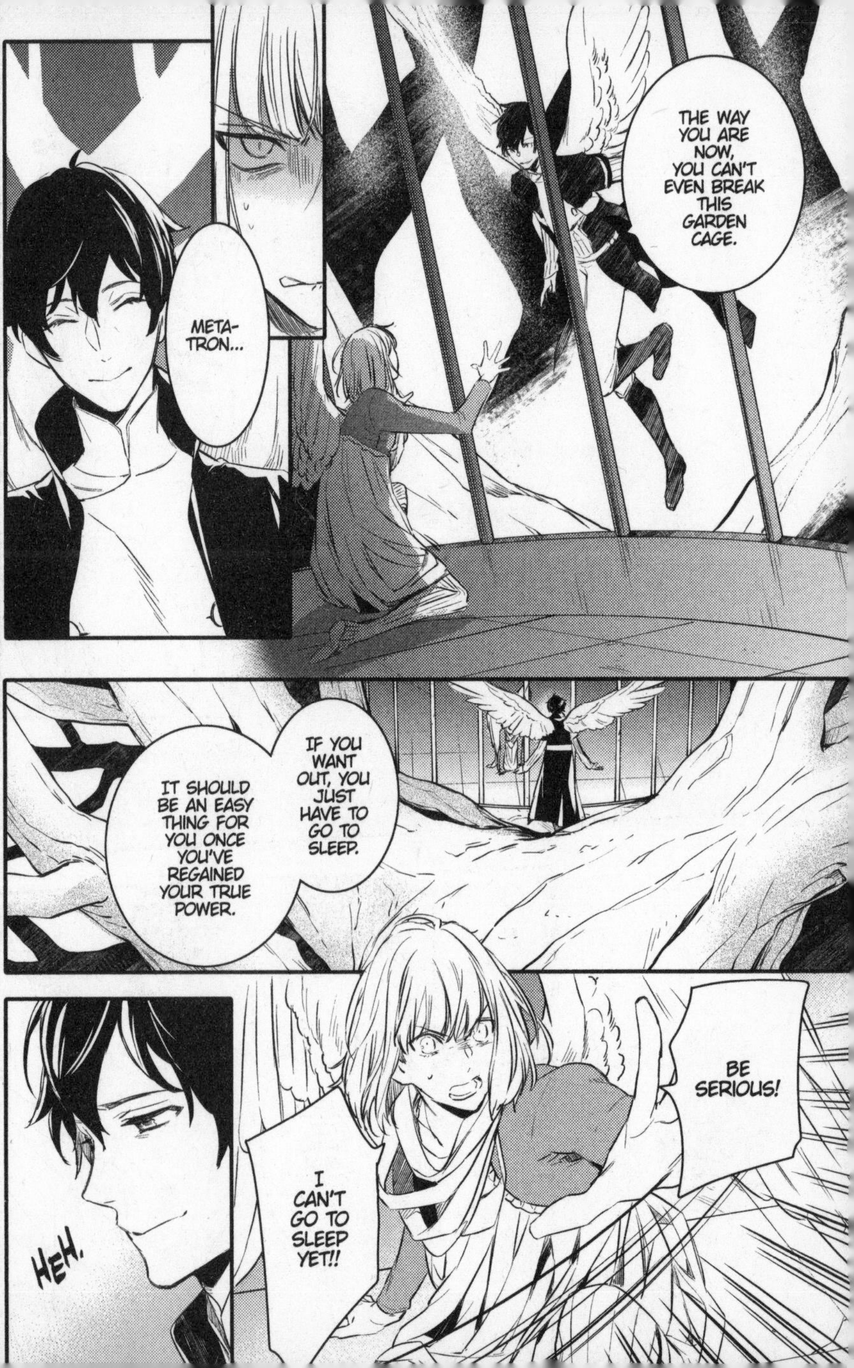
THE WAY YOU ARE NOW, YOU CAN'T EVEN BREAK THIS GARDEN CAGE.
METATRON...
IF YOU WANT OUT, YOU JUST HAVE TO GO TO SLEEP.
IT SHOULD BE AN EASY THING FOR YOU ONCE YOU'VE REGAINED YOUR TRUE POWER.
BE SERIOUS!
I CAN'T GO TO SLEEP YET!!
HEH.

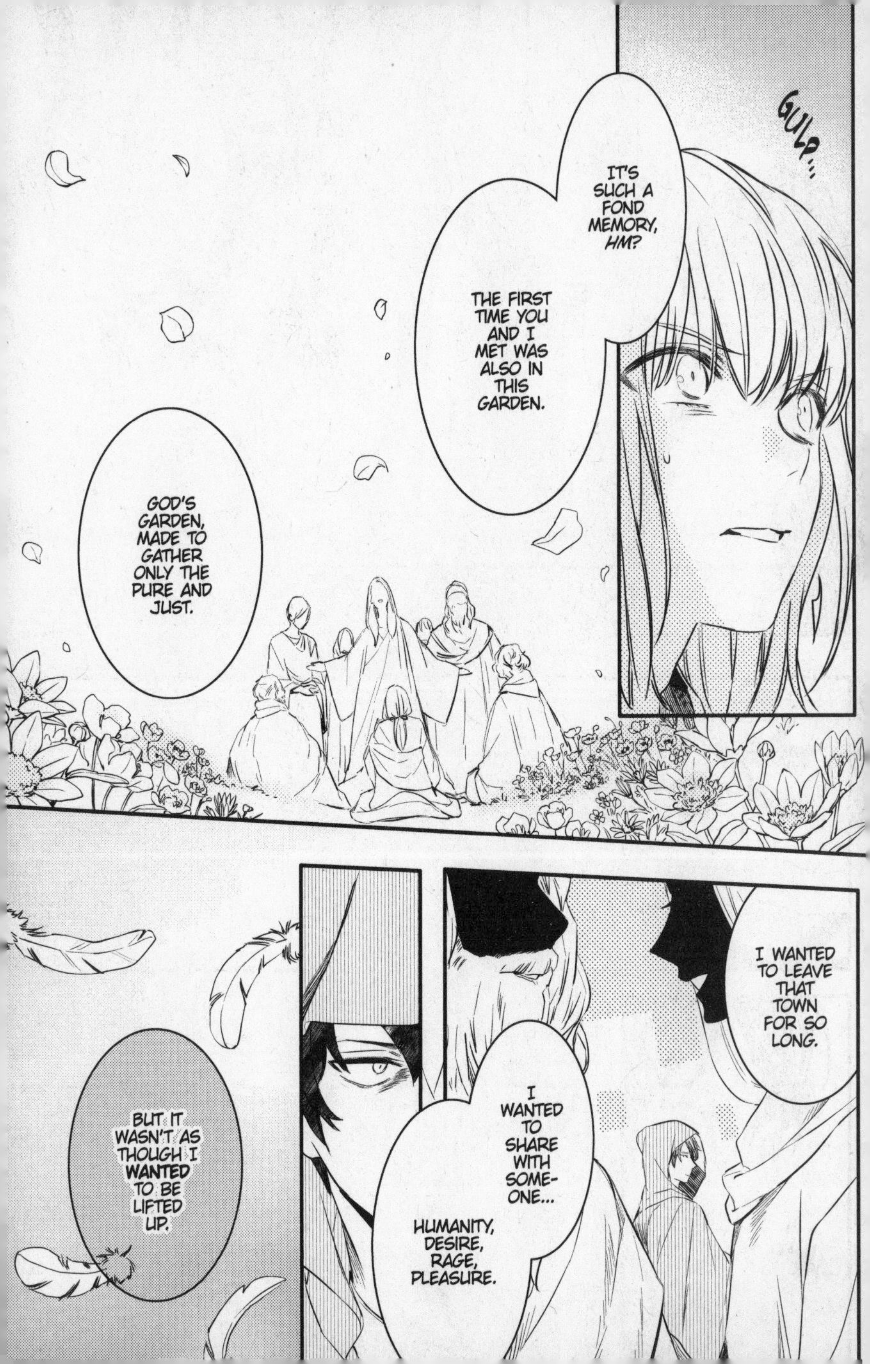
GULP...
IT'S SUCH A FOND MEMORY, HM?
THE FIRST TIME YOU AND I MET WAS ALSO IN THIS GARDEN.
GOD'S GARDEN, MADE TO GATHER ONLY THE PURE AND JUST.
I WANTED TO LEAVE THAT TOWN FOR SO LONG.
I WANTED TO SHARE WITH SOME-ONE...
HUMANITY, DESIRE, RAGE, PLEASURE.
BUT IT WASN'T AS THOUGH I WANTED TO BE LIFTED UP.

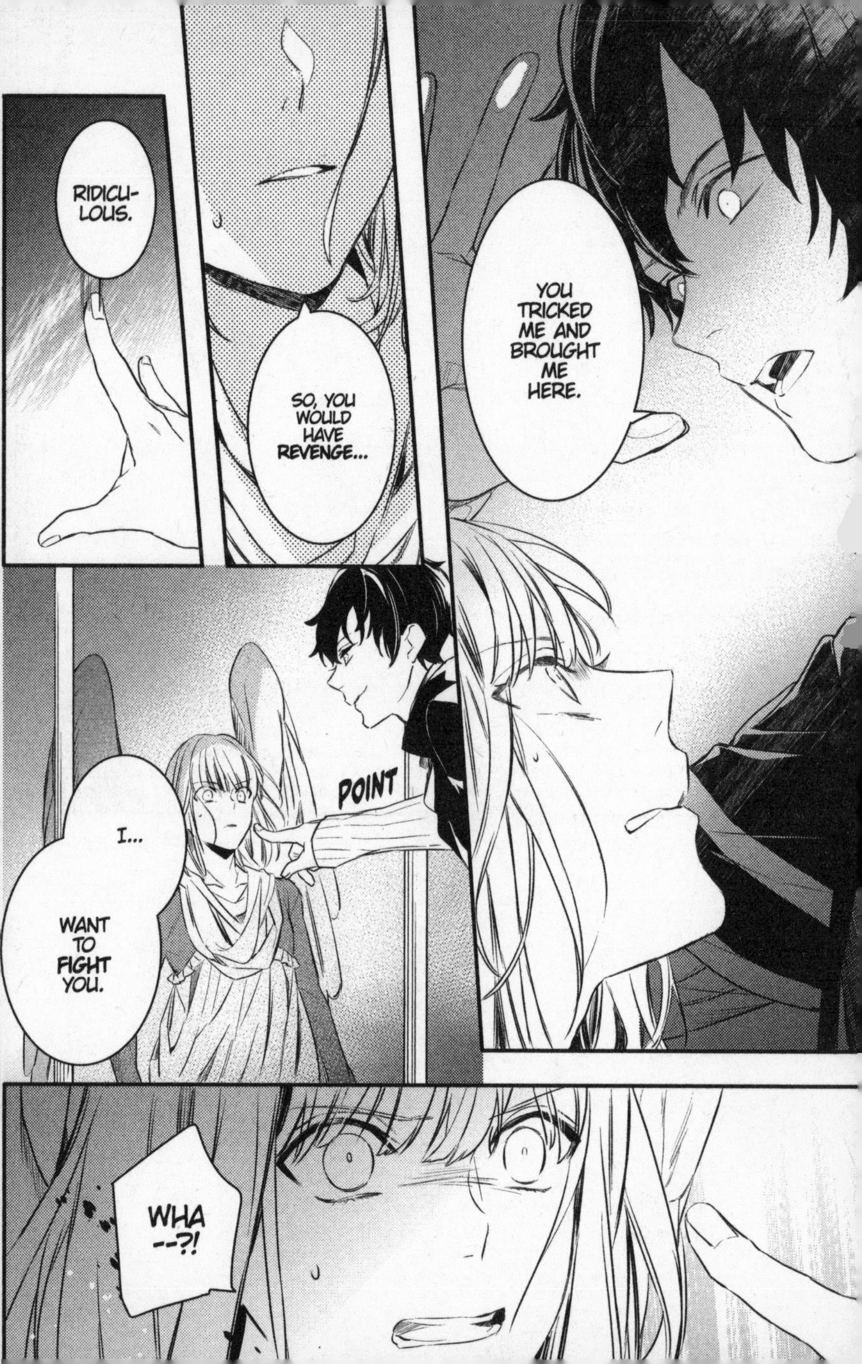
YOU TRICKED ME AND BROUGHT ME HERE.
SO, YOU WOULD HAVE REVENGE...
RIDICULOUS.
POINT
I...
WANT TO FIGHT YOU.
WHA--?!

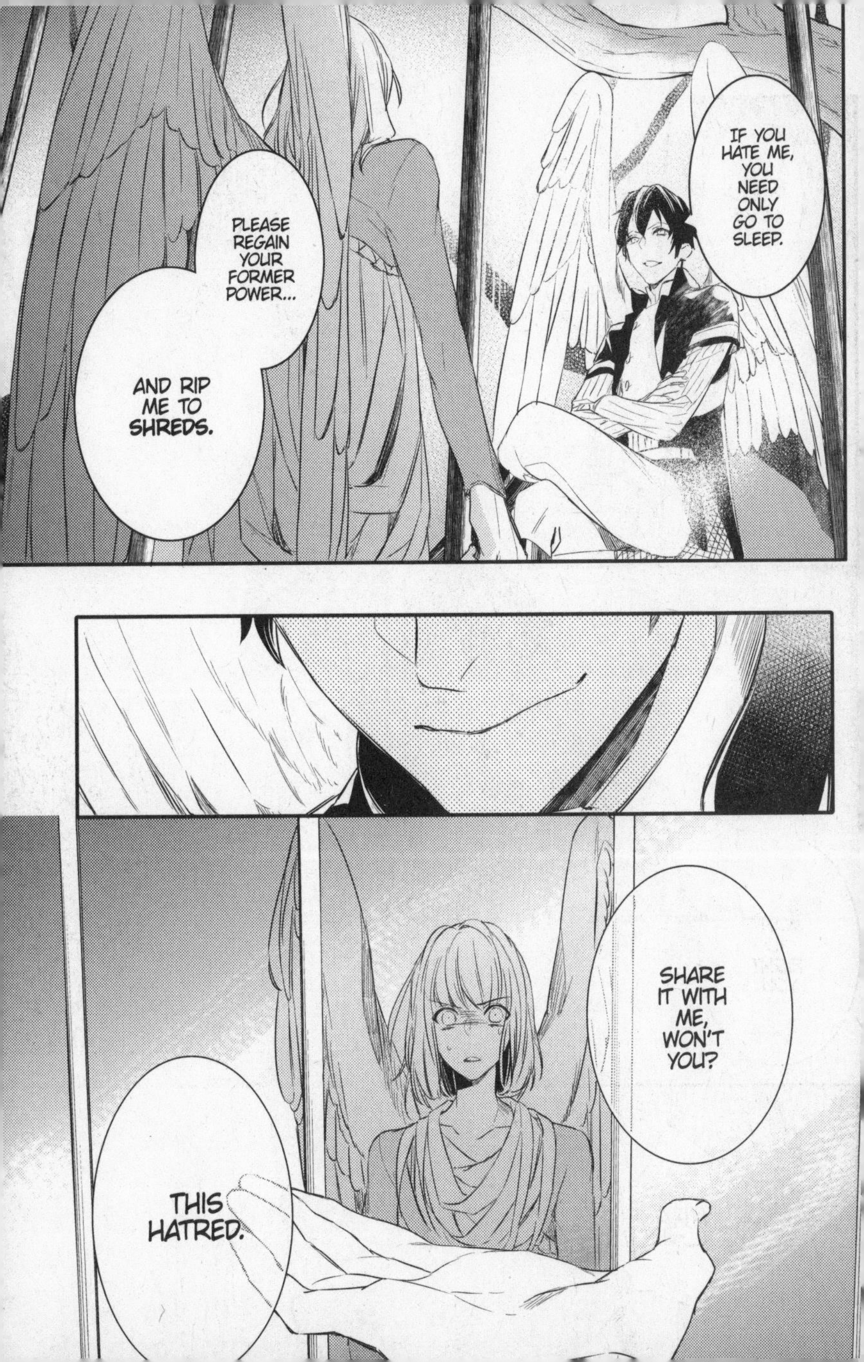
IF YOU HATE ME, YOU NEED ONLY GO TO SLEEP.
PLEASE REGAIN YOUR FORMER POWER...
AND RIP ME TO SHREDS.
SHARE IT WITH ME, WON'T YOU?
THIS HATRED.

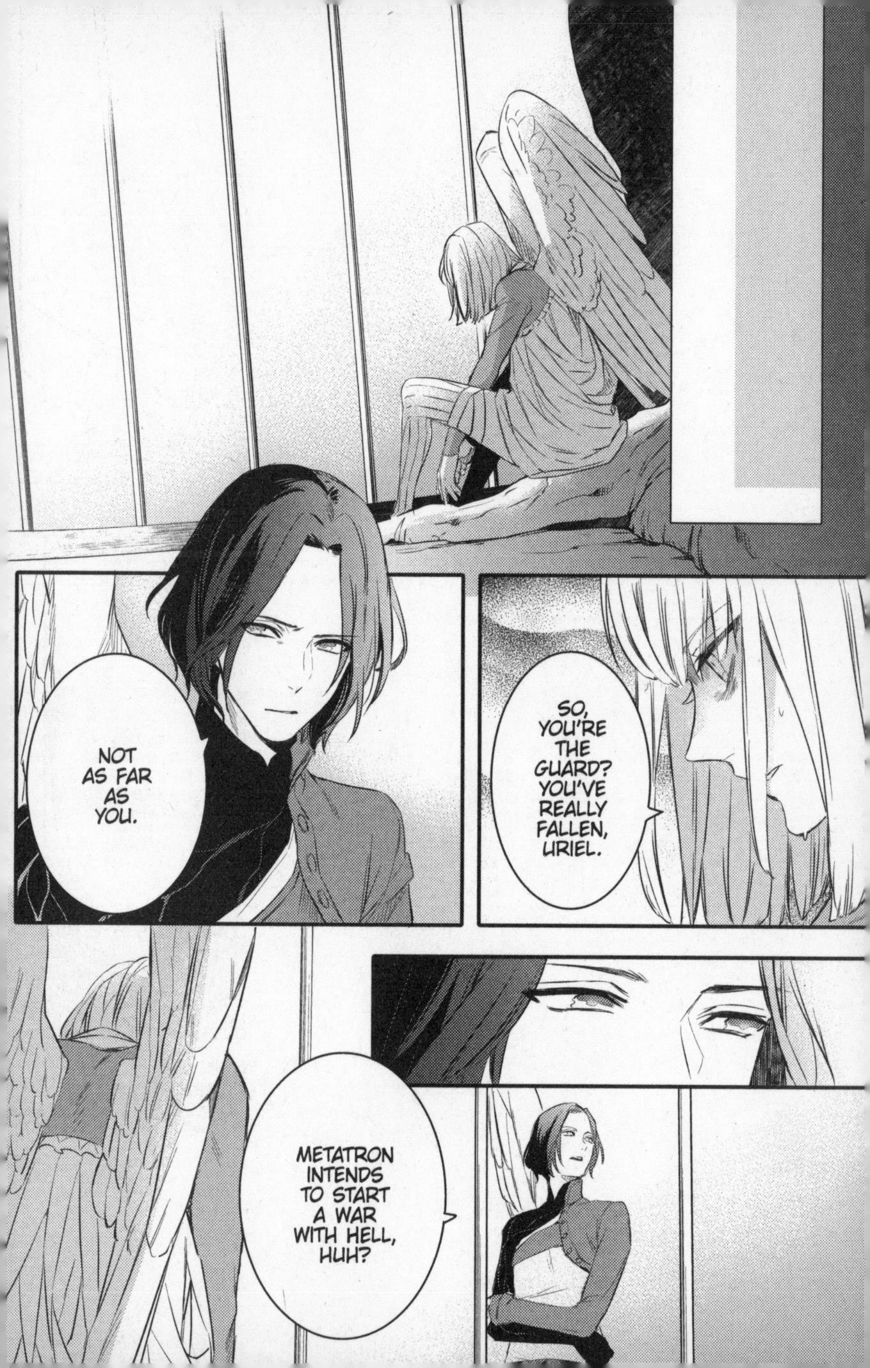
SO, YOU'RE THE GUARD? YOU'VE REALLY FALLEN, URIEL.
NOT AS FAR AS YOU.
METATRON INTENDS TO START A WAR WITH HELL, HUH?

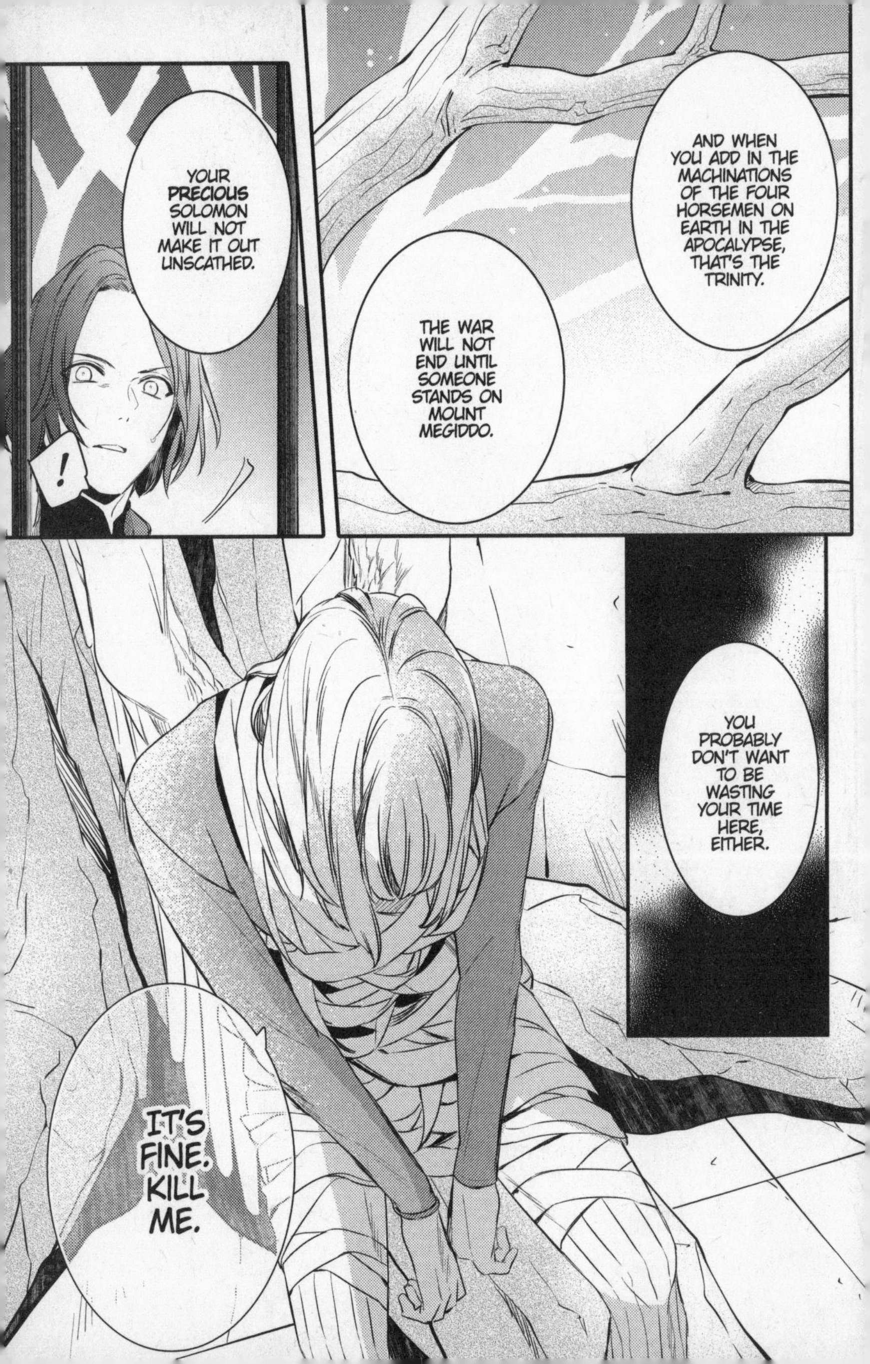
AND WHEN YOU ADD IN THE MACHINATIONS OF THE FOUR HORSEMEN ON EARTH IN THE APOCALYPSE, THAT'S THE TRINITY.
THE WAR WILL NOT END UNTIL SOMEONE STANDS ON MOUNT MEGIDDO.
YOUR PRECIOUS SOLOMON WILL NOT MAKE IT OUT UNSCATHED.
!
YOU PROBABLY DON'T WANT TO BE WASTING YOUR TIME HERE, EITHER.
IT'S FINE. KILL ME.

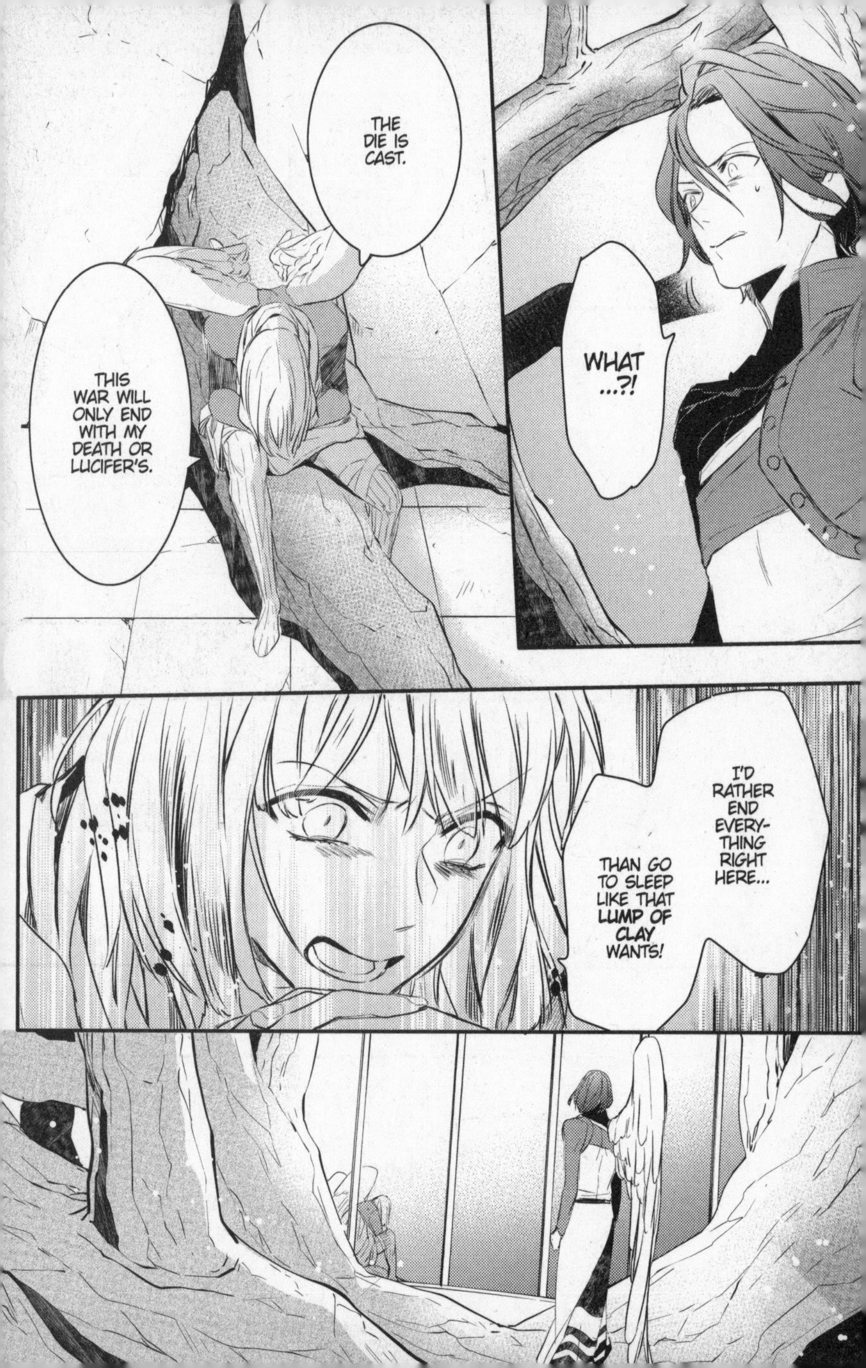
WHAT ...?!
THE DIE IS CAST.
THIS WAR WILL ONLY END WITH MY DEATH OR LUCIFER'S.
I'D RATHER END EVERYTHING RIGHT HERE...
THAN GO TO SLEEP LIKE THAT LUMP OF CLAY WANTS!

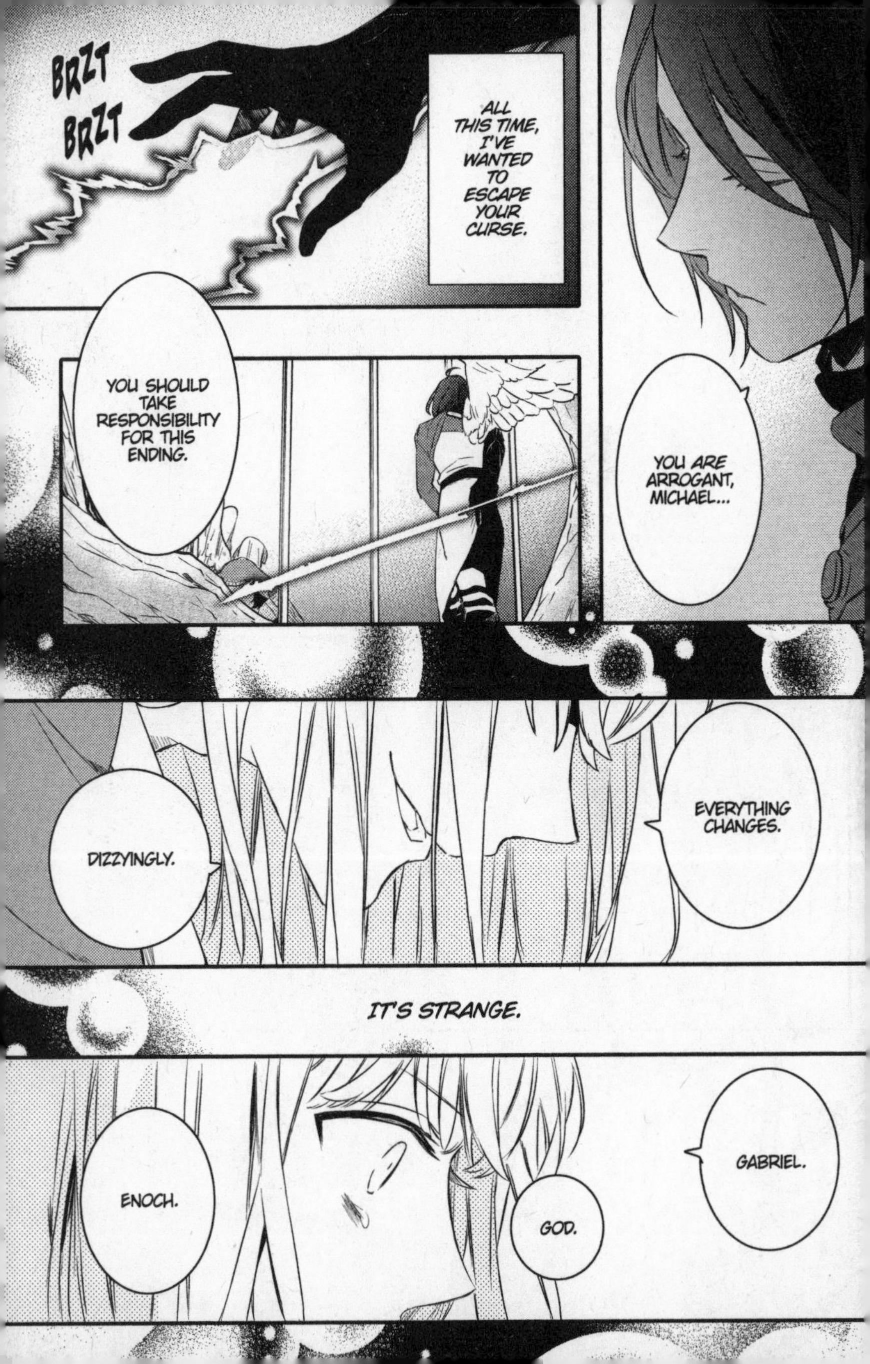
YOU ARE ARROGANT, MICHAEL...
BRZT BRZT
ALL THIS TIME, I'VE WANTED TO ESCAPE YOUR CURSE.
YOU SHOULD TAKE RESPONSIBILITY FOR THIS ENDING.
EVERYTHING CHANGES.
DIZZYINGLY.
IT'S STRANGE.
GABRIEL.
GOD.
ENOCH.

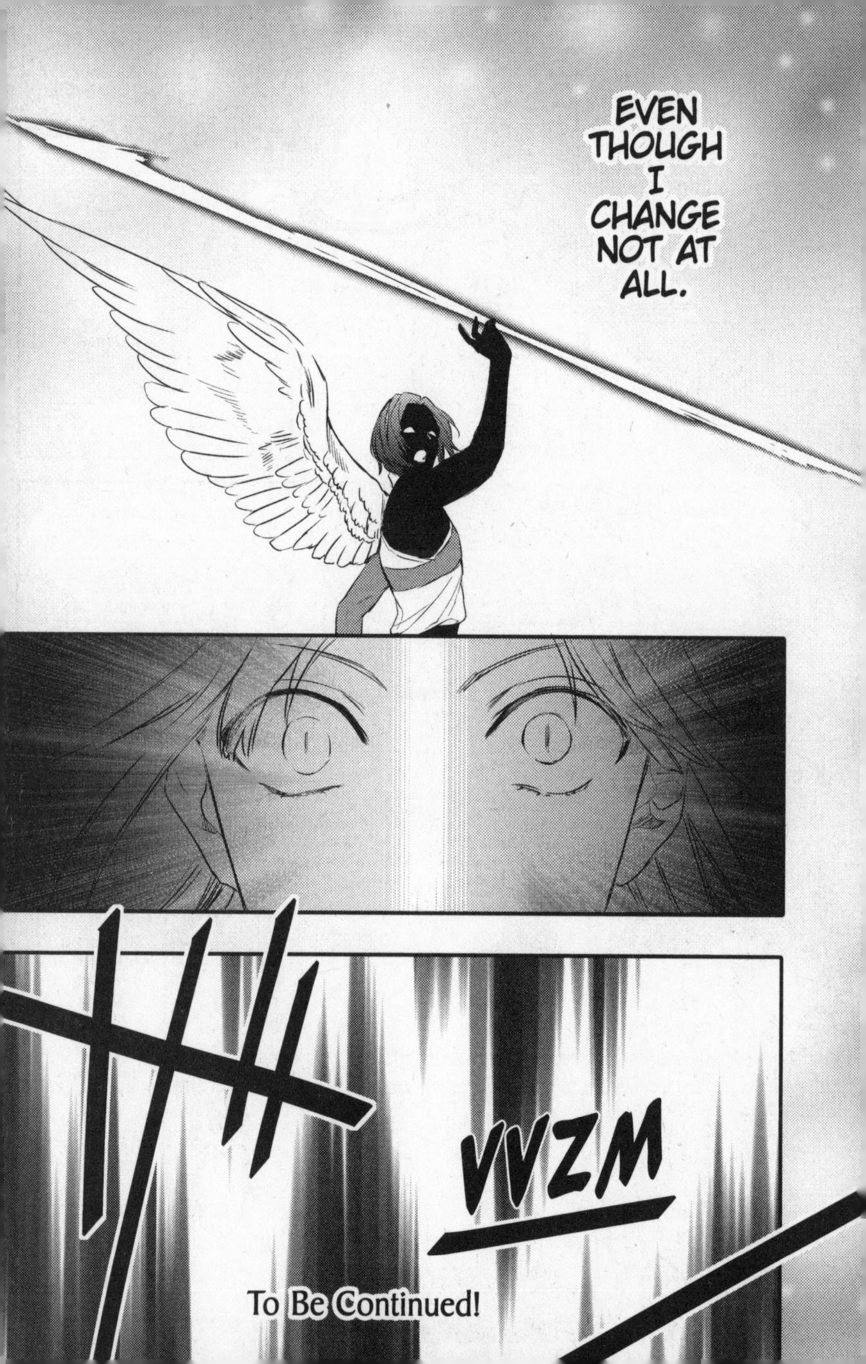
EVEN THOUGH I CHANGE NOT AT ALL.
VVZM
To Be Continued!

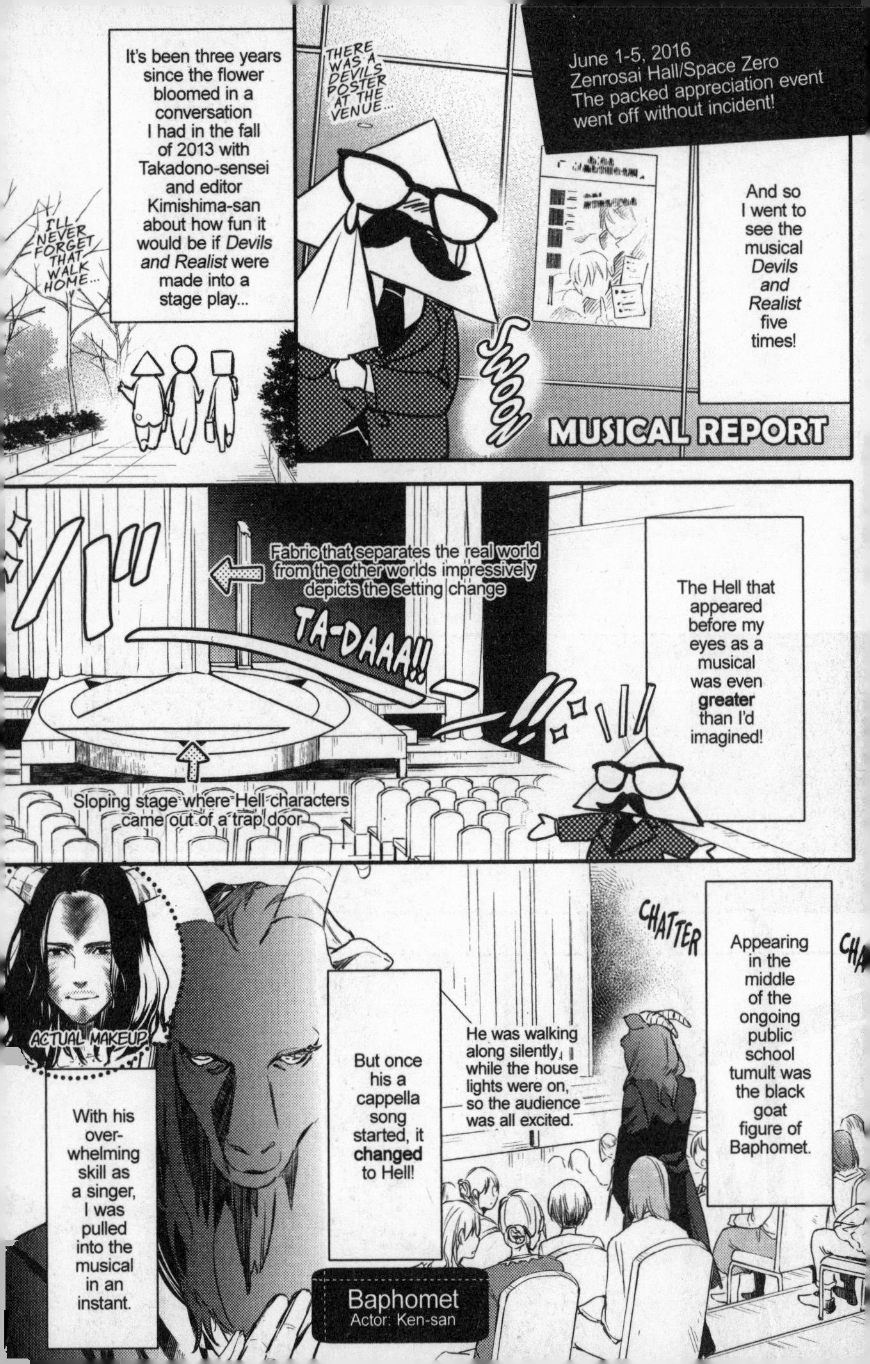
June 1-5, 2016
Zenrosai Hall/Space Zero
The packed appreciation event went off without incident!
And so I went to see the musical *Devils and Realist* five times!
MUSICAL REPORT
THERE WAS A DEVILS POSTER AT THE VENUE...
SWOON
It's been three years since the flower bloomed in a conversation I had in the fall of 2013 with Takadono-sensei and editor Kimishima-san about how fun it would be if *Devils and Realist* were made into a stage play...
I'LL NEVER FORGET THAT WALK HOME...
The Hell that appeared before my eyes as a musical was even **greater** than I'd imagined!
TA-DAAA!!
Fabric that separates the real world from the other worlds impressively depicts the setting change
Sloping stage where Hell characters came out of a trap door
Appearing in the middle of the ongoing public school tumult was the black goat figure of Baphomet.
CHATTER
CHA
He was walking along silently while the house lights were on, so the audience was all excited.
But once his a cappella song started, it **changed** to Hell!
With his over-whelming skill as a singer, I was pulled into the musical in an instant.
ACTUAL MAKEUP
Baphomet
Actor: Ken-san

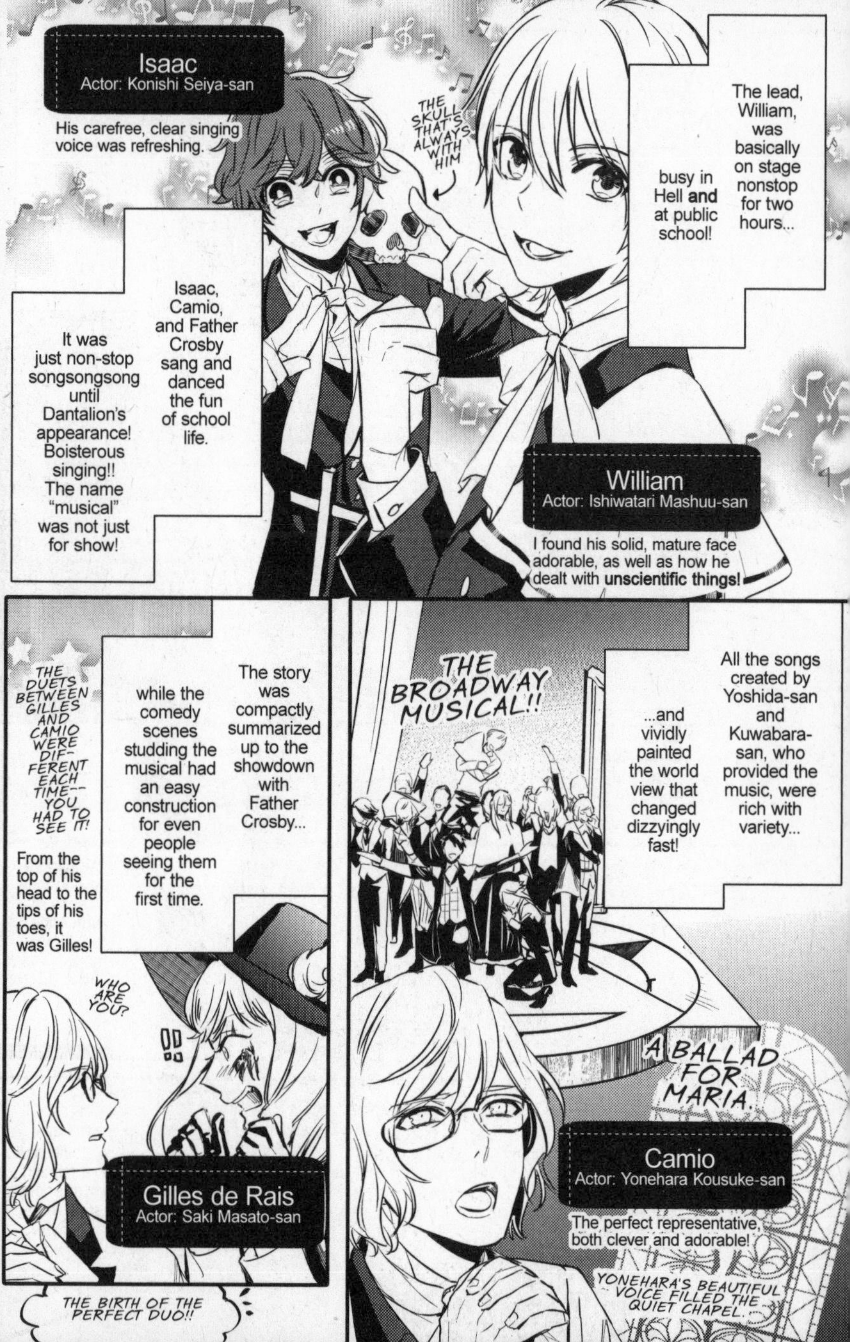
The lead, William, was basically on stage nonstop for two hours...
busy in Hell and at public school!
THE SKULL THAT'S ALWAYS WITH HIM
Isaac
Actor: Konishi Seiya-san
His carefree, clear singing voice was refreshing.
Isaac, Camio, and Father Crosby sang and danced the fun of school life.
It was just non-stop songsongsong until Dantalion's appearance! Boisterous singing!! The name "musical" was not just for show!
William
Actor: Ishiwatari Mashuu-san
I found his solid, mature face adorable, as well as how he dealt with unscientific things!
All the songs created by Yoshida-san and Kuwabara-san, who provided the music, were rich with variety...
...and vividly painted the world view that changed dizzyingly fast!
THE BROADWAY MUSICAL!!
A BALLAD FOR MARIA.
Camio
Actor: Yonehara Kousuke-san
The perfect representative, both clever and adorable!
YONEHARA'S BEAUTIFUL VOICE FILLED THE QUIET CHAPEL.
The story was compactly summarized up to the showdown with Father Crosby...
while the comedy scenes studding the musical had an easy construction for even people seeing them for the first time.
THE DUETS BETWEEN GILLES AND CAMIO WERE DIFFERENT EACH TIME--YOU HAD TO SEE IT!
From the top of his head to the tips of his toes, it was Gilles!
WHO ARE YOU?
!!
Gilles de Rais
Actor: Saki Masato-san
THE BIRTH OF THE PERFECT DUO!!

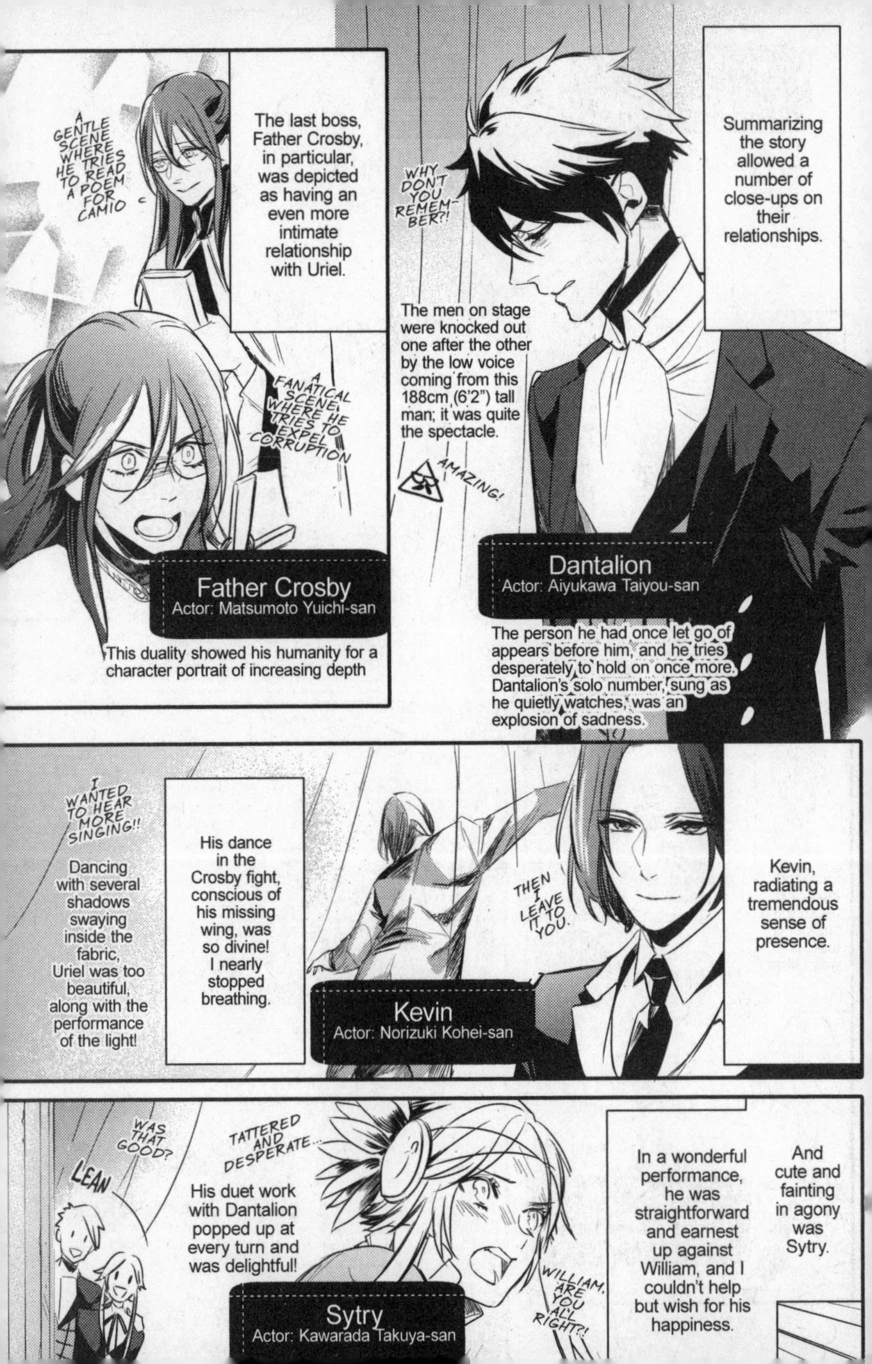
Summarizing the story allowed a number of close-ups on their relationships.
WHY DON'T YOU REMEMBER?!
The men on stage were knocked out one after the other by the low voice coming from this 188cm (6'2") tall man; it was quite the spectacle.
AMAZING!
Dantalion
Actor: Aiyukawa Taiyou-san
The person he had once let go of appears before him, and he tries desperately to hold on once more. Dantalion's solo number, sung as he quietly watches, was an explosion of sadness.
The last boss, Father Crosby, in particular, was depicted as having an even more intimate relationship with Uriel.
A GENTLE SCENE WHERE HE TRIES TO READ A POEM FOR CAMIO
A FANATICAL SCENE WHERE HE TRIES TO EXPEL CORRUPTION
Father Crosby
Actor: Matsumoto Yuichi-san
This duality showed his humanity for a character portrait of increasing depth
Kevin, radiating a tremendous sense of presence.
THEN I LEAVE IT TO YOU.
Kevin
Actor: Norizuki Kohei-san
His dance in the Crosby fight, conscious of his missing wing, was so divine! I nearly stopped breathing.
I WANTED TO HEAR MORE SINGING!!
Dancing with several shadows swaying inside the fabric, Uriel was too beautiful, along with the performance of the light!
And cute and fainting in agony was Sytry.
In a wonderful performance, he was straightforward and earnest up against William, and I couldn't help but wish for his happiness.
WILLIAM, ARE YOU ALL RIGHT?!
TATTERED AND DESPERATE...
Sytry
Actor: Kawarada Takuya-san
His duet work with Dantalion popped up at every turn and was delightful!
WAS THAT GOOD?
LEAN

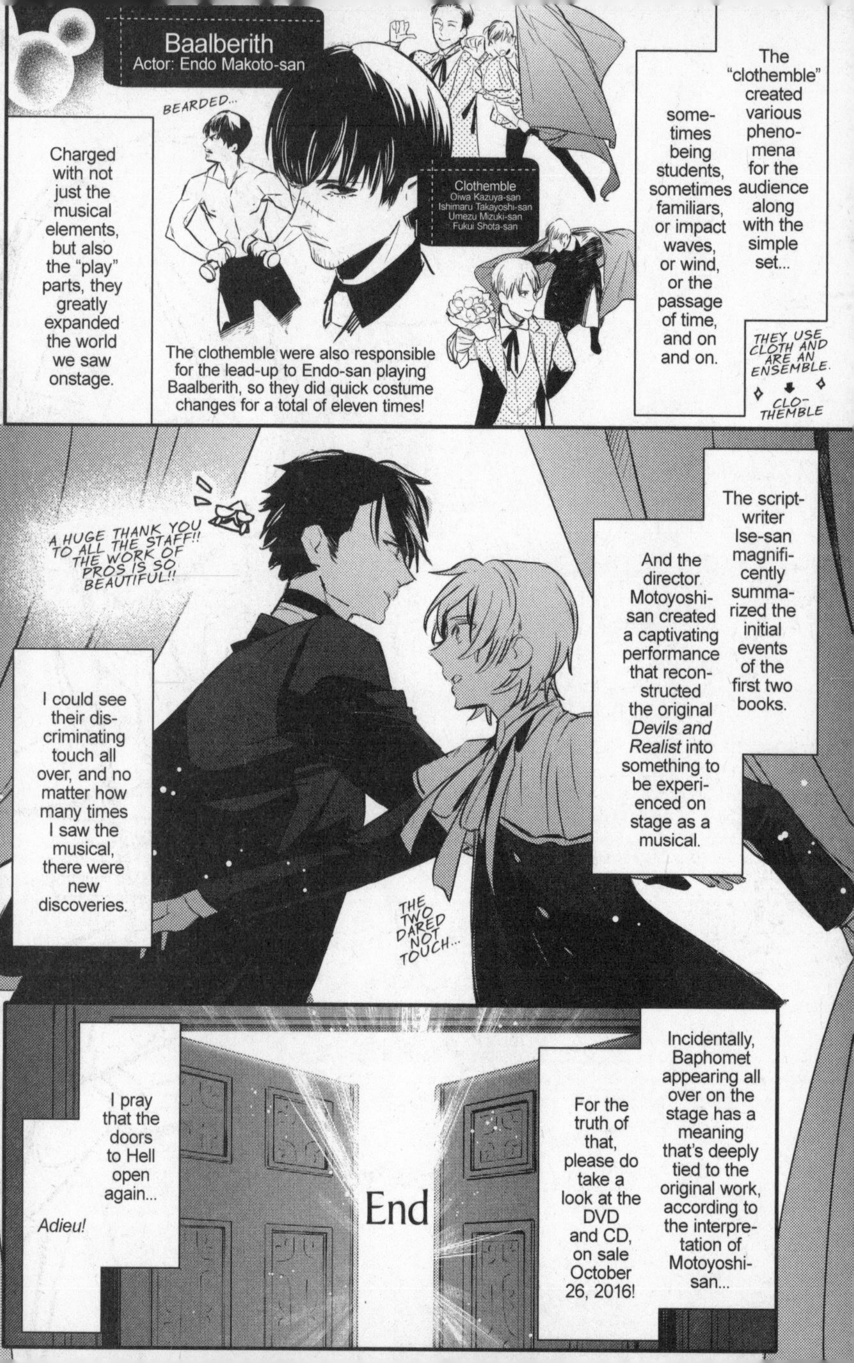
The "clothemble" created various phenomena for the audience along with the simple set...
sometimes being students, sometimes familiars, or impact waves, or wind, or the passage of time, and on and on.
THEY USE CLOTH AND ARE AN ENSEMBLE.
CLOTHEMBLE
Baalberith
Actor: Endo Makoto-san
Clothemble
Oiwa Kazuya-san
Ishimaru Takayoshi-san
Umezu Mizuki-san
Fukui Shota-san
BEARDED...
Charged with not just the musical elements, but also the "play" parts, they greatly expanded the world we saw onstage.
The clothemble were also responsible for the lead-up to Endo-san playing Baalberith, so they did quick costume changes for a total of eleven times!
The script-writer Ise-san magnificently summarized the initial events of the first two books.
And the director Motoyoshi-san created a captivating performance that reconstructed the original *Devils and Realist* into something to be experienced on stage as a musical.
A HUGE THANK YOU TO ALL THE STAFF!! THE WORK OF PROS IS SO BEAUTIFUL!!
I could see their discriminating touch all over, and no matter how many times I saw the musical, there were new discoveries.
THE TWO DARED NOT TOUCH...
Incidentally, Baphomet appearing all over on the stage has a meaning that's deeply tied to the original work, according to the interpretation of Motoyoshi-san...
For the truth of that, please do take a look at the DVD and CD, on sale October 26, 2016!
End
I pray that the doors to Hell open again...
Adieu!

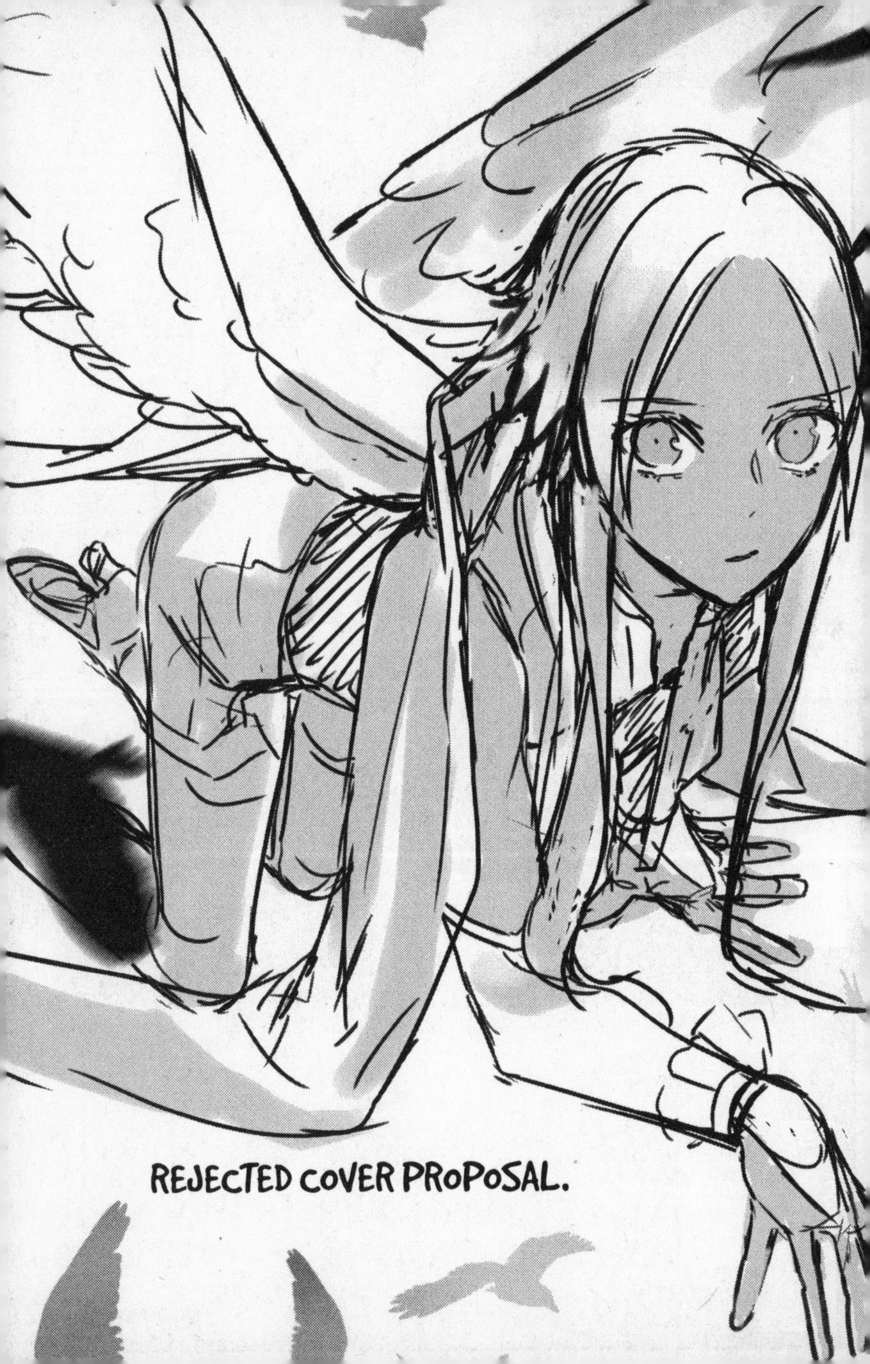

REJECTED COVER PROPOSAL.

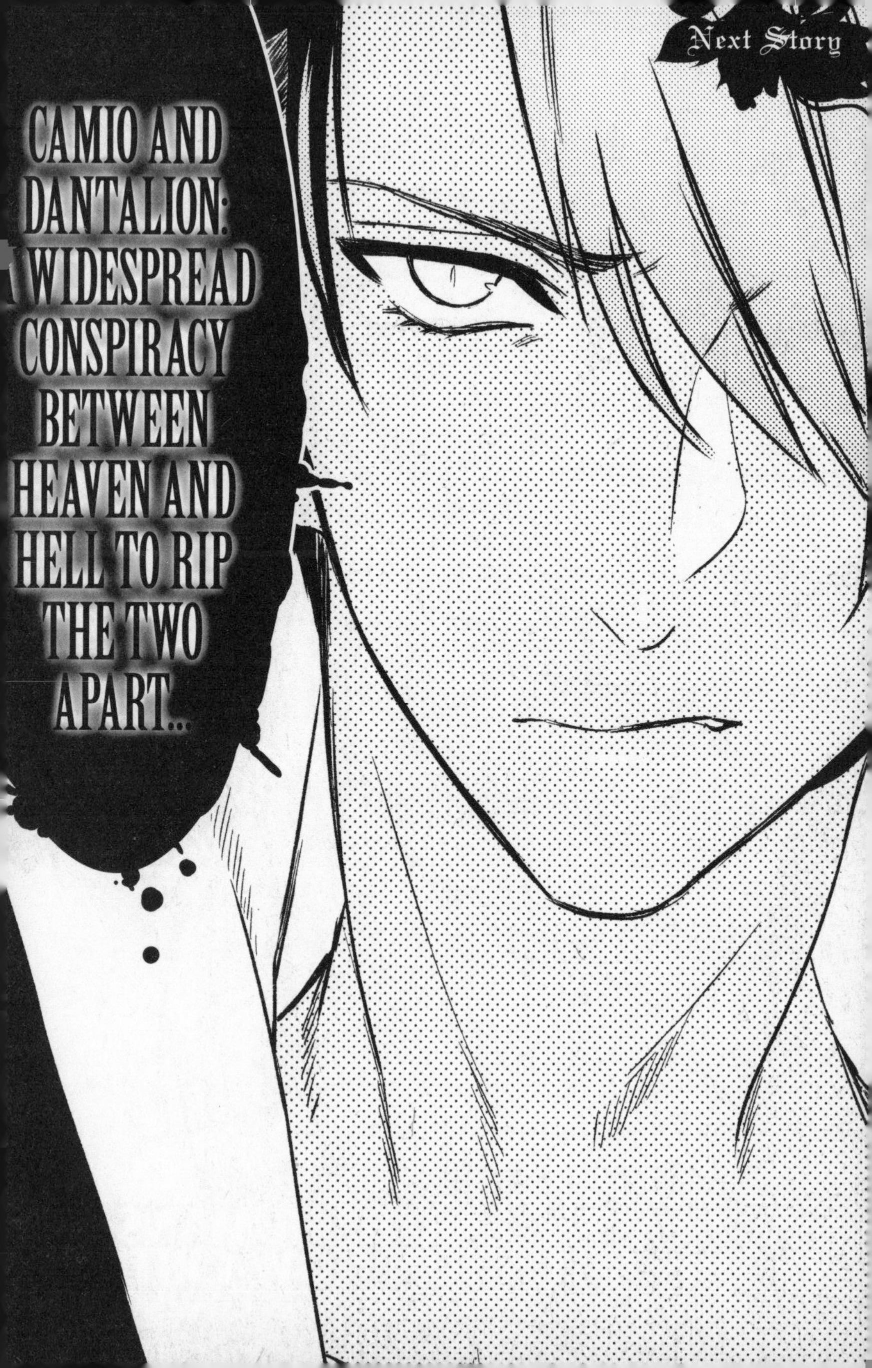
Next Story
CAMIO AND DANTALION: A WIDESPREAD CONSPIRACY BETWEEN HEAVEN AND HELL TO RIP THE TWO APART...

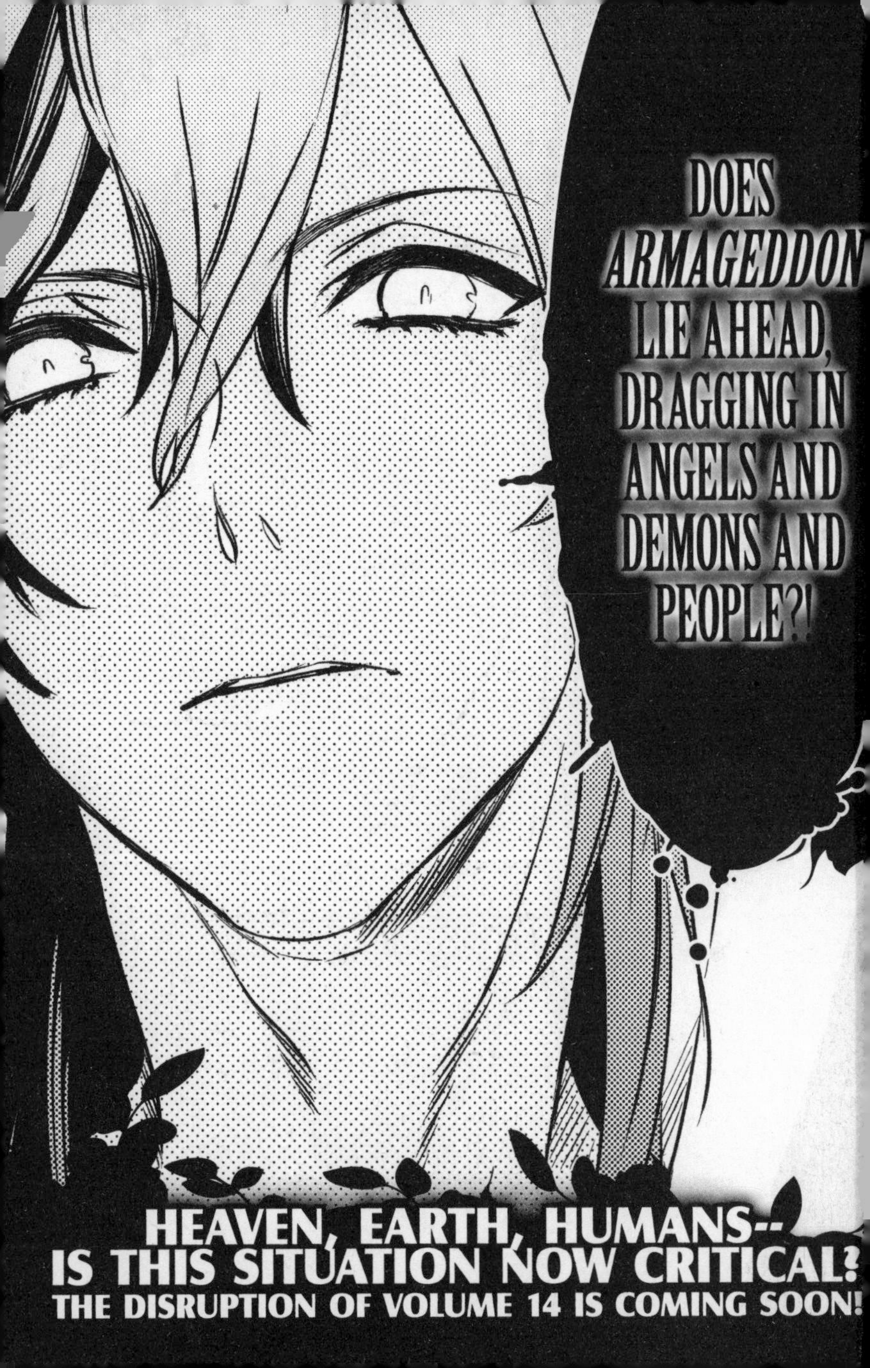
DOES ARMAGEDDON LIE AHEAD, DRAGGING IN ANGELS AND DEMONS AND PEOPLE?!
HEAVEN, EARTH, HUMANS-- IS THIS SITUATION NOW CRITICAL?
THE DISRUPTION OF VOLUME 14 IS COMING SOON!

SEVEN SEAS ENTERTAINMENT PRESENTS

Devils and Realist

art by **UTAKO YUKIHIRO** / story by **MADOKA TAKADONO**   VOLUME 13

TRANSLATION
Jocelyne Allen

ADAPTATION
Danielle King

LETTERING AND RETOUCH
Roland Amago
Bambi Eloriaga-Amago

COVER DESIGN
Nicky Lim

ASSISTANT EDITOR
Jenn Grunigen

PRODUCTION ASSISTANT
CK Russell

PRODUCTION MANAGER
Lissa Pattillo

EDITOR-IN-CHIEF
Adam Arnold

PUBLISHER
Jason DeAngelis

MAKAI OUJI: DEVILS AND REALIST VOL. 13
© Utako Yukihiro/Madoka Takadono 2016
First published in Japan in 2016 by ICHIJINSHA Inc., Tokyo.
English translation rights arranged with ICHIJINSHA Inc., Tokyo, Japan.

Seven Seas books may be purchased in bulk for promotional, educational, or
business use. Please contact your local bookseller or the Macmillan Corporate
and Premium Sales Department at 1-800-221-7945, extension 5442, or by
e-mail at MacmillanSpecialMarkets@macmillan.com.

Seven Seas and the Seven Seas logo are trademarks of
Seven Seas Entertainment, LLC. All rights reserved.

ISBN: 978-1-626925-13-7

Printed in Canada

First Printing: November 2017

10 9 8 7 6 5 4 3 2 1

FOLLOW US ONLINE: *www.gomanga.com*

READING DIRECTIONS

This book reads from *right to left*, Japanese style.
If this is your first time reading manga, you start
reading from the top right panel on each page and
take it from there. If you get lost, just follow the
numbered diagram here. It may seem backwards at
first, but you'll get the hang of it! Have fun!!

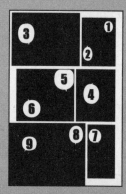